# *Into Teachers' Hands*

## Table of Contents

| | |
|---|---|
| Developmental/Early Childhood Education | 3-30 |
| Differently Abled | 31-68 |
| Multiage | 69-90 |
| Integrated Language Arts | 91-237 |
| Assessment | 238-284 |
| Professional Development | 285-295 |
| Whole Language Resources | 296-316 |
| Index | 317 |

This book is printed on recycled paper.

FIFTH EDITION

Executive Director: Jim Grant
Edited by Deborah Sumner
Cover Design: Susan Dunholter
Cover Photo courtesy of: *Teaching/K-8* (April 1991 edition)
                                40 Richards Avenue
                                Norwalk, CT 06854

                                Rob Nelson, photographer
                                      and
                               Phoebe Ingraham, teacher

SDE Design Director: Susan Dunholter
Production Coordinator: Deborah Fredericks

ISBN 09627389-3-X (paperback)

# America 2000: Taking The Next Step

**THE VISION: AMERICA 2000**
**President George Bush**
**and the nation's governors have**
**outlined the following six goals**
**for America 2000:**

*By the year 2000:*

*1) All children in America will start school ready to learn.*

*2) The high school graduation rate will increase to at least 90 percent.*

*3) American students will leave grades four, eight, and twelve having demonstrated competency in challenging subject matter including English, mathematics, science, history, and geography; and every school in America will ensure that all students learn to use their minds well, so they may be prepared for responsible citizenship, further learning, and productive employment in our modern economy.*

*4) U.S. students will be first in the world in science and mathematics achievement.*

*5) Every adult American will be literate and will possess the knowledge and skills necessary to compete in a global economy and exercise the rights and responsibilities of citizenship.*

*6) Every school in America will be free of drugs and violence and will offer a disciplined environment conducive to learning.*

*The following excerpt is taken from* America 2000: An Education Strategy *distributed by the U.S. Department of Education.*

## Goal 1: The Objectives

• All disadvantaged and disabled children will have access to high quality and developmentally appropriate preschool programs that help prepare children for school.

• Every parent in America will be a child's first teacher and devote time each day to helping his or her preschool child learn; parents will have access to the training and support they need.

• Children will receive the nutrition and health care needed to arrive at school with healthy minds and bodies, and the number of low birthweight babies will be significantly reduced through enhanced prenatal health systems.

## Necessary Changes and Restructuring

*The Preschool Years:*

"American homes must be places of learning. Parents should play an active role in their children's early learning, particularly by reading to them on a daily basis. Parents should have access to the support and training required to fulfill this role, especially in poor, undereducated families.

"In preparing young people to start school, both the federal and state governments have important roles to play, especially with regard to health, nutrition, and early childhood development. Congress and the Administration have increased maternal and child health coverage for all families with incomes up to 133 percent of the federal poverty line. Many states go beyond this level of coverage, and more are moving in this direction. In addition, states continue to develop more effective delivery systems of prenatal and postnatal care. However, we still need more prevention, testing, screening, and early identification and treatment of learning disorders and disabilities.

"The federal government should work with the states to develop and fully fund early intervention strategies for children. All eligible children should have access to Head Start, Chapter 1 or some other successful preschool program with strong parental involvement. Our first priority must be to provide at least one year of preschool for all disadvantaged children."

*The School Years*

"As steps are taken to better prepare children for schools, we must also better prepare schools for children. This is especially important for young children. Schools must be able to educate effectively all children when they arrive at the schoolhouse door, regardless of variations in students' interests, capacities, or learning styles.

"Next, our public education system must be fundamentally restructured in order to ensure that all students can meet higher standards. This means reorienting schools so they focus on results, not procedures; giving each school's principal and teachers the discretion to make more decisions and the flexibility to use federal, state, and local resources in more productive, innovative ways that improve learning; providing a way for gifted professionals who want to teach to do so through alternative certification avenues; and giving parents more responsibility for their children's education through magnet schools, public school choice, and other strategies. Most important, restructuring requires creating powerful incentives for performance and improvement, and real consequences for persistent failure. It is only by maintaining this balance of flexibility and accountability that we can truly improve our schools...."

*Below, SDE Executive Director Jim Grant reflects on the importance of America 2000's first goal, school readiness, and what it means for children and educators today.*

### Jim Grant's Response:

"President Bush and the governors should be strongly commended for a 'first things first' position. Goals 2-6 will not be achieved until Goal 1 is in place.

"They are saying that we need to look at the whole child, physically, socially and emotionally as well as intellectually. The goal addresses important issues such as nutrition and medical attention and identifies parents as the child's first teacher. Teachers who have promoted developmental education have believed in those ideas for decades and our teaching reflects those beliefs.

"The goal reflects America's neglect of our children, including lack of social services, proper nutrition, and prenatal, health and dental care. It doesn't seem to take into account the poverty and the "pinwheel" population of mobile kids who are in and out of school. It recognizes that parents are the child's first teacher but ignores the fact that many children are now brought up in single parent families with Mum having to work long hours to make things work. I'm not sure parents are going to pick up the ball that is being thrown back in their court.

"I am in concert with the idea that children come to school ready to learn. But I'm concerned that Goal 1 focuses solely on children before they come into school. There is virtually no help offered to American public school educators to address the goal once children are in

school. It's the old 'here they come, ready or not' situation, and the teachers virtually have nothing they can put their arms around. We're not really doing what needs to be done to help teachers address the different levels of readiness in the classroom.

"I'm also concerned that many of the proposals either won't happen or won't be funded, and teachers are still going to feel the burden of dealing with a very diverse population.

"There is a strong danger that the committee will continue to be top heavy with people who don't work with children and that the teaching force won't be represented.

# GOAL 1
# *BY THE YEAR 2000, ALL CHILDREN IN AMERICA WILL START SCHOOL READY TO LEARN*

"People who have been appointed to the committee are the same folks who have been detractors from the readiness concept. They seem to be moving away from the concept of readiness and want to change the name to 'early childhood assessment,' which is sad, I think, because virtually all parents and teachers understand the term 'readiness.'

### Assessment

"I'm concerned that the assessment will become the main focus. I would rather spend the time and energy on teaching rather than testing.

"There's an emphasis to assess children to find out progress on the goals. But we're not going to make any progress unless there's help for the teacher in the classroom.

"In some ways I think that testing is a smoke screen to avoid really tackling the other issues. The main issue is that school is too rigidly structured — K-12, 180 days per increment, 5 1/4 hours per day, 30 pounds of curriculum per kid, tested at regular intervals. It's really a production model that we're trying to use to educate children. Our diverse population doesn't fit the structure we've had in place for the past 150 years.

---

*The main issue is that school is too rigidly structured — K-12, 180 days per increments 5 1/4 hours per day, 30 pounds of curriculum per kid, tested at regular intervals. It's really a production model that we're trying to use to educate children. Our diverse population doesn't fit the structure we've had in place for the past 150 years.*

---

"I feel that all six of the America 2000 goals are going to filter down to one focus, to have a national test. That will be the beginning of the end for the American public school. In my experience working in all the states, it is not very likely that one assessment is going to fit the needs of all our children.

"We don't have equality for all. There are a lot of children who, for many reasons, will not function well on a standardized test. I'm concerned that all the other important things will be lost as national testing becomes the focus.

"The national test is indoor work with no heavy lifting. It sounds glorious to those who don't actually have to work with children. Because it's something you can see and it sounds good on the surface, I think people will readily bond to the idea as many business people already have. I also think that teachers will be held solely responsible for the passing scores. The danger is that the amount of teacher bashing in the media will escalate as the scores become available, and people won't look below the surface to see why the kids are struggling.

### Hope at the Local Level

"People at the grassroots level are at a disadvantage because they do not have access to the media. But I think the saving grace in education is going to be a strong grassroots movement of teachers and parents working together and pushing for change such as we had in 1966 with the New Hampshire movement for developmental education. I think that's going to be a long, long battle. But if we wait for the state and the federal government to produce the solution, we'll lose one generation of children. We need local groups, school by school, classroom by classroom, to take charge, take control and make the needed changes."

---

*From* The SDE NEWS, *Vol. 2 No.1, spring 1992.*

---

## Voices

*Cooperative learning is now a widely used and supported strategy within classrooms, and the same principles should be modeled by the adults involved in the education system. Infighting, profiteering, and political grandstanding should not be excused as part of the American way. At a time of growing international competition and intense need on the part of our children, Americans must work together effectively to improve our education system.*

*Jim Grant*
**Developmental Education in the 1990's**

**Reprinted with permission of Modern Learning Press, Rosemont, NJ. © 1991. ISBN O- 935493-42-5**

# Ready to Learn: A Seven-Step Strategy

## A distinguished educator presents a comprehensive blueprint for achieving the nation's first education goal.

### Ernest L. Boyer

*I*n Ready to Learn: A Mandate for the Nation, *Ernest L. Boyer, president of the Carnegie Foundation for the Advancement of Teaching, examines the challenges posed by the first of the national education goals—that by the year 2000 all children will come to school "ready to learn." The following is a summary of the book's seven-step strategy for achieving this goal.*

### Step 1. A Healthy Start

Good health and good schooling are inextricably interlocked, and every child, to be ready to learn, must have a healthy birth, be well nourished, and well protected in the early years of life.

• Today's students are tomorrow's parents; every school district in this country should offer all students a new health course called "The Life Cycle," with study units threaded through every grade.
• The federal nutrition program for women, infants, and young children, known as WIC, should be fully funded so that every eligible mother and infant will be served.
• A network of neighborhood-based Ready-to-Learn Clinics should be estab-

Ernest L. Boyer is president of the Carnegie Foundation for the Advancement of Teaching.

Excerpted with permission from *Ready to Learn: A Mandate for the Nation,* published in 1991 by the Carnegie Foundation for the Advancement of Teaching, Princeton, New Jersey. Copyright © 1991, The Carnegie Foundation for the Advancement of Teaching.

lished in every underserved community across the country to ensure access to basic health care for all mothers and preschool children.
• The National Health Service Corps should be expanded to ensure that a well trained health and education team is available to staff the proposed clinics.

---

*"Every child should live in a language-rich environment in which parents speak frequently to their children..."*

---

• Every state should prepare a county-by-county Maternal and Child Health Master Plan to assure that all regions are covered and that existing resources are well used.
• Funding for two key federal health programs—Community and Migrant Health Centers and Maternal and Child Health Block Grants—should be significantly increased, with awards made to states that have justified the need based on a master plan.

### Step 2. Empowered Parents

The home is the first classroom. Parents are the first and most essential teachers; all children, as a readiness requirement, should live in a secure environment where empowered parents encourage language development.

• Every child should live in a language-rich environment in which parents speak frequently to their children, listen carefully to their responses, answer questions, and read aloud to them every day.
• A new Ready-to-Learn Reading Series, one with recommended books for preschoolers, should be prepared under the leadership of the American Library Association.
• A comprehensive parent education program should be established in every state to guarantee that all mothers and fathers of preschool children have access to such a service.
• A national Parent Education Guide, focusing on all dimensions of school readiness, should be prepared collaboratively by state departments of education and distributed widely to parents.
• Every community should organize a preschool PTA—supported and encouraged by the National Congress of Parents and Teachers—to bring parents of young children together and to build a bridge between home and school.

### Step 3. Quality Preschool

Since many young children are cared for outside the home, high quality preschool programs are required that not only provide good care, but also address all dimensions of school readiness.

• Head Start should be designated by Congress as an entitlement program and

be fully funded by 1995 to ensure that every eligible child will be served.

• Every school district in the nation should establish a preschool program as an optional service for all three- and four-year-olds not participating in Head Start.

• The new federal initiative—the Child Care and Development Block Grants—should be used by states to start new programs that expand the quality of care for small children, especially in disadvantaged communities.

• A National Forum on Child-Care Standards should be convened by the National Association for the Education of Young Children. The Forum's recommendations should be adopted by all states, so that by the year 2000 every day care center in the country is licensed to meet these standards.

• Every community college should make

it a special priority to establish an associate degree called the Child-Care Professional and also establish a collaborative relationship with local day care and preschool programs, offering inservice programs for teachers and providers.

### Step 4. A Responsive Workplace

If each child in America is to come to school ready to learn, we must have workplace policies that are family-friendly, ones that offer child-care services and give parents time to be with their young children.

• All employers should make at least 12 weeks of unpaid leave available to parents of newborn or adopted children, to allow time for the bonding that is so essential to a child's social and emotional well-being.

• Flexible scheduling and job sharing should be available to employees to help them better balance work and family obligations.

• Parents of preschool children should be given at least two parenting days off each year, with pay, to visit with their children in day care and preschool programs, and to consult with teachers.

• All employers should help their workers gain access to high quality child-care and preschool services, either on-site or at local centers. A child-care information and referral service also should be available to workers.

• A national clearinghouse should be established, perhaps by the National Alliance of Business, to help employers promote family-friendly work policies.

## Step 5. Television as Teacher

Next to parents, television is the child's most influential teacher. School readiness requires television programming that is both educational and enriching.

• Each of the major commercial networks—CBS, NBC, ABC, and Fox—should offer, at an appropriate time, at least one hour of preschool educational programming every week.

• A Ready-to-Learn television guide should be prepared, listing programs on all channels that have special educational value for young children.

• Companies producing and selling products geared to young children—toys, breakfast cereals, fast foods—should help underwrite quality educational television for preschoolers.

• Every hour of children's programming on commercial networks should include at least one 60-second Ready-to-Learn message that focuses on the physical, social, or educational needs of children.

• Twenty million dollars should now be appropriated to the National Endowment for Children's Educational Television to support the creation of educational programs for preschoolers.

• A Ready-to-Learn cable channel should be established, working collaboratively with public television, to offer programming aimed exclusively at the educational needs and interests of preschool children.

• A National Conference on Children's Television should be convened to bring together broadcast executives, corporate sponsors, educators, and children's advocates to design a decade-long school-readiness television strategy.

## Step 6. Neighborhoods for Learning

Since all children need spaces and places for growth and exploration, safe and friendly neighborhoods are needed, ones that contribute richly to a child's readiness to learn.

• A network of well designed outdoor and indoor parks should be created in every community to give preschoolers opportunities for exercise and exploration.

• "Street playgrounds" should be established in every urban area to make open spaces for creative play and learning immediately available to children.

• Every library, museum, and zoo should establish a school readiness program for preschoolers. The funding of such services should be given top priority by each community.

• Every major shopping mall should include in its facility a Ready-to-Learn Center, an inviting, creative space where young children can engage in play and learning.

• A Ready-to-Learn Youth Service Corps should be organized to make it possible for school and college students to serve as volunteers in children's Ready-to-Learn Centers, libraries, and playgrounds in every community.

## Step 7. Generation Connections

Connections across the generations will give children a sense of security and continuity, contributing to their school readiness in the fullest sense.

• Schools, day care centers, and retirement villages should redesign their programs to bring young and old together, building bridges across the generations.

• A "Grandteacher Program" should be created in communities across the country, one in which older people participate as mentors in day care centers and preschools.

• Every community should organize a series of intergenerational projects—called "Grand Days" perhaps—in which senior citizens engage in activities and excursions with young children.                ☐

FOR FURTHER INFORMATION

Copies of *Ready to Learn: A Mandate for the Nation*, from which this article is excerpted, are available for $8 each (30% discount for bulk orders) from the Princeton University Press, 3175 Princeton Pike, Lawrenceville, NJ 08648. Telephone 609-896-1344.

### A Roll Call of the Unready

According to a survey of kindergarten teachers taken by the Carnegie Foundation in 1991, a nationwide average of 35 percent of their students were not ready to participate successfully in school. The state averages were:

| State | % of students not ready | State | % of students not ready |
|---|---|---|---|
| Alabama | 36% | Montana | 28% |
| Alaska | 34 | Nebraska | 29 |
| Arizona | 35 | Nevada | 39 |
| Arkansas | 42 | New Hampshire | 29 |
| California | 38 | New Jersey | 27 |
| Colorado | 32 | New Mexico | 40 |
| Connecticut | 24 | New York | 36 |
| Delaware | 42 | North Carolina | 39 |
| Florida | 38 | North Dakota | 23 |
| Georgia | 41 | Ohio | 33 |
| Hawaii | 47 | Oklahoma | 40 |
| Idaho | 26 | Oregon | 32 |
| Illinois | 31 | Pennsylvania | 29 |
| Indiana | 32 | Rhode Island | 40 |
| Iowa | 25 | South Carolina | 40 |
| Kansas | 27 | South Dakota | 29 |
| Kentucky | 40 | Tennessee | 39 |
| Louisiana | 39 | Texas | 37 |
| Maine | 30 | Utah | 26 |
| Maryland | 31 | Vermont | 28 |
| Massachusetts | 26 | Virginia | 34 |
| Michigan | 27 | Washington | 33 |
| Minnesota | 24 | West Virginia | 34 |
| Mississippi | 41 | Wisconsin | 32 |
| Missouri | 33 | Wyoming | 26 |

**This article appeared in the May 1992 edition of *Principal*. Reprinted with permission of the Carnegie Foundation for the Advancement of Teaching.**

8

# Making the Transition to Kindergarten

## Administrative support and leadership can smooth a child's bumpy road from home and preschool to kindergarten.

### Mary Ellin Logue and John M. Love

*Like the majority of children in her half-day kindergarten, Angela entered with no preschool experience. She and her mother had attended the kindergarten orientation the previous spring and were assured that being five years old was the only requirement.*

*Angela cried inconsolably several times a day, sometimes because she missed her mother, other times because she was hungry but was told it was not time to eat. She became irritable and drowsy during the late morning when she typically napped at home. She demanded attention by yelling or pulling on the teacher's clothing when the teacher was busy with other children.*

*Angela had no experience with scissors, crayons, or pencils, and little with books. She did not have a "school sense" about waiting her turn or sitting in her seat, and showed little readiness for the formal kindergarten curriculum.*

\* \* \*

*Following Head Start, Daniel entered a full-day kindergarten in the same building that the principal describes as "academically focused," with emphasis on basic skills in a predominantly teacher-directed environment. Daniel knew his letters, numbers, and colors, could write his name, and passed the kindergarten readiness test with flying colors.*

*In Head Start, with teachers and parent volunteers, there were always adults in the room, ready to intervene when Daniel's boundless energy needed redirection. In kindergarten, however, he soon earned a reputation as a fighter and troublemaker. He would wander off to play with blocks during seatwork time, and he cried when the teacher brought him back. He sang to himself while working and resisted resting after lunch.*

*The Head Start teachers had written a detailed report about Daniel's learning style and how best to engage him, but the kindergarten teacher had not read it. Daniel threatened the teacher that unless school got better soon, he would "pack up his cubby and move back to Head Start."*

\* \* \*

*After a year in a highly developmental preschool, Sarah entered kindergarten in a suburban elementary school. She and her family had visited the kindergarten program the previous spring, and the school phased in kindergarten children during the first week to help them adjust to the larger class size. Sarah had begun to read in preschool, using a whole language approach, and her learning continued in kindergarten, where a similar approach was used.*

*Sarah began having bathroom "accidents" during her first few weeks of school, which concerned her teacher and baffled her mother. When the community preschool and kindergarten teachers met at the end of September to discuss children's adjustment problems, the kindergarten*

*teacher discussed Sarah's difficulty with her former preschool teacher, who remarked that the different classroom structure of the two programs might be responsible for the problem.*

*In kindergarten, children wishing to use the bathroom had to leave the classroom and travel down a hall alone to a facility shared with older children. By calling on one of the parent volunteers or another child to accompany Sarah to the bathroom, what could have become a more serious problem was quickly solved.*

The experiences of Angela, Daniel, and Sarah are hypothetical, but the events they describe are very real and illustrate some of the factors that influence the quality of a child's transition to kindergarten. Those influences may range from simple structural considerations, such as location of bathrooms or timing of snacks, to more complex issues such as pedagogical inconsistency between programs, attitudes toward parents, and the effects of poverty.

Children enter kindergarten each year with a wide range of prior experiences and skills, and are subjected to programs that vary considerably in sensitivity to their individual differences. While quality preschool programs can provide important benefits, they don't always do so, nor do such benefits necessarily endure.

One way to enhance the benefits of early childhood programs may be for schools to provide programs and services that smooth

Mary Ellin Logue is a research associate at RMC Research Corporation in Portsmouth, New Hampshire.

John M. Love is director of the Center for Early Childhood Research and Policy of the RMC Research Corporation.

Kathleen Marie Menke/Crystal Images 1992

*Establishing communication between prekindergarten and kindergarten staffs.* Only 10 percent of schools reported systematic communication between kindergarten teachers and previous caregivers or teachers about entering kindergarten children.

*Providing joint training for preschool and kindergarten staffs.* Three-fourths of the schools reported that less than 25 percent of preschool staff participate in such training.

Transition activities like these, involving parents, are somewhat easier to implement:

*Welcoming incoming children and their parents.* While only 47 percent of schools have a formal program for school visits by parents, 81 percent reported that at least half of the incoming children and their parents visit the school before the beginning of the kindergarten year.

*Informing parents of entering students about their rights and responsibilities.* More than a third (39 percent) of the schools provided this information through written documents, meetings, or a designated contact person.

*Involving parents in classroom activities designed to facilitate a smooth transition.* Only 13 percent of schools made *no* effort to involve parents in such activities.

## Schools that Support Transition

Transition activities are more likely to be found in schools with certain characteristics: The presence of a prekindergarten program in the school; a high level of poverty among families served; and a high degree of administrative support.

When there is a prekindergarten program in the school (*e.g.*, a state-funded preschool, local day care program, Head Start, or special education programs), the following activities occur more frequently:

• Transfer of records from the prekindergarten program to kindergarten
• Communication between kindergarten and prekindergarten teachers about students
• Communication between teachers at both levels about curriculum issues
• Coordination of prekindergarten and kindergarten instructional programs

the discontinuity children frequently experience when making the transition from preschool or home into kindergarten, and the National Association of Elementary School Principals regards the issue of continuity for children with sufficient concern to include it as one of the standards for quality programs for young children (NAESP 1990).

NAESP expects principals to initiate communication and coordination with the various organizations in the community that serve young children, arrange joint staff development opportunities with these organizations, invite parents and children to visit the school before enrollment, familiarize themselves with what incoming children have been learning, and strive to provide continuity between the two experiences.

How well are our nation's schools progressing toward the goal of creating continuity between preschool and kindergarten? The recently published final report of the National Transition Study sponsored by the U.S. Department of Education (Love, Logue, Trudeau, and Thayer 1992) concludes that public schools do not place a high priority on transition activities. In the study, conducted midway through the 1989–90 school year, the RMC Research Corporation surveyed nationally representative samples of 830 school districts and 1,169 schools with kindergarten classes. In addition, researchers visited eight schools to analyze their transition activities and the contexts in which they occur.

The transition activities fall into two distinct categories: Those that involve coordination or communication between school and preschool levels, and those that include parents as participants. The former are difficult to implement and only limited efforts were found in the following areas:

*Coordinating prekindergarten and kindergarten curricula.* Only 12 percent of schools had kindergarten curricula designed to build on preschool programs.

• Participation of prekindergarten program staff in transition activities such as joint workshops, sharing information, assisting children with adjustment problems, and preparing individual children and parents.

The types of transition activities found in schools often reflects the proportion of children from low-income families served by the schools. There are usually more transition activities involving coordination and communication between preschool and school levels in high-poverty schools, and more activities that involve parents in higher-income schools.

It may be that high-poverty schools, in spite of their many challenges, have resources through state and federal sources that facilitate coordination and communication. Also, high-poverty schools are more likely to house prekindergarten classes and to receive children from Head Start programs.

Administrative support and leadership are also important factors in promoting transition efforts. For example, the schools found to have more coordination and communication with preschools usually had staff who were responsible for transition activities. The study suggests that principals and district administrators have greater influence over schoolwide transition activities than do individual teachers.

There is also more coordination and communication between prekindergarten and kindergarten levels when there is a positive school climate—when school personnel have more positive attitudes toward children and parents, and have higher expectations for children's success in school.

**What Can Schools Do?**

The survey indicates that while most schools consider their kindergarten programs to be developmental, they rate themselves relatively low on some of the key classroom activities that early childhood educators associate with good developmental practice. For example, activities such as using daily worksheets, keeping children quiet in class, and instructing children primarily in large-group arrangements were not seen as incompatible with such developmental activities as creative play, use of blocks and manipulatives, and an emphasis on child-initiated learning.

We see three major implications of the study's findings:

1. *There is no single way to implement transition activities that is appropriate for all schools.* They must tailor their transition activities to the needs of the children and families they serve. It is especially important to know where the majority of incoming children spent the year before entering kindergarten in order to plan appropriately.

Do you know which prekindergarten programs send children to your school, and do you include them in coordination activities?

Do you identify activities that would best meet the needs of both preschool and kindergarten teachers?

What transition efforts are currently under way?

Are most of the parents included in transition activities?

What other activities would meet their needs?

2. *Schools serving higher proportions of students from low-income families may need to exert special efforts to create preschool-kindergarten continuity.* While high-poverty schools are more likely to implement activities that involve preschool-kindergarten coordination (e.g., teacher communication and transfer of records), they are less likely to focus on parents in planning and implementing transition activities.

Because of the barriers many low-income parents experience in coming to school, we may need new strategies to reach them. But we must make the effort because more than two-thirds of children from low-income families enter kindergarten without formal preschool experience, and these children, their families, and teachers need support in dealing with the adjustment to a formal school setting.

Although the study found that staff members of high-poverty schools generally have less positive attitudes toward children's future achievement, parent-teacher relationships, and teacher-teacher relations, it also found that better levels of communication are accompanied by more positive expectations for children. These findings imply that a school climate marked by open communication can positively affect children's kindergarten experience.

3. *Schools must ensure that their kindergarten programs are of the highest possible quality.* There is little point in carefully planning transition activities for children and families if the kindergarten program children enter is not of equal or better quality than their preschool experience. The study found a clear gap between administrators' understanding of developmentally appropriate practice and the activities implemented in their kindergartens.

If principals and teachers believe they have already adopted a developmental orientation, they are less likely to see the need to change. It is therefore critical for principals not only to understand but to explain, organize, and implement quality early childhood programs in their schools, and to provide an environment where such programs can be successful.

While the challenge to principals to assume leadership in this area is enormous, so too are the potential benefits for children, families and schools. □

REFERENCES

Administration for Children, Youth and Families. *Easing the Transition from Preschool to Kindergarten: A Guide for Early Childhood Teachers and Administrators* (pamphlet). Washington, D.C.: U.S. Department of Health and Human Services.

Caldwell, B. "Continuity in the Early Years: Transitions Between Grades and Systems." In S. L. Kagan (ed.), *The Care and Education of America's Young Children: Obstacles and Opportunities*. Chicago: National Society for the Study of Education, 1991.

Love, J. M.; Logue, M. E.; Trudeau, J. V.; and Thayer, K. *Transitions to Kindergarten in American Schools*. Washington, D.C.: U.S. Department of Education, 1992.

National Association of Elementary School Principals. *Standards for Quality Programs for Young Children: Early Childhood Education and the Elementary School Principal*. Alexandria, Va.: The Association, 1990.

FOR FURTHER INFORMATION

To order a copy of the study, *Transitions to Kindergarten in American Schools,* on which this article is based, write to U.S. Department of Education, Office of Policy and Planning, Planning Evaluation Service, 400 Maryland Ave., S.W., Room 3127, Washington, DC 20202-4244, or call 202-401-0590.

# Is Your Child Ready For School?

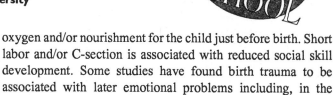

## by JAMES K. UPHOFF, Ed.D.

**College of Education and Human Services Wright State University**
**Dayton, OH 45435 • (513) 873-2107**

The school bells ring in late summer and thousands of children march through the school house doors without anyone having given any thought as to whether or not these children are ready—physically, socially, emotionally, academically—for the curriculum awaiting them. This document aims to provide you, the parent, with a number of major elements which should be considered as you make this vital decision. These same considerations are also relevant when parents are thinking about giving their child the *gift of time* another year in the current grade in order to grow and mature, or a year in a readiness, K or a transition K-1 program. Too often parents and school officials alike confuse verbal brightness with readiness for school. *Being bright and being ready for school are not the same thing!* An inappropriate start in school too often "tarnishes" that brightness.

Today's K-3 curriculum has been pushed down by our American "faster is better" culture to the point that what is often found in today's kindergarten was found in late first or early second grade just three decades ago! Many schools are trying to change from the "sit-still, paper-pencil" approach of the present to a more active, involved, manipulative curriculum which enables young children to learn best. However, until this latter learning environment is available for your child, you must consider whether or not the child is ready. The material which follows is presented to help you make this very tough decision!

Each of the factors below indicates a potential for problems. The more of these factors which apply to an individual child, the more likely he/she is to encounter difficulty—academically, socially, emotionally, and/or physically—and each of these areas is crucial to a well-rounded human being. No one factor should be the only basis for making a decision. Look at all of the factors, then decide.

## READINESS FACTORS

**Chronological Age at School Entrance:** My own research and that of many others indicates that children who are less than five and one-half years of age at the time of school entrance into kindergarten are much more likely to encounter problems. This would put the date at about March 25th for many schools. The younger the child is, the more likely the current academic paper/pencil kindergarten curriculum is inappropriate.

**Problems at Birth:** When labor lasts a long time or is less than four hours; or when a C-section is used regardless of length of labor; or when labor is unusually difficult, the child is more likely to experience problems. Long labor too often results in reduced oxygen and/or nourishment for the child just before birth. Short labor and/or C-section is associated with reduced social skill development. Some studies have found birth trauma to be associated with later emotional problems including, in the extreme, suicidal tendencies.

**Early General Health & Nutrition:** Poor nutrition in the preschool years puts the child at greater risk in terms of school success. The child who experiences many serious ear infections during these years has been found to have more difficulty in learning to read. Allergies, asthma, and other similar problems can also inhibit such learning. Any type of illness or problem which results in a passive child—in bed or just "being very quiet" day after day—is more likely to result in a physically delayed development. Lack of body and muscle control can be a major problem for learners.

**Family Status:** Any act which lessens the stability of the child's family security is a problem and the closer such acts/events occur to the start of school, the more likely that start is to be a negative one. Such destabilizers as the following should be considered.

1. **Death** of anyone close to the child. This includes family, friends, neighbors, pets, etc.
2. **Moves** from one house/apartment to another even though the adults may see it as a positive relocation —   more space, own bedroom for child, etc. The child may miss friends, neighbors, the dog next door, etc.
3. **Separation** from parents or close family members whether by jobs, military duty, divorce, prison, remarriage, moves, etc., can create problems for child in early school experiences.
4. **Birth of a Sibling** or the addition of new step-family members can be very upsetting.

**Birth Order:** If the gap between child #1 and #2 is less than three years, then #2 is more likely to have problems in school. When there are more than 3 children in a family, the baby of the family (last born) often experiences less independence and initiative. There are exceptions to these factors as with the others, but they remain as predictors, never-the-less.

**Low Birth Weight:** A premature child with low weight often experiences significant delays in many aspects of his/her development.

**Sex:** Boys are about one month behind girls in physiological development at birth; about 6 months behind at age 5; and about 24 months behind girls at age 11-12. (Some contend that we males never catch up!) Boys need extra time more than girls, but research shows that girls actually benefit from it more. Their eyes, motor skills, etc., etc., are ahead by nature, and when given time become even "aheader"! Boys fail far more often than do girls and have many more school problems than do girls.

**Vision:** Being able to see clearly does NOT mean that a child's vision is ready for school work. It is not until age 8 that 90% of children have sufficient eye-muscle development to do *with ease* what reading demands of the eyes. The younger the child is, the more likely he/she does NOT have all of the vision development required. For example, many children have problems with focusing. Their eyes work like a zoom lens on a projector zooming in and out until a sharp focus is obtained. Much time can be spent in this process and much is missed while focusing is taking place. Other eye problems include the muscle ability to maintain focus and smooth movement from left to right, lazy eye, and mid-line problems.

**Memory Level:** If a child has difficulty remembering such common items as prayers, commercials, home address/telephone number, etc., then the child may well experience problems with the typical primary grades curriculum. Many times memory success is associated with one's ability to concentrate—attention span, thus this factor is related to the next one.

**Attention Span:** Research has clearly shown a strong connection between the amount of time a child spends working on skill content (three Rs) and the achievement level reached. The child who is easily distracted and finds it difficult to focus attention for 10-15 minutes at a time on a single activity is also a child who is probably going to experience much frustration in school. Discipline problems are likely as are academic ones. Sitting still is very difficult for the typical 5½- to 6½-year-old child and this normal physiological condition is at great odds with the typical sit still/paper-pencil curriculum imposed after Sputnik went up over 30 years ago!

**Social Skills:** The child with delayed social development is often reluctant to leave the security of a known situation (home/sitter/pre-school/etc.). This child is very hesitant about mixing with other children, is passive, and slow to become involved. Non-involvement is often associated with lower learning levels. Tears, urinary "accidents," morning tummy aches, a return to thumb sucking, etc., are all signals of such a delay. Some research has found correlations between C-section and/or short labor deliveries and problems such as these.

**Speaking Skills:** The ability of a child to communicate clearly is closely related to maturation. In order to pronounce sounds distinctly and correctly, muscle control is essential. Hearing must also be of good quality and this has often been reduced by early ear infections, allergies, etc. Inappropriate speech patterns (baby talk) and/or incorrect articulation (an "r" sounds like a "w") are major concern signals.

**Reading Interest:** If a child does not like to be read to, has little desire to watch a TV story all the way through, or rarely picks up a book to read to him/herself, then the odds are high that this child is not ready for the curriculum of the typical kindergarten. Few of us do well those things in which we are not yet interested and our children are no different!

**Small Motor Skills:** The ability to cut, draw, paste, and manipulate pencils, colors, etc., are very important in today's pushed-down kindergarten. The child who has some difficulty with these, uses an awkward grip on the pencil (ice-pick, one or no finger tips on the pencil, etc.), and/or has trouble holding small cards in the hand during a game is a candidate for frustrations. Eye/hand coordination is vital for a high degree of success.

**Large Motor Skills:** It is typical for a 5- to 6-year-old child to "trip over a piece of string," yet the typical curriculum assumes major control over one's body movements. Ability to skip, jump on one foot at a time, walk a balance beam, hop, jump from a standing position, etc., is an ability which research has found to be related to overall sucess with some particular skills tested just before starting school predicting reading success levels in 5th and 8th grades!

## SUMMARY

Ready or not for school? is a major question for parents to answer. This small document merely highlights some of the key factors one should consider when making such a decision. I urge all schools to adopt a thorough assessment procedure which checks all of these factors so as to provide parents with more information upon which to base their decisions. The book, *Summer Children: Ready or Not For School* (1986), which I co-authored, has been used by thousands of educators and parents to help them in this process. The 1987 book which I have edited, *Dialogues on Developmental Curriculum: K and 1* (1987), focuses on what an appropriate curriculum should be. A third book *Changing to a Developmentally Appropriate Curriculum—Successfully: Four Case Studies*, which I edited, was published in spring, 1989. It shares the actual procedures and methods used by four very different school districts as they moved from the paper-pencil approach to a curriculum, which gave many more children an opportunity to learn in the best way! All are available through Programs For Education, Inc., Rosemont, NJ 08556, 1-800-627-5867.

A child's self-concept needs to be positive. He/she should see school as a good place to be, a place where he/she finds success and support. Giving the child the best start in school demands that the parent and school work together to be sure that the curriculum available will enable this child to find success and positive experiences. Parents can also provide support for the school in its efforts to reduce the amount of paper work in the early grades. Working together, the home and the school can help each child establish a firm foundation for a lifetime of learning.

# Smaller Classes Really Are Better

*This research in Tennessee says class size definitely does make a difference in student achievement*

BY BARBARA A. NYE, JAYNE BOYD-ZAHARIAS, B. DEWAYNE FULTON, AND MARK P. WALLENHORST

IF YOU'VE BEEN A school board member for any length of time, you know there are certain recurring topics in education and certain perennial pleas. One of the pleas, offered by many parents and educators, is to reduce class sizes. Smaller classes, they argue, mean more effective teaching, and more effective teaching means improved learning for students.

But is this really so? Our own research, conducted in Tennessee classrooms, says Yes: Class size does definitely make a difference in student achievement, with smaller classes resulting in higher performance. But nationwide there is—and, in fact, always has been—great controversy over the subject of class size.

In fact, if you and your fellow school board members contemplate making classes smaller, you no doubt will be bombarded with criticism. People will say that reducing class size is little more than a way to make teachers' work less demanding, or that nothing really changes when classes are smaller. Few of these criticisms are grounded in empirical evidence. But research is available demonstrating the educational advantages of small classes.

## Small classes put to the test

In recent years, several states have opted to test the theory that small class sizes mean better student performance. And the tests show some promising results. Indiana, for one, tried in its kindergarten through second grade classes an initiative called Prime Time between 1981 and 1983. During those years, the state reduced classes from an average of 23 students for each teacher to anywhere from 14 to 18 students per teacher.

The results were impressive. On standardized reading and mathematics achievement tests, 14 percent more students in the small classes scored above average than did students in larger classes. As for teachers, those working in

*Barbara A. Nye is research director, Jayne Boyd-Zaharias is research associate, and B. DeWayne Fulton and Mark Wallenhorst are research specialists at Tennessee State University's Center of Excellence for Research in Basic Skills in Nashville.*

the smaller classes reported marked improvements in student behavior and participation, as well as increases in their own productivity.

Although Indiana's results are encouraging, they aren't without criticism. Prime Time's outcome has been questioned because the program wasn't a controlled or experimental study. The program leaders didn't account for extraneous variables (such as the effects of school location, demographics, teaching styles, or the degree of parent involvement), making it impossible to conclude definitively that performance improved because of the small classes.

Tennessee has attempted to go a step better. In 1984, Helen Pate-Bain of Tennessee State University completed a study on the effects of small class size in one Nashville school. Her findings persuaded the Tennessee legislature to commit more than $12 million to a major study in grades K-3 from 1985 to 1989. The legislation specified the project study class-size variables and include schools from inner-city, suburban, urban, and rural areas.

All Tennessee school systems were invited to participate in the Student/Teacher Achievement Ratio (STAR) Project, and 79 schools in 42 systems were selected to proceed. Participating schools agreed to a couple of conditions: First, they would not group students by ability; and second, they would assign teachers and students at random to one of three types of classrooms: (1) *small*, one teacher for from 13 to 17 students; (2) *regular*, one teacher for from 22 to 25 students; and (3) *regular-with-aide*, one teacher for from 22 to 25 students with a full-time teacher aide.

Project STAR continued for four years, involving more than 6,000 students each year. To determine the effect of small classes on student achievement, program leaders considered scores from the Stanford Achievement Test and from Tennessee's Basic Skills First test.

The results were striking. At each grade level in each of the four specified settings, the small classes performed better than both the regular classes and the regular classes with a full-time teacher aide. Although the advantage declined slightly in the second and third grades, the small-class effect remained strong across all variables. The effect was most dramatic for inner-city students, who experienced the greatest gains during each year of the study. Furthermore, students of low socioeconomic status (as determined by participation in free or reduced-price lunch

*Critics say reducing class size
isn't worth the costs. They
maintain other
approaches are more cost-effective*

programs) benefited more than did students of high socioeconomic status.

Tennessee's Department of Education is currently funding a follow-up study—the Lasting Benefits Study, or LBS—on the continued benefits of small-class participation. From our involvement in this study, we found positive benefits for fourth-grade students who previously had been in small classes in grades kindergarten through three. The benefits of small classes—as measured on test scores—were still evident one full year after students returned to regular-sized classes. LBS will continue to track the academic achievement of STAR students through 12th grade.

## The debate

The Tennessee study seems unequivocal in its support for the contention that small is better when it comes to class size. But the research on class size can be confusing, because the results have been contradictory. A landmark analysis conducted in 1978 is a case in point: After considering 77 research projects on reduced class size, Gene V. Glass and Mary Lee Smith concluded smaller classes can increase academic performance. Yet an Educational Research Service (ERS) review of the Glass and Smith analysis found their results to be a faulty interpretation of mean-

ingful information. ERS says the two researchers compared uncontrolled experiments with controlled experiments and analyzed one-on-one tutorials and other small-group activities as though they were small classes. Furthermore, says ERS, the Glass and Smith analysis combined grade levels, ranging from kindergarten through college, for the statistical analysis.

In 1986, Glen E. Robinson of ERS (with James H. Wittebols) took a second look at the Glass and Smith study and concluded there are benefits to small classes in the early primary grades. And in a 1990 study looking at research focusing on kindergarten through third grades, Robinson concluded the most significant benefits of small classes occur during these formative years.

Nevertheless, critics say reducing class size isn't worth the costs. They maintain techniques such as peer tutoring, computer-aided instruction, and increased instructional time are more cost-effective than decreasing class size.

But studies exist to refute those notions. A comparative cost-effectiveness analysis conducted by Stanford University's Henry Levin, Gene V. Glass, and Gail R. Meister found increased instructional time to be much less cost-effective and computer-aided instruction only about equally cost-effective as small classes for math. Other

# Want more on class-size research?

Want to know more about the effects of class size on student learning? The following articles and publications are a good place to start:

Theodore A. Chandler, "Here's What to Try When You Can't Shrink Class Size Enough To Matter." *The American School Board Journal*, October 1988, pages 33, 51.

Educational Research Service, *Class Size Research: A Critique of Recent Meta-analyses.* Arlington, Va.: Educational Research Service, 1980.

Gene V. Glass and Mary Lee Smith, "Meta-analysis of Research on Class Size and Achievement." *Educational Evaluation and Policy Analysis*, 1 (1979): pages 2-26.

John M. Johnston, "Relations Between Reduced Class Size and Reduced Teacher/Pupil Ratio and Developmentally Appropriate Practice in Kindergarten through Third Grade." Paper presented at the annual meeting of the American Educational Research Association, Boston, April 1990.

Henry M. Levin, Gene V. Glass, and Gail R. Meister, *Cost-Effectiveness of Four Educational Interventions* (Report No. 84-All). Stanford, Calif.: Stanford University, Center for

Education Research, 1984. (ERIC Document Reproduction Service No. ED 246 533.)

Barbara A. Nye, Jayne B. Zaharias, B. DeWayne Fulton, et al. *The Lasting Benefits Study: A Continuing Analysis of the Effect of Small Class Size in Kindergarten Through Third Grade on Student Achievement Test Scores in Subsequent Grade Levels.* Nashville, Tenn.: Tennessee State University, Center of Excellence for Research in Basic Skills, 1991.

Helen Pate-Bain and Roseanne Jacobs, "The Case for Smaller Classes and Better Teachers." *Streamlined Seminar* (published by the National Association of Elementary School Principals), September 1990, pages 1-8.

Glen E. Robinson, "Synthesis of Research on the Effects of Class Size." *Educational Leadership*, April 1990, pages 80-90.

Glen E. Robinson and James H. Wittebols, *Class Size Research: A Related Cluster Analysis for Decision Making.* Arlington, Va.: Educational Research Service, 1986.

Robert E. Slavin, "Chapter 1: A Vision for the Next Quarter Century." *Phi Delta Kappan*, April 1991, pages 586-89.—B.A.N., J.B.-Z., B.D.F., and M.P.W.

# *We find this much is clear: Smaller classes allow educators to lay the foundation for improving achievement*

researchers have shown that peer tutoring, a popular intervention, is both cost-effective and educationally effective. How useful it is in the early primary grades is somewhat questionable, however, because students in those grades need trained adult supervision.

Those who cling to the argument that small classes aren't cost-effective tend to overlook two important points: the economic costs and the education costs that stem from low teacher morale, job dissatisfaction, and increased teacher turnover. Each of these costs is incurred in overcrowded classes.

One study, in particular, points up the hidden costs of not reducing class size. John M. Johnston of Memphis State University found discrepancies in the perceptions and attitudes of those teachers who taught small classes and those teachers who taught regular-size classes. Teachers of small classes said they were more relaxed and less pressured because they were able to complete their daily lesson plans. In addition, they said they felt more satisfied with their jobs because they had more personal and academic interactions with students, fewer classroom control problems, and more opportunities to accommodate individual student needs.

A common criticism of small-class research studies is the limited scope of the investigations. And this criticism is often justified: Most projects consist of small samples in uncontrolled environments. And there hasn't been a consistent definition of what constitutes a small class. These design problems might account for the divergent and contradictory results associated with small-class research.

In our eyes and in much of the research findings, though, this much is clear: Smaller classes allow educators to lay the necessary foundation for improving basic student achievement. Reducing the number of children per class will allow teachers to apply techniques we know to be successful teaching strategies.

Pate-Bain has shown that, compared to a teacher with 25 or more students, a teacher with only 15 students is much more likely to monitor students' performance closely and provide immediate feedback. In addition, small classes are more likely to stress activities that provide children with hands-on experience. Small classes also result in increased individualized instruction and create a family atmosphere where students participate and take initiative more frequently. Moreover, the teacher can increase parent contacts and involvement.

## More than one solution

Traditionally, finding adequate funding has been one problem with reducing class sizes. The process isn't inexpensive, but those who have reduced class sizes in their school systems say the action is well worth the dollars.

Cocke County, Tenn., is one example. Eight of the county's 10 elementary schools reduced classes from as many as 25 students to as few as 15 students per teacher. The program required hiring 18 additional teachers at $26,000 each (including fringe benefits). The total cost: $468,000, or approximately $400 per child.

Some resources are available to help with these costs. School systems across the country have benefited from the new Chapter 1 flexibility allowed by the Hawkins-Stafford Amendment of 1988. The STAR results encouraged at least 10 Tennessee school systems—including Cocke County—to use Chapter 1 funds to reduce class sizes. Memphis, Tennessee's largest inner-city school system and the nation's 15th largest system, also decided to use Chapter 1 funds to reduce class size.

School systems that don't have access to Chapter 1 funds or other large funding sources can consider other ways to reduce class size that do not require great sums of money. One strategy is to shift teacher workloads: Staff members—principals, reading specialists, and librarians, as well as special education, music, and art teachers—can free their morning schedules to teach regular academic curricula (such as reading and math) in small classes, and then teach their specialized subjects in larger classes in the afternoon. This redistribution of teachers and staff can considerably reduce the number of children in the academic classes where small student-teacher ratios offer the greatest benefits.

Another way to achieve small work groups is to recruit trained volunteers from the community. Local college professors, education students, and retired teachers—among other possible volunteers—can effectively reduce student-teacher ratios by freeing up the teacher to conduct small work groups. This strategy also frees the teacher to address the needs of individual students while the rest of the class continues its work under the supervision of a trained volunteer.

In the end, it comes down to this: Providing the best possible education environment is either an expensive proposition—or a wise investment in children. The choice falls to school board members. You are the ones who must weigh the costs and benefits of reducing class size, along with alternatives to this strategy. You are the ones who must consider all the evidence and then make informed choices that aim to improve student achievement.

Well-controlled, longitudinal research on Project STAR and the Lasting Benefits Study indicates that smaller classes can provide substantial gains in student achievement, especially in the early grades. The results can include higher self-esteem among students and higher morale among teachers—plus lower retention rates and less need for special education facilities. Aren't outcomes such as these worth the extra effort and the extra cost? **SB**

# Children Don't Need Better Teachers . . . They Need Better Childhoods

## The State of America's Children

### Family/Societal Factors Affecting Today's Children:

- Divorce
- Developmentally delayed children
- Dysfunctional families
- Lack of community connectedness
- Violence — home/school/community
- Lack of manners, respect, sense of propriety
- Lack of social services
- Homeless children
- Lack of health services
- Latch key children
- Mobile population
- Poor quality day care
- Harried, hurried children
- Abused/neglected children
- Discrimination
- Blended families
- Lack of spiritual guidance
- Alcohol/drug related issues
- Children's stress — fear — anxiety
- Television
- Poverty
- Hungry children

**The Discipline/Self-Esteem Connection**

# Misbehaviors

- Attention-seeking behavior

- Power-seeking behavior

- Avoidance-of-failure behavior

**The Discipline/Self-Esteem Connection**

# Points to Discuss:

- Discipline Philosophy

- Punishment

- Consequences

- Corporal Punishment

- School Rules

- The Difficult Child

- Self-Esteem

- Teacher stress . . . the high cost of caring

- 

- 

- 

**The Discipline/Self-Esteem Connection**

Jim Grant

# Avoiding Practices That Cause Discipline Problems in the Classroom

**"We have met the enemy and he is us."**
Pogo

- Discipline programs that are suppressive in nature
- Unfair competition
- A-B-C report cards
- Test-driven curriculum
- Escalated curriculum
- Untrained teachers
- Rigid classroom structure
- Teachers who don't like children
- Inconsistency in the classroom
- Humorless classroom — no fun
- Hostile classroom environment
- Inactivity . . . no movement
- Lack of classroom management skills
- Discriminatory practices
- Boring instruction
- Meaningless irrelevant curriculum
- Large class size
- Lack of aide support in classes with high number of "at risk" children
- Lack of support staff: social worker, counselor and special education services
- Inflexible teachers
- Fixed point curriculum in a fixed amount of time
- Wide developmental range
- School rules that make no sense
- Group standardized achievement tests

**The Discipline/Self-Esteem Connection**

**Jim Grant**

# Discipline/Self-Esteem Building Techniques That Work

- Chimes/lights/musical notes
- Humor as a tool
- Time-out — classroom, office, home
- "Car Wash" to promote self-esteem
- Rewards — stickers, stars, tickets, etc.
- Moving the student
- The thinking chair
- Lower your voice
- Cease teaching
- Talk to a puppet
- Send a note/letter/card/"happy gram"
- Peer modeling
- Bibliotherapy
- "Crumb of the week"
- In-house field trips
- Positive time-out
- Reading children's names into a children's story
- The forgiveness I.O.U.
- Telephone I.O.U.
- Gift certificates, e.g., extra gym, music, recess and art
- Proximity posture
- Memorizing phone numbers
- Teacher-to-student phone visit
- 
- 
- 

**The Discipline/Self-Esteem Connection**

Jim Grant

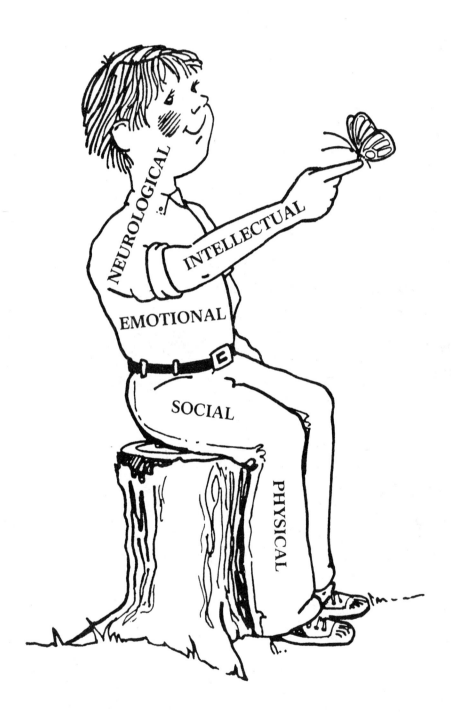

# Dispelling the Myth of Developmental Education

- Developmental Education Philosophy

- Staff Training/Selection Process

- Parent Education

- Entrance Age

- Curriculum

- Physical Setting

- Graded/Nongraded School

- Multi-age Grouping

- Discipline

- Cooperative Learning

- Tracking

• Retention

• Extra Time Programs

• Class Size

• Recess/Play/Time on Task

• Report Cards

• Authentic Assessment vs. Artificial Assessment

• Textbook/Basals/Workbooks/Dittos

• Departmentalized Elementary School

# Developmental Education

## Bibliography
### Compiled by SDE presenters

**If you would like help locating any of these books, contact Crystal Springs Books, 1-800-321-0401or in N.H., 603-924-9380.**

Ames, Louise Bates. *Arnold Gesell — Themes of His Work*. New York: Human Science Press, 1989.

_____. *Questions Parents Ask*. New York: Crown, 1988.

_____. *What Do They Mean I'm Difficult?* Rosemont, NJ: Programs for Education, 1986.

Ames, Louise Bates, and Ilg, Frances L. *Child Behavior*. New York: Barnes & Noble Books, 1955.

_____. *School Readiness*. New York: Harper & Row, 1964, 1965, 1972.

_____. *The Child From Five to Ten*. New York: Harper & Row, 1946.

_____. *Your Two-Year-Old (Terrible or Tender)*. New York: Dell, 1980.

_____. *Your Three-Year-Old (Friend or Enemy)*. New York: Dell, 1980.

_____. *Your Four-Year-Old (Wild and Wonderful)*. New York: Dell, 1980.

_____. *Your Five-Year-Old (Sunny and Serene)*. New York: Dell, 1981.

_____. *Your Ten-to Fourteen-Year-Old*. New York: Dell, 1989.

Ames, Louise Bates, and Chase, Joan Ames. *Don't Push Your Pre-Schooler*. New York: Harper & Row, 1980.

Ames, Louise Bates, and Haber, Carol Chase. *He Hit Me First (When Brothers and Sisters Fight)*. New York: Dembner Books, 1982.

_____. *Your Seven-Year-Old (Life in a Minor Key)*. New York: Delacorte, 1985.

_____. *Your Eight-Year-Old (Lively and Outgoing)*.

_____. *Your Nine-Year-Old* (Thoughtful and Mysterious). New York: Delacorte, 1990.

Ames, Louise Bates; Baker, Sidney; and Ilg, Frances L. *Child Behavior (Specific Advice on Problems of Child Behavior)*. New York: Barnes & Noble Books, 1981.

Ames, Louise Bates; Gesell, Arnold; and Ilg, Frances L. *Youth, the Years from Ten to Sixteen*. New York: Harper & Row, 1956.

Ames, Louise Bates; Ilg, Frances L.; and Haber, Carol Chase. *Your One-Year-Old (The Fun-Loving 12-to 24-month-old)*. New York: Delacorte, 1982.

Ames, Louise Bates, et al. *The Gesell Institute's Child from One to Six*. New York: Harper & Row, 1946.

_____. *Your Six-Year-Old (Loving and Defiant)*. New York: Delacorte, 1979.

Arent, Ruth P. *Stress and Your Child*. Englewood Cliffs, NJ: Prentice-Hall, 1984.

Armstrong, Thomas. *In Their Own Way*. Los Angeles: J.P.Tarcher, 1987.

Baratta-Lorton, Mary. *Mathematics Their Way*. Reading, MA: Addison-Wesley, 1989.

_____. *Workjobs*. Reading, MA: Addison-Wesley, 1989.

_____. *Workjobs II*.

_____. *Workjobs for Parents*. Reading, MA: Addison-Wesley, 1987.

Barbe, Walter. *Growing Up Learning*. Reston, VA: Acropolis, 1985.

Bettelheim, Bruno. *A Good Enough Parent*. New York: Alfred A. Knopf, 1987.

Bluestein, Jane. *Being a Successful Teacher — A Practical Guide to Instruction and Management*. Belmont, CA: Fearon Teacher Aids, 1988.

_____. *21st Century Discipline — Teaching Students Responsibility and Self-Control*.

Bluestein, Jane and Collins, Lynn. *Parents in a Pressure Cooker*. Rosemont, NJ: Programs for Education, 1990.

Boyer, Ernest. *Ready to Learn: A Mandate for the Nation*. Princeton, NJ: The Foundation for the Advancement of Teaching, 1991.

Brazelton, T. Berry. *Working and Caring*. Reading, MA: Addison-Wesley, 1985.

_____. *To Listen to a Child — Understanding the Normal Problems of Growing Up*. Reading, MA: Addison-Wesley, 1986.

_____. *What Every Baby Knows*. New York: Ballantine, 1988.

Bredekamp, Sue, ed. *Developmentally Appropriate Practice in Early Childhood Programs Serving Children from Birth through Age 8*. Washington: NAEYC, 1987.

Coplan, Theresa and Frank. *The Early Childhood Years*. New York: Putnam Publishing Group, 1983.

*Dialogues on Development. A Wide Spectrum of Persuasive Articles, Facts and Figures*. Rosemont, NJ: Programs for Education, 1986.

Dodson, Fitzhugh. *Give Your Child a Head Start in Reading*. New York: Simon & Schuster, 1981.

Elovson, Allana. *The Kindergarten Survival Book*. Santa Monica, CA: Parent Ed Resources, 1991.

Gilmore, June E. *The Rape of Childhood: No Time to Be a Kid*. Middletown, OH: J & J Publishing, 1990.

Gold, Svea J. *When Children Invite Child Abuse*. Eugene, OR: Fern Ridge Press, 1986.

Grant, Jim. *Childhood Should Be a Precious Time*. (poem anthology) Rosemont, NJ: Programs for Education.

_____. *I Hate School*. Rosemont, NJ: Programs for Education, 1986.

_____. *Jim Grant's Book of Parent Pages*. Rosemont, NJ: Programs for Education, 1988.

_____. *Worth Repeating*. Rosemont, NJ: Programs for Education, 1989.

_____. *Developmental Education in the 1990's*. Rosemont, NJ: Programs for Education, 1991

Grant, Jim, and Azin, Margot. *Every Parent's Owner's Manual*. Mini-booklets. (for 3-to-7-year-olds.)

Grant, Jim, and Johnson, Bob. *Childhood Should Be a Journey . . . Not a Race: Kindergarten Readiness*. Peterborough, NH : Crystal Springs Books, 1992.

_____. *Childhood Should Be a Journey . . .Not a Race: First Grade Readiness.* Peterborough, NH: Crystal Springs Books, 1992.

_____. *Childhood Should Be a Journey . . .Not a Race: Second Grade Readiness.* Peterborough, NH: Crystal Springs Books, 1993.

_____. *Childhood Should Be a Journey . . .Not a Race: Third Grade Readiness.* Peterborough, NH: Crystal Springs Books, 1993.

Hayes, Martha, and Faggella, Kathy. *Think It Through.* Bridgeport, CT: First Teacher Press, 1986.

Hoffman, Carol M. *Curriculum Gone Astray.* Lancaster, PA: Technomic Publishing Co., 1987.

Holt, John. *How Children Fail.* New York: Dell Publishing, 1964, 1982.

Horowitz, Janet, and Faggella, Kathy. *Partners for Learning.* Bridgeport, CT: First Teacher Press, 1986.

Kentucky Education Association. *The Wonder Years.* Frankfort, KY: KEA.

Labinowitz, Ed. *The Piaget Primer.* Reading, MA: Addison-Wesley, 1980.

LaBritta, Gilbert. *I Can Do It! I Can Do It! — 135 Successful Independent Learning Activities.*

Lansky, Vicki. *Divorce Book for Parents.* New York: New American Library, 1989.

LeShan, Eda. *When Your Child Drives You Crazy.* New York: St. Martin's Press, 1986.

Linderman, C. Emma. *Teachables from Trashables — Homemade Toys That Teach.*

Miller, Karen. *Ages and Stages.* Marshfield, MA: Telshare Publishing, 1985.

Moore, Dorothy N., and Moore, Raymond. *Home Grown Kids.* Irving, TX: Word Books, 1984.

National Association of Elementary School Principals. *Early Childhood Education and the Elementary School Principal.* Alexandria, VA: NAESP, 1990.

Nelson, Jane. *Positive Discipline.* New York: Ballantine, 1987.

Nichols, Elisabeth. *Young Children at Work.* Rosemont, NJ: Programs for Education, 1988.

Northeast Foundation for Children, Inc. *A Notebook for Teachers: Making Changes in the Elementary Curriculum.* Greenfield, MA.

Ohio Department of Education. *The Ohio Early Childhood Curriculum Guide.* Columbus, OH: Ohio Department of Education, 1991.

Shickedanz, Judith A. *More Than ABC's.* Washington: NAEYC, 1986.

Singer, Dorothy, and Revenson, Tracy. *How a Child Thinks: A Piaget Primer.* Independence, MO: International University Press, 1978.

Szasz, Suzanne. *The Unspoken Language of Children.* Toronto, Ont.: George J. McLeod, 1978.

Uphoff, James K., ed. *Changing to a Developmentally Appropriate Curriculum — Successfully: 4 Case Studies.* Rosemont, NJ: Programs for Education, 1989.

_____. *Dialogues on Developmental Curriculum: Pre-K-1.* Rosemont, NJ: Programs for Education, 1987.

Vail, Priscilla L. *Clear and Lively Writing*. New York: Walker & Co., 1981.

White, Burton L. *The First Three Years of Life*. New York: Avon Books, 1979.

Wolf, Elizabeth Kjorlaug. *Meanwhile Back to the Child*.

# For Children, Too

Cohen, Miriam. *First Grade Takes a Test*. New York: Greenwillow Books, 1980.

_____. *No Good in Art*. New York: Greenwillow Books, 1980.

_____. *See You in Second Grade*. New York: Dell, 1990.

_____. *When Will I Read*? New York: Greenwillow Books, 1977.

_____. *Where's George?*

_____. *Will I Have a Friend?* New York: Collier Books, 1967.

Kraus, Robert. *Leo the Late Bloomer*. New York: Windmill Books, 1971.

_____. *Leo the Late Bloomer Bakes a Cake*. New York: Windmill Books, 1981.

_____. *Leo the Late Bloomer Takes a Bath*. New York: Windmill Books, 1971.

Pass, Linda. *Taking a Test: The Inside Story*. Rosemont, NJ: Programs for Education, 1988.

Reavis, George H. *The Animal School*. Rosemont, NJ: Programs for Education, 1988.

Ross, Pat. *Molly and the Slow Teeth*. Peterborough, NH: Crystal Springs Books, 1992.

Trisler, Alana, and Cardiel, Patricia Howe. Words I Use When I Write. Rosemont, NJ: Programs for Education, 1989.

# Anti-Hurrying

Elkind, David. *All Grown Up & No Place to Go*. Reading, MA: Addison-Wesley, 1984.

_____. *The Hurried Child*. Reading, MA: Addison-Wesley, 1981.

_____. *Miseducation*. New York: Alfred A. Knopf, 1987.

_____. Grandparenting: *Understanding Today's Children*.

Healy, Jane. *Endangered Minds*.

Packard, Vance. *Our Endangered Children*. Boston: Little, Brown & Co., 1983.

Postman, Neil. *The Disappearance of Childhood*. New York: Dell, 1982.

Winn, Marie. *Children Without Childhood*. New York: Penguin Books, 1984.

# Grade Re-Placement

Ames, Louise Bates. *What Am I Doing in This Grade?* Rosemont, NJ: Programs for Education, 1985.

_____. *Is Your Child in the Wrong Grade?* Rosemont, NJ: Modern Learning Press, 1978.

Ames, Louise Bates; Gillespie, Clyde; and Streff, John W. *Stop School Failure.* Rosemont, NJ: Programs for Education, 1972

Grant, Jim. *I Hate School.* Rosemont, NJ: Programs for Education, 1986.

_____. *Worth Repeating.* Rosemont, NJ: Programs for Education, 1989.

Healy, Jane M., Ph.D. *Your Child's Growing Mind.* New York: Doubleday & Co., 1987.

Hobby, Janice Hale. *Staying Back.* Gainesville, FL: Triad, 1950.

Moore, Sheila, and Frost, Roon. *The Little Boy Book.* New York: Clarkson N. Potter, 1986.

Osman, Betty B. *No One to Play With.* New York: Warner Books, 1982.

Sachar, Louis. *Someday Angeline.* New York: Avon Camelot Books, 1983.

Uphoff, James K., and Gilmore, June E. *Summer Children — Ready or Not for School.* Middletown, Ohio: J&J Publishing Co., 1986.

# Early Childhood/
# Developmental Education Publications

*Childhood Education*
Journal of the Association for Childhood
  Education International
Suite 315
11501 Georgia Ave.
Wheaton, MD  20902

*Early Childhood News*
Peter Li, Inc.
2451 E. River Rd.
Dayton, OH  45439

*Early Childhood Research Quarterly*
Ablex Publishing Corp.
355 Chestnut St.
Norwood, NJ  07648

*Pre-K Today*
730 Broadway
New York, NY 10003

*A Newsletter for Teachers*
Northeast Foundation for Children
71 Montague City Rd.
Greenfield, MA 01301

*Young Children*
National Association for the Education of Young
  Children (NAEYC)
1834 Connecticut Ave. NW
Washington, DC 20009

# Audio/Video Resources

Ames, Louise Bates. *Part I: Ready Or Not: Here I Come!*, video.

_____. *Part II: An Evaluation of the Whole Child*, video. (Available from Programs for Education)

Bluestein, Jane. *"Win-Win" Discipline for Parents (and Teachers) in a Pressure Cooker*, video. (Programs for Education)

Coletta, Anthony. *Developmental Parenting*, audio tape. (Programs for Education)

*Gesell Institute of Human Development. Ready or Not Here I Come!* Video/16mm film, 1984. (Programs for Education)

Grant, Jim. *Jim Grant Live*, audio tape. 1985.

_____. *Grade Replacement*, audio tape.

_____. *Worth Repeating*, video.

_____. *Do You Know Where Your Child Is?*, video, 1985. (All four available from Programs for Education)

Haines, Jackie. *Gesell Seminar*, audio tape. (Programs for Education)

Johnson, Robert. *Implementing a Developmental Program*, audio tape. (Programs for Education)

Page, William. *The Basics: Time, Play and You*, audio tape, 1986. (Programs for Education)

Uphoff, James K. *Readiness for School: Setting the Stage for Success*, audio tape. (Programs for Education)

Vail, Priscilla L. *Raising Smart Kids: Commonsense, Uncommon Needs*, audio tape, 1986. (Programs for Education)

Webb, Gwen. *Is Your Child Ready?*, filmstrip, audio tape, video.

_____. *Questions Parents Ask*, video.

Address of Order Department:
    Programs for Education
    P.O. Box 167
    Rosemont, NJ 08556
    1-800-627-5867

# Child Advocacy Organizations

Children's Defense Fund
122 C Street NW, 4th Floor
Washington, DC 20001

Privately supported child advocacy organization.

Child Trends, Inc.
2100 M Street NW
Washington, DC 20037

Research organization that studies social changes affecting children.

# DIFFERENTLY ABLED

## Teach Me: Don't Label Me

Barbara K. Given, Ph.D

I am not "disabled."
I learn differently.
I am not "handicapped."
I take in and use information
    that is somewhat unique to me.
Others may see me as handicapped
    when they insist on teaching me
    in ways through which I cannot learn
    or when they insist that I demonstrate my abilities
    in ways that are comfortable for them
    but not for me.
It is not I who is out of step, inadequate, handicapped or disabled.
It is the system.
I don't want my teacher to be my pal, but
    I do want a model and a friend.
I don't want my teacher to make life easy for me, but
    I do want a teacher filled with a conviction that what
    he or she teaches is important enough for me to learn
    and
I do want a teacher who has enthusiasm that encourages
    me to keep working until I learn.
I don't want to be the teacher's pet, but
    I do want to be treated as a person worthy of respect
    in spite of my learning style or because of it.
I don't want a teacher who demands praise, but
    I do want a teacher who understands my respect even
    if I show it in an awkward and sometimes hostile way.
I don't want a brain transplant, but
    I do want to learn as much as I am able.
I don't want a label, but
    I do want an appropriate education.
I don't want to be called "learning disabled," but
    I do want to learn.
Teach me.
Don't label me.

*Associate Professor Barbara K. Given is coordinator of the Learning Disabilities Teacher Preparation Program and co-director of Southeast Learning Styles Center, George Mason University, Fairfax, VA 22030-4444.*

Academic Therapy                                                                        May 1988

# Whole Language with LD Children

by Paul M. Hollingsworth and D. Ray Reutzel

*Practices consistent with whole language theory*
*to help LD students become literate users*
*of language as a communication medium*

The debate among educators over how to best help learning disabled children who have difficulty learning to read and write continues unabated right up to the present moment and is unlikely to subside in the near future. Recently the debate has begun heating up once again with the two sides lining up for another major battle. On the one side, the teacher, the curriculum, and the scope and sequence of skills are considered to be at the center of the schooling process; while on the other, the children, their skills, competencies, and needs are at the heart of schooling. The intent of this article is not to further debate this issue but to elaborate the research and theoretical foundation established in our previous article, "Whole Language and the Practitioner," which was published in the March 1988 issue of *Academic Therapy*.

The search for solutions to help the language-learning disabled must be multi-disciplinary in nature if these children are to be best served. For many years, the diagnosis and treatment of the language-learning disabled was the exclusive domain of special education or remedial reading clinicians. Programs designed for and delivered in these settings were outgrowths from a strong dependence on the tenets of behavioristic psychology. Behaviorists used task analysis to simplify the tasks of reading and writing by breaking them down into smaller subsets or subskills (Dudley-Marling 1986). Each sub-skill in reading and writing was taught in a predetermined sequence until students could demonstrate mastery. This practice created the problem of having children practice the very skills in which they experienced the least success (Pearson 1985). The assumption was that if each skill was practiced and mastered individually, the collective or unitary nature of reading and writing would naturally emerge as the outgrowth of such instruction. This has proven to be a false assumption (Altwerger, Edelsky & Flores 1987). Furthermore, the teaching of reading and writing skills in fragmented skill sequences cannot be supported from the research literature since no validated skill hierarchy has ever been established in reading and writing (Samuels 1976).

Stripping reading skills away from the holistic act of reading and writing into separate lessons that often do not relate to processing a complete piece of text made literacy learning even more difficult (Reutzel & Daines 1987). When the learning disabled child is presented with fragmented bits and pieces of written language, he is often led to the conclusion that learning reading and writing skills lacks real purpose or at best is aimed at completing workbook pages and ditto sheets

(Dudley-Marling & Rhodes 1986; Smith 1986). In fact, when the reading and writing process is broken down into isolated and arbitrarily sequenced instructional objectives, the process of becoming literate is made increasingly abstract and complex (Poplin 1986). Thus when the skill and mastery driven approach to helping the language-learning disabled child began to show signs of failure, children with language related disabilities were considered to be disabled users of language (Ramsey 1985).

This conclusion was accepted by many when, in fact, language-learning disabled children may not be language disabled at all (Smith 1986). They may just have had a difficult time making sense out of a teaching system that arbitrarily established learning sequences and hierarchies and divorced the learning of reading and writing skills from their real and functional use in society. Rather than examining the instructional program, philosophy, and practices used to treat the language-learning disabled child, the diagnosis and evaluation of educators in the past was usually focused on the child and what was organically, intellectually, or functionally inadequate within the organism. A language-learning disability was viewed as something innately wrong with the child and not a manifestation of the potential inadequacies of a particular program, philosophy or practice (Goodman 1986).

In contrast, Mary Poplin (1984) indicated that the learning disabled child often learns best through his collective experiences which is best accounted for by the use of a holistic learning model. Under a holistic model, the emphasis on a deficit driven approach to the learning disabled is shifted toward a strengths, ability, and child-needs-oriented perspective. Poplin clarifies this position by explaining that several factors are crucial to a

successful learning experience for the learning disabled child: (a) linking instruction to past and present experiences, (b) arranging physical variables to serve the functional needs of the child, and (c) carefully considering personality traits of the learner and the teacher, and the child's natural interests, abilities, and aptitudes.

*The language-learning disabled child learns naturally from exposure and use rather than from isolated instructional drills.*

Learning disabled children can best learn to read and write in much the same way they learned to speak (Holdaway 1979). LD children become familiar with meaningful printed materials and find support for naturally progressing toward a state of cognitive clarity regarding the functions and purposes for using printed language through immersion in a print-rich environment (Downing 1984; Hiebert 1986). The language-learning disabled child extracts from the print-rich environment that which is personally relevant to him. Thus, the learning progresses from the meaningful whole of language to an understanding of the parts of the language transaction. The language-learning disabled child learns naturally from exposure and use rather than from isolated instructional drills. Simply put, learning occurs best where there is active involvement in an

interesting and functionally relevant language-learning opportunity (McNutt 1984; Carbo 1987). Knowing this brings us to the next important element associated with helping the language-learning disabled child — changing the language-learning environment.

### The Whole Language Learning Environment: Modifying the Resource Room

The learning environment is an essential element in the learning process for LD children (Poplin 1986). No longer should teachers and children be carelessly placed in a learning environment that just happens to be vacant at that hour of the day or in a space resembling a closet in the basement. The resource room can no longer be that "other room for those other children," but must look much like any other appropriately designed language classroom in the school. This raises the question — what does an appropriately designed language classroom look like?

First, a well designed language-learning classroom will exhibit a home-like environment with tables, chairs, bean bag chairs, couches, and special carpeted areas arranged into areas intended for silent reading and writing as well as areas designated specially for discussion and interaction. Second, space on bulletin boards, chalkboards, windows, doors, and walls should become display and publishing areas to be covered with children's compositions, dictations, and art work which are the natural outgrowths of LD children's reading and writing.

Third, the room would contain interest centers that focus on a single topic, theme or literature selection. These thematic or literature centers would deal with topics or literature in which the LD children in the resource room express an interest. The children and the resource teacher could make or bring to the interest center books, magazines, specimens and exhibits, magnets, aquariums, games, puzzles, their art work and compositions, etc., to be shared and to add interest to the resource room. From the use of these materials and the production of other materials, the LD child learns naturally. Not only do LD children learn in these interest centers, but they extend their interests and enrich their experiential base. Often in the regular classroom, LD children seldom get to work in these centers because they must complete their workbook assignments before they can participate in interest and learning centers.

Fourth, the resource room should not be the exclusive habitat of the LD child. In order to erase the stigma attached to this room, "normal or average" learners should be ushered into this room to participate and share in the learning experiences of their LD peers. One potential outcome of this modification may involve a demand by normal students to be placed in the resource room! Last, the term "learning disabled" should be eliminated. If one truly believes it is the program, philosophy, and practices that are disabled, then labeling the child learning disabled is certainly inappropriate. Some special educators feel that no child is learning disabled, but rather some children have been the victims of teaching disabilities (Hammill 1976).

**Selected Pedagogical Practices Consistent with Whole Language Theory**

Many instructional practices are or can be considered consistent with whole language theory and are highly interactive and social in nature, thus helping the LD child acquire the social skills necessary to function in the resource room as well as the regular classroom. Among these are: (1) Impress Method, (2) Oral Reading Variations, (3) Reading Aloud, (4) Language Experience Approach, (5) Predictable Story Books, (6) Word Rubberbanding, (7) the Shared Reading Experience, (8) the Writing Process Approach, (9) Sustained Silent Writing, (10) Sustained Silent Reading, (11) Contextual Reading Clues or Cloze, and (12) Logo Language or Environmental Print.

---

*Some special educators feel that no child is learning disabled, but rather some children have been the victims of teaching disabilities.*

---

*Impress Method*

Research has indicated that the Impress Method can help students in reading fluency and assist them through modeling fluent reading. This method is especially suitable for remedial or learning disabled children (Heckelman 1962; Hollingsworth 1978). The child chooses the book that he has an interest in reading.

The Impress Reading Method is a unison reading technique in which the teacher and the child read aloud simultaneously. The teacher and the child hold the same book so that the student's one hand is free to use his finger as a guide to how fast or slow the reading is. The finger should be directly below the words as they are read and then moved with a smooth, continuous motion while reading. During the first session using this technique, the teacher may need to slide her finger under the words until the child understands the procedure or the teacher could slide the child's hand and finger while reading. During the reading period, no instruction is given in word attack, comprehension, or any other reading skills. The goal is to read as much as possible without causing any physical discomfort for a fifteen-minute period. When reading is finished, the teacher does not quiz the child. The child may discuss with the teacher what was read if he wishes. Variations to the Impress Method include choral reading, teacher/student reading, and student/student reading (Hollingsworth 1970).

*Oral Reading Variations*

Pearson and Fielding (1982) emphasize that oral reading can help children comprehend what they read by placing attention on the rhythm, tempo, and melody of written language. Wood (1983) recommends an oral reading variation called four-way oral reading. After reading a story or selection silently in preparation for oral reading, the teacher tells the students they will be called on to read randomly rather than in sequence as in round robin. Children may be called on individually, in pairs, or in groups to read aloud. The first oral reading variation involves students reading in pairs. Here a pair of students read aloud in unison, and the teacher provides help with difficult words. The second oral reading variation uses choral reading. Everyone in the group reads in unison until the teacher indicates a stopping point. The third oral reading variation employs a technique called imitative reading. The teacher reads a sentence or two aloud and tells the children to read the sentences back to her just as she read them. In essence, the children echo the sentence reading of the teacher. Finally, children can become involved in mumble reading, the fourth oral reading variant. This is defined as reading aloud quietly or mumbling.

These four oral reading strategies can be used to add variety to the reading of any story or text. For example, a teacher might begin the reading of a selection by having several pairs of students read a paragraph or two each. Next, she could have the entire group read the next few paragraphs in choral. After that, the students might be asked to read a few sentences echoing the teacher's reading. And finally, the students might mumble read to the end of the story individually. An important fact to remember about oral reading is that oral reading is performance. These oral reading variations provide a psychological safety net for students when they read aloud, thus eliminating or at lease reducing the risk of public failure and embarrassment generally associated with solo oral reading in the round robin reading circle.

### Reading Aloud

In a whole language resource room, time should be set aside for the teacher or the children to read aloud to each other. This is an opportunity for the children and the teacher to share favorite books they have read or to share their writing activities. A reader's theatre provides an excellent opportunity for LD children to rehearse an oral reading selection in preparation for an audience-oriented presentation. The repeated readings along with the added motivation of performance give necessary practice and repetition as well as extra motivation to read.

### Language Experience Approach

The Language Experience Approach (LEA) helps the learning disabled student in reading, writing, spelling, and language even if he is not proficient in these skills. In the resource room, either real-life or vicarious experiences are provided as stimuli to elicit the compo-

sition of a story. Either type of experience can produce excellent results. The sharing of a literature selection can also serve as a basis for language experience compositions. LEA can be done for one child, a small group, or all of the children at once. The procedures for LEA are: (1) the children participate in an experience, (2) a through oral discussion of the experience is held, (3) the children write or dictate about the experience, and (4) the children share their writing experiences with others by displaying them in the resource room and by reading them to their classmates. During step three, the entire procedure for the writing process can be utilized.

### Predictable Story Books

Predictable story books are excellent for reading with remedial or learning disabled children. Predictable books exhibit two primary characteristics. First, the text is supported by the pictures and vice versa. Second, the books contain repeated language patterns such as those found in books like *The Gingerbread Man* and *The Three Billy Goats Gruff*. These books provide children with a view that reading is predictable and patterned. Often these books are popular with LD children because they can be successful with their first try. They enjoy the stories and usually read the entire book at one time. This is a feat few LD children experience or are allowed to experience.

### Word Rubberbanding

When LD children participate in shared reading experiences, they will begin to relate letters to sounds, and the patterns of language written down. If they are still having difficulty with sounds in words, the "rubberbanding" procedure is very effective not only for reading but also for writing (Calkins 1986). When a child needs help, the teacher or other children

in the classroom stretch out the sounds of the words much like stretching a rubber band. From the word "man," the helper would say "mmmmmmm — aaaaaaa — nnnnnnn, mm — aa — nn, man." From this rubberbanding, the child begins to pay greater attention to the sounds that make up words he needs to read and spell.

### The Shared Reading Experience

The Shared Reading Experience (Holdaway 1979; Slaughter 1983) is an excellent method for helping LD children gain an understanding of fluent reading and the purposes and conventions of printed language. The key to using a Shared Reading Experience is to enlarge the text of familiar poems, songs, books, etc., so that the entire group can see and share in the reading experience. The SRE is designed to imitate the bedtime story reading episode that occurs in many homes. First, the teacher reads the small text aloud to the group. Second, the enlarged text is displayed for the group and read aloud by the teacher. Next, the children are invited to join in reading the text while the teacher points to each word as it is read. Extensions of the approach include having children point to the words, discussing important language elements such as phonic clues, text structure, word endings, etc. Commercially prepared "big books" are an easy way to incorporate this practice into every LD resource room.

### The Writing Process Approach

Self-selection of the writing topic is central to the writing process approach (Graves 1983; Calkins 1986). Students begin by brainstorming alone, with peers, or the teacher about topics for writing that can be recorded and kept in a folder for each child. Children are then encouraged to write, plan or even draw during the prewriting phase of the writing process without interruption for correction or revision. After a draft has been prepared, students and teacher participate in a writing conference where suggestions and support are given for revision. Elements of the writing convention such as neatness, punctuation, and spelling are dealt with during the writing conference. Next, the child revises if he feels sufficient involvement with the topic to complete the second draft. Otherwise another topic for writing is selected from the folder. If a revision ensues from the conference, the second draft is submitted to an outside editor such as a peer or even the teacher for final suggestions. Finally, the work is published. Hence, the process includes prewriting or planning, writing, conferencing, revision, and publication. The form of the writing can also vary from the authoring of cards, notes, and recipes to books, posters, and poetry.

*Silent Sustained Writing*

This is a time of the day that is reserved for everyone, including the teacher, to engage in self-selected writing. Often times this centers on the practice of journal writing. A nice variation on this approach can involve the use of dialogue journals where the student writes to the teacher in his journal and the teacher responds in writing to the child's journal entry. Thus the student and teacher engage in a dialogue in the child's journal.

*Sustained Silent Reading*

Most learning disabled children after they have experienced success in reading will like to read for some part of the day in a quiet, informal area. This is especially true when they have learned to successfully read the stories and books that are available in the classroom. Sustained silent reading occurs when everyone in the class, including the teacher, is reading for a period of time.

*Contextual Reading Clues or Cloze*

From the whole language per-

spective, reading and writing instruction should always take place in sentence level units or higher levels of language. When children need help in reading, the words or sounds are taught in a meaningful context. Sounds or words are not presented in isolation, but are taught in the context of whole texts, phrases, or sentences. Such an approach to language instruction helps LD children see the proper relationship between letter sounds and words as they relate to the context of the materials read. Even if the child cannot read the entire sentence with absolute oral accuracy, the children learn how these units work together to produce messages that they can understand. The children are naturally drawn to letters, sounds, and parts of words as they search for meaning. An excellent process for helping LD children learn to properly use contextual clues in print is called the "cloze procedure." This is essentially a fill-in-the blank procedure where students must infer from the text a deleted word. Many variations on the cloze include successive cloze, maze, modified cloze, etc. (Aulls 1982).

*Logo Language or Environmental Print*

LD children are bombarded with print from their environment. Television advertisements make it possible for them to go to the store and pick out the item advertised. Labels and signs of all kinds can be used effectively to teach reading in a whole language resource room. Children are readily familiar with these labels and signs, thus capitalizing on the LD child's collective life experiences (Poplin, 1986).

**Conclusions**

A crucial consideration in the Whole Language Approach for LD students is to help them know they are already successful language users and that reading and writing are just another way they can use the language to communicate. In

the resource room, the children need to feel it is all right to risk and make mistakes for that is the way we all learn. They need to guess, take risks, and test out their reading and writing skills in a supportive environment. The solution to the problem for many learning disabled children is putting language together again and helping them rediscover the meaningful relationships that exist in our language.

**References**

Altwenger, B., Edelsky, C. and Flores, B.M. 1987. Whole Language: What's New? *The Reading Teacher*, 41, pp. 132-137.

Aulls, M.W. 1982. *Developing readers in today's elementary school.* Boston: Allyn & Bacon, Inc.

Calkins, L. 1986. *The art of teaching writing.* Portsmouth, NH: Heinemann.

Carbo, M. 1987. Matching reading styles — correcting ineffective instruction. *Educational leadership,* 45, pp. 55-62.

Downing, J. 1984. Task awareness in the development of reading skill. In Downing, J. and Valtin, R., (Eds.) *Language awareness and learning to read.* New York: Springer-Verlag.

Dudley-Marling, C. 1986. Assessing the reading and writing development of learning disabled students: An holistic perspective, *Canadian Journal of Special Education,* 2, pp. 33-43.

Dudley-Marling, C. & Rhodes, L.K. 1986. Teachers must create an environment for literacy instruction. *Teaching Exceptional Children,* 18, pp. 289-291.

Goodman, K. 1986. *What's whole in whole language?* Portsmouth, NH: Heinemann.

Graves, D.H. 1983. *Writing: Teachers & children at work.* Portsmouth, NH: Heinemann.

Hammill, D.D. 1976. Defining learning disabilities for programmatic purposes. *Academic Therapy,* 12, pp. 29-37.

# ATTENTION DEFICIT DISORDERS
## (ADD/ADHD)

by Edna D. Copeland, Ph.D.
Child/Clinical Psychologist
Coauthor of *Attention Without
Tension: A Teacher's Handbook*

*The teacher leaves the room, and
Johnny impulsively throws his pencil
across the room.*

*Susie, endearingly called, "my little
dreamer," is in a world of her own.
While her attention can be refocused
on the teacher, constant gentle
reminders are necessary.*

*Tommy can't sit still during storytime.
Instead, he crawls on the floor or
under the table and frequently bothers
other children.*

*Carolyn is disorganized and forgetful.
Lost sweaters, forgotten books and
crumpled papers have become expected.*

*Frank is overactive and aggressive
and bullies his classmates.*

These and other scenes involving
preschool and early elementary
children with attention disorders are
repeated hundreds of times daily in
every school in the nation. Why
don't these children pay attention?
Why are they so disorganized?
Why are some overactive and
impulsive, while others are underactive and lethargic?

### What Are Attention Disorders?

Attention disorders, both those
with hyperactivity (ADHD) and
those without hyperactivity
(undifferentiated ADD), are neuro-
physiological disorders generally
believed the result of deficiencies
or imbalances in the neurotransmitters, or brain chemicals, which
affect the parts of the brain important for alertness, focusing, attention, organization, and inhibition.
ADHD/ADD is a medical disorder.
It is not a psychological problem, a
learning disability, poor parenting,
or an overly demanding teacher, as
is often mistakenly thought.

It is conservatively estimated that
3-6% of the 45 million children in
the United States under the age of
18 have an attention disorder.
These disorders occur in children of
every ability level and in every
socioeconomic group throughout
the world. They occur four to eight
times more frequently in boys than
in girls. However, girls are thought
to be greatly underidentified.

Attentional problems usually
begin in early childhood or in the
elementary school years. They
often continue into adolescence and
adulthood and can last a lifetime.
They can be difficult to recognize,
for the symptoms frequently
masquerade as other kinds of
difficulties. Often children, adolescents, and even adults with ADHD/
ADD are thought to be "lazy,"
"disinterested," or "uncooperative."

Attention disorders are receiving
much attention at the present time.
In September, 1991, the U.S.
Department of Education issued a
memorandum stating that Attention
Deficit Disorders are considered a
handicapping condition under the
*Other Health Impaired (OHI)*
category of P.L. 94-142. Those who
do not meet eligibility criteria for
P.L. 94-142 assistance can receive
assistance under Section 504 of
P.L. 93-112. This clarification of

> **It is conservatively
> estimated that
> 3-6% of the 45
> million children in
> the United States
> under the age of 18
> have an attention
> disorder.**

the law, now known as the *Individuals With Disabilities Education
Act* or *IDEA,* designed to assist
those with ADHD or ADD, was of
major importance, for untreated
attention disorders create significant learning, emotional and social
problems for children and adolescents. Schools are meeting the
challenge of ADHD/ADD with
increased education of teachers and
parents and greater understanding
of how to assist students with
attention disorders maximize their
potential.

Teachers of preschool and early
elementary children must be aware
of attention disorders. The implica-

tions of ADHD/ADD in language and reading disorders have received increasing attention as it has become apparent that attentional deficits affect the preschooler's selective and sustained attention to the language he hears. Since 1985, the link between early oral lan-

> ## Developmental readiness becomes an especially crucial issue for students who have attentional problems.

guage skills and reading has been clearly demonstrated, as well as the interaction of language, memory and attention on later reading ability. Since attention shows a very high correlation with reading success, it is important that we identify those children with ADHD/ADD in the preschool years and effectively intervene in the attention disorder.

Developmental readiness becomes an especially crucial issue for students who have attentional problems, whether on the day-dreaming, underactive end of the continuum, or the more restless, distractible, overactive end. Children with attention disorders tend to be neurologically, socially, and developmentally immature. Adding chronological immaturity to this constellation can be especially devastating. The assessment of readiness for kindergarten and first grade is thus crucial. Many of these children will do best if they have an additional year at the K-4 level.

## CHARACTERISTICS OF CHILDREN WITH ATTENTION DISORDERS

Each child with ADHD or ADD has a unique set of symptoms and characteristics. It is crucial that you, as a teacher, recognize the symptoms of attention disorders in your students. After understanding the difficulties associated with ADHD, you should be able to recognize the symptoms. If you do suspect that a student has an attention disorder, encourage his/her family to seek professional assistance from someone thoroughly familiar with this disorder. Proper diagnosis is crucial to establishing appropriate and effective treatment interventions.

The major symptoms of ADHD/ADD, originally described by the American Psychiatric Association and ones which continue to be viewed as major problems, are divided into three categories. These are (1) inattention and distractibility, (2) impulsivity, and (3) problems with activity level — either overactivity or underactivity. Other characteristics include: noncompliance, attention-getting behavior, immaturity, school problems, emotional difficulties, poor peer relationships, and family interaction problems.

*For a comprehensive list of symptoms of ADHD and ADD, you may obtain the Copeland Symptom Checklist for Attention Deficit Disorders from the 3 C's of Childhood, P.O.Box 12389, Atlanta, GA 30355.*

**Reprinted with permission of Edna D. Copeland.**

> ### Voices
>
> *Children do not care what you know until they know that you care.*

# That Kid Who Drives You Crazy!

**by Jane Hersey, Executive Director**
**Feingold Association of the United States**

*You could run through an alphabet of symptoms: aggressive, belligerent, clumsy, distractable, emotional, forgetful, gauche, hyperactive, impulsive...*

*There is evidence to indicate that many children like this are reacting to everyday substances; fortunately a great deal can be done to help them.*

Do you wake up some days and wonder why you ever chose to be a teacher? Of all the challenges you face, let's isolate one and take a closer look at it — and in this case "it" is a child we'll call Jeremy. He's bright. The tests show that, but you wouldn't know it from looking at his work. He understands a concept one day and is bewildered by it the next.

He does foolish/destructive things even though he knows better. When you ask him why, and he responds, "I don't know," his answer seems genuine.

His hands, legs and mouth appear to possess a life of their own. He says the wrong things, too loud, and at the wrong time. Most of the other children avoid him; although a few find him an easy target and convenient scapegoat.

As you speak with Jeremy's mother you listen carefully for clues that would explain where she went wrong. But she's as exasperated as you are, and her other children are fine. "Poor parenting" just doesn't fit.

Is there "something wrong" with this little boy — something in his brain which doesn't work properly? Is there a defect he was born with? This is not a comfortable fit either, as his behavior is inconsistent. On some days he functions quite

well, and on others he's impossible. Similarly, his mother notes there are wide variations at home. She also mentions that Jeremy was a contented baby during the time she was breastfeeding, but he had difficulty sleeping after she introduced table food. Both of you notice he's worse after holidays and parties but conclude that he is just over stimulated.

Although various tests show Jeremy's brain is perfectly normal, your suspicion is correct that something is wrong with his "internal environment." A relatively new branch of science deals with this. It's called "behavioral toxicology" and looks at the way a sensitive individual's behavior can be affected by external substances.

While the formal study of behavioral toxicology is new, the examples are as old as recorded history. Take an external substance called "wine." If a person consumed a large quantity of wine, and then behaved abnormally or couldn't remember how to solve a math problem, we wouldn't be mystified by the cause.

> **A relatively new branch of science . . . called "behavioral toxicology" looks at the way a sensitive individual's behavior can be affected by external substances.**

If we were to conduct an experiment with many individuals, we would see wide variations in the ability to tolerate this substance (wine). The reactions to it would depend upon the amount consumed and each person's degree of sensitivity to it — in other words, the individual's chemical make-up would be an important factor.

There are many substances besides wine which can affect a person's behavior and ability to focus and learn. Some are believed to be transient and some are known to be permanent. Examples include heavy metals such as lead, mercury and cadmium; alcohol of all types; nicotine; caffeine; drugs — both legal and illegal; solvents and glues, such as airplane glue; petroleum.

---

*We eat, breathe, and surround ourselves with the by-products of crude oil every day, and some of us are having a hard time coping with these powerful substances.*

---

Petroleum!? Who thinks about this, except when we fill our gas tank or read about OPEC? Few people are aware that 37% of the crude oil used in the United States goes into the manufacturing of other products with which we come in contact every day. Derivatives of petroleum and crude oil are in our clothing, cosmetics, shampoos, detergents, perfumes, paints, plastics, pesticides, and — most significant of all, our food. We eat, breathe, and surround ourselves with the by-products of crude oil every day, and some of us are having a hard time coping with these powerful substances.

Let's take a look at the typical morning in Jeremy's life as he gets ready for school. (Every substance which is likely to be an irritant for a chemically-sensitive person is noted with an*.)

He wakes up between sheets which have been exposed to scented fabric softening strips.* He walks down the hall on new carpeting,* which still retains the smell of the chemicals used in its manufacture. An air freshener* adorns the bathroom and competes with scented soap* and scented tissue.* The tub has been cleaned with a miracle spray,* and the scent of chlorine* clings to the tile floor. His toothpaste is green.* Breakfast is a bowl of sugar frosted grains and synthetically-colored marshmallow bits,* all treated with the preservative BHA.* The cereal floats in a sea of low fat milk, which has BHT* hidden in the added vitamin A. What looks like juice is a blend of water, sugar, and synthetic dyes,* plus artificial orange flavoring.* An artificially colored and flavored vitamin* tops off the meal. If Jeremy is having one of his frequent ear infections, his mother gives him a spoonful of bright pink, bubble gum-flavored medicine.* He runs past the fragrant potpourri,* out the door, across the lush green lawn treated with powerful pesticides,* across the newly paved asphalt* street. He has forgotten his homework and his lunch money (for the third time this week), and Jeremy's mother wonders why her son simply can't get his act together.

## The Research
### Food Allergies Can Trigger Symptoms of Hyperactivity and Attention Deficit Disorder

British and German researchers placed 185 children who showed symptoms of hyperactivity and ADD on a very restricted diet. During the four-week period that the children ate a limited number of foods, 116 improved significantly — a positive response of nearly 63%. When the children were challenged with the suspect foods/additives, the symptoms returned. The test was double-blind, placebo-controlled.

Although care was taken to exclude several food dyes and two preservatives, this was primarily a study of food allergies. The results, however, document that diet can trigger hyperactive and ADD symptoms. Egger, J.; Stolla, A.; McEwen, L.: "Controlled trial of hyposensitisation in children with food-induced hyperkinetic syndrome." *The Lancet*, 339:1150-53. May 9, 1992.

## Diet Similar to Early Version of the Feingold Program Helps More Than Half of the Preschool Children Tested

Canadian researchers worked with 24 preschool-aged boys diagnosed as hyperactive. By making changes in the children's diet, including the removal of some food additives, they achieved an improvement in the behavior of 58% of the children.

The authors conclude: "Our research...demonstrates a larger potential impact of diet than previously reported." Kaplan et al, *Pediatrics,* January 1989.

## Double-Blind Study Demonstrates Yellow No. 5 Triggers Hyperactivity in Majority of Diagnosed Children

British researchers tested one synthetic food dye, one preservative, as well as some foods, on a population of boys diagnosed as hyperactive. When the children were challenged with the dye and the preservative, 79% of them reacted with hyperactive behavior.

The authors report: "The suggestion that diet may contribute to behavior disorders in children must be taken seriously."

Egger et al, *The Lancet,* March 9, 1985.

## Animal Studies Show Artificial Food Dyes Associated with Hyperactivity

"Animal studies indicate that certain food dyes interfere with chemical communication in the brain, adding further support to the theory that they are associated with hyperactivity in children. The researchers found that, in low doses, the dye enters the brain readily, inhibiting the uptake of neurotransmitters by nerve cells. Neurotransmitters are chemicals that convey messages from one nerve cell to another, regulating the activity of the nervous system."

(From *News & Features from NIH,* March, 1981, published by the National Institutes of Health).

## Food Dyes Impair Performance of Hyperactive Children on a Laboratory Learning Test

"Forty children were given a diet free of artificial food dyes and other additives for five days. Twenty of the children had been classified as hyperactive by scores on the Conners Rating Scale and were reported to have favorable responses to stimulant medication.... Oral challenges with large doses (100 or 150 mg) of a blend of FD&C approved food dyes or placebos were administered on days four and five of the experiment. The performance of the hyperactive children on paired-associate learning tests on the day they received the dye blend was impaired by the challenge with the food dye blend."

Swanson and Kimsbourne, *Science Magazine,* Vol. 207, March 28, 1980.

## Study Connects Nutrition and Learning

Over a four-year period major synthetic food additives were removed from the foods served to children in 803 New York City public schools.

In 1979 the schools ranked in the 39th percentile on California Achievement Test scores. By 1983 the scores had risen to the 55th percentile, with the only change being dietary.

Schoenthaler, et al, *International Journal of Biosocial Research,* Vol. 8, No 2, 1986.

---

The Feingold Association of the United States is a nonprofit volunteer support group made up of parents and professionals. The Association provides members with step-by-step instruction on how to test for sensitivities to foods and synthetic chemicals. Membership materials include books listing brand name products which have been researched and are acceptable for use. The Association also generates public awareness of the potential role of foods and food additives in behavior, learning and health problems. Additional information for parents and professionals is available from the Feingold Association of the United States, P.O. Box 6550, Alexandria, VA 22306 (703) 768-FAUS.

# The Cocaine-Exposed Children Are Here

*Ms. Gregorchik hopes that the early interventions that Carl and his mother needed and the school programs that Carl needs today will finally be in place for Carl's little sister when she starts school a few years down the road.*

By LAMEECE ATALLAH GREGORCHIK

ONE COOL spring evening in 1982, a woman we'll call Evelyn went out on her back steps to snort cocaine with friends. They snorted some, talked some, and snorted some more until about half an hour later when Evelyn felt the urgent push of a labor contraction. She was eight months pregnant. Her friends walked her the five blocks to the city hospital, where, within 2½ hours of snorting her last line of coke, Evelyn delivered a baby boy weighing four pounds, 12 ounces.

Aside from his early arrival and low birth weight, tiny Carl Marcus Williams appeared to be healthy. Nurses working in the nursery did notice that he seemed easily startled and was slightly oversensitive to their touch. He also seemed more irritable than the other newborns. But Carl's mother was not addicted to cocaine on a daily basis and had used no other drugs during her pregnancy except for alcohol, so Carl presented none of the typical signs of newborn drug addiction and withdrawal. Once his weight

*LAMEECE ATALLAH GREGORCHIK teaches kindergarten at U.B. Kinsey/Palmview Elementary School in West Palm Beach, Fla.*

improved, he was discharged and went home with his mother.

> **At first glance, Carl seemed small for his age, a bit thin, and noticeably hyperactive.**

Five years and six months later, that same little boy walked into my kindergarten classroom for his first day of school. At first glance, Carl seemed small for his age, a bit thin, and noticeably hyperactive. In time he would prove to be a little powder keg of problems: inattentive, lacking in motor coordination, frustrated, and aggressively demanding of my attention.

As school opens each fall, more and more cocaine-exposed children like Carl will be arriving on educators' doorsteps, carrying their invisible luggage with them into the classrooms of America.

Long thought to be a harmless drug, cocaine has emerged as one of the most insidious drugs on the illicit market. Whether snorted, free-based, shot intravenously, or smoked as crack, cocaine triggers a rapid, euphoric high. Because of its relatively low cost per high ($3 to $10) and its easy availability, crack has been attracting an ever-increasing number of users from all socioeconomic groups.

Unfortunately, pregnant women constitute a growing segment of users. In 1987 a survey of callers to the 1-800-COCAINE help hotline revealed that *20% of the women who called said they had used cocaine during pregnancy.*

Inner-city teens facing unwanted pregnancies have been using cocaine as an abortifacient for years. Studies now confirm that placental vasoconstriction (narrowing of the blood vessels in the placenta) is directly caused by maternal cocaine use and can prompt spontaneous abortion, particularly during the first trimester of pregnancy. Cerebral infarction (destruction of the cerebrum because of blood loss to that part of the brain) has also been attributed to maternal cocaine use, as has stillbirth due to abruptio placentae (the placenta separating from the walls of the uterus). Doctors at Boston City Hospital now frequently order blood tests when women deliver prematurely, because prematurity is so common an indicator of cocaine-induced labor.

Crack's high wanes in about 10 minutes; a user must smoke repeatedly in order to prolong the feeling. This pattern could lead to high levels of fetal exposure. While the half-life of cocaine is short, and the mother's liver quickly metabolizes most of the cocaine she takes in, the stabilization of the fetus can take much longer.

We know now that the placenta is freely crossed by many drugs taken during pregnancy, and cocaine easily diffuses across the placental barrier. The fetus' liver and kidneys, being immature, are slow to metabolize and excrete drugs passed into them by the mother. This can mean that *drugs ingested by the mother may remain longer in the fetus than they do in the mother's own system.*

In a study conducted on 39 newborns of women who used only cocaine in its various forms throughout their pregnancies, 34 babies had neurological abnormalities.* Other studies have shown that lower birth weight, smaller head circumference, and shorter height are common among cocaine-exposed infants. Recent long-term studies suggest, however, that — with good prenatal care and early intervention — the majority of such infants seem to develop normally through the first three years of life.

The state of Florida became concerned about the number of babies with problems related to drugs showing up in neonatal intensive care units. In 1987 Florida instituted the Health and Rehabilitative Services Substance-Abused Newborn Regulation, which requires all places of birthing to refer to the Florida Abuse Registry any baby suspected to be a victim of substance abuse. In 1988-89 alone an astounding 10,425 infants were logged into the registry as being at risk because of either suspected or actual intrauterine substance abuse. A follow-up study of all identified newborns is being carried out by the health department of Palm Beach County and Health and Rehabilitative Services.

Seven years ago there may have been an occasional drug-addicted baby born in the neonatal nursery at St. Mary's Hospital in Palm Beach County, but now the rate is up to one per day, reports neonatologist Dr. Arnold Mackles. "These babies may look okay at birth, although they may be premature and have cocaine

---

*Tatiana M. Doberczak et al., "Neonatal Neurologic and Electroencephalographic Effects of Intrauterine Cocaine Exposure," *Journal of Pediatrics,* vol. 113, 1988, pp. 354-58.

in their blood, but they're not going to be okay," he says.

IF THE medical profession has been caught unawares by the climbing number of cocaine-exposed babies, educators are stupefied. "We are in no way ready to accommodate the numbers of these children who are appearing," says Diane Kornse, educational psychologist for the Palm Beach County School District.

> # Educators are stupefied by the climbing number of cocaine-exposed children.

The big question, according to Nancy Fontane, drug-free school director for the state of Florida, is, Do we separate these children out or not? "These children have a lot of the same characteristics as children in special education classes," Fontane says. "Yet behavior reinforcements that might work for other handicapped children do not necessarily work with drug-exposed children. Since 1975 educators have been trying to mainstream handicapped students into regular classes, but teachers like me are finding that just one cocaine-exposed child in a class of 30 is enough to strain the learning environment; four or five in the same classroom can be a disaster for everyone involved."

Some preschools and kindergartens are using parent screening inventories to provide valuable information on the child's birth, infancy, and early medical problems. An alert teacher can learn to read between the lines of these forms to understand a child's behavior. For instance, Brandie's inventory was completed by her aunt, who had guardianship of her. Answers checked as *yes* included: pregnancy was less than nine months, baby weighed less than six pounds at birth,

baby was sick in hospital (in the "explanations" column was written "premature at birth"), baby was slow in talking, and baby was slow in walking.

However, aberrant behavior may be an elementary teacher's first warning of prenatal cocaine exposure. Exposed children show a conspicuous inability to concentrate and to process information. Their fine motor skills are poor, and they have trouble following directions. Nationwide, only a few pilot programs have been started to study and find solutions to the problem. Because drug testing of newborns and pregnant mothers is relatively new, children who are already in school may never have access to all the help they will need for success in school or, for that matter, in life.

Donna Miller, a registered nurse, is a practicing specialist in infant development and is concerned about the delay in providing help for those children already in the schools. "It's really hard at 5 years of age to do what should have been done from birth," she acknowledges. "Often these children are raised in an environment so deprived of any stimulation during their preschool years that, when they arrive in the classroom, they get so bombarded with sensory activities that they can't handle it — they just freak out."

Her words reminded me of little Carl's actions when he first entered my classroom. While I introduced myself to his mother, he ran to a small, portable chalkboard, opened his crayon box to choose a crayon, and excitedly began coloring all over the chalkboard.

During the year Carl tried hard to meet the challenges that school presented to him, but he always seemed acutely aware that he was not on the same wavelength as the rest of us. Once, after working on adding sets of objects together, he abruptly stood up, stretched his hands toward the ceiling, and did a little song and wiggle-dance in place for about 20 seconds — then sat himself back down, picked up his blocks, and calmly continued his adding.

Another child, Tyrone, seemed always to be battling within himself between the child he could be if he had not been affected by cocaine and the child whose fate had been altered in his mother's womb. For about two months he made efforts to finish his work on time, neatly and accurately. He was keeping up with the

**43**

class and staying on an even keel emotionally. Then suddenly he would lose control, throw his pencil down, drop his head dejectedly, and sigh, "I'm tired! I can't do this anymore!"

A fellow kindergarten teacher told me of her frustration with these children's seesaw approach to learning: "Barbara could do this puzzle with me — every day we sat and put it together. Then one day she looked at it and just had no idea which pieces fit together! When it came time for me to give her a final evaluation on the skill, she could not focus on the task long enough to finish. Now should I pass Barbara on this particular skill or not? One day she can do it; another day, she can't."

Teachers need to be aware of some classic symptoms of drug-damaged children so that they can alter their teaching strategies. These symptoms include:

• attention deficit disorder (the child has difficulty concentrating and is easily distracted);

• hyperactivity (the child is unable to sit still, to be quiet, or to control movements);

• poor coordination (the child is clumsy, unable to control crayons or scissors);

• low tolerance level (the child is easily frustrated by tasks and gives up quickly);

• unpredictability (the child has mood swings, temper tantrums);

• poor memory (the child has trouble following three-step directions); and

• indications of drug use in the home.

---

**The keys to helping these children are consistency and structure ... along with an abundance of love.**

---

THE YELLOW Brick Road Learning Center operates as a pilot preschool program supported by a yearly grant administered by the Parent-Child Center in West Palm Beach, Florida. To be admitted to the school, children must be in foster care or under the supervision of child protective services and show developmental delay. Cocaine is the reason that 90% of the children between the ages of 2½ and 5 are in the program. Some have even been "kicked out" of other day-care centers because of their behavior. Once enrolled at Yellow Brick Road, the child — as well as his or her family — undergoes extensive testing and therapy. Although most of the children prove to be of average or above-average intelligence, they cannot cope in the usual preschool setting.

The keys to helping these children are consistency and structure, say the teachers at the school, along with an abundance of love. "We're here every day for them," says teacher Karen Markwith. "School is at least one part of their life that is the same every day, and they know they can count on us even if their home life is somewhat chaotic." Structure is so crucial to the children that any change in the school day or in personnel is immediately reflected in their behavior.

Much of the school day at Yellow Brick Road emphasizes sitting in chairs, getting in a line, or participating in simple group activities — skills a normal 2-year-old can master easily. Markwith explained that the teachers are trained to steer the children toward positive behavior with individually tailored reinforcements. For those children with the tolerance to wait until the end of the day for rewards, there is a token economy system. But for children who cannot wait, there are edible reinforcers for immediate, ongoing behavior modification. Behavior contracts are drawn up verbally between the children and their teachers.

The Los Angeles Unified School District led the nation in preparing its teachers for the influx of cocaine-exposed children, largely because of the research and influence of Dr. Judith Howard, director of the Suspected Child Abuse and Neglect Team at the University of California at Los Angeles. Eleven years ago Dr. Howard began studying the abnormal play patterns of babies born to addicted mothers. Her findings led to the creation

of the Salvin Special Education School, the first of its kind in the nation.

Carol Cole, a teacher at Salvin, is convinced that cocaine-exposed children need to be separated from children in the mainstream. "Their preschool and kindergarten environments need to be more protective," she said. Cocaine-exposed children often thrive in pilot programs because their teachers, unlike regular classroom teachers, are able to handle their temper tantrums and short attention spans. A set routine is important, and sudden transitions, even from one activity to another, can unsettle the children. Lots of old-fashioned loving and touching seem to help immeasurably.

But such care comes with a high price tag. Most child specialists agree that, even if the drug-exposed child is mainstreamed into normal classes, he or she will need additional meetings with a social worker, a psychologist, a speech and language therapist, and a pediatrician.

How can we afford the special services these children need? Neonatologists are taking the measures necessary to save the lives of these drug-exposed babies, as is their job. Now health and education professionals will be asked to take the measures that will help them adjust to the world around them. We know that the cocaine epidemic will get worse before it gets better, leaving thousands of children with neurological disorders and developmental disabilities. Even now it takes up to one year to test a child who needs special education and to place him or her in an appropriate learning environment. What happens when the demand for testing increases and alternative therapies are needed as well? The costs to us as taxpayers may become astronomical.

Little Carl will be entering the second grade this next school year. He continues to be hyperactive, easily distracted, lagging in language skills, aggressive toward other students, and a challenge to his teachers, none of whom have been able to convince administrators that Carl needs to be tested by the school psychologists for special help. Carl's mother picked him up at the school gate on the last day of school in June, and she appeared to be reaching the ninth month of pregnancy. Perhaps the early interventions that Carl and his mother needed and the school programs that Carl needs will be in place for his little sister. **K**

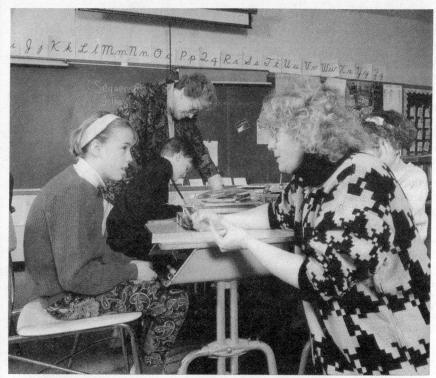

Why pull students *out* of a regular classroom when you can bring the special-ed teacher *in*?
That's the thinking behind a different vision of mainstreaming, known as co-teaching. It's catching on in schools across the country—with impressive results for kids and teachers, too!

# The New Mainstreaming

BY MARILYN FRIEND and LYNNE COOK

These days, more and more schools are experimenting with a new take on an old idea: Instead of pulling mainstreamed students *out* of the regular classroom for additional help in a resource room for part of the day, special-education teachers are coming *into* regular classrooms. The result, called *co-teaching*, creates a dynamic, high-energy classroom situation that promotes increased learning for students *and* teachers.

## HOW DOES CO-TEACHING WORK?

In co-teaching, two teachers plan lessons and deliver instruction together and share the responsibility for assessing students' mastery. Here are some of the ways in which this happens:

• One teacher teaches the large group while the other teacher circulates around the room, paying particular attention to the needs of the students with disabilities.

• The teachers divide the class in half, each teaching the same information to a smaller group.

• One of the teachers provides remediation for students who need it (those with disabilities and those without), while the

---

MARILYN FRIEND, Ph.D., *is associate professor of education at Indiana University—Purdue University at Indianapolis, Indiana.*
LYNNE COOK, *Ph.D., is director of the National Clearinghouse on Professions in Special Education in Alexandria, Virginia.*

other provides enrichment for the rest of the class.

• Both teachers teach the whole group at the same time—one modeling a skill while the other describes it, or both role playing for the students or sharing a presentation.

In some schools, students with disabilities are grouped into a single class at each grade level for subjects like reading and language arts, and the special-education teacher co-teaches in that classroom every day. Sometimes special-education teachers split time among several classrooms, perhaps co-teaching in social studies in a third-grade class on Mondays and Wednesdays and in a fifth-grade class on Tuesdays and Thursdays, with Fridays set aside as flexible time to be used according to need.

Some schools find that co-teaching works well when scheduled by units. For example, if a teacher who has mainstreamed students in her class is teaching a concept that many children find difficult, she might ask the special-education teacher to co-teach that concept.

## WHAT'S THE PAYOFF FOR STUDENTS?

Through co-teaching, special-education students avoid the stigma associated with daily journeys in and out of the regular classroom. Their learning is less fragmented, not only because they don't miss any time in the regular classroom, but also because the special-education teacher is better able to relate remediation to regular instruction. Students with learning disabilities report that they like school better in a co-teaching situation, and they say that when two teachers share a classroom, there's always a teacher available to help them. Anecdotally, principals and teachers alike report that behavior problems decrease for students in co-taught classes. And all students, those with disabilities and those without, benefit from having two teachers in the classroom who can provide extra help and more options for learning, such as flexible grouping, hands-on experiences, and modeling of interactions.

But it's important to realize that co-teaching may not be the best option for all students with disabilities. That decision must be made by the team of professionals, including the regular classroom teacher, who write the child's educational program.

## WHAT'S IN IT FOR TEACHERS?

Think of how teaching and learning in your classroom would change if you had a co-teacher. Perhaps you would tackle the integrated language arts and social studies unit you've been meaning to try. Or maybe you could provide the extra assistance you know would make the difference to some of your students. You might even convince your co-teacher to join you in teaching fundamental concepts by putting on classroom skits.

A co-teacher also becomes a supportive teaching partner, someone who understands and shares both the successes and the frustrations associated with trying something new. For some teachers, this is the greatest personal benefit of co-teaching.

# How It Really Works

## A special-ed teacher and a classroom teacher discuss the ups and downs of teaming in the mainstream.

For the past two years, Candy Passaglia and and Judy Alford have co-taught at Maplewood Elementary School in Cary, Illinois. As the special-education teacher, Candy comes to Judy's fifth-grade class four mornings a week for language arts and two afternoons a week for social studies. The rest of the time, Candy is either co-teaching with others or serving students with disabilities in her special-education classroom. At those times, Judy teaches alone in her classroom.

Judy has six students with learning disabilities mainstreamed into her classroom for at least half of the day. Occasionally, these students still work with Candy in the special-education classroom, but that need has significantly decreased as the result of the school's co-teaching program.

Recently, Marilyn Friend asked Judy and Candy to speak with her about both the benefits and the drawbacks of co-teaching. A portion of their conversation follows.

**Marilyn Friend:** *Tell me about your early experiences with co-teaching. What was it like for the two of you at first?*

**Candy:** I had some trouble in the beginning because I was accustomed to working in my little protected room with a few children in the pull-out program. Now I had to go into a regular classroom—and into someone else's territory.

**Judy:** And from my standpoint, someone coming in and watching me was intimidating. It took a while for us to feel we could be honest with each other and take risks together. We had to get through what I call the "comfort continuum." You have to learn to feel comfortable with each other before you can start exacting changes in the classroom.

**MF:** *Obviously, planning is important to the success of a co-teaching arrangement. How do you two get at the planning?*

**Candy:** The first year that this program was in place, there was no planning time built in. And we needed that time. After all, the L.D. teachers in our school were struggling with new roles and trying to figure out how we'd fit into the district's

Co-teachers Judy Alford (left) and Candy Passaglia share a light-hearted moment in Judy's fifth-grade classroom. Candy says, "Sometimes you just tell the kids, 'This [co-teaching] is improvisation.'"

plan. I think we may have been able to speed up the process had there been more planning time. Then, during our second year, a grant enabled us to hire a floating substitute so we could sit down with the classroom teachers for one full day, an hour per teacher for formal planning. I can't tell you what a difference that has made. We'll start out with a simple idea, then watch it ripple outward like a pebble in water. We feed off each other, back and forth, until we arrive at a wonderful idea for presenting a lesson to the class.

**Judy:** In addition to our formal planning time, we usually check in with each other every day to touch base and catch up. And because we're in contact with each other every day, we can use our informal planning time for talking fast and exploring ideas. But I'm the one who keeps an eye on the district curriculum and who directs the lesson plans.

**Candy:** And I need Judy to do that, to captain the ship, so to speak. I'm the first mate, but I rely on her to call out

## "Now we truly have a team approach to teaching the children, in which all of the specialists are involved in a kind of co-ownership of each child."

the directions. Because I work with several teachers, I've found that what happens in a co-teaching situation differs from class to class. You're dealing with different personalities, with people who are at different points in their careers, and with varying degrees of comfort with the whole idea of co-teaching. It's not easy, so you have to stay focused on the kids and try to get past egos and personality differences.

**MB:** *Why should any classroom teacher and special-ed teacher sit down one day and say, "Let's co-teach?"*

**Candy:** Definitely because of the difference it makes for the kids. Now that the kids with learning disabilities are spending a bigger chunk of their day with their peers in a regular classroom, they're developing more maturity and are demonstrating more acceptable behaviors. They have better role models. They feel better about themselves. The improvement in their self-esteem would be enough. And they're not losing academically.

**Judy:** Now we truly have a team approach to teaching the children, in which all of the specialists are involved in a kind of co-ownership of each child. Working together, we can look at a child from all different angles and really concentrate on meeting that child's needs in the least restrictive environment. Candy and I share the philosophy that all children can learn. But we know that different kids need different methods and approaches. So at any given time, we may be balancing a large presentation, individual work, and small-group work. This way, all kids experience many different ways to learn. Co-teaching provides us with the energy it takes to do that.

**MF:** *Some people worry that co-teaching may put the students without disabilities at a disadvantage because not as much material might be covered and because they don't get as much attention as the special-needs kids. How would you respond to that?*

**Judy:** Maybe it depends on how you look at curriculum. If you believe that the curriculum amounts to pages in a book, then, yes, sometimes you don't cover as much material for any of the children. But one of the things we know about learning is that it's better to cover a given area and cover it well than to go through an additional 100 pages insufficiently. And if you feel that learning to work with other people is an important part of the curriculum, then you think it's important for all kids—not just those with special needs. And in my classroom, I provide a 25-minute period after lunch every day for kids to work independently on projects of their choosing. It's an opportunity for any child to run as far as he or she wants to run with a concept or an idea.

**MF:** *How have parents reacted to this program?*

**Judy:** Parents of students with special needs will tell me that they want their child to be a "regular kid." And yet, they know their child may need some specific assistance. With this program, parents know their children can feel like "regular kids" and still get that special help. And the same goes for the very bright children. In this situation, every child has two adults to bounce ideas off of and to get extra help from when it's needed.

**Candy:** I think parents react so positively because they see the results, the success stories. And our building as a whole communicates well with parents. In fact, the whole atmosphere in our building is based on responding to parents and making them feel like important members of the team.

**Judy:** And with two people in the classroom you increase your ability to communicate with parents. You've got one other person who saw how the day went and can make a good-news call. So it's easier to increase parent contact.

**MF:** *What have both of you taken away from this experience so far?*

**Candy:** Having spent so much time in a pull-out situation, working with a small group of kids, I'd forgotten so much about timing and pacing and managing cooperative groups. But Judy has helped me work that out, and so has our school's peer-coaching program, which is now in its second year. The formal peer-coaching situation gives me opportunities to watch other teachers. And Judy has helped me fine-tune my teaching even more in the classroom.

**Judy:** Now that I have a co-teacher, when I start to run down, there's a second person who comes up with the ideas or the suggestions—and I do the same for her. We feed off one another. And the kids get two perspectives, though we both know where each lesson is heading. I was getting tired and I guess co-teaching brought back some of the excitement I felt as a

> **"When I start to run down, there's a second person who comes up with the ideas or the suggestions. I was getting tired and I guess co-teaching brought back some of the excitement I felt as a new teacher."**

# Tips For Successful Co-Teaching

*If you're thinking of co-teaching, keep these points in mind:*

**1** *Planning is the key.* It's important that you make time to plan lessons and discuss exactly how you will work together throughout your co-teaching experience. Some co-teachers set aside one lunch period each week for this purpose. Others meet biweekly after school. And in some schools, specific planning periods are built into the teachers' schedules.

**2** *Discuss your views on teaching and learning with your co-teacher.* What are your goals for students for the lessons you are teaching? Do you expect all students to master all of them? Experienced co-teachers agree that to be effective, the teachers should share basic beliefs about instruction.

**3** *Attend to details.* When another professional is teaching with you, you'll need to clarify classroom rules and procedures, such as
• class routines for leaving the room, using free time, turning in assignments;
• discipline matters;
• the division of such chores as grading student work or making bulletin boards;
• pet peeves such as gum chewing.

**4** *Prepare parents.* A few parents may wonder what a co-taught classroom means for their children. Does this mean you'll be teaching less material? Will expectations for behavior be lower? Does the special-education teacher work with all children? The answers to these questions should be *no, no,* and *yes.* Explain to parents that having two teachers in the class gives every child the opportunity to receive more attention than before.

**5** *Make the special-education teacher feel welcome in your classroom.* Clear a place in your room for the other teacher's belongings and be sure to display his or her name. Also, plan how you will introduce the special-education teacher to students. Many co-teachers decide that the special-education teacher can be described as a teacher who helps students learn how to learn.

**6** *Avoid the "paraprofessional trap."* The most common concern about co-teaching is that the special-education teacher becomes a classroom helper. This quickly becomes boring for the special-education teacher. More important, it is a very limited use of the talents of two professionals. Having two teachers in a class opens teaching opportunities you may never have had before—the excitement of co-teaching comes from taking advantage of these.

**7** *When disagreements occur, talk them out.* To have some disagreements in co-teaching is normal. What is important is to raise your concerns while they are still minor and to recognize that both of you may have to compromise to resolve them.

**8** *Go slowly.* If you begin with co-teaching approaches that require less reliance on one another, you have a chance to learn each others' styles. As your comfort level increases, you will try more complex co-teaching approaches. Above all else, periodically stop to discuss with your co-teacher what is working and what needs revision.

## "Co-teachers are not always going to get along. You're not always going to see eye to eye. When that happens, you need to remember why you're doing this—that it's for the kids."

new teacher. Also, it's been great to know that another person sees and shares my frustrations and that there's someone I can bounce my feelings off of. It keeps both of us from feeling like we can't deal with the problems.

**Candy:** I think we've both learned to be open to new ideas and open to each other. In the beginning, I had to realize that I was going to have to function in the classroom teacher's arena and that she has a vast knowledge of the children in her class and how they interact. I had to be open to those ideas and know that maybe my own great ideas weren't going to work in a full classroom situation. And that was new for me.

**MF:** *What are the most difficult and most challenging aspects of co-teaching?*

**Judy:** It's still a big time commitment. I know it would be a lot easier if I could just sit down with my planbook and stay until 7:00 one night and just do it all myself without worrying about what someone else is going to do or say. Another difficulty centers on the fact that my classroom is set up for two adults and our lessons are planned around two adults. When one of us is absent for whatever reason, that can cause new problems. And I guess another frustration revolves around grading. Again, it would be much easier for me just to decide on a grade for a child myself without having to worry about whether someone else is going to agree with me. It's the difference between making a decision by committee and just making it yourself.

**Candy:** My first thought is so many kids, so little time. I now have more than 15 children in my caseload and I find it challenging to remember the needs of all those children at any given point in any given day. I also have to remember what I told teacher X I'd prepare for her lesson. And on top of that, I still

have to do testing and take care of all the other things I had to handle in my old job. I won't kid you—this approach takes a lot more time. But that frustration is balanced by the excitement of working with teachers who are excited about teaching, spending more time with people who share my philosophy, and bouncing all these wonderful ideas off each other.

**MF:** *What advice would you give to teachers who have been asked to co-teach or who may want to experiment on their own?*

**Judy:** You need to have a mentor who's already been through it. Someone who will listen to your frustrations and not be judgmental about your fits and starts. When we started out, we wanted it to be perfect. But it wasn't perfect. So it was helpful to have a third set of ears to vent our frustrations to.

**Candy:** Absolutely. Co-teaching is like a marriage, and once in a while you need a marriage counselor. Also, it helps to remember that co-teachers are not always going to get along, you're not always going to see eye to eye. When that happens and you start to lose your focus, you need to remember why you're doing this, that it's all for the kids.

**Judy:** I also think it's important to work on building trust. We all mess up in the classroom from time to time. But when you've got another adult watching you mess up, it's important to know that she's not going to run around the building telling everyone what happened. I guess I'd also say that you don't have to co-teach every lesson. Start out small, with one little area, one little math lesson, one little social studies lesson. When you feel good about that, let it grow.

**Candy:** Just like the kids. You build on their successes. We build on our successes. ■

**Reprinted with permission of Marilyn Friend, Lynne Cook, *Instructor Magazine* and Scholastic Inc.**

# Slow Learners: Students at Risk

by Kaye Johns, Executive Director,
*The Center for Success in Learning*

*The following is an address by Kaye Johns, founder and executive director of The Center for Success in Learning before the Commissioner of Education's Advisory Committee on the 1990-94 Long-Range Plan for Public Education. Johns, a well-known author and topic presenter on the subject of slower learners, has served on three TEA Advisory Committees during the development of rules for Alternatives to Social Promotion and frequently testifies before the State Board of Education.*

We believe it is important for the State Board of Education, its Long-Range Plan, and individual school districts to clearly delineate slower learners as part of the at-risk student population.

When slower learners are not mentioned specifically, it is presumed that they should be able to do grade level work, to keep up academically with their peers — and when they don't, it is their fault because they are not motivated, or not trying hard enough. They are blamed because they don't learn as quickly as other children. They are set up to fail.

If they are not identified as a group with significant learning problems, there is no call to action, no reason to do anything differently in the classroom. The assumption is that all children with learning problems are served by special education, and all other students should be able to master nine months of information in nine months' time in a traditional classroom setting.

The basic presumption of "Alternatives to Social Promotion" is that being "at risk" is a temporary condition for students, who should be "remediated" or caught up, when placed in alternative programs or given modifications in classrooms. Slower learners have problems that are not temporary and that are not resolved in one year's time in the classroom. These students are likely to remain academically at risk from kindergarten through grade 12.

And yet, without an acknowledgment of the severity of their problems, slower learners are expected to maintain passing grades of 70, stay on grade level with their peers, earn 21 Carnegie Credits to graduate, and pass the TEAMS Exit Exam just like the other students. Is this realistic?

It didn't used to be. That's why slower learners were so often socially promoted before educational reform. They couldn't keep up and stay on grade level with their peers. If they were unable to keep up *before* educational reform raised the standards, *how will they keep up now?*

Slower learners have not changed. The world has changed. Education has changed, standards have risen — but these students, with their limited capacity to learn, are still the same.

Are we saying these students cannot learn? Cannot one day graduate?

Absolutely not! But we are saying that unless we change the way most of them are being taught, particularly in secondary schools, many of them may not have a chance.

## Who is the Slower Learning Student?

We acknowledge that there is no agreed-upon definition of the slower learner. But in general, educators agree that these students are caught in that grey area between average and retarded, generally IQ 70-89.

*We are talking about 22% of the population who fall within this IQ range, one in five.*

We are the first to acknowledge that IQ scores are imperfect and can be biased. But IQ scores are used to qualify students for special education as well as gifted/talented programs, so they are respected in the educational community.

IQ does not measure a student's grit, drive, determination, ambition, tenacity or perseverance. It doesn't tell us whether the student is lazy or motivated, an under-achiever or an over-achiever — because slower learners are as individual as the rest of us. Nor does it tell us what kind of home students come from, what kind of love and support they receive.

IQ tests do not guarantee a student's success in life — b*ut they are one of the best predictors we have to indicate a student's likely difficulty in learning, in doing grade level work in school.*

## Students Learn at Different Rates

Although the following chart illustrates how far behind slower learners typically are by the time they enter the ninth grade, we know this doesn't just happen in the 8th grade. These students are usually not fully on grade level at the end of their first or second grade, and they fall gradually further behind every year

|         | **9th Grade**      | **12th Grade**     |
| ------- | ------------------ | ------------------ |
| IQ 75   | 5th grade, 5 months | 7th grade, 7 months |
| IQ 80   | 6th grade, 2 months | 8th grade, 6 months |
| IQ 85   | 6th grade, 9 months | 9th grade, 5 months |

This chart is surely our challenge. What would happen if slower learners were picked up in kindergarten and given individualized instruction according to what we know works with these students? Examples are: multi-sensory teaching, peer tutoring, small group techniques, accommodations for learning styles and perceptual strengths, modifications to supplement textbooks with study guides and other materials on an appropriate reading level, tests adapted for clarity, and appropriate study skills. If so, might these students do much better than this chart predicts?

Still, this chart stands on historical data as an illustration of the frustration and sense of failure that is constantly reinforced as we expect these students to do grade level work — and their teachers to be able to "catch them up." Here are educators' comments:

"Students whose mental ability places them in the slow learner range (IQ 70-90) are — because of their limited ability — low achievers. Yet the general public (including the press, state legislators, and members of boards of education) in the current push for minimum competency testing for high school graduation seems largely unaware that no amount of testing, no setting of competencies, and no establishment of standards and remedial programs can cause these students to achieve beyond the limits of their intellectual capacity.

"The public expects that students not in special education should achieve at grade level or at the national average. They do not realize that, by definition of the word `average,' as many students must be below this mark as above it."
Howard G. Dunlap, "Minimum Competency Testing and the Slow Learner," *Educational Leadership*, Vol. 367, pp.327-328.

## Slower Learners — More Than Half of the Dropouts

If we accept that most slower learning students will be 2-4 years below grade level in their basic skills when they *enter* high school, it is easy to see how they fit into the at-risk population.

"The single best predictor of whether or not a student will drop out of school is his or her level of academic achievement. The typical at-risk student has mathematics or reading skills two or more years below grade level and is not maintaining a scholastic average of 70%."
"Characteristics of At-Risk Youth," *TEA Practioner's Guide*, Series No. One, p. 26.

"The most common reason for leaving school is poor academic performance....A majority of all dropouts in the National Longitudinal Survey had basic skills in the bottom 20% of the score distribution."
Andrew Hahn, "Reaching Out to America's Dropouts: What to Do?" *Phi Delta Kappan*, Dec. 1987, pp.256-263.

"It has been estimated that as many as one-third of all students attending school today will drop out before graduation. Of these, more than half could be described as slow learners."
H. Hodgkinson, "Today's Numbers, Tomorrow's Nation." *Education Week*, May 14, 1986, pp.14-15.

## Many Other At-Risk Programs

As at-risk students and their problems are studied, programs are springing up everywhere to help with identified problems — drug and alcohol abuse, teenage pregnancy, counseling for students who are abused, depressed, suicidal. We see a renewed emphasis on helping students with self-esteem; we are working with cultural issues; we are addressing students' needs when they have English as a second language.

When a problem is identified, we develop programs, policies, and strategies to deal with it. Everyone — from the Legislature to the local school board to the district administrative staff, local campus administrators, teachers, parents — even the public — is aware of the need to do something to solve the problem.

When the problem is not identified, it is overlooked at best, or considered not to exist at worst.

This is the primary reason we feel it is imperative that we let parents, teachers and the public know that some children who are not served by special education still have significant problems learning.

We must do something to help teachers learn what works with these children — because research is showing us many things do.

## What Works with Slower Learners, Works with Many Other At-Risk Students

Slower learners and other at-risk students do not do well in traditional classroom settings (straight rows, no moving, not talking) with a standard textbook/lecture format. They need multi-sensory teaching through high school.

It is clear from both research and classroom application that the following strategies work for slower learners and other at-risk students, and most students in general:

- Multi-sensory teaching
- Peer and cross-age tutoring
- Small group techniques
- Mixed ability classes, heterogeneous groupings
- Increasing the time spent on a single subject
- Teaching to students' perceptual strengths
- Informal classroom design
- Changing the time of day for testing
- Matching student's strongest period of day with testing time and major academic subjects
- Smaller student/teacher ratio
- Technology/media-assisted instruction
- Extending the classroom to the community

### But Aren't Those Simply Good Teaching Principles, Period?

Of course they are. And based on the feedback received from teacher workshops, these techniques are much more likely to be utilized by elementary teachers, although by no means are all elementary teachers taking advantage of these strategies. Why not? Why do many classes still fall into the traditional textbook/lecture pattern at the fourth grade level, or sooner? Why are 95% of academic high school classes still taught in the traditional classroom setting with a textbook/lecture format?

One reason is that even though most students will do better with the above techniques, they will not be hurt if these techniques are not used. Students with average, or above average intelligence have been making it through school academically for a long time. Some of them may not be excelling as they could and should and probably would if these strategies were used, but they haven't been pushed out of school because they weren't.

Slower learners, on the other hand, are students living on the edge. For them, the difference between a teacher who utilizes the previously mentioned techniques and one who doesn't can make the difference between passing and failing, graduating or not.

Let's identify slower learners specifically as students who have needs to be addressed. Otherwise, where will the impetus, the urgency, for changing what happens in the classroom come from?

But wait! We shouldn't label students!

And yet, we do. We have "labeled" students gifted and talented, honors, learning disabled, emotionally disturbed, visually, auditorily or physically impaired, mentally retarded, minority, transient, economically disadvantaged, non-English speaking, home ec, vocational, and so on.

Why do we have these labels? Because they provide access into services in the school. They describe the program that the student has which has been identified, or they describe the program where the student in placed.

Who says we haven't already labeled slower learners?

- Ask anyone who the "students who fall through the cracks" are.
- Or ask about "shadow children," slower learners in the shadow of the system.
- Or the students in the grey area.
- Or the "dull."
- Or the "borderline."
- Or the "marginal."

We prefer *slower learner* because it emphasizes a positive — these students learn, but they learn slowly.

Think of the cost to the students when we don't identify their problem. Parents often punish them for not trying. Teachers crack down because the children aren't paying attention. Other kids think they're dumb because they don't have any apparent problem. The students feel it's all their fault. If they were better, tried harder, worked longer, then they could learn.

Learning disabled and mentally retarded students don't have to face that. They know they have a problem that isn't their fault, that it is something they have to come to terms with.

### All Children Can Learn

We must have high expectations for all children, just as we must believe that all children can learn. But all children cannot learn in the same way, or at the same rate, or even with the same amount of information. More time will not make a slower learner a brain surgeon. We must recognize, respect and support the learning differences in children.

And we must have high but realistic expectations. We do not expect our "C" students to win scholarships to Harvard or Yale, and we do not hold average students to the same goals and expectations as our gifted/talented students. Why then, must we insist that students with below average intelligence meet the same expectations as students with average and above average intelligence? Why do we set them up to fail over and over again? It doesn't take long until they don't even try.

As long as we don't use the term "slower learner" — or some other legitimate, identifying term — to describe these children, we leave them and their parents and their teachers shadow boxing. They can't attack the problem because they don't even know what it is.

When we don't say "slower learner," we're saying it isn't okay to be a slower learner. And it must be. It has to be, because all children are not alike. They cannot be the same.

*This article appeared in* Instructional Leader, *a publication of the Texas Elementary Principals and Supervisors Association, February 1990. For further information, contact The Center for Success in Learning, 4949 Westgrove, #180, Dallas, TX 75248, 1-800-488-9433.*

# Inclusiveness Transforms Special Education for the 1990s

**By Richard Schattman and Jeff Benay**

Despite debate within the educational community as to its value, many school districts throughout the United States and Canada are using inclusionary models, where all children — regardless of the type or severity of their disability — are fully educated in regular education classes. While such schools differ in size, location, and wealth, they have some common characteristics.

The first of these involves the relationship between inclusion and the broader issues of school reform. Since these schools are often engaged in other reform or restructuring efforts, they often embrace well-articulated mission statements reflecting the values and beliefs of those involved in the school community. In inclusive schools, district mission statements speak to the needs of all children.

A second point of similarity is that these schools often use a teaming approach for problem solving, planning, and program implementation, breaking professional isolation by linking teachers, parents, and administrators. Student-centered planning teams are essential for inclusive programs because:

• Teams provide all parties with a support network. No one individual has all the skills needed to meet the educational needs of severely disabled children.

• Teams are a powerful tool for problem solving. When a collaborative team approach uses specific problem-solving techniques, solutions to complex issues are more likely. In addition, the quality of outcomes resulting from multiple perspectives is usually greater than those from unilateral efforts.

• Teams involve parents meaningfully. Few schools organize themselves in ways that make them accessible to most parents; teams allow parents to meet with professionals regularly, share responsibility, and develop a meaningful relationship.

• Teams enable the group to share responsibility. No one team member has all the answers. When a group of individuals works together with common goals, complex programs can be developed and implemented in regular education classes.

Thus, teaming allows teachers, parents, related service providers, and administrators to recognize the complexity of their task and organize personnel and resources for success. Adoption of a team-based model reflects a more holistic view of the system, whereby teachers, administrators, and parents must be linked in an interdependent manner to succeed. Adoption of teaming not only alters a school's approach to educating the disabled but fundamentally changes how schools operate, how decisions are made, how instruction is delivered, and how individuals relate to each other.

In a team-based approach, roles of teacher, administrator, and parent are different from how they appear in more separate and segregated models. Thus, a third characteristic of schools with an integrated approach to educating all children is that these traditional roles change.

Schools without teaming often have much specialization among professionals. In a team model, teachers, parents, and administrators share responsibility for a range of activities and embrace parents as equal partners. The parent's role is elevated in importance and function, and professional roles expand from specialist to generalist. Where this transformation has occurred, teachers and administrators have discovered that a team approach is both professionally enriching and more efficient.

In inclusive schools, administrators report that they participate on teams, are involved in instructional decisions, and share responsibility for achieving collaboratively established goals. They are no longer responsible for making unilateral decisions related to resource allocation or accessing outside technical assistance and support. When they share their power with the team, decisions are more child-centered, they reflect the multiple perspectives of those involved, and all parties are invested in the decisions made because all have participated.

Richard Villa and Jacqueline Thousand, in *Strategies for Educating Learners with Severe Disabilities within Their Home Schools and Communities*, identify a number of important roles for the building and central administration in a team-based model supporting fully inclusive practices. They include:

• Challenging teams to make decisions that align with the mission and philosophy of their school;

• Modifying master schedules to support teachers with the time needed to meet as teams;

• Creating job descriptions that reflect the new roles of professionals working in a team-based system;

• Hiring personnel who embrace the district's philosophy and have appropriate technical and communication skills;

• Supervising and evaluating staff in a manner that supports the district's commitment to all children;

• Arranging for inservice and training for staff.

In addition, administrators need to support staff in the self-evaluation of their performance as a team and address their inservice needs related to improving teaming skills.

---

*Districts that have embraced inclusive practices assign a top priority to the staff development needs of team members, including parents.*

---

Teacher roles also change in inclusive schools. The teacher provides direct instruction, consults with other team members, supervises paraprofessionals, and coordinates related services. Teachers in integrated schools also participate in training colleagues.

The role of a special education teacher also changes in an integrated school — to that of a team member co-teaching with regular class teachers, sharing in the responsibility of providing training, support, and supervision to paraprofessionals, and participating on teams as an equal member with parents, class teachers, and administrators.

In some northern Vermont school districts, responsibilities of regular and special education teachers have become less distinct, participation in a team process resulting in teachers learning skills from each other. Moving from teacher specialist to teacher generalist reflects an upgrading of skills among all professional staff.

Teaming encourages this. When teaming results in a professionalization of all staff, integration is modeled by adults to students. In districts where student and staff integration has occurred, all instructional staff are regarded as teachers rather than special education teachers, regular education teachers, speech language pathologists, and psychologists.

Two of the most important contributors to these transformations are new knowledge and staff develop-

ment. Districts implementing integrated approaches have an increased need for ongoing staff development. Most districts have an enormous supply of expertise on staff and can tap into it to provide training. Yet, traditional organizational strategies often isolate staff from each other and make it less likely they will share knowledge and expertise.

Districts that have embraced inclusive practices assign a top priority to the staff development needs of team members, including parents. Strategies include linking with other districts, giving teachers and parents time to meet, involving staff with institutions of higher education, and participating in professional organizations.

Inclusive education has multiple benefits:

• It offers the child with disabilities the opportunity to be a meaningful member of the community, to be exposed to talented teachers, to develop social relationships with nonhandicapped peers, and to have quality educational programs taught in a "normal" school setting.

• It offers teachers the opportunity to use their skills with a wide range of students, to join other teachers for support, to work with administrators on decisions that affect their ability to teach, and to link with parents.

• It brings administrators into the arena of instruction as members of a team, linking them with teachers and parents so quality decisions benefiting all children may be made.

• It offers parents the opportunity to develop ongoing relationships with a small group of school professionals working on behalf of their child. For parents to be meaningfully involved, and for schools to benefit from their insight, parents must have an ongoing relationship and a forum for open and honest discussion. The student-centered planning team enables this level and quality of involvement to occur.

Inclusive education offers the school the opportunity to be truly effective. Ultimately, if a school is to be successful, it must provide equity and excellence for all children. Education in a democratic society requires no less.

*Richard Schattman, a research associate with the National Study of the Implementation of Least Restrictive Environment, is in the Department of Special Education, University of Vermont, Burlington. Jeff Benay is Director of Indian Education, Franklin Northwest Supervisory Union, Swanton, Vermont. This article has been condensed from* The School Administrator, *49 (February 1992), 8-12.*

---

# Every teacher is a special education teacher

## By Paula Wasserman

I teach learning disabled and emotionally disturbed students every day. So does every teacher in the U.S. at each grade level. And I contend regular classroom teachers need and want help with the task.

According to Harold B. Levy, M.D., from 10 percent to 15 percent of the students in the nation's total classroom population have learning disabilities. According to the Texas Education Ageny, approximately 2 percent are severely emotionally disturbed, and from 10 percent to 20 percent will need mental health services at some point during their school years. Compare the number of students in your school with the number of children classified as learning disabled (LD) or emotionally disturbed (ED) and assigned to your special education program. If your school is typical, you'll find mainstream classes probably have many unidentified students with these disabilities.

What instruction have your teachers received enabling them to teach these students effectively? Do your teachers know strategies that would aid a student with an auditory receptive difficulty? (These children can hear what you say but have trouble interpreting it.) Have your teachers been trained to handle the behavioral outbursts of an emotionally disturbed child?

Because colleges of education typically do not include this information in their courses for mainstream classroom teachers, special education teachers usually are the only ones who can answer these questions. School districts could ease their teachers' jobs by providing staff development in this area for teachers of all grade levels.

As a special education teacher,

*Paula Wasserman is a special education teacher in the Round Rock Independent School District, Austin, Texas.*

---

*As a special education teacher, I see a powerful need for other teachers to learn about students with learning problems*

---

I've seen a powerful need for other teachers to learn about students with special learning problems. I've been appalled by the ignorance of some regular education teachers about the students who receive both regular and special instruction during different periods of the day. One teacher, when referring to my LD classes, asked me, "Don't all of your students have IQs in the 70s?"

In fact, most learning disabled children test normal or above normal on intelligence measures, and I was upset to find a classroom teacher who still believed the old myth. I wondered what expectations she had of the LD students in her class. And I doubted she would spend much time trying to help students whose capabilities she grossly underestimated.

Throughout the school year, teachers corner me in the hallway, asking me to explain the difference between the child labeled LD and the one referred to as ED. During lunch periods, teachers often collar me and describe a specific student's difficulty, asking for advice. Social studies and science teachers question how dyslexic students will be able to read the textbook and what can be done if they can't.

These content-area teachers ask questions because they are conscientious and caring educators. They want to feel good about their ability to deal with these children. But these teachers fear they're not equipped to handle the various special needs in their classrooms. The underlying question behind all these inquiries, I believe, is this: "Is it realistic to expect these students to learn in my classroom?"

Your school district's special education teachers and counselors have the knowledge and practical experience to conduct staff development in this area. Let them do it: This is one workshop your teachers need. Areas to cover in such a workshop should include the following:

• Definitions and descriptions of LD and ED students.

• Referral procedures teachers can follow to find out if a student should be placed in special education.

• Legal restrictions applying to all teachers with special education students in their classes.

• Teaching strategies to use with these students in regular classrooms.

Teachers should be heartened and encouraged to know these students aren't lost causes. Henry Ford and Albert Einstein both had learning problems, as did Charles Darwin, Sir Isaac Newton, and Sir Winston Churchill. Woodrow Wilson didn't learn to read until he was nine years old. Nelson Rockefeller wrote an article based on his experiences as a learning-disabled person. Its title: "Don't Accept Anyone's Verdict that You Are Lazy, Stupid, or Retarded."

We can't afford to let people like these slip through school without providing them the educational opportunities they deserve. Your teachers desperately want to help these kids succeed. It's up to you to ensure all teachers in your district receive this essential training. 𝐄𝐄

# Inclusion Myths and Truths: The Game

As we learn about what works and what doesn't for inclusion, a number of myths and truths are being discovered. As a way to actively engage people in thought and talk about issues raised in the name of inclusion (hopefully with an element of fun) Inclusion *Myths and Truths: The Game* was developed. To enjoy and learn the most, play the game with others. Also, adapt the game and add the myths and truths you have discovered in your own efforts to create inclusive school communities.

**Instructions: For each statement indicate "M" for MYTH or "T" for TRUTH.**

1. _____ Teams need about one school year to plan for the inclusion of one student in a general education class.

2. _____ The initial objectives of inclusion for students are safety and participation ... for the teachers, survival!

3. _____ It is possible to finalize the curricular, instructional, social, and management aspects of a student's education before she or he is included.

4. _____ Socialization is the only reason for students with disabilities to be included in general education classes.

5. _____ Learning equals acquiring specified curricular outcomes.

6. _____ Textbooks define curriculum.

7. _____ Only students with disabilities present diverse needs that require individual accommodations.

8. _____ Inclusion means that students spend 100% of their school days in general education classrooms.

9. _____ Collaboration is second nature for most adults.

10. _____ The people who experience the most anxiety in the change to inclusion are the classmates. They are also the biggest barriers.

11. _____ If children are excluded from school communities, they are at risk for lifetime exclusion from the community at large.

12. _____ Initially, designing a fully inclusive program, like any change, requires new learning and is therefore inefficient and requires additional time.

13. _____ The excessive need to plan and meet decreases over time.

14. _____ Having an extra adult in the classroom is always a support to the classroom teacher and always promotes inclusion of the student.

15. _____ It is difficult for team members to work concurrently in segregated and integrated models of service provision.

16. _____ There are recipes for making inclusion work, it is just that the cookbook is not published yet.

17. _____ If I just wait long enough, inclusion too will pass.

18. _____ Concerns about class size are specific to inclusion.

19. _____ Inclusion is an initiative related to students with severe disabilities only.

20. _____ Inclusion is about building school communities where all children are welcomed, accepted, and successful.

**Answers:**

**(1) Myth.** Of course, it would depend on how frequently the planning team would meet throughout the year. Generally, a few meetings between the family and the core team members are sufficient to map out a preliminary schedule and supports.

**(2) Truth.** Well ... mostly. It seems to take a couple weeks for everyone to get comfortable enough to move on to program specifics.

**(3) Myth.** Context has a tremendous effect on how students behave and on what team members identify as the most important instructional priorities.

**(4) Myth.** Socialization is just one of the important reasons for student to learn together. Further, implying that a classroom teacher need not be concerned about a student learning the curriculum frequently raises anxiety. The paradigm operative in most of general education is that learning is defined by the acquisition of specified curricular outcomes. Gains made in socialization, therefore, frequently (and unfortunately) do not make teachers feel that they have contributed to a student's learning.

**(5) Myth**...although held as a truth in many schools.

**(6) Myth** — ideally.

**(7) Myth.** In fact, one important outcome of general and special educators working together in the same learning environment is greater individualization and support for all students.

**(8) Myth.** No students — labeled or not — should spend 100% of their school days in classrooms. Classrooms are irrelevant environments in the long run. In the short run, they serve as gathering places.

**(9) Myth. Myth. Myth**.

**(10) Myth.** Mostly the classmates are tremendous supports, especially when invited to contribute and support one another.

**(11) Truth.** If we cannot figure out how to include kids in communities ... it is not very likely they will figure it out for themselves as they get older.

**(12) Truth.** By definition, the acquisition stage of learning is inefficient. The process of inclusion requires learning many new skills.

**(13) Truth.** Almost always. Again, early on there is so much learning, more support from team members is needed.

**(14) Myth.** Always is a sure clue to indicate myth ... Extra adults can be tremendously supportive if the reason for their participation is clear — to facilitate inclusion of the student. Otherwise, they can isolate students.

**(15) Truth.** Both personally and organizationally. Personally, once the beneficial outcomes of inclusion are observed for a few students, it is difficult (if not painful) to "go back" and work with students who remain segregated. Organizationally, the scheduling flexibility required for special educators and related services personnel to provide support in integrated learning environments cannot be realized when they are tied to rigid direct instruction or therapy schedules.

**(16) Myth**. There are some general strategies that work well. But for each student there is a unique application.

**(17) Myth**...at lease for the historians and optimists among us.

**(18) Myth.** Class size has been an issue for eternity.

**(19) Myth.** See next item.

**(20) Truth.**

*Developed and contributed by Jennifer York, Assistant Professor, Department of Educational Psychology and Institute on Community Integration, University of Minnesota.*

**Reprinted with permission from *What's Working: Inclusive Education in Minnesota*, Fall/Winter 1991-92, published by the Institute on Community Integration (UAP), University of Minnesota, Minneapolis, MN.**

# Achieving Inclusion

- **Integrate Students**

- **Adapt Curriculum**

- **Remain Flexible**

- **Use Support Facilitators**

- **Develop School Philosophy**

- **Principles of Natural Proportion**

- **Include All**

- **Develop Networks (TEAM)**

- **Teachers Team**

- **Students in Mainstream**

- **Challenging Yet Assistive**

- **Supportive Community**

- **Respect Selves**

- **Accept Responsibilities**

- **Success Breeds Success**

# Creating Friendly Classrooms

- **Eliminate Competitive Symbols**

- **Use Inclusive Language**

- **Build Community**

- **Use One Another as Resources**

- **Applaud Accomplishments**

- **Employ Children's Literature**

- **Encourage cooperative learning**

- **Develop Peer Partners**

# Self-Esteem Strategies

- **Pupil Conferences**

- **Punch Cards**

- **Responsible Time Out**

- **Parents as Resources**

- **Amnesia**

- **Multiple Response**

- **Yarn Ball Activities**

# Organizing

- H.O.W.

- Calendars

- Chunking

# Classroom Rescripting

- Tape Recorders

- Chunking

- Block Outs

- Highlight

- Cut Corners

- Sequence Steps

- Signal Responses

- Homework Options

- Card Games

- Group Games

- Focus Techniques     1.                    2.

                       3.                    4.

# Reading Strategies

1. 144 Things to Read

2. Alphabet Clues

3. % of Known Words

4. Sequence Strategies

5. Five Finger Approach to Word Attack

6. Comprehension Strategies

7. Story Frame

8. Drill Sandwich

9. Repeated Reading

10. Information Organizer

11. Index Cards

12. Structured Study Guides

Gretchen Goodman

# *Math Strategies*

- **Numeration**
    1.
    2.

- **Rounding Off**

- **Preparation of Pages**
    1.
    2.

- **Fractions**

- **Organizers**

- **Learning Ladders**

- **Multiplication Clues**
    1.
    2.
    3.

- **Graphs**
    1.
    2.

# Spelling / Writing Strategies

1. Writing Paper

2. Folder Organizer

3. Address Labels

4. Magnetic Letters

5. Letter Charts

6. Configuration Clues in Spelling

7. Fitzgerald Spelling

8. Formats for Automatic Writing

9. Grafitti Boards

10. Clueing

11. Other

# Tests

1. Format

2. Content

3. Adaptations

4. Alternatives

# Grading

1. Contracts

2. Pass/Fail System

3. Letter or Numerical Grades

4. Checklist

5. Report Cards

# Inclusive Education Checklist

All across the nation, classroom teachers and specialists are being asked to meet the daily challenge of educating all children within the "regular" classroom setting. In order to be truly inclusive, children need to be included in all activities of the classroom and their home school setting. Neighborhood schools will now welcome back a variety of children who previously had been excluded. The following checklist will provide an expedient avenue for the initial inclusive project.

## School Community

_____ 1. The school is physically able to include all (ramps, elevators, wheel chair access, lavatories, desks, etc.).

_____ 2. All staff members have received adequate inservice (teachers, teacher-assistants, nurses, janitors, secretaries, administrators, cafeteria workers, bus drivers).

_____ 3. The school's mission statement is in line with the inclusive philosophy.

_____ 4. Support teams have been initiated to ease staff, parents, and community into a "we" philosophy as opposed to an "I" philosophy.

_____ 6. The needs and I.E.P.'s of included children have been described in simplified terms.

_____ 7. The staff is able to positively model the inclusive, accept-all philosophy.

_____ 8. Parents and community task-force members have been inserviced.

_____ 9. The special education and regular education teacher have been provided with time to plan and implement.

_____ 10. Art, music, library, and physical education teachers have become part of the teaming process.

_____ 11. The school is able to grasp the concept of "all education is special" and all teachers are special teachers and begin to dissolve staff and student labels.

## Classroom Environment

_____ 1. The children have been prepared for the inclusive project.

_____ 2. A variety of literature has been used to enable the children to see and discuss acceptance of all.

_____ 3. The children have been exposed to speakers, videos, and movies in which people share information about disabilities.

_____ 4. The classroom is set up to facilitate movement for all children.

_____ 5. There are a variety of activities and centers available to meet a variety of learning styles.

_____ 6. Friendship is an integral part of the school-wide curriculum.

_____ 7. All students are provided with opportunities to socialize and interact with one another.

_____ 8. Classroom rules and consequences are written in simple language. They are displayed for all to see and are frequently reviewed.

_____ 9. Children and teachers are able to communicate with each other and employ assisting devices as needed.

_____ 10. The classroom philosophy is one that encourages cooperative learning, peer partners and cross-age study buddies.

_____ 11. There are positive peer role models for all children.

# Students' Bill of Rights

_____ 1. Children enter the classroom at approximately the same time.

_____ 2. Students are situated in the classroom to facilitate their individual learning styles.

_____ 3. Children engage in similar activities at the same time.

_____ 4. Children, regardless of their label, receive the aid of a teacher assistant or specialist as needed within the regular classroom setting.

_____ 5. Children are made to feel welcome and are seen as participating members of a classroom society.

_____ 6. Children are involved actively in classroom routines.

_____ 7. Members of the class assist each other only when needed, yet allow for individual independence as needed.

_____ 8. All students are taught at a developmentally appropriate level.

_____ 9. Student successes are celebrated equally.

_____ 10. Adequate time is provided for peer interactions. Positive interactions are fostered.

_____ 11. Students are able to accomplish individual goals in regular classroom settings.

_____ 12. Children are set up to succeed in the regular classroom setting.

_____ 13. Parents and support staff are available to help children rehearse for expected educational outcomes.

_____ 14. Children are provided with immediate, positive feedback.

_____ 15. There has been documented evidence of a variety of children being included in after school socializing activities.

*Developed by Gretchen Goodman*

# Hershey Primary School — IST Progress Report

Name | Grade | Teacher | School Year 19 ___ - 19 ___

**Accommodations Checklist**

1. Test read orally for students
2. Test explained to student in detail
3. Material taped for the student
4. Instructional material altered or changed to meet student's needs
5. Content material retaught
6. Some individual instruction needed at times
7. Other

**Type of Support**

LS - Accommodations for learning support student
CS - Accommodations initiated by classroom teacher
IS - Accommodations planned by instructional support team
RS - Accommodations planned by remedial teacher

| | 1st Period | | 2nd Period | | 3rd Period | | 4th Period | |
| --- | --- | --- | --- | --- | --- | --- | --- | --- |
| | Type Support Code | Accommodations | Type Support Code | Accommodations | Type Support Code | Accommodations | Type Support Code | Accommodations |
| Reading | | | | | | | | |
| Process Writing | | | | | | | | |
| Math | | | | | | | | |
| Spelling | | | | | | | | |
| Science | | | | | | | | |
| Health | | | | | | | | |
| Social Studies | | | | | | | | |

# Differently Abled

## Bibliography
### Compiled by SDE Presenters

**If you would like help locating any of the books, contact Crystal Springs Books, 1-800-321-0401 or in N.H., (603) 924-9380**

Bain, Lisa J. *A Parent's Guide to Attention Deficit Disorders*. New York: Delta, 1991.

Copeland, Edna D., and Love, Valerie L. *Attention Without Tension: A Teacher's Handbook on Attention Disorders (ADHD and ADD)*. Atlanta, GA: 3 C's of Childhood, 1990.

Fagan, S.A.; Graves, D.L. and Tressier-Switlick, D. *Promoting Successful Mainstreaming: Reasonable Classroom Accommodations for Learning Disabled Students*. Rockville, MD: Montgomery County Public Schools, 1984.

Greene, Lawrence J. *Kids Who Underachieve*. New York: Simon & Schuster, 1986.

Harwell, Joan. *Complete Learning Disabilities Handbook*. New York: Simon & Schuster, 1989.

Hunsucker, Glenn. *Attention Deficit Disorder*. Abilene, TX: Forrest Publishing, 1988.

Lerner, Janet. *Learning Disabilities*. Boston: Houghton Mifflin, 1981.

Lipsky, D.K.,& Gartner, A. *Beyond Separate Education — Quality Education For All*. Baltimore: Paul H. Brookes, 1989.

McGuinness, Diane. *When Children Don't Learn*. New York: Basic Books, 1985.

Moss, Robert A., and Dunlap, Helen Huff. *Why Johnny can't Concentrate: Coping with Attention Deficit Problems*. NewYork: Bantam Books, 1990.

National Association of State Boards of Education. *Issues in Brief*. Vol.11, # 16. Alexandria, VA: NASBE.

Perske, R. & Perske, M. *Circle of Friends*. Nashville, TN: Abingdon Press, 1988.

Phinney, Margaret. *Reading with the Troubled Reader*. Portsmouth, NH: Heinemann, 1989.

Rhodes, Lynn, and Dudley-Marling, Curt. *Readers and Writers with a Difference: A Holistic Approach to Teaching Learning Disabled and Remedial Students*. Portsmouth, NH: Heinemann, 1988.

Rosner, Jerome. *Helping Children Overcome Learning Difficulties*. New York: Walker & Co, 1979.

_____. Visual Motor Program, Auditory Motor Program. New York: Walker & Co., 1979.

Stainback, S. and Stainback, W. *Curriculum Considerations in Inclusive Classrooms: Facilitating Learning for All Students*. Baltimore, Paul H. Brookes, 1992.

_____.*Support Networks for Inclusive Schooling*. Baltimore: Paul H. Brookes, 1990.

Stainback, S.; Stainback, W., & Forest, M., eds. "Classroom Organization for Diversity Among Students," *from Educating All Students in the Mainstream*. Baltimore: Paul H. Brookes, 1989.

Thousand, J., & Villa, R. "Strategies for Educating Learners with Severe Handicaps Within Their Local Home, Schools and Communities." *Focus on Exceptional Children*, 23 (3), 1-25, 1990.

Vail, Priscilla. *The World of the Gifted Child*. New York: Walker & Co., 1979.

_____. *Gifted, Precocious, or Just Plain Smart*. Rosemont, NJ: Programs for Education, 1987.

_____. *Smart Kids with School Problems*. New York: E.P. Dutton, 1987.

_____. *About Dyslexia*. Rosemont, NJ: Programs for Education, 1990.

Villa, R. et al. *Restructuring for Caring and Effective Education: Adminstrative Strategies for Creating Heterogeneous Schools*. Baltimore: Paul H. Brookes, 1992.

## Inclusive Education Resources

Paul H. Brookes Publishing Co.
  (catalog available)
P.O. Box 10624
Baltimore, MD 21285-0624
!-800-638-3775

Impact
Institute on Community Integration
University of Minnesota
6 Patte Hall
150 Pillsbury Dr. SE
Minneapolis, MN 55455
(612) 624-4848

---

### Voices

Working well with others is the key to success whether the others are students, parents, or educators. Sometimes, belief in a philosophy like whole language can lead to zealotry, with others being attacked or put down for holding opposing or even slightly different points of view. I find that sharing, supporting, and modeling are far more effective means of accomplishing goals, outside the classroom as well as inside.

*Jay Buros*
**Why Whole Language**

Reprinted with permission of Modern Learning Press, Rosemont NJ © 1991. ISBN 0-935493-44-1

# Questions About Implementing Mixed-Age Grouping

by Lillian G. Katz, Demetra Evangelou and
Jeanette Allison Hartman, coauthors of
*The Case for Mixed-Age Grouping in Early Education*

Research indicates that cross-age interaction among young children can offer a variety of developmental benefits to all participants. However, merely mixing children of different ages in a group will not guarantee that benefits will be realized. Four areas of concern are the optimum age range, the proportion of older to younger children, the time allocated to mixed-age grouping, and the appropriate curriculum. None of these concerns has been examined by empirical studies. We attempt here a preliminary exploration of questions.

## What is the optimum age range?

Although no systematic evidence has been found concerning the beneficial effects of the age range within a group, experience suggests that the range is likely to affect the group in several ways. We hypothesize that there is an *optimal* age range and that children too far apart in age will not engage in enough interaction to affect each other. If the age span within a group goes beyond the optimal range, then the models of behavior and competence exhibited by the oldest member may be too difficult for younger members to emulate. Indeed, there may be a risk that the eldest children will

intimidate the youngest members. Furthermore, we suggest that customary age-segregation practices provide too narrow a range of competence for maximum learning across much of the curriculum. For example, in a class composed entirely of three-year-olds, the children may not be able to engage in play as complex as they would engage in if in a class including four-year-olds. However, in many schools and child care centers, the mixture of age groups is more likely to be determined by the actual enrollments than by empirically-derived formulae.

Research is needed to illuminate the dynamic factors that operate in various age ranges. Comparative studies of classes with a two - versus a three-year age spread could identify the effects of age range on the frequencies, structure, and content of cross-age interaction. It would also be useful to know whether the types and frequencies of prosocial behavior (e.g., nurturance, leadership, tutoring) that older children exhibit in interactions with younger ones are related to the spread in ages. Of course, in many situations, the age range may not be a matter of choice, but rather a function of demographic factors beyond the school's control. The advantages or risks associated with age ranges are not clear from any available data.

## What is the best proportion of older to younger children in a class?

There is at present no empirical basis on which to predict what proportions of older to younger children within a class are optimal. Real conditions are unlikely to allow teachers to have one-half the class age four and the other half age five. It seems likely that if the class consists of five four-year-olds and 15 five-year-olds, the youngest members might easily be overwhelmed by their older classmates. However, if the proportions are reversed, might the demands of the younger children overshadow the needs of the older ones, and the acceptance of behavior appropriate from the younger children give the older ones license to behave in these less mature ways as well? In either case, the teacher's role includes not only fostering cooperative and constructive interaction across the age groups, but also minimizing the potential risks of the uneven distribution of the age groups and the kinds of behavioral characteristics associated with them. We have only indirectly related evidence on these issues — from cross-cultural studies on peer interaction (Whiting & Whiting, 1975). The Whitings' classical study describes a wide age range of peer interaction found in other cultures. The Whitings report that prosocial behaviors tend to emerge, and relationships among children of all ages are characterized by cooperation.

### What proportion of time ought to be spent in mixed-age groups?

There is as yet no evidence to indicate what proportion of the time children spend in an early childhood setting should be spent in mixed-age groups. However, we might consider possible mixtures of ages in early childhood settings and elementary schools. An ideal elementary school that has provisions for four-year-olds could be organized to provide an early childhood section or department for children four to six years old. (The National Association of State Boards of Education, 1988, recommends a unit composed of four- to eight-year-olds.) In such an early childhood department, the children might spend all of their time in mixed groups, depending to a large extent on the nature of the curriculum. If the curriculum is mainly informal and includes spontaneous play, learning centers, project work, and individual assignments as needed, children's progress in acquiring basic literacy and numeracy skills will not be jeopardized.

Another plan might be to set aside particular periods during which the teacher offers specific learning and instructional activities for small, flexible subgroups of children with relatively homogeneous abilities, knowledge, or competence. Members of these groups might work on specific individual assignments and receive systematic instruction as needed. While these small groups are receiving special instruction (see Katz & Chard, 1989. pp. 10-11), others in the class can continue to work on projects or play together in spontaneous groups.

On the other hand a school might want to have a home room for several periods of the day. For example, the children might be in mixed-age groups during an opening period, an extended lunch and rest time at midday, and perhaps during the last half-hour of school. The main advantages to the age mixture in this arrangement stem from opportunity for social interaction rather than from various kinds of cross-age tutoring or mixed-age project work.

The teaching staff of an early childhood department can allocate some time each day that cooperative learning groups use to work on assigned learning tasks. We suggest that the staff plan together the allocation of time and their own efforts in such a way that a balanced grouping results. When such a balance exists, mixed-and same-age groups have the opportunity to form spontaneously, and the teacher can organize assigned groups (more or less mixed in age) for specific instructional purposes. Each child would spend her first three years in the department, participating in a variety of peer groups. In this way, the uneven development and progress of many young children could be addressed by the flexibility of placement both in same-age and within mixed-age groups.

Efforts to maximize family grouping seem to be especially appropriate in child care centers in which many young children spend the majority of their waking hours. A class in a center could be composed of three-, four-, and five -year-olds. The early part of their day could be spent participating together in the morning meal.

*Maximizing the advantages and minimizing the risks of mixed-age grouping and making proper use of time will depend largely on the judgment and skillfulness of the teacher.*

The children could take a real role, appropriate to their level of competence, in setting the table and cleaning up after the meal, and could undertake real household chores before starting to play. Of course, the group does not have to be mixed in age to create this kind of family or community atmosphere. This plan would enhance the homelike quality of child care settings and reduce the temptation to "scholarize" the lives of very young children in child care. If, as is often the case, their siblings are enrolled in the center, increasing the opportunities for sibling contact is desirable. Many young children in institutions may find contact with siblings during the day a source of comfort.

Thus far, there is no data that suggests the optimal allocation of time to mixed-versus homogeneous-age grouping. There is therefore no reason to believe that time must be allocated to either one or the other age-grouping arrangement. Maximizing the advantages and minimizing the risks of mixed-age grouping and making proper use of time will depend largely on the judgment and skillfulness of the teacher.

## What about curriculum and mixed-age groups?

One of the possible benefits of mixing ages in the early childhood classroom may be a reduction of teachers' and administrators' tendency to adopt a unidimensional curriculum consisting of exercises and assignments that all children must complete within a given time. Instead of a formal academic curriculum for a whole class or age cohort, we recommend an informal curriculum with ample group project work, opportunity for spontaneous play and systematic instruction for individual children as needed.

Unless the curriculum has a significant amount of time allocated to informal group work and spontaneous interactive play in naturally occurring groups, the benefits of the age spread are unlikely to be realized. Katz and Chard (1989) propose that the curriculum for all young children should include opportunities for children to work on extended group projects in which individuals contribute differentially to the effort at many levels of competence.

If a class includes five-and six-year-olds in a family grouping arrangement some fives will be closer to six-year-olds than to other fives in a given skill and will profit from small-group instruction that involves six-year-olds as well. Similarly, some six-year-olds may benefit from small-group experiences that involve certain activities with five-year-olds for a while. The composition of the groups can be fluid, depending on the tasks and the rate of progress of each child.

One of the important potential advantages of a mixed-age early childhood department is the minimization of grade retention and repetition. Any child who had spent two or three years in such a department and was still judged unlikely to profit from the subsequent grade, which might be called Year 1 of primary school, could be referred for special services. Any curriculum for which more than 10% of the age-eligible children are judged unready is probably inappropriate (Katz, Raths, & Torres, 1987; Graue & Shepard, 1989).

## Summary

Although mixed-age grouping is a straightforward concept, the practical details of implementation are not well researched. Experience and some research, however, suggest that 1) an optimum age range is larger than the customary range in current classrooms, yet not so wide that children cannot share interests, 2) the proportion of older to younger children should be large enough to keep the older children from regressing, 3) no particular proportion of time needs to be allocated to mixed- and same-age grouping, and 4) an informal, multidimensional, non-age-based curriculum is most appropriate to a mixed-age group.

## References

Graue, M.E., & Shepard, L. (1989). Predictive Validity of Gesell School Readiness Tests. *Early Childhood Research Quarterly*, 4, 303-315.

Katz, L.G., & Chard, S.C. (1989). *Engaging Children's Minds: The Project Approach.* Norwood, NJ: Ablex.

Katz, L.G., Raths, J.D., & Torres, R.D. (1987). *A Place Called Kindergarten.* Urbana, Il: ERIC Clearinghouse on Elementary and Early Childhood Education.

National Association of State Boards of Education (1988). *Right from the Start: The Report of the NASBE Task Force on Early Childhood Education.* Alexandria, VA: Author.

# The Pros and Cons of Mixed-Age Grouping

### There are times when two age groups in a classroom are better than one—and times when they are not.

### Richard Lodish

Multi-age grouping had its roots in the one-room village school which, in an earlier time, combined age groups out of necessity. But in recent years, a number of larger, graded schools have tried to recapture the potential advantages of a wide age range in their classrooms.

The educational benefits of mixed-age grouping have been discussed by reformers from Montessori and Pestolozzi to Dewey. Since the 1930s, as educators have become increasingly aware of the limitations of a rigidly graded system, they have introduced more flexible organizational patterns. They have found that the nongraded organizational system recognizes and plans for a wide range of pupil abilities, provides for differential rates of progress, and adjusts to individual emotional and social needs.

A number of public and private schools that began as nongraded, emphasizing concern for individual continuous progress, have gradually changed to a multi-age vertical organization pattern. Increasing understanding of the developmental approach to education has resulted in renewed interest in Kentucky, Mississippi, and Oregon, where state legislatures have mandated multi-age classes for grades K–3. A number of other states, including Pennsylvania, Florida, Alaska, Georgia, California, Texas, Tennessee, and New

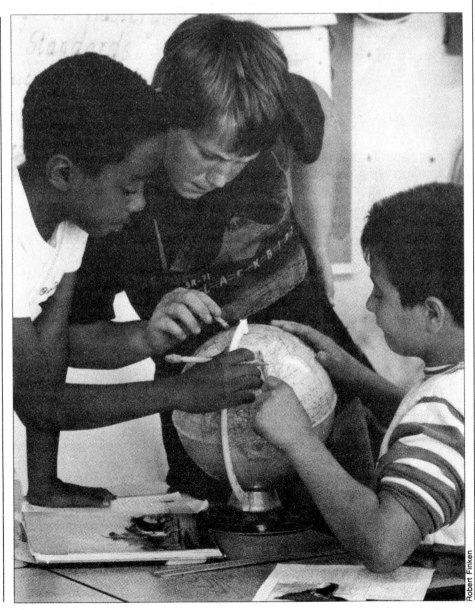

Robert Finken

Richard Lodish is principal of Sidwell Friends Lower School in Washington, D.C.

York, are reported to be developing similar programs.

## Defining Mixed-Age Grouping

Mixed-age or multi-age groupings should not be confused with combination classes, in which two or more age groups are combined for administrative reasons, such as overcrowded conditions or small enrollments at one grade level (*see accompanying article*). Where combination classes mix ages out of necessity, multi-age groupings do it for perceived benefits.

Ironically, combination classes that began as a stopgap arrangement have become, in many instances, the preferred arrangement. Changes in teaching methods, concern for individual differences, and concern for the social needs of children have prompted some teachers of combination classes to see the long-term advantages of mixed-age groupings.

A rationale frequently proffered for mixed-age grouping is that a larger age span is more reflective of the child's society outside school, and that children are accustomed to associating with groups covering a wide age range. A related rationale is that such classes substitute for the children's experience within an "age-segregated society." Advocates of this view see multi-age grouping as a reaction to changes in family structure and a decrease in contact among age groups in other settings, such as nursery schools and day care centers.

## Four Misconceptions

At Sidwell Friends, we have had to deal with several misconceptions about multi-age grouping. One is that multi-age vertical groups are less structured than single-grade horizontal ones. In my view, the tightness of structure in a classroom depends more on the style of teaching and organization than on the nature of the grouping.

Assuming that there is the same teacher-student ratio in both types of classes, and there are equal opportunities for individual attention and challenging learning experiences, the most important factor in determining if a child should be in a vertical or horizontal classroom is the fit of the teacher's teaching style and the student's learning style.

A second misconception is that mixed-age classrooms are meant to equalize chil-

---

### A Choice of Groupings

For the past several years Sidwell Friends Lower School, has offered a single-age and a mixed-age option at each Pre-K–4 grade level, with no classroom spanning more than a two-year age range. At present, the mixed-age classes are: PK–K, K–1, 1–2, 2–3, and two 3–4 classes. We find that a combination of vertical and same-age grouping allows us greater scope in meeting the needs of individuals and eliciting the greatest contribution from each student.

This combination of groupings also gives us a greater number of placement options each year. We have 13 classrooms, and if all were single-age classrooms, we'd have 13 placement choices. Because of mixed-age grouping, however, we have 19 options every year—an increase of almost 50 percent.

---

dren of different ages and abilities. In fact, vertical grouping offers children with a wide range of abilities and rates of progress a chance to work together. We do not track children by ability or age. We do not, for example, place "weak" or younger second graders with first graders, and "strong" or older second graders with third graders.

A third misconception is that the younger child in a mixed-age class will be "stretched" more than in a single-age class. Parents arguing in favor of this view incorrectly employ a sports metaphor: "I like to play tennis with someone just a little better than I am. It keeps me on my toes and improves my game." My response is: "How would you like to lose every game by just a little bit for the next five years, no matter how much you improve?"

Older children are as academically challenged in the top half of a mixed-age class as they would be in a single-age class when there is an equally demanding curriculum and individual attention to learning style and academic level. Additionally, when older children "teach" newly learned skills to younger classmates, they strengthen their own understanding of these skills.

The last misconception is that, once children begin a mixed-age class in the younger of two grades, they must stay with the class

---

for the second year. At Sidwell Friends, we follow our regular placement procedure at the end of each year, with teachers from adjacent grades discussing each child and determining the most suitable placement for the following year. Such factors as individual student needs, interests, temperament, and learning styles are balanced with logistics that make for a cohesive class. As a result, some children in the lower age span of a mixed-age class may move into single-age classes, while some in horizontal groupings may be placed in the upper age span of a vertical group.

## The Pros of Mixed-Age Grouping

Many of the studies done in the last 30 years have been supportive of mixed-age grouping. In their 1990 study of the subject, Katz, Evangelou, and Hartman found that:

1. The wide range of competencies in a mixed-age group provides students with opportunities to develop relationships and friendships with others who match, complement, or supplement their own needs and styles. Children in vertical groupings have a wide selection of models from whom they can learn—some older, some younger, some the same age. Mixed-age grouping provides older children with leadership opportunities and younger children with opportunities for more complex pretend play than they could initiate themselves.

2. Although some parents express concern about the likelihood of competition in a multi-age group, research indicates the opposite—that greater cooperation is often the result. And because such grouping appears to minimize competitive pressure, discipline problems that seem inherent in competitive environments are often substantially reduced.

3. Since most young children are not equally mature in areas of development at a given time, mixed-age grouping can be an effective strategy for dealing with their different rates of development. This grouping can be very helpful for children functioning below age-group norms in some developmental areas.

4. As a child interacts with children at different levels of cognitive maturity, intellectual growth is stimulated. Some proponents of mixed-age classes argue that the

cognitive conflict likely to arise in mixed-age interaction provides situations for significant learning for younger children as they strive to accommodate to the more advanced understanding of their classmates.

Other studies have determined that:

• Vertical grouping means that many children can have the same teacher or teaching team for more than one year, enabling teachers to use the knowledge they have gained about a child during the first year to plan learning experiences for the next year. Mixed-age grouping minimizes the get-acquainted time at the beginning of the year and provides children with strong continuity.

• In mixed-age groups, teachers' tendencies to teach all children the same lessons at the same time are reduced. Mixed-age grouping compels educators to organize learning activities and curriculum so that individuals and small groups of children can work on different tasks together.

### The Cons of Mixed-Age Grouping

There are, of course, some disadvantages to mixed-age grouping that have been mentioned in research or personally observed:

1. When the number of children in a mixed-age classroom is small, it may be difficult for same-age, same-sex children to develop friendships. This problem can be lessened by encouraging cross-age friendships and by providing opportunities for same-age children in different classes to come together at recess, snack time, lunch, or for joint projects.

2. There can be a tendency for teachers of mixed-age groups to provide fewer challenges for older children. Sometimes it's easier for a teacher to step back and let an older child help the younger ones. Teachers must make an effort to consistently provide enriching experiences for older children in mixed-age classes.

3. Some younger children, especially if very competitive, may be frustrated by the perceived gap between their work and that of older students.

4. A mixed-age class may encounter more difficulty in scheduling times for individual students to work with special teachers.

5. Teachers must do more work in planning instruction for a wide age range of students.

In the final analysis, putting children of different ages together in the same space does not necessarily bring about either beneficial or negative experiences. The external organizational method of single-grade or mixed-age grouping is less significant in influencing the relationships among children and their learning than the quality of the classroom environment.

As a K–1 teacher in a Vermont school puts it, ''The less we expect kids to be the same, the more they will accept and enjoy the differences among them. When that type of atmosphere is achieved, kids are free to learn from each other, and teachers have more time to teach.''  □

REFERENCES

Harkins, J. *Vertical Grouping Ten Years Later.* Germantown, Pa.: Germantown Friends School, 1977.

Katz, L. G.; Evangelou, D.; and Hartman, J. A. *The Case for Mixed-Age Grouping in Early Education.* Washington, D.C.: National Association for the Education of Young Children, 1990.

Lodish, R. ''Cross-Age Relationships in an After-School Center: An Observational Study of Children's Interactions with and Perceptions of Different Age Groups.'' Ph.D. diss., Harvard University, 1976.

Mitchell, J. ''Two Grades Are Better Than One.'' *Teacher,* April 1991.

**Voices**

## MARCELLUS CENTRAL SCHOOL DISTRICT MISSION STATEMENT

The Marcellus Central School District believes that all students can learn and that learning involves the whole person, physical, emotional, social, intellectual and aesthetic. Our task as a school community is to assist the child in discovering and actualizing his/her own talents/abilities and acquiring the skills and knowledge necessary to function productively in a diverse and changing world. The Marcellus Central School District recognizes that education is the responsibility of the entire community and is committed to fostering an interdependent relationship between school and community to enhance the educational experience.

*The Marcellus Central School District*
**Marcellus, New York**

# Teaching Combined Grade Classes: Real Problems and Promising Practices

*A Joint Study by the Virginia Education Association and Appalachia Educational Laboratory*

The concept of the multi grade class — also known as grade combination, split level, mixed grade, multiage, ungraded, non-graded, vertical, and family grouping — is not new. It has its roots in the one-room school of the early days of education in the United States. Multigrade classes are defined here as the assignment of two or more grade levels of students as one teacher's instructional responsibility. Since the term multi-grade class is the one most frequently discussed in the literature, it will be used throughout this rationale.

Current trends in demographics and economics, such as decreasing student population and rising costs of building construction and maintenance, have motivated educators to consider school reorganization and consolidation to deal with the problems of uneven student distribution, limited instructional resources, and inadequate facilities. Multigrade classes are often a result of such reorganization.

Recent research findings support multigrade grouping, indicating it can provide both cognitive and social benefits for students (e.g., Pratt & Treacy, 1986; Rule, 1983; Milburn, 1981) In response to the demands of changing demographics, particularly a decreasing and shifting student population, as well as to recent research, several state legislatures — including Kentucky, Mississippi, Florida, and

Louisiana — have called for implementation of multigrade programs. For example, the Kentucky State Legislature, in its Education Reform Act of 1990, mandated the implementation of ungraded primary programs (K-3) by September 1992; and the Mississippi State Legislature in 1990 mandated mixed-aged classrooms in elementary schools to be phased in over the next few years.

Although multigrade classes are an educational reality, and the literature reveals positive effects from this type of instructional organization, little research exists on teacher strategies for delivering instruction to two or more grades of students at one time.

"Throughout its history the concept of 'non-gradedness' has been presented as an ideal to which schools may aspire rather than as a specific program which they may implement" (Slavin, 1986, p. 47). Consequently, efforts to capture the ideal have been largely unsuccessful (Miller, 1989).

## Effects of Multigrade Classes

Research indicates no negative effects on social relationships and attitudes for students in multigrade classes. In fact, in terms of affective responses, multigrade students outperform single-grade students in more than 75 percent of the measure used (Miller, 1989, pp. 4-13). Results from several studies re-

viewed by Miller show positive effects of multigrade classes when measures of student attitude toward self, school, or peers are compared across a range of schools and geographic areas (Pratt & Treacy, 1986; Milburn, 1981; Schrankler, 1976; Schroeder & Nott, 1974). For example, Milburn (1981) found that children of all ages in the multigrade school had a more positive attitude toward school than did their counterparts in traditional grade-level groups. Schrankler (1976) and Milburn (1981) found multigrade students have significantly higher self-concept scores than students in single grades. A trend toward more positive social relations is indicated also (Sherman, 1984; Mycock, 1966; Chace, 1961). Sherman (1984) found that multigrade students felt closer to their multiage classmates than did single-grade students. Chace (1961) and Mycock (1966) determined that multigrade students had significantly better teacher-child relationships and better social development than single-grade students. These studies indicated that students in multigrade classes tend to have significantly more positive attitudes toward themselves, their peers, and school.

In terms of academic achievement, the data clearly support the multi-grade class as a viable, effective organizational alternative to single-grade instruction (Miller, 1989, p. 113). Little or no difference in student achievement in the single or multigrade class was found in the studies. In a study conducted in 1983, Rule found in general that multigrade students scored higher on standardized achievement tests in reading than did single-grade students. Milburn (1981) found little difference in basic skills achievement levels between students in multigrade and grade-level groups, but multigrade classes did score significantly higher on the vocabulary sections of the reading test administered. To account for this, Milburn concluded that teachers in multigrade classes may have placed greater emphasis on oral language, or that teachers working in multigrade settings may tend to speak at a level geared to the comprehensive abilities of the older children. In all cases in Milburn's study, children in the youngest age group in the multigrade class scored higher on basic skills tests than their age-mates in single grade classes. The findings of Milburn's study suggest that multigrade classes may be of special benefit to slow learners. Such children may profit from the tendency to emulate older students. Also, if they are in the same classroom with the same teacher for more than one year, slow learners have more time to assimilate learning in a familiar environment. Furthermore, multigrade grouping enable youngsters to work at different developmental levels without obvious remediation — a situation that can cause emotional, social, or intellectual damage — and without special arrangements for acceleration (Milburn, 1981, pp. 513-514).

A number of other studies indicate that multigrade grouping can provide remedial benefits for at-risk children. For example, it has been established that children are more likely to exhibit prosocial behaviors (Whiting, 1983) and offer instruction (Ludeke & Hartup, 1983) to younger peers than to age-mates. Brown and Palinscar (1986) make the point that the cognitive growth stemming from interaction with peers of different levels of cognitive maturity is not simply a result of the less-informed child imitating the more knowledgeable one. The interaction between children leads the less-informed member to internalize new understandings. Along the same lines, Vygotsky (1978) maintains that internalization of new concepts takes place when children interact within the "zone of proximal development, the distance between the actual developmental level and the potential developmental level as determined through problem solving under adult guidance or in collaboration with more capable peers." Slavin (1987) suggests that the discrepancy between what an individual can do with and without assistance can be the basis for cooperative peer efforts that result in cognitive gains, and that children model in collaborating groups behaviors more advanced than those they could perform as individuals. Brown and Reeve (1985) maintain that instruction aimed at a wide range of abilities allows novices to learn at their own rate and to manage various cognitive challenges in the presence of "experts."

## Obstacles to Multigrade Instructional Organization

In view of the advantages to multigrade instruction cited in the literature, the reader may wonder why more schools have not been organized into multigrade classes. One response is *tradition*. Although schools of the 1800s were nongraded, with the beginning of the industrial revolution and large scale urban growth, the practice of graded schools was established as the norm for organizing and classifying students. Educators found it easier to manage increased numbers of students by organizing them into grades or age divisions. Other factors, such as the advent of graded textbooks, state supported education, and the demand for trained teachers, have further solidified graded school organization. The graded school system was largely a response to a need for managing large numbers of students rather than an effort to meet individual student needs (Goodlad & Anderson, 1963).

Although the graded school developed as a result of demographics and economics, it has become the predominant way educators and parents think about schools. Ironically, changes in demographics and economics are now necessitating different school organizational patterns. However, the expectations created by the norm of graded schools have created a handicap for anyone seeking to operate a multigrade school (Miller, 1989). Also, most teachers receive training for teaching single-grade classes organized around whole-class instruction and/or small ability-grouped instruction, which are characterized by low student diversity. Different and more complex skills in classroom management and discipline, classroom organization, instructional organization and curriculum, instructional delivery and grouping, self-directed learning, and peer tutoring are needed to deliver instruction successfully in a multigrade class (Miller, 1989). Lack of attention to these skills in teacher education programs is a problem to teachers who are assigned multigrade classes (Miller, 1988; Horn, 1983; Jones, 1987; Bandy & Gleadow, 1980). Too frequently, the teacher skill deficit and the need to develop community understanding and support of multigrade instruction are overlooked by administrators or policymakers when decisions to implement multigrade classes are made and teacher assignments to these classes are given.

### Teaching Strategies

The Northwest Regional Educational Laboratory's (NWREL) Rural Education Program recognized the need for material to assist the multigrade teacher in 1987 when concerns were raised about the availability of research and training materials to help rural, multigrade teachers improve their skills. As a result, the Rural Education Program developed a handbook which contains a comprehensive review of the research on multigrade instruction, key issues teachers face in a multigrade setting, and resource guides to assist multigrade teachers in improving the quality of instruction. Twenty-one multigrade teachers reviewed a draft of this handbook and provided feedback, strategies, and ideas which were incorporated into the final version completed in September 1989. *The Multigrade Teacher: A Resource Handbook for Small, Rural Schools* by Bruce A. Miller has been of benefit to the VEA-AEL Study Group in preparing its study. Particularly helpful were the bibliographies and the overview of current research on the effects of multigrade instruction on student and teacher performance.

Teaching a multigrade class is a demanding task requiring a special type of individual. It also requires training, communication with parents and community members, and support. *Teaching Combined Grade Classes: Real Problems and Promising Practices* suggests types of training, resources, and support that facilitate multigrade instruction; effective strategies and practices employed by teachers experienced in

multigrade class instruction; and state and local policy initiatives that can support and assist teachers in multigrade class settings. The teachers who prepared this study, as well as those who responded to the study group's survey, have experience teaching multigrade classes. Their suggestions can be valuable to novice teachers in the multigrade approach, to administrators who are reorganizing schools, to those who plan professional development activities, and to those who recommend or initiate educational policy.

## Perceived Advantages and Difficulties of Grade Combination Teaching

In addition to identifying experience characteristics of grade combination teachers, the survey was designed to assess respondent perceptions of grade combination teaching. Perceived advantages and difficulties were recorded in response to questions 15 and 16 of the survey. Following the questions is a description of respondent data.

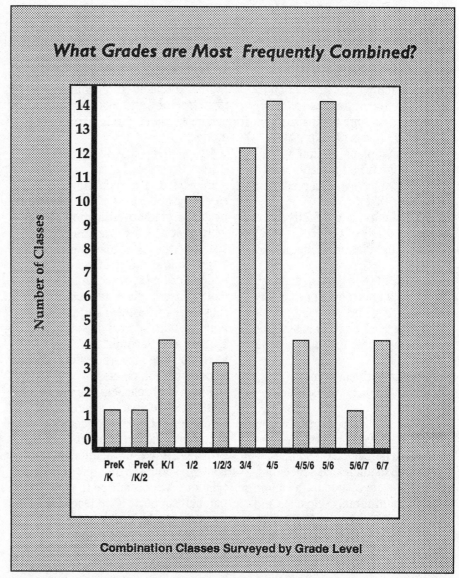

**What Grades are Most Frequently Combined?**

Number of Classes (y-axis)

Combination Classes Surveyed by Grade Level (x-axis: PreK/K, PreK/K/2, K/1, 1/2, 1/2/3, 3/4, 4/5, 4/5/6, 5/6, 5/6/7, 6/7)

15. Please describe any difficulties you have experienced in teaching curricula of two grade levels.

16. Please describe advantages you perceive to teaching grade combination classes.

## Difficulties

The consensus on difficulties experienced by 83 percent of the respondents can be capsulated in the response "*double* planning, *double* teaching, *double* grading, and *double* record keeping." These teachers cited specific difficulties indicating, as one teacher stated, "The time factor is most critical — in terms of covering materials with students." The individual difficulties reported by teachers that relate to the "time factor" in daily class instruction in order of frequency are as follows:

- lack of class time for instruction of two grade levels (71%);
- insufficient planning time (62%);
- not enough time for teachers to master two curricula in preparation to teach (48%);
- insufficient time to effectively cover two sets of curricula (45%);
- never caught up on written work (38%);
- insufficient time to remediate or work on a one-to-one basis with a child (24%); and
- inability to go beyond basics (e.g., not enough time for science experiments) (7%).

After time, the next most frequently cited difficulties, identified by 38 percent of the respondents, were fragmentation, scheduling, and grouping. Several responses illustrate these perceived difficulties. Two teachers indicated scheduling problems were related to the number of pull-out programs. Science and social studies were specific areas mentioned as difficult to schedule. Two teachers noted that in subjects such as family life, health, and sex

education, the curriculum for one grade is not appropriate for the other grade. Therefore, teachers must "farm out" children before they can teach certain lessons. Three other teachers said they could not arrange field trips because the subject would not be appropriate for both grade levels.

The third most frequently experienced difficulty in teaching curricula of two grade levels was the inability of one group of children to work independently while the teacher instructed the other group (20 percent). For example, one teacher stated there was constant competition between the groups for the teacher's time, and another described problems with children who fit in no group. However, three teachers identified problems related to scheduling for team teaching and working with teachers who they felt were uncooperative.

Respondents also identified difficulties related to how children were placed in combination classes. Concerns about how children were placed in grade combination classes were raised by six teachers who specified that class size was too large; children were inappropriately added during the year; children felt isolated from others in their grade, thus their self-esteem suffered; and children with special needs such as English as a Second Language students were inappropriately placed in combination classes.

Finally, 11 teachers described difficulties related to supports and resources. Three respondents specified a lack of support from their principal, and four mentioned concern about the amount of public relations work required to gain parental support. Two teachers mentioned a lack of support and assistance in general, and two responses described insufficient resources and materials to teach and

to integrate two curriculum levels.

## Advantages

In describing advantages to teaching grade combination classes, the consensus of 26 percent of the 69 teachers who responded to this question was that peer tutoring is the greatest benefit. In contrast to a perceived disadvantage mentioned by one teacher, 14 percent of the teachers who responded to this question stated that having the children two consecutive years allowed them the advantages of knowing the children's strengths and weaknesses and of being able to group ahead of time. One teacher responded, "Keeping students for a second year is great — no lost time!"

Integration of language arts and other curricula was identified as an advantage by 14 percent of the teachers. Six of these 10 responses specified the particular benefit combination classes had to integrating the reading curricula.

Respondents perceived a wide variety of other advantages. However, each was mentioned by only one or two persons. These advantages are categorized below under the headings of grouping, academic, behavioral, and resource and support advantages.

### Grouping advantages:
- Children are always taught in small groups.
- Gifted and talented programs, differentiation, and general grouping are no problem.
- Class size is always smaller.
- You get the top notch students academically and no behavior problems.
- All children can read.

### Academic advantages:
- Upper grade can review what is taught to the lower grade.

- One group motivates the other group.
- Children in the lower grade get enrichment by listening to what is taught to the upper group.
- Children in the lower grade are better prepared for the next year.

### Behavioral advantages:
- Different ages learn to socialize.
- Teacher can observe nine- and 10-year olds interacting.
- More independent work habits are developed.
- Upper grade children act as role models for lower grade children.

### Resource and support advantages:
- I received an extra computer for my room.
- Help from an aide was provided.

Although 24 percent of the 69 teachers who answered this question responded negatively with "no advantages," one teacher noted, "Kids learn from kids. I use students to help other students with word recognition, spelling, math, etc." However, this teacher went on to say, "This isn't really an advantage because this could be done in a one-grade class." Another respondent stated, "After 12 years of teaching combination grades, I can see no advantages. Because of time limitations, you cannot reach all students and meet their needs. They become angry and 'turned off.' Teachers are left frustrated and emotionally and physically drained."

In summary, a diversity of difficulties and advantages to grade combination classes were perceived by survey respondents. Difficulties identified by respondents in teaching curricula of two grade levels fall into five categories; time, scheduling/grouping, children's inability to work independently, student placement, and supports/resources. Teachers cited specific difficulties, most notably lack of planning and instructional time, relating to the most frequently identified problem — time. In contrast, a number of advantages to grade combination classes were identified, most frequently peer tutoring. Moreover, problems cited by some respondents were perceived as advantages by others, although there was greater consensus on specific difficulties. For example, 83 percent of the respondents identified "double planning, teaching, grading, and record keeping" as a difficulty, while 14 percent identified curriculum integration as an advantage. Also, some teachers indicated grouping was a problem, while others perceived grouping as an advantage to grade combination classes. Although they also may have identified difficulties, a majority of the respondents perceived some advantages to teaching grade combination classes.

## Bibliography

Brown, A.L., & Palinscar, A. (1986). *Guided Cooperative Learning and Individual Knowledge Acquisition* (Technical Report No. 372). Champaign, IL: Center for the Study of Reading.

Brown, A.L., & Reeve, R.A. (1985). *Bandwiths of Competence: The Role of Supportive Contexts in Learning and Development* (Technical Report No. 336). Champaign, IL: Center for the Study of Reading.

Chase, E.S. (1961). *An Analysis of Some Effects of Multiple-Grade Grouping in an Elementary School.* Unpublished doctoral dissertation, University of Tennessee.

Ludeke, R.J., & Hartup, W.W. (1983). Teaching Behavior of 9 and 11 year-old Girls in Mixed-age and Same-age Dyads. *Journal of Educational Psychology*, 75(6), 908-914.

Milburn, D. (1981). A Study of Multiage or Family-Grouped Classrooms. *Phi Delta Kappan*, 64, 306-319.

Miller, B.A. (1989). The Multigrade Classroom: A Resource Handbook for Small, Rural Schools. (Contract No. 400-86-0006). Portland, OR: Northwest Regional Educational Laboratory.

Mycock, M.A. (1966). A Comparison of Vertical Grouping and Horizontal Grouping in the Infant School. *British Journal of Educational Psychology*, 37, 133-135.

Pratt, C., & Treacy, K. (1986). *A Study of Student Grouping Practices in Early Childhood Classes in Western Australia Government Primary Schools.* (Cooperative Research Series No. 9). Nedlands, Australia: Education Department of Western Australia.

Rule, G. (1983). Effects of Multigrade Grouping on Elementary Student Achievement in Reading and Mathematics (Doctoral dissertation. Northern Arizona University). *Dissertation Information Service* No. 8315672.

Schrankler, W.J. (1976). Family Grouping and the affective Domain. *Elementary School Journal*, 76, 432-439.

Schroeder, R. & Nott, R.E. (19974). Multiage Grouping — It Works! *Catalyst for Change*, 3, 15-18.

Sherman, L.W. (1984). Social Distance Perceptions of Elementary School Children in Age-Heterogeneous and Homogeneous Classroom Settings. *Perceptual and Motor Skills*, 58, 395-409.

Slavin, R.E. (1986). *Using Student Team Learning*. Third edition. Baltimore, MD: John Hopkins University.

Slavin, R.E. (19887). Developmental and Motivational Perspectives on Cooperative Learning: A Reconciliation. *Child Development*, 58, 1161-1167.

Vygotsky, L.S. (1978). *Mind in Society: The Development of Higher Psychological Processes*. Edited by M. Cole, V. John-Steiner, S. Scribner, and E. Souberman. Cambridge, MA: Harvard University Press.

Whiting, B.B. (1983). The Genesis of Prosocial Behavior. In D. Bridgeman (Ed.), *The Nature of Prosocial Development*. New York: Academic Press.

**An excerpt from Teaching Combined Grade Classes: Real Problems and Promising Practices, September 1990, by the Virginia Education Association and Appalachia Educational Laboratory. Reprinted with permission of AEL.**

# Policy Briefs

## AEL

A publication of the
APPALACHIA EDUCATIONAL LABORATORY
STATE POLICY PROGRAM ❖ 1991

## UNGRADED CLASSROOMS— FAIL-SAFE SCHOOLS?

Too many students are not succeeding in school, and education reformers want to eliminate practices that, they believe, cause kids to fail. Some say doing away with grade levels, especially for young children, is one way to do that.

Advocates of ungraded classes argue that eliminating grade levels can help "curb ability tracking and grade retention, two factors that a growing number of educators identify as the detrimental precursors to failure for some young children."[1] Also, ungraded classes are a way "to steer schools away from competitive and overly academic instruction in the early grades and toward methods grounded in hands-on learning, play, and exploration"[1]—practices that research tells us are developmentally appropriate for 5- to 8-year-olds. Finally, ungraded primary programs eliminate the need to screen children to see if they are ready for school—a practice that flies in the face of what is known about the uneven and varied ways children develop.[2]

California and New York have appointed task forces to recommend changes in the early grades, but Kentucky is the only state to mandate the ungraded primary statewide. Part of the Kentucky Education Reform Act of 1990, the mandate was a response to an "overwhelming demand to reexamine our educational practices," says Linda Hargan of the Kentucky Department of Education and head of a task force charged with designing the implementation of the new primary school program. Hargan added:

> The way we are doing it now is not getting the job done. Somewhere between 20 and 30 percent of our children are being retained in kindergarten, first, and second grade, and we know there is a high correlation between children who are retained and those who drop out of school.[3]

❖

### DEFINING TERMS

The terms ungraded, nongraded, mixed-age, multigrade, or combined classes are used interchangeably. This results in a lot of confusion about just what the terms mean.

An ungraded or nongraded school is a school that abandons grade levels. (This is not to be confused with schools that eliminate the use of letter "grades" to report student progress.) In ungraded programs, children of different ages and abilities "work together in an environment conducive both to individual and group progress without reference to precise grade-level standards or norms."[4] Teachers help children progress as far and as fast as they can. That's why Goodlad and Anderson also call such programs "continuous progress."[5] Ungraded schools grow out of a philosophical belief that schools should meet children where they are in their growth process and provide a developmentally appropriate program for them, a program in which they can learn and not fail.

In contrast, terms such as multiage, multigrade, split-grade, or combined classes refer to classrooms that contain students from more than one grade level and where students continue to be identified by their grade level. Student groupings that follow this pattern grow out of economic and geographic necessity, particularly in rural areas.

Although teachers in multigrade, split-grade, or combined-grade classes can group their students across age, grade, or ability levels, they seldom do. Instead, they tend to group students by grade and teach each grade separately.[6,7] While research shows that students in these multigrade classes benefit from being with children of different ages, maintaining separate grade levels results in an unnecessary burden for teachers. Yet, these teaching practices persist because of a "strong organizational expectation that student grade-level identities be maintained."[6] For example, state curriculum regulations require certain material to be taught at specific grade levels, students are tested on grade-level material, state reporting procedures require information by grade level, and promotion and retention policies remain in place.

## ❖ ESSENTIAL INGREDIENTS OF UNGRADED PROGRAMS

Since ungraded classrooms are child-centered, they will not all look alike. But they can be expected to have at least six essential ingredients in common.

**Goals of schooling.** In ungraded schools, people think of the primary years as a developmental period when some children will move more rapidly than others.[1] They need to see each child as a whole person who needs help to grow socially, emotionally, physically, aesthetically, and intellectually.[5,8,9,10]

**Curriculum.** Ungraded schools structure the curriculum to focus on learning to learn—concepts and methods of inquiry—not specific content. Ungraded curriculum is integrated, not compartmentalized; it is age-appropriate and individual-appropriate.[5,7,10]

**Teaching.** Teachers' roles change dramatically in ungraded settings. They prepare the environment for children to learn, work with each other to plan the curriculum, and put kids in groups so they learn from each other.[8,10]

**Materials.** Ungraded classrooms have a wide variety of books and manipulative materials for a wide range of interests, ages, learning styles, and reading abilities. Grade-level textbooks are stumbling blocks to change, but some materials for whole-language reading, mathematics manipulatives, and technology-based writing are suitable for the ungraded, mixed-age approach.[6,10]

**Assessment.** Children's progress in ungraded programs is measured not in terms of grade-levels but in terms of each child's past individual performance. Assessment is continuous and comprehensive—taking into consideration all aspects of growth.[10,11]

**Grouping patterns.** Children in ungraded settings work in small groups with flexible age boundaries. Those groups provide opportunities for children to have frequent contact with other children of different personalities, backgrounds, abilities, and interests, as well as different ages. They come in contact with as many sensory, concrete experiences as possible.[10,11]

That's what Kentucky wants. The state ungraded the K-3 "to allow the 5-, 6-, and 7-year-olds to see what 8-year-olds can do and to learn from that," says Jack Foster, Kentucky Secretary for Education and the Humanities. "It replicates real life in the classroom because every one of those kids goes out there not to learn what other kids their same age can do, but to be like the big kids."[12]

## ❖ NATIONWIDE INTEREST

Interest in ungraded programs may be the result of several related groups urging a more developmentally sound way to teach young children. For example, the National Governors' Association challenges schools to allow "more varied grouping arrangements that promote student interaction and cooperative efforts but are not limited to conventional age-grading practices."[13]

The Council of Chief State School Officers observes that ability grouping in elementary classrooms results in considerably different learning environments among groups, while heterogeneous grouping can make these inequitable learning environments less likely.[14]

The National Association of State Boards of Education supports new primary units that provide developmentally paced learning for 4- to 8-year-olds.[15]

The National Association for the Education of Young Children (NAEYC), which stops short of promoting ungraded primary schools, identifies ungradedness as one aspect of developmentally appropriate practice.[16]

## ❖ OVERWHELMING RESEARCH

While we don't have a lot of research on ungraded programs, "we've made remarkable breakthroughs in understanding the development of children, the development of learning, and the climate that enhances that," says Ernest Boyer of The Carnegie Foundation for the Advancement of Teaching.[18] Kentucky's Hargan concurs, "We have a sound research base about how young children learn. What we lack now is a change in our practices to match what we know."[3]

**How children learn.** Young children learn best through active, hands-on teaching methods like games and dramatic play. "What looks like play to adults is actually the work of childhood, developing an understanding of the world."[1] The most effective way to teach young children is to capitalize on their natural inclination to learn through play.

Data on attitudes and peer relations have "tended overwhelmingly to favor" classes with students of mixed ages—graded or ungraded. But comparisons of student performance in graded and ungraded schools are inconclusive, partly because researchers failed to establish clear distinctions between the graded and ungraded settings they were comparing. Researchers agree, however, that students in ungraded classrooms do not fall behind and that they are more likely to enter the fourth grade with their classmates. Also, minority students, boys, underachievers, and low-income students benefit most from ungraded classrooms, but all students attending ungraded schools are more likely to have good mental health and positive attitudes toward school. Further, the likelihood of positive attitudes and better academic achievement improves the longer students are in an ungraded program.[5]

**Classroom practices.** Ungraded programs in the 1960s were associated with a lack of structure.[17] Since that time, the NAEYC and the National Association of Early Childhood Specialists in State Departments of Education have researched developmentally appropriate practices and clearly articulated the necessary structure on which to build a good program.[11]

In addition peer-tutoring—encouraging children to learn from one another—is a practice especially compatible with ungraded classrooms. More important, it is likely to have a positive effect on student learning. Research shows that organized and focused tutoring benefits tutors and learners. Further, students who are tutored outperform students who have not been tutored.[6]

Cooperative learning—small student groups that permit every student to participate in the completion of a clearly assigned task—is another practice that, research shows, can result in significant increases in student achievement, interpersonal relations, motivation to learn, and student self-esteem. For these groups to be effective, students need to be trained in cooperative work behaviors, and teachers must orchestrate the implementation of group work.[6]

❖
## What States Can Do

What is best for young children and their education is well-known, but putting all of those principles into practice is not easy.

To improve the chances of success for ungraded programs, states can encourage the use of new developments, as well as tried-and-true strategies. Some of these strategies are discussed below.

**Put computers in the classroom.** Computers facilitate learning, information gathering, and management activities in the classroom. With computers, students can learn independently, retrieve information from computer databases, and use the computer word processor to organize that information. Teachers can use the computer not only as a teaching tool, but also as a convenient way to document the work children do and how they do it.[6]

**Permit site-based decisionmaking.** Site-based decisionmaking—the shifting of authority for certain education decisions from state and district offices to school building staff—gives teachers the latitude to design the most appropriate education program for that school's students. This not only strengthens the implementation of ungraded programs, it also permits diversity from one school to another.

**Provide for teacher training and involvement.** Reaching children at their individual level of development requires sophisticated, skillful teaching—the most critical variable in the effectiveness of ungraded, multiage grouping.[6] Some teachers have difficulty implementing this kind of approach. The reason? "Our teachers are not all trained for it," says Sharon Kagan, Yale University.[17] Not only do teachers need training, they also need to be involved.

Schools that have instituted an ungraded program find that teachers adjust better when they're involved in the planning and decisionmaking.

**Encourage parent education and involvement.** Parent acceptance of ungraded programs is essential. When parents of students in ungraded classrooms see that their children like school, get along with other children, and learn to be good thinkers, "they become convinced."[17]

**Provide for ungraded materials.** Teachers need access to and information about appropriate materials for a variety of age and developmental levels. Teaching in an ungraded classroom can seem overwhelming when all the standard classroom materials are geared to single grades.

❖
## Summary

Moving to ungraded programs—a developmentally appropriate practice for 5- through 8-year-olds—is a fundamental change. Kentucky's Hargan sums it up this way:

> It's a change from conformity to diversity; from sequential, step-by-step approaches to self-paced and developmentally paced approaches; from age and ability grouping to multiage, multiability grouping. It means moving from the notion that the child should fit the school to a notion that the school should fit the child, from segregating special programs to integrating special programs, from competition to cooperation, and from failure-oriented to success-oriented schools.[2]

# REFERENCES

1. Cohen, D. L. (1989, December 6). First stirrings of a new trend: Multiage classrooms gain favor. *Education Week*, pp. 1, 13-15.

2. Shepard, L. A. & Smith, M. L. (1986). Synthesis of research on school readiness and kindergarten retention. *Educational Leadership*, pp. 78-86.

3. Hargan, L. (personal communication, March 15, 1991).

4. Yates, A. (Ed.) (1966). *Grouping in education: A report sponsored by the Unesco Institute for Education, Hamburg*. New York: John Wiley and Sons.

5. Goodlad, J. I. & Anderson, R. H. (1987). *The nongraded elementary school*. New York: Teachers College, Columbia University.

6. Miller, B. A. (1989, September). *The multigrade classroom: A resource book of small, rural schools*. Portland, OR: Northwest Regional Educational Laboratory.

7. Galluzzo, G., Cook, C. R., Minx, N. A., & Neel, J. H. (1990, October). *The organization and management of split-grade classrooms* (AEL Minigrant Report Series No. 19). Charleston, WV: Appalachia Educational Laboratory.

8. National Association for the Education of Young Children. (1986, September). Position statement on developmentally appropriate practice in early childhood programs serving children from birth through age 8. *Young Children*, 41(9), 4-17.

9. Katz, L. G. (1988). *Early childhood education: What research tells us*. (Phi Delta Kappa Fastback). Bloomington, IN: Phi Delta Kappa Educational Foundation.

10. Appalachia Educational Laboratory & Kentucky Education Association. (1991, April). *Ungraded primary programs: Steps toward developmentally appropriate instruction*. Charleston, WV: Author.

11. National Association for the Education of Young Children. (1991, March). Guidelines for appropriate curriculum content and assessment in programs serving children ages 3 through 8: A position statement of the National Association for the Education of Young Children and the National Association of Early Childhood Specialists in State Departments of Education. *Young Children*, 46(3), 21-38.

12. Foster, J. (1990, October). *Reflections on the legislation and its underlying considerations*. Presentation at the Regional Laboratory Symposium on Kentucky Education Reform. Lexington, KY.

13. David, J. L., Purkey, S. & White, P. (1989). *Restructuring in progress: Lessons from pioneering districts*. Washington, DC: Center for Policy Research, National Governors' Association.

14. Harris, C. (1989, November). *Success for all in a new century: A report by the Council of Chief State School Officers on Restructuring Education*. Washington, DC: Council of Chief State School Officers.

15. The National Association of State Boards of Education. (1988, October). *Right from the start: The report of the NASBE Task Force on Early Childhood Education*. Alexandria, VA: Author.

16. National Association for the Education of Young Children. (1988, January). NAEYC Position Statement on Developmentally Appropriate Practice in the Primary Grades, Serving 5- Through 8-Year-Olds. *Young Children*, 43(2), 64-68.

17. Krantrowitz, B. & Wingert, P. (1989, April 17). How kids learn. *Newsweek*, p. 50-56.

Reprinted with permission of Appalachia Educational Laboratory, P.O. Box 1348, Charleston, WV 25325, 1-800-624-9120.

# *Multiage*

## Bibliography
### Compiled by SDE Presenters

**If you would like help locating any of the books, contact Crystal Springs Books, 1-800-321-0401 or in N.H., (603) 924-9380**

Canadian Education Association. *Multiage Classes: Myths and Realities*. Toronto, Ont.: CEA.

Goodlad, John I., and Anderson, Robert H. *The Non-Graded Elementary School*. New York: Teachers College Press, 1987.

Katz, Lillian G.; Evangelou, Demetra; and Hartman, Jeanette Allison. *The Case for Mixed-Age Grouping in Early Education*. Washington, DC: NAEYC, 1990.

Kentucky Education Association. *Ungraded Primary Programs: Steps Toward Developmentally Appropriate Instruction*, Frankfort, KY: KEA.

Smith, Lee. *A Practical Approach to the Nongraded Elementary School*. West Nyack, NY: Parker Publishing Co., 1988.

Virginia Education Association and Appalachia Educational Laboratory. *Teaching Combined Grade Classes: Real Problems and Promising Practices*. Charleston, WV: Appalachia Educational Laboratory, 1990.

# Multiage Programs That Work

- **Goals**

- **Framework**

Adapted from Barbara Nelson Pavan's research

Elizabeth Lolli

- **Materials**



- **Curriculum**



- **Teaching Methods**



- **Evaluation and Reporting**


Adapted from Barbara Nelson Pavan's research

# Central Academy Nongraded
*Together Everyone Achieves More*
## (T.E.A.M.)

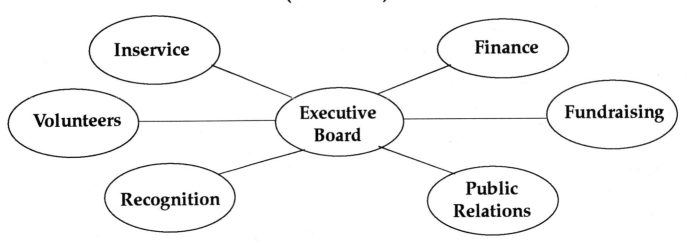

All parents participate on at least one of the committees to accomplish the year-long goals.

# Daily Schedule

8:00  Attendance, lunch count

8:15  Exercise video

8:30  Language arts

11:25  Lunch/recess

12:15  Math

1:00  Content projects

1:45  Specials/teachers plan

2:30  Oral reading

2:45  Dismissal

Elizabeth Lolli

# Parent Goal Sheet

**Please fill out the goal sheet, using the information you have about your child's needs.**

## Academic

1. What are your child's strongest academic areas?

2. What are your child's interests in the strongest academic area? Is there something in this area that your child really likes or excels in?

3. What would you like to see your child learn about the strongest academic area?

4. What does your child need additional work on, academically?

5. Is there a topic that your child dislikes in the area(s) he/she needs additional work in? If so, what topic?

6. What should be your child's three main academic goals for the first nine weeks?

7. What should be the three long-term goals for your child's academic progress for the school year?

8. Please make any other comments necessary about your child's academic abilities.

## Social

1. What are your child's strongest social skills?

2. What would you like to see your child learn about social skills?

3. What does your child need additional work on, socially?

4. What should be your child's three main social goals for the first nine weeks?

5. What should be the three long-term goals for your child's social progress for the school year?

6. Please make any other comments necessary about your child's social skills.

# Physical

1. What are your child's strongest physical abilities?

2. What are your child's interests in the strongest area?   Is there something in this area that your child really likes or excels in?

3. What would you like to see your child learn about the strongest physical area?

4. What does your child need additional work on, physically?

5. Is there a topic that your child dislikes in the area(s) he/she needs additional work in?  If so, what topic?

6. What should be your child's three main physical goals for the first nine weeks?

7. What should be the three long-term goals for your child's physical progress for the school year?

8. Please make any other comments necessary about your child's physical abilities.

# Emotional

1.  Is there anything that makes your child very happy or excited?  If so, what?

2. Is there anything that makes your child sad?  If so, what?

3. Does your child have a fear of anything which would relate to school?  If so, what?

4. What should be the three emotional goals for your child for the school year?

5. Please make any additional comments you feel appropriate.

*Developed by Elizabeth Lolli, Central Academy/Nongraded.*

# Questions and Answers about Multiage Programs

• **What is non graded?**

• **Why multiage?**

• **Why whole language?**

• **Where do skills fit in?**

• **What kinds of groups?**

# Cooperative Learning Groups

- **Pairs Check**

- **Numbered heads**

- **Co-op co-op**

- **Jigsaw**

- **Numbered corners**

# INTEGRATED LANGUAGE ARTS

## Children's Whole Language Bill of Rights

**EVERY CHILD HAS THE RIGHT TO:**

1. Be literate.

2. A child-centered classroom where the development of language and literacy results from integrated reading, writing, listening and speaking.

3. Teachers who understand the whole language approach; who actively involve parents, and who are empowered by their administrators to be key decision makers.

4. A curriculum that meets the individual's needs and that is organized around broad themes integrating language arts with mathematics, science, social studies, music, art and physical education.

5. High interest, language rich, meaningful reading material such as trade books, which take the place of workbooks and worksheets in the practice of reading skills.

6. Write about subjects that interest him or her without fear of criticism, and to scribble, reverse letters, and to invent spelling and punctuation as a part of his or her growth in literacy.

7. Speak and be heard in the classroom as an important step toward reading, writing and thinking.

8. Active involvement in learning through interaction with other children, manipulatives, toys and appropriate materials.

9. Abundantly supplied libraries, both school and classroom, that include predictable, printless, and pop-up books, poetry, fiction and non-fiction.

10. Progress assessment based on appropriate measurements such as writing portfolios, miscue analysis, book lists, peer reports and student-teacher interviews rather than norm-referenced, standardized tests.

## Judith M. Newman
## Susan M. Church

# Myths of whole language

*Newman, a writer, education consultant, and professor at Mount Saint Vincent University, Halifax, Nova Scotia, is concerned about helping teachers become more reflective and responsible for their own teaching. Church is a curriculum supervisor at Halifax County – Bedford District School Board and works to provide support to teachers in the process of making changes in their classrooms.*

It seems everywhere we turn these days, someone has something to say about "whole language." The term has become prominent in journal articles, books, conference presentations, publishers' advertising, and the media. Teachers, school administrators, researchers and theoreticians, parents and politicians have all contributed to the whole language literacy discussion. The problem is, however, that a good deal of what people have had to say reflects a serious misunderstanding of what whole language is really about. A number of myths and misconceptions are causing confusion and anxiety among both educators and the public.

The myths take a variety of forms. There are misconceptions about specific instructional decisions. There are overgeneralizations that keep teachers from seeing what their students are trying to accomplish. There are

orthodoxies that undermine students' learning. And there are large overriding myths that conflict dramatically with the theoretical underpinnings of whole language philosophy. We feel very much like Frank Smith must have felt when he wrote his "Myths of Writing" in 1981: "Not all teachers harbor all or even many of these misconceptions. Nevertheless [we] believe they are sufficiently egregious both in school and out to warrant their exposure and examination" (p. 792).

What follows is a close look at some of the myths about whole language. These myths are widespread. We've met them head-on all over the continent – here at home in Nova Scotia, in Alberta and Ontario, in Texas, Maine, and California. We present the myths not to criticize teachers but to help us all examine our pedagogical assumptions and to learn from the contradictions we find there. (We have written as "we" to make it clear that although we as authors have other responsibilities, we are first and foremost whole language teachers ourselves.)

### Myths about skills

**Myth:** *You don't teach phonics in whole language.*

**Reality:** No one can read without taking into account the graphophonemic cues of written language. As readers all of us use information about the way words are written to help us make sense of what we're reading. But these cues aren't the only clues readers use. We use

---

Commentaries are peer refereed submissions in which authors express their opinions on a variety of current issues in literacy education. The opinions expressed in commentaries do not necessarily reflect those of the Editors, nor are they necessarily endorsed by IRA.

---

a variety of other language cues: cues about meaning (semantic cues) and cues about the structure of a particular text passage (syntactic cues). We use pictorial cues when they're available, we bring our general knowledge about the subject into play, and we bring all our previous experience with reading and writing to bear when we read. Whole language teachers do teach phonics but not as something separate from actual reading and writing. We might offer students some phonics hints at an appropriate moment when they are writing and aren't sure how to spell something; we might draw their attention to graphophonic cues after they've successfully figured out an unfamiliar word. Readers use graphophonic cues; whole language teachers help students orchestrate their use for reading and writing.

**Myth:** *You don't teach spelling or grammar in a whole language classroom.*

**Reality:** Within a whole language framework, these aspects of language are a means to an end rather than an end in themselves. Spelling, punctuation, and handwriting are important because they help the writer to make meaning clearer for readers. Knowledge of grammar is helpful to both readers and writers as they construct meaning. Learning to read and write begins with engaging reading and writing experiences that have strong personal and shared meaning rather than with instruction in isolated skills. As children use language, they learn about language, discovering much on their own and through interaction with peers. When it seems appropriate, the teacher might provide information or assistance through short, focused lessons with individuals, groups, or the whole class. When children have real audiences for their writing, they have reasons to pay attention to the conventions of written language. They have reasons to learn how to revise and edit. As they become more proficient, they become increasingly independent at using conventional spelling and punctuation in final drafts.

## Myths about instruction

**Myth:** *Whole language means a literature-based curriculum.*

**Reality:** Although many whole language teachers often use literature as a vehicle for shaping classroom learning, we don't limit ourselves to activities that fit into a particular theme or even to texts of a particular genre. Many whole language teachers plan their literacy curriculum around investigations in math, science, and social studies. We try to capitalize on opportunities prompted by our students' interests in the world outside the classroom. We encourage students to be on the lookout for important current community or world events around which to develop learning enterprises. Because we believe it's important to offer our students multiple texts and different genres in conjunction with a broad range of hands-on experiences, we don't worry about forcing everything that goes on in the classroom into a single theme. A number of investigations may be going on simultaneously. The students may be in-

*Whole language teachers do teach phonics but not as something separate from actual reading and writing.*

volved in the exploration of some aspect of measurement or classification while at the same time investigating family issues from a number of different perspectives. Or they may be engaged in a project on fables as well as conducting a local community census using a broad range of tools to help them organize and interpret their data.

**Myth:** *Whole language is a way of teaching language arts; it doesn't apply to other subject areas.*

**Reality:** Whole language philosophy underlies the entire curriculum. Inquiries in science, social studies, and mathematics provide many opportunities for learners to be actively involved in solving meaningful problems. Students can explore with concrete materials, carry out investigations, relate what they learn outside and inside the classroom, and, in the process, use oral and written language as well as other communication systems to reflect upon and extend their learning. A look at an African legend, for example, might lead to the investigation of legends in the students' own culture. The exploration of legends could raise an interest in the function of musical instruments in African societies. This interest in musical instruments could move to the exploration of the physics of sound and the making of instruments. To consolidate their investigation, students might write their own legends, compose some accompanying music, and then publish and/or perform their efforts. In such a curricular enterprise, the students' knowing is strengthened by exploration between and among these many diverse perspectives.

**Myth:** *In a whole language classroom you don't have to teach.*

**Reality:** Teachers working from a whole language perspective are active participants in the learning context. We continually work at structuring an environment in which learners can engage in purposeful activities. We collect curriculum resources such as trade books, magazines, science, math, and social studies support materials, and we consider and reconsider their location in the classroom. We initiate learning activities. We pose questions, offer procedural suggestions, and suggest explorations. We are ever on the alert for opportunities to present learners with challenges that gently push them beyond their current strategies and understanding. We are constantly observing our students, asking questions, and inviting contributions from all members of the class in order to judge when learners can best use particular information. We make time to reflect on how learning is proceeding and change direction when it becomes apparent that things aren't going as well as expected or when students propose better alternatives. All of these activities are integral aspects of teaching.

**Myth:** *A whole language classroom is unstructured.*

**Reality:** A whole language classroom is highly structured. Both teachers and students contribute to the organization. The teacher has thought about the placement of furniture, what specific resources to offer and their location within the classroom, the grouping of the students, the nature and flow of activity, the approximate amount of time to allocate, and some possible ways for students to present what they have learned. While long-range objectives have been carefully considered, the moment-to-moment decision-making is fluid. Students are encouraged to suggest alternative

strategies or to propose new directions for themselves. Whole language teachers make every effort to merge students' interests with overall instructional goals thereby creating a flexible, yet comprehensive curriculum.

## Myths about evaluation

**Myth:** *There's no evaluation in whole language.*

**Reality:** Teachers working from a whole language perspective are always evaluating. We observe and interact with students to discover not only what but how they're learning. We are constantly gathering information that we use to make decisions about future instruction. We notice when a student tries a new strategy or demonstrates awareness of a writing convention. We keep tabs on how groups are progressing. We examine students' work often, looking for evidence of their latest discoveries. We share what we learn with students so they, in turn, can learn to judge how they're doing for themselves. When this kind of ongoing evaluation occurs, both teachers and students have a clear understanding of accomplishments and needs. Moreover, we can communicate this understanding to parents and others.

**Myth:** *In whole language classrooms there are no standards; anything goes.*

**Reality:** In open, generative learning environments the standards are set by the situation and the participants. When the focus of learning and teaching is the construction and communication of meaning, standards are intrinsic. When learners are engaged in purposeful experiences, success lies in fulfilling the intended purpose and progress is judged on the basis of students' ability to handle increasingly complex language and thinking tasks. Teachers who are guided by a whole language framework set expectations based upon our theoretical knowledge, and we encourage learners to impose increasingly demanding expectations for themselves.

**Myth:** *Whole language teachers deal just with process; the product doesn't matter.*

**Reality:** Whole language teachers are very concerned about the quality of our students' efforts. However, we also value the process whereby assignments, stories, reports, and projects are produced. We know the value of distinguishing between work-in-progress and finished products. Work-in-progress is allowed to be rough. The point of taking some assignments, stories, reports, and projects through to completion is to help students learn the strategies for making sure that their intended meaning is clear, that conventions have been followed, and that the format is attractive and appropriate. But not all work needs to be perfected. Many assignments and written efforts are intended to increase fluency—to help students discover and articulate ideas. The important thing is assisting students to discern when conventions matter and when they don't.

## Myths about learners

**Myth:** *Whole language philosophy applies only to teaching children in the early grades.*

**Reality:** Although the majority of teachers who are attempting to implement whole language philosophy in their classrooms are elementary teachers, the theoretical arguments apply equally to the teaching of 15-year-old and 35-year-old students. The principles guiding whole language instruction are appropriate regardless of the learner's age. Whether in primary classrooms or in graduate classes, students need to be actively engaged in making sense for themselves.

**Myth:** *Whole language won't work for kids with special needs.*

**Reality:** Children having difficulty in school for whatever reason are the very ones who benefit most from a learning context that encourages them to take risks and to experiment. For so many of these children their problems have been exacerbated by the fragmented, right answer skills-based literacy instruction they've been receiving. The instruction, rather than helping them sort out what reading and writing are all about, has interfered with their strategies for making sense, rendering them dependent, cautious learners. Many of these children have stopped believing they can learn. A whole language-based learning environment invites these children to see themselves as learners once again.

## Other myths

**Myth:** *There is little research to support whole language.*

**Reality:** The research base for whole language philosophy is broad and multidisciplinary. It includes research in linguistics, psycholinguistics, sociology, anthropology, philosophy, child development, curriculum, composition, literary theory, semiotics, and other fields of study. Increasingly, we are gaining insights into language learning and language instruction through collaborative classroom inquiry, wherein teachers and researchers pursue issues of common concern. Through this kind of research, teachers and researchers alike have made, and are continually making, important discoveries about what happens in highly complex, multifaceted classroom and real-world environments.

**Myth:** *All you need for whole language is a "whole language" commercial program.*

**Reality:** Published programs attempt to provide short-cuts for teachers. Many publishers are now prepackaging reading materials and lessons that incorporate aspects of methodology associated with whole language philosophy. There is nothing intrinsically wrong with these materials—many programs use high quality literature and a range of interesting activities. But they do not, in themselves, create a whole language learning environment. Furthermore, to use any materials in a way that is supportive of individual learners, we must first understand some of the theoretical basis of whole language. We must question our beliefs about instruction, and we must be willing to watch and learn from our students. The danger with adopting a commercially-prepared reading program is that teachers will apply sets of procedures rather than structure experiences appropriate for their particular students and their individual needs. To create a whole language-based classroom, we must learn to observe our students closely and be reflective about our teaching.

**Myth:** *Whole language is a methodology.*

**Reality:** Whole language is a philosophy of learning and teaching based on a number of fundamental assumptions. Some of these include the following:

Learning
  is social;
  requires risk-taking and experimentation;
  involves constructing meaning and relating

**95**

new information to prior knowledge;
occurs when learners are actively involved,
  when they have real purposes,
  when they make choices and share in
     decision-making;
uses language, mathematics, art, music,
  drama, and other communication systems
  as vehicles for exploration.

Teachers working from these assumptions try to create open learning environments. Our methodology is dynamic and continually evolving—guided by our observations of students and our ever-changing understanding of theory. We use a variety of teaching strategies and materials depending upon the needs of individual students. We base our instructional decisions upon what we know about learning and about the individual learners in our classroom. Whole language is practical theory. It argues for theoretically-based instructional practice.

## Myths about becoming a whole language teacher

**Myth:** *Giving teachers a few whole language tips makes them into whole language teachers.*

**Reality:** The difficult part of becoming a whole language teacher is learning to recognize the beliefs that underlie instructional decisions. The trouble with presenting teachers with 50 nifty tips is that it leaves people believing whole language merely consists of using particular materials or doing certain specific activities. Tips perpetuate unreflective teaching; they misrepresent the complexity of what is involved in creating a learner-centered classroom. In fact, every teaching action, every decision, every response in the classroom is based on some set of assumptions about teaching. Helping people become whole language teachers means helping everyone engage in a serious and ongoing examination of pedagogical beliefs and instructional practices.

**Myth:** *You need only a few inservice sessions to change teaching practice.*

**Reality:** Since whole language is a philosophy rather than a methodology, teachers need ongoing opportunities to explore both the theory and implications for classroom practice. Traditional, one-shot inservices may give teachers a few new ideas, but they leave people without the analytic tools to be able to

figure out where to go next or why. This kind of inservice does not lead to the examination of assumptions so necessary for change in beliefs and practice. Anyone taking a leadership role—principals, curriculum supervisors, as well as classroom teachers—must recognize the complexity of the process and consider realistic time expectations. Curriculum leaders need to create many different kinds of learning situations so that everyone is supported in a long-term exploration of learning and teaching.

**Myth:** *Whole language simply involves a change in classroom practice; it's business as usual for administrators.*

**Reality:** Because whole language is not a program to be defined and mandated but a belief system that is in a constant process of evolution and implementation, everyone involved in implementing whole language philosophy has to become a learner. Administrators need to recognize that changing one's philosophical stance involves the same learning processes that teachers are trying to establish for students in the classroom. Like students, teachers also need to be helped to identify their strengths and to build upon them. Teachers need to feel it's safe to take risks and to experiment. That means providing a supportive environment. It's not enough to tell people what *they* should be doing. It means everyone should be working together to identify a specific curricular problem we would like to address and then explore possible instructional alternatives. We all need to reflect on what happens in a collaborative, learning-focused environment. And that can't happen unless administrators are working from the same philosophical position they are attempting to help teachers implement. Therefore, principals and district-level administrators must also examine their beliefs about learning and teaching and about teacher development.

## The grand myths

**Myth:** *There is one right way to do whole language.*

**Reality:** This grand myth subsumes a long list of misconceptions about whole language: "You only work in small groups." "Every piece of writing has to go through the '3' or the '5' steps in the writing process." "You never spell a word for a child." "You never tell them what a word is." "You never do any grading." Statements like these are easily identified as misconceptions—each represents an orthodoxy. They embody the belief that there is some magic, correct solution to the many complexities of instruction. But the reality is that there is no one right answer to any question about teaching. Every question can and must be answered by "It depends." It depends on what has gone on before, on what the students seem to know, on the strategies they have at their disposal at the moment, on how ready they seem to be to forge ahead, on the resources at hand, on how much time is available, on how far we teachers think we can push the conventional expectations and values of the school and the community. Every instructional decision requires a judgment—a judgment made at the moment, by the teacher who is right there in the classroom. And as with all judgments, sometimes they'll be wrong. However, as we teachers become more adept at examining assumptions and learning from students, we will become better able to take new theoretical ideas and explore them in our classrooms.

**Myth:** *Whole language is only for super-teacher.*

**Reality:** Although lots of people think you've got to be a special, intelligent, well-read, ambitious, sensitive, brilliant person to teach from a whole language perspective, the truth is that anyone willing to take some risks can begin the exploration. Any teacher can handle the decision-making. Every teacher can create the subtle structures that help shape the learning context. Every teacher can discover that there is no elusive right way for implementing whole language. With some support, every teacher can find his or her own way.

## Dispelling the myths

So how do we begin to dispel the myths? We begin by assuming responsibility for our personal ongoing professional development. It's as difficult and as simple as that.

Taking charge of our own professional development is not easy. From our own schooling experiences to preservice education and through much of our graduate education and inservice, we teachers have been faced with a transmission view of learning and teaching. At every turn we are told how and what we should teach. Rarely are we encouraged and helped to think a situation through for ourselves. Instead, district-wide adoption of published programs in all areas of the curriculum conveys the not-so-subtle message that we can't be trusted to make sensitive, intelligent instructional decisions; someone else is the expert.

However, it is possible to learn to value our own experience and trust our own instructional judgments. The strategies are varied yet simple. Some people have become researchers in their own classrooms (see Bissex & Bullock, 1987). Not big R researchers, but careful observers. We have made a commitment to finding out for ourselves. We have begun with a question, "I wonder how predictable books support these beginning readers?" "Can journal writing help develop students' writing fluency?" "How does freewriting help my students learn science?" We do our best to keep track of what is happening: jotting notes to ourselves during the day about what we've seen going on, keeping track of students' conversation and written work and examining it regularly for indications of progress or difficulty, interviewing students periodically to ascertain how they see themselves progressing. Through our research efforts, we have uncovered some of the contradictions inherent in our assumptions about teaching and between espoused beliefs and instructional practices. As a result of careful observation, we have been able to eradicate some personally-held misconceptions about whole language-based instruction.

Another useful reflective strategy is the recording and sharing of critical incidents (Newman, 1987; 1990). A critical incident is an occurrence that lets us see with new eyes some aspect of what we're doing. When we're unsettled about something that's happened and reflect on it, we can learn both about our students and about the impact our teaching might be having on them. A comment overheard, a direct question, a reaction in a journal or personal log, something we read that conflicts with our experience or opens possibilities we haven't considered previously can allow us to examine our pedagogical assumptions and refine what we do with students. "I didn't think I was allowed to do that," says a student and the teacher questions what she has done to have conveyed a particular orthodoxy. "The teacher said I should," remarks another student, and we're forced to reconsider the assistance we have just offered. "The difficulty with teaching is to find a balance between imposing judgment and allowing for students' spontaneity, between controlling students' actions and offering free rein," writes a researcher, and we think about an assignment we've just given. Moments like these, if examined, may help us clarify our assumptions and contemplate contradictions within our practice. Potential critical incidents can be found everywhere, not just in the classroom, and they present important opportunities for us to become reflective practitioners. But first we have to become aware of these moments and the possibilities they offer.

Whole language teachers have made a commitment to professional development in a variety of ways. We take courses to help sort out the issues and debates about literacy instruction. We make time to read new books and professional journals in order to stay current with research on theories of literacy development and instructional implementation. We have formed study groups that meet regularly both to share ideas for practice and to discuss classroom, school, and school district problems. A few of us have written about our experiences as a way of sorting out what we have learned and to offer insights to fellow teachers. All of these activities lead to reflective practice and help dispel the myths.

In turn, as we become more strongly reflective, we find ourselves in a position to help others become reflective: our students, their parents, administrators, as well as the public at large. It's important for students to become reflective about what they know and how they learn. By openly sharing our ways of finding out with them, we allow them to become independent and responsible learners. Parents, too, need to understand the theoretical basis of a whole language perspective. By inviting them to participate in class projects by allowing them to share in the celebration of the learning, we can help them understand how a whole language-based instructional context really supports their children's learning and let them see the many different ways their children are developing. Administrators need to

become reflective as well. They are responsible for the tone and morale of a school or school district. By inviting them to participate in the students' learning, either directly or vicariously through our writing, we can help them consider contradictions between their pedagogical assumptions and their administrative practices. And the public needs to be informed about what is really happening in whole language classrooms. We can share our students' achievements and involve the public in celebrating their accomplishments.

Whole language is founded on the belief that learning is a collaborative venture and that we are implicated in each other's learning. Whole language isn't an add-on. It's not a frill. We can't just do a little bit of whole language and leave everything else untouched. It's a radically different way of perceiving the relationships between knowledge and the knower, between compliance and responsibility, between learner and teacher, between teacher and administrator, between home and school. Taking a whole language stance makes for a very different classroom—a classroom in which both teachers and students have a voice.

It's seductive to think we're making some headway when we incorporate new activities or set aside published basal reading series. But these changes are merely surface ones (Shannon, 1989). Real change is far more complex. Real change involves a critical appraisal of our instructional practices, trying to identify contradictions within our theoretical assumptions and their impact on our students. There is no safe middle ground, no convenient compromise. We won't make much progress toward developing a whole language stance, or toward discrediting the myths, unless we are willing to make ourselves vulnerable and become learners too.

**References**

Bissex, G.L., & Bullock, R.H. (1987). *Seeing for ourselves.* Portsmouth, NH: Heinemann Educational Books.

Newman, J.M. (1987). Learning to teach by uncovering our assumptions. *Language Arts, 64,* 727-737.

Newman, J.M. (1990). Finding our own way. In J.M. Newman (Ed.), *Finding our own way: Teachers exploring their assumptions* (pp. 7-24). Exeter, NH: Heinemann Educational Books.

Shannon, P. (1989). The struggle for control of literacy lessons. *Language Arts, 66,* 625-634.

Smith, F. (1981). Myths of writing. *Language Arts, 58,* 792-798.

**Reprinted with permission of Judith M. Newman and the International Reading Association.**

**The Society for Developmental Education©**
Northgate, Route 202, P.O. Box 577, Peterborough, NH 03458 (603) 924-9621

# The Whole Language Newsletter for Parents

ANTHONY D. FREDERICKS

Assistant Professor of Education • York College • York, PA

VOL. 1, NO. 1 AUGUST/SEPTEMBER 1991

## Welcome Aboard!

Welcome to the first issue of "The Whole Language Newsletter for Parents." In this issue and the other issues to follow, we'll provide you with information on what "whole language" is, how it works, and what you can do at home to develop your child's reading and writing. We hope that you'll find this information helpful so that you'll be able to work with your child's teachers in promoting literacy—both in the classroom and at home.

We welcome your support and comments. If there's anything we can do to help you help your child, feel free to contact us through *Teaching K-8*. By working together, we can help all children grow to the maximum of their educational potential.

### Questions and Answers

*What is "whole language"?*
Whole language is a philosophy of teaching in which reading, writing, listening and speaking are integrated and taught throughout the elementary curriculum. It is not a program, but rather a way in which children's literature, writing activities and communication activities can be used in every subject.

Whole language provides a natural learning environment based on the individual learning needs of each child. It is child-based education, which means that children begin to assume some of the responsibility for what they learn in the classroom.

*What about skills?*
For many children, "skill work" means circling words or filling in the blanks on worksheets. Since this work is often separate from a complete story or lesson, many students have difficulty seeing how the words they have circled relate to anything else.

In a whole language classroom, skills are not eliminated; rather, they are taught in a context that is meaningful to the child. For example, instead of having the child circle all the adjectives on a worksheet, the teacher might ask the students to write about a favorite toy. The teacher will then note whether each child has used a variety of adjectives and will work individually with each child making suggestions on adjective use. This approach relies on the child's experiences instead of skill sheets that may not relate to the child's life.

*What do children do?*
Whole language programs are as varied as the teachers and students who participate in them. However, they usually include a variety of the following elements: lots of time for individual writing; silent reading; sharing of good books; frequent read-alouds by the teacher; small group work and reading conferences; oral dictation by students; good writing modeled by the teacher.

These activities are used in every subject and throughout the school day. It's the teacher's responsibility to make sure that every child is able to participate and share in a whole language classroom. It's each child's responsibility to be involved in activities that meet his or her special needs and abilities.

*How can parents help?*
Parents can play a major role in helping their children become competent readers and writers. The environment you establish at home has much to do with how successful your child will be in school.

Home activities that support the whole language classroom include reading to your children every day; sending your child lots of notes or letters; listening to the things your child does every day; making frequent trips to the library; buying books as presents for your child; letting your child see you reading and writing; and talking with your child about things that are important to him or her.

### Whole Language Activities

Here are some activities you and your child can do at home. The emphasis is on sharing and fun. Try not to turn your home into a "school away from school."
*Tape recording.* As you and your child read stories together, record them on cassette tape. Later, your child can hear you read a favorite story again and again.
*Letters and notes.* From time to time, post a note on the refriger-

### Activities *(Continued)*

ator door, tuck one into your child's lunch box, or leave one on the pillow. You can tell your child how proud you are of him or her, remind him or her about an upcoming event, or suggest a special book to read.

*Children's magazines.* One of the most valuable gifts you can give your child is a children's magazine subscription. Check with the school librarian for addresses and subscription information.

*Journals.* Schedule several sessions during the week when you and your child can share some thoughts in a notebook or journal.

*Modeling.* You serve as a positive role model for your child. Be sure he or she sees you reading a newspaper or magazine, writing letters, or sharing a book or story with another family member.

*Storytelling.* Plan some time each day when you and your child can share a good book together. You can read the book to your child or have your child read to you. Be sure to check with the school or public librarian for some good recommendations.

*Family calendar.* Post a large wall calendar in the living room or kitchen. Put your child in charge of recording family appointments, celebrations and holidays. Have your child provide "reminders" to family members in the form of small notes.

*Collages.* Ask your child to cut out magazine pictures of items mentioned in a favorite story or book. These can be fashioned into a collage and posted on the refrigerator door. Have your child supply a title for the collage.

*Card collection.* Ask your child to draw illustrations of favorite book characters on 4" x 6" index cards. On the back of each card, your child can write a short description of the character, similar to the descriptions found on baseball cards. Have your child keep a permanent collection of these cards.

*Before and after.* What events could have occurred before the start of a favorite story? Challenge your child to put them in writing. He or she may also enjoy writing a sequel to the story.

*Interviews.* Have your child talk to family members, relatives or neighbors about some of the ways they use reading and writing in their jobs or hobbies. What kinds of reading materials must they use every day? How often must they write a letter or a memo? What about at home?

### Books for Parents

*What's Whole in Whole Language?* by Kenneth Goodman (Heinemann Books, 1986).

*Notes from a Schoolteacher* by James Herndon (Simon & Schuster, 1986).

*Learning All the Time* by John Holt (Addison-Wesley, 1990).

*The New York Times Parents' Guide to the Best Books for Children* by Eden R. Lipson (Random House, 1988).

*Reading Together: Helping Children Get a Good Start in Reading* by B. Taylor and D. Monson (Scott, Foresman, 1991).

*The New Read-Aloud Handbook* by Jim Trelease (Viking Penguin, 1989).

### Books for Children

*The Jolly Postman* by Janet and Allan Ahlberg (Little, Brown, 1986). A marvelous story filled with special letters and lots of surprises.

*The Great Kapok Tree* by Lynne Cherry (Gulliver Books, 1990). A man begins to cut down a kapok tree until the animals of the jungle convince him otherwise.

*The Magic School Bus Inside the Earth* by Joanna Cole (Scholastic, 1987). What happens when a school bus full of students and their teacher travel to the depths of the earth.

*Miss Rumphius* by Barbara Cooney (Puffin Books, 1985). Miss Rumphius longs to travel around the world—but when she returns, she must do something very important.

*Sam Johnson and the Blue Ribbon Quilt* by Lisa C. Ernst (Lothrop, Lee and Shepard, 1983). Sam Johnson decides he enjoys sewing and wants to join the women's quilting club.

*In Coal Country* by Judith Hendershot (Knopf, 1987). The story of a child growing up in an Ohio coal mining community in the 1930's.

*Days with Frog and Toad* by Arnold Lobel (Harper and Row, 1979). A collection of five stories about the special friendship between a frog and a toad.

*Shaker Lane* by Alice and Martha Provensen (Viking Penguin, 1987). Shaker Lane contains a collection of some of the oddest people you'd ever want to meet.

*When I Was Young in the Mountains* by Cynthia Rylant (Dutton, 1985). An endearing story of the special times one girl experienced growing up in rural America.

*Aurora Means Dawn* by Scott Sanders (Bradbury Press, 1989). A family of nine makes a perilous journey from Connecticut to Ohio in 1800.

*Mitchell Is Moving* by Marjorie Sharmat (Collier, 1978). Mitchell the dinosaur is moving away from his good friend Margo.

*Once There Were Giants* by Martin Waddell (Delacorte Press, 1989). A newborn girl sees giants all around her until one day she "turns into" a giant herself.

**Reprinted with permission of the publisher, Early Years, Inc., Norwalk, CT 06854. From the Aug./September 1991 issue of *Teaching/ K-8.***

## Jerry Harste

# Jerry Harste speaks on reading and writing

*Harste, a professor in the Language Education Department at Indiana University, is known internationally for his research and writing on young children's acquisition of literacy.*

During the past decade or two, a revolution has occurred in what we know about the development of literacy. Recently my colleagues and I had the opportunity to summarize what we saw as some key insights into literacy based on our studies of early literacy (Harste & Woodward, 1989; Harste, Woodward, & Burke, 1984). Our analysis led to the following conclusions:

- Language is learned through use rather than through practice exercises on how to use language. The more frequently children experience a particular language setting, the more successful they will be in producing appropriate texts for that particular context.

- Because the markings (writing attempts) 4-year-old children produce prior to formal schooling reflect the written language of their culture, we can no longer assume that children come to school without some knowledge of written language.

- Because the markings 3-year-old children make when asked to draw a picture of themselves look quite different from the markings they make when asked to write their name, we can no longer dismiss these efforts as mere scribbling. By age 6, children move freely between communication systems in producing a text.

The "Distinguished Educator" series provides prominent literacy educators an opportunity to present their personal views on topics about which they are recognized experts.

- By age 5 and 6, most children have sorted out how language varies by context of use and have begun to explore the graphophonemic system of language. Their phonetic writing has been called *invented spelling* and has been found to progress systematically and predictably.

- By age 4, the texts that children produce when asked to write a story, as opposed to a letter, are beginning to be distinctive. Their stories sound like stories, look like stories, and function like stories. Their letters sound like letters, look like letters, and function like letters. By age 6, these distinctions are well developed and much more marked.

- Most children as young as 3 can read *Stop* on a stop sign, *McDonald's* when shown the golden arches, and *Crest* when shown a Crest toothpaste carton. By 6, all children can read these and other items of environmental print they frequently encounter. The findings mean that we do not have to teach young children to read, but rather we need to support and expand their continued understanding of reading.

- By age 3, when asked to read or pretend to read a book, children start to vary their normal speech to sound like "book talk." By age 6, children who have been read to frequently have internalized the structures of stories in their culture and can produce many fine stories of their own.

- Learning proceeds from the known to the unknown. Comprehension and learning are now seen as a search for patterns that connect, and growth is seen as a search for ever wider patterns. Children need to be given opportunities to make language their own by making connections with their lives and background information. In short, there is no better way to begin instruction than in terms of the learner's language and current background experience.

- Language learning is risky business. Children learn best in low-risk environments where exploration is accepted and current efforts are socially supported and understood. Language is a social event. Most of what we know about language has been learned from being in the presence of others.

Although teaching reading and writing should not be the primary purpose of preschool and kindergarten, a well designed program can enhance children's already considerable language skills by providing ample opportunities for them to use reading and writing in their daily activities. The following recommendations grow out of these insights and are designed to explore curriculum as a potential for language learning.

*A literacy curriculum needs to support the success of each learner.* The soundest preschool programs are based on the knowledge that children learn best from firsthand experience. In addition to clay, sand, water, and other materials to touch, pour, sift, mold, pound, and manipulate, there should be lots of printed materials around to provide opportunities for the same kind of experience with language.

Preschool and kindergarten programs that highlight literacy are places where storytime and books play a prominent role; where children are encouraged to draw and write independently or with their teachers and peers; where signs made by teachers and students are

---

*Preschool and kindergarten programs that highlight literacy are places where storytime and books play a prominent role.*

---

posted; and where mailboxes, charts, schedules, and sign-in activities serve a functional purpose. Centers such as housekeeping, music, art, dramatic play, blocks, math, and manipulatives contain appropriate material. General materials such as magazines, menus, message pads, typewriters, and blank paper are provided. The centers serve as open invitations for children to use language and other sign systems in their play.

Visitors and planned excursions are provided to widen young children's views of the world. Children are encouraged and helped to use language to express their ideas, feelings, and frustrations. There are opportunities to choose individual activities or play with others.

*A literacy curriculum needs to be focused on learning.* Invitations to read and write must be open-ended. Open-ended activities allow children to enter and exit at their own level of interest and involvement. Books and pencils should be in children's hands from the first day in school. Invitations to talk about reading and writing experiences can help children see reading and writing as tools for learning: "How are you different now from who you were before? What do you know now that you didn't know before?" Literature should be seen as a way for children to view their world through new eyes, rather than as a vehicle for teaching reading per se.

In the final analysis, our interest in reading and writing is an interest in learning. Reading is not so much taking meaning from texts as it is sharing meaning about texts. Writing is not simply a process of recording on paper already-perfected ideas but also a vehicle for organizing thought.

*A literacy curriculum needs to let learners explore language in all its complexity.* Children are capable of monitoring and direct-

---

> **Curriculum development must be placed in the hands of the classroom teacher. For curricula to be dynamic, children need to be our curricular informants.**

---

ing their own literacy learning when they have many opportunities to encounter oral and written language in familiar situations. To be strategic, readers and writers must vary their cognitive processes by content and context. Different strategies are brought to the foreground when reading and interpreting a poem than when reading a content area selection.

Classrooms must be places where children can see others using language for real purposes. It is important that children be put in situations where they can see the strategies of successful written language use and learning demonstrated. Teachers should write with their children as well as invite parents, administrators, professional writers, and others into the classroom on a regular basis.

A literacy curriculum should help children expand their communication potential through the use of language as well as art, music, and other sign systems. There are many forms of authorship. Learning in one sign system supports learning in another. Students should be encouraged to use various forms of communication to express themselves in all subject areas. Beginning literacy instruction should provide opportunities to interact with print in all these contexts using a multitude of expressive forms: listening to stories, sharing and talking about books, writing and illustrating stories, composing stories in block play, enacting stories through drama, interpreting stories in art and music, reading and writing recipes for cooking, interpreting music through dance, composing and writing music, writing math problems, reading poetry, and reading and writing predictable books.

These recommendations mean that curriculum and curriculum development must be placed in the hands of the classroom teacher. A good curriculum sets directions and provides examples of the kinds of settings believed to permit children to take the mental trips we associate with successful language use and learning. For curricula to be dynamic, children need to be our curricular informants. Administrators must support teachers in reclaiming their classrooms. Trying new ideas is risky. But just as children take risks as they explore language, teachers need to be free to take risks as they explore literacy instruction.

These are but a few of the curricular implications that might be explored given recent insights into early literacy. I close by inviting interested teachers to read *Emerging Literacy: Young Children Learn to Read and Write*, edited by Dorothy Strickland and Leslie Mandel Morrow (1989), where these and other ideas are explored more fully.

**References**

Harste, J.C., & Woodward, V.A. (1989). Fostering needed change in early literacy programs. In D.S. Strickland & L.M. Morrow (Eds.), *Emerging literacy: Young children learn to read and write* (Chapter 12). Newark, DE: International Reading Association.

Harste, J.C., Woodward, V.A., & Burke, C.L. (1984). *Language stories and literacy lessons*. Portsmouth, NH: Heinemann.

Strickland, D.S., & Morrow, L.M. (Eds.). (1989). *Emerging literacy: Young children learn to read and write*. Newark, DE: International Reading Association.

# Look What They've Done to Judy Blume!: The 'Basalization' of Children's Literature

**Kenneth S. Goodman**

One of Judy Blume's first published books, republished by Dell in 1981, was called *The One in the Middle is the Green Kangaroo*. Recently, as I was doing research on basal readers for *Report Card on Basal Readers* (Goodman et al., 1987), I came across a revision of this story in a basal reading program. Here's how her original began and how the revision began.

Original: (Blume, 1981) *The One in the Middle is the Green Kangaroo*

> Freddy Dissel had two problems. One was his older brother Mike. The other was his younger sister Ellen. Freddy thought a lot about being the one in the middle. But there was nothing he could do about it. He felt like the peanut butter part of a sandwich, squeezed between Mike and Ellen.

Revision: (Holt, Level 8) *Maggie in the Middle*

> Maggie had a big sister, Ellen.
> She had a little brother, Mike.
> Maggie was the one in the middle.
> But what could she do?

How could they have done this to Judy Blume? The answer is that it was done by design. It was done to fit within a basal reader built on the premise that to teach reading the language of what children read must be controlled. This revision illustrates how basals change literature to fit their self-imposed constraints.

Even the title has been changed in the basal version. It's now become *Maggie in the Middle*. That's because the central character, *Freddy,* has been changed to a girl, *Maggie*. Basal publishers have been under pressure to remove sex bias from their books. So it is likely that this change took place when the editors charted the main characters in stories at this level and decided here was an opportunity to have a female with active non-stereotypic traits. Apparently to maintain balance, Ellen has been promoted to older sister and Mike is now the little brother.

These are not the only character name changes. Ms. Gumber, Freddy/Maggie's teacher in the original, becomes Mrs. Cook in the revision. This carries through an old tradition in basals to use real words as proper last names wherever possible. That stems from the view that exposure to a word is extra practice no matter where it occurs in the text. The drama teacher moves from Ms. Matson to Mrs. Chang in the revision. That provides for more ethnic balance.

The theme of this story, "it's tough to be a middle child," remains but it's purged of both the pain and the sibling conflict in the revised version. Just being in the middle is not the same as feeling squeezed between siblings, "like the peanut butter part of a sandwich." Here, again, is Blume's original:

Original: (Blume, 1981)

> Once Freddy tried to join Mike and his friends. But Mike said, "Get out of the way kid!" So Freddy tried to play with Ellen. Ellen didn't understand how to play his way. She messed up all of Freddy's things. Freddy got mad and pinched her. Ellen screamed.
> "Freddy Dissel!" Mom yelled. "You shouldn't be mean to Ellen. She's smaller than you. She's just a baby."

Revision:

> Maggie tried to play with Ellen
> and her friends.
> But Ellen said, "Go away, Maggie.
> Run and play with your own friends.
> This is not a game for little girls."
> Maggie tried to play with Mike.
> It was no fun.
> Mike would not play right.
> He ran away with Maggie's games.
> He put them in his room.

The original, "Get out of the way, kid!", rings truer than the alternate, "Go away, Maggie." And the scene with Freddy pinching Ellen and Mom yelling at him for it isn't quite the same. In the revised version Mom doesn't yell. "Mike is too little to play with you," said Mother. "Let him play with his own games."

But the biggest change to Judy Blume's original is the reduction of the text through the avoidance of less frequently used words and the use of short sentences. In the process of controlling the vocabulary and syntax, the style and wit of the original is lost and the language becomes much less natural and thus less predictable.

## Why Include Authentic Children's Literature in Basals and Then Change It?

If you look at the current crop of basal readers which dominate reading instruction in American classrooms, it's clear that some effort has been made to bring into the program current, popular children's literature. That's not new entirely, but it got a boost when there was a shift in the sixties and seventies away from the vaguely suburban middle class family including Dick, Jane, baby Sally, Mother in apron, and Father in suit and tie (or their counterparts, Tom, Betty et al.) in the stories written "in house." One force behind that shift was the demand by minority and women's groups for more representative and realistic representation of American people, life-styles, and cultures.

Publishers work hard to include a range of selections written by well-known children's authors, but for reasons having to do with the fundamental structure of basal readers, most of what eventually winds up in the anthologies to be read by the pupils is either adapted or specially written for the purpose. It might seem surprising that children's authors let their work be changed. In many cases it is likely that permission does not even involve the author's consent. The original publisher may control permission rights. Furthermore, though authors of previously published children's stories selected for inclusion are not getting rich on the fees they share with the original publisher, their initial royalties may not have amounted to much, and the added income is probably quite tempting. Graham reports an average of $500 is paid for stories and $150 for poems (Graham, 1978).

Most of the material in the kindergarten and first grade levels is still written by basal staff members. These are less likely to involve a continuing cast of characters. But they may involve retold folk tales. The texts themselves are still created synthetically from the word lists and readability formulas that grew out of the research of the 1920s by Thorndyke, Gray and others. Use of folk tales, animal characters, and cartoon-like illustrations may give a look of literature to those beginning basal levels, but there is a clear focus on the "stories" being vehicles to practice words and skills. There is no invitation to the world of literature in these synthetic texts.

Here's the beginning of a version of the classic folk tale, *Little Red Riding Hood,* that appears in one basal. In this rendition, when a character is speaking, a picture of the head appears before the quotation and quotation marks are thus not needed. Some words are superimposed on a picture of what the word represents. In this selection, *basket* and *bird* are new words highlighted in that manner.

Original:
  Red Riding Hood wants to see Grandma.
  (RR) I can put apples into my [basket]. I can put red apples into my [basket] for Grandma.
  I will walk to see Grandma. I like to hear the red [bird]. Grandma likes to hear the [bird]. Grandma will come out to hear the red [bird].
  (Wolf) Hello, Red Riding Hood, Hello.
  (RR) I have red apples. I have big red apples for Grandma. I put the apples into my [basket].
  (Wolf) Red Riding Hood will walk to see Grandma. I will not walk. I will run to see Grandma.

Scott, Foresman, *Focus,* Level 2c, 1985

In this basalized version there is clearly more concern for controlling the vocabulary than telling the story. Words like *red, bird, basket, apples* are repeated even when they are inappropriate to the story line. On the last page of the basal version of *Red Riding Hood*, after the woodcutter has chased the wolf away and saved her life, Red Riding Hood concludes the episode and the story by proclaiming:

Revision:
  (RR) I like you, Woodcutter.
  Come have some apples.
  I put red apples into my [basket].
  I put big red apples into [basket].(sic)

Scott, Foresman, *Focus,* Level 2c, 1985

This is not simply a badly written version of this folk tale. It is deliberately synthesized according to criteria designed to teach skills and words. "Thank you for saving my life" might have been more appropriate or predictable but it would not have afforded the extra opportunity to use the target words that "I put red apples into my basket" provides.

In some synthetic "stories" there is even less cohesion and story line. The following synthetic text, taken from a pre-primer, is accompanied by cartoon-like illustrations. The *pony* is balloonish, the *dog* is rather serpentine.

A pony asked a dog to go to the zoo.
  The pony said, "We can ride the bus now."

The dog said, "You can't ride and ride.
You have to jump and walk, too."
The pony said, "You do?"
"Read that!" said the dog.
  PETS!
 WE CAN HELP!
  WALK,
 KICK, JUMP!"
The dog said, "We can?"
The cat said, "I can show you the kick and jump."
The pony said, "Dog, did you see that fish jump?"

Macmillan *Reading Express.* p.3, 1985.

This synthesized text constitutes a particular genre. It could only occur in a basal reader and its only justification is that it fits the peculiar constraints of the basal. Yet is has more in common with the basalized version of Judy Blume than might be evident.

Beyond first grade most of the material in basals is from literature already published for children, but it is adapted to conform with the same criteria used to generate the synthetic stories of the basals. Publishers start out seeking the best available material to make the program attractive to young readers and those who select them for use. Editors follow the reviews of books carefully. They know which authors are winning awards, which are popular with children, and which are selling best. They search children's literature for stories that will provide a broad representation of people, cultures, and lifestyles.

But then the process of self-censorship and revision begins. There are two major types of revision. The first is intended to make the literature fit the readability, vocabulary, and skill criteria of the publisher. Selections may be shortened, simplified, or rewritten. Vocabulary may be changed, sentences shortened, and the story line modified. The editors try to make the selections fit the charts developed for each grade. In the hands of even the most skillful editors, it often results in unpredictable, awkward, and quite inauthentic texts.

The second kind of revision is to make sure the stories fit the publishers' standards of acceptability for content, language, and values. This is a self-censorship to avoid criticism from an array of groups. There is concern to avoid ethnic stereotypes, racism, and sexism. But there are also groups who see witches, communists, and secular humanists lurking in children's literature. Even selections which will only be listed for suggested further reading are purged if anyone thinks they might be offensive.

Even before any revision takes place, many selections are considered and rejected. Program authors and editors nominate selections. Screening editors reject some and pass other selections on to supervising editors who may reject some and tentatively assign others to grade levels. Then story characteristics such as genre, content, location, ethnic representation, sex of characters, readability rating, and ethnicity of the author are noted to seek a predetermined balance.

It's then likely that authors of the program, as well as editors higher up the chain of command, will be asked to consider the selections. Graham estimates that only 10% of what is reviewed is actually used. I found in my own review of current basals that, with the major exception of an occasional poem, literature that is included is almost always revised. Sometimes this revision only involves an occasional word change or abridging. But at times it would be hard for the original author to recognize the adaptation. During the continuous winnowing out and reediting of the selections, each selection according to Graham, is read and edited at least 40 times in the process, as it is "pounded into house requirements."

### Focus on Learning Words and Skills

So Judy Blume's story, like the synthetic texts of the basals, is shaped by revision to fit the basal word lists and skill sequences. But there is another thing that happens to what once was literature. The story now becomes part of a lesson sequence. The purpose for the pupils reading the story in its new incarnation is to learn words and skills. Word lists are provided in the basals for every story so that teachers and learners will know which words are to be learned.

Before permitting pupils to read *Maggie in the Middle*, the basal teacher's manual directs the teacher, under the heading *Developing Vocabulary*, to focus pupils' attention on particular words. The stated objectives for reading this story are to increase vocabulary, to understand literal meaning in sentences, and to apply decoding skills.

Two types of words are to be specifically taught: "Special Attention Words": *Maggie, middle, Ellen, clothes, room, away,* and "Easily Decoded Words": *Mike, Ellen, fit, ones, own, run, Maggie's.* According to the manual, the teacher must place the new words on the chalkboard or in pocket charts and follow an instructional sequence provided for each word. For example:

> Display the word **middle**.
> Have the children notice the double consonants and the le ending that is pronounced as it is in little. Then have them read the words in this sentence.
> **Maggie is in the middle.** (Holt, Level 8, p. T-133)

While pupils read the story their focus is also to be kept on these words; in the margin of each reproduced page from the pupil's text in the teacher's manual, again under the heading of Vocabulary Development, is a note as each of these introduced words occurs. For example:

### Mike

**Decode** *Mike* by combining the initial/m/as in the picture-word *man* with the graphemic base *-ike*

Then, just to make sure, on the last page of the story, the teacher's manual provides a review exercise. Each of the "special attention words" is again to be written on the board. The teacher is to read sentences with missing words and asks the children to fill in the blanks by pointing to the story. Then the teacher is expected to write all the "easily decodable words" on the board and read a series of words that rhyme with those, asking children to point to and read the words that rhymes with each (i.e., fiddle/middle).

There is also instruction intended to teach "comprehension skills" through *Maggie in the Middle*. Under a heading of "Comprehension/Literary Skills," These objectives are listed for the story: Reading vocabulary, Sentence meaning, Cause and effect; Recalling details: characters. Here vocabulary is included under comprehension and separately from phonics/decoding. Teaching comprehension is accomplished by asking a series of questions before, during, and after the reading.

For each page of this story there are almost as many questions in the comprehension check-up as sentences. There is a question paradigm being followed here, which we found typical of the basals we examined, that appears to be based on a view that children comprehend to the extent that they agree with the question writer's view of the text meaning. Even when the question is intended to draw on "background knowledge," or require "critical thinking," a simple conformist answer is suggested as a model for the teacher of what answers to accept. Frequently, it is hard to see consistency in the categorization of the questions, particularly when, as in this series, each question is put in a single category.

Requiring conformity to a single correct answer is not a minor issue. And it is complicated by a tendency for questions and answers to be inappropriate for the text. The question "Who is bigger, Ellen or Maggie?" seems simple and straight-forward. But children know that a big sister is not the same as a bigger sister. Furthermore, the pictures on the page with the text show a much larger view of Maggie with a smaller picture of Ellen as if behind her. On the second page of the story there's a more serious problem. The picture shows Maggie bundled up in coat, scarf, cap, and mittens. The text says:

> Ellen got too big for her clothes.
> Ellen's clothes fit Maggie.
> Maggie got the old clothes.
> Ellen got new ones.

Two questions, both labeled "inferential thinking," relate to this sentence.

> 1. Why does Maggie look funny in the picture? (Because the clothes she is wearing are too big.) *Picture Clues* 2. Why is Maggie wearing clothes that are too big? (Because she is wearing her sister Ellen's clothes, which Ellen has outgrown.) *Cause and Effect*

The text says Ellen's clothes fit Maggie, and though the picture may suggest otherwise, the "literal" response the pupils might make is likely to be at odds with the inference the question writer expects them to make. The questions used in teaching and assessing comprehension in the basals we looked at suggest that a categorization system has been used to produce them, that the categorization system has not been used well, and that the questions themselves are often problematic. Since both the teaching and assessment of comprehension in the basals are confined almost entirely to the questions the teachers are instructed to use, the quality of the questions must be a major concern.

Frequently, children have mentioned to me how they identified with the characters in Judy Blume's stories and their experiences. That shows a high level of comprehension. They can match their own schemas to those of the story. But the basals redefine comprehension. It no longer belongs to the reader. It is predetermined by the teachers' manual. The teacher is to judge comprehension by the ability of pupils to produce answers to questions which usually have single correct responses. When children's contacts with literature are confined to basals, they build some distorted concepts. I once asked a Navajo boy in the sixth grade why he thought Scott O'Dell had written *Sing Down the Moon,* a historical story of the Navajo people which he'd just read. "To teach me new words," he responded. It's not difficult to see how he might have arrived at this idea.

Recently a teacher shared with me a vignette from his sixth grade class room. They had just finished reading a basal revision of a Jack London story. The children were complaining about some of the questions that followed the story in their basal. On a hunch, he said to them, "Who do you think wrote the questions?" They all agreed that the author did. "You think Jack London wrote those questions?" he asked. They assured him that they believed Jack London wrote the questions at the end of the his story. When he asked them why there weren't questions at the end of Jack London's stories that weren't in basals, they said that was because in this story he was teaching them to read. "Besides," said one young man, "he wants to be sure you're paying attention."

So I've got news for Judy Blume. There are a lot of kids out there that think she writes questions at the end of her stories when they're in basal readers.

## Fracturing and Narrowing Language

Linguists generally agree that to be language there must be three systems present. Halliday calls these three levels the symbolic system (phonology in speech, orthography in writing), the lexico-grammatical system, and the meaning system. The middle system includes both the wording of the text and its structure. (Halliday, 1975)

Basals have tended to isolate sounds, letters, and words from the systems. And they have given little attention to the systems and how they relate in natural texts. In pulling out letter-sound relationships these become distorted abstractions. And words out of context lose textual meaning and grammatical function. Again, they become abstractions. Furthermore, the value of the information in the parts is not the same as it is in the whole natural text. The whole is more than the sum of its parts. And it is the system that gives unity to the whole. An authentic text is cohesive; there is a unity to it that comes from the lexico-grammatical and the semantic meaning structure.

If we compare the beginnings of the original and revised versions of the Judy Blume story above we get a sense of what makes a text a text and why focus on parts rather than the whole makes language less predictable and less comprehensible. There are reasons why authentic stories are worded the way they are. Some of them have to do with the style and voice of the author. But some of them have to do with the way the system of language works.

In basals, language is not likely to be authentic; that is, it is not likely to be a functional, cohesive text which has a communicative purpose for the reader and which is embedded in a real literacy event. Pupils are continually encountering reduced language shaped to fit the scope and sequence chart. Even when what they are assigned to read starts out as a real story written by a real author, it is likely that it has been transformed considerably before the child encounters it.

## Adapted and Synthetic Texts

Lest you think what happened to Judy Blume is unique or unusual, consider some data we assembled for the Report Card on Basal Readers (1987). It is the exception rather than the rule when the text has not been revised before the pupil reads it in the basal. Table 1 shows the degree to which two basals we examined are adapted.

The table shows the kinds of texts used in two basals. Almost all the authentic texts in both series are poems or songs. In some of the early levels, though these appear in the pupils' texts, they are to be read to the pupils by the teacher. In some other programs, other poems appear primarily in the teacher's guide for reading to the pupils. Most of the first grade selections in all series, as in these two, are synthetic. In third and fifth grade most of the selections are adapted, that is revised, abridged, or both.

The reason that so little in the basals is authentic language and so much is synthetic or revised is that the focus on words and skills commits the publisher to controlling the language of what pupils read. Harcourt, like the other basal publishers, says that keeping language natural is important, but they seem to feel that it can be both natural and controlled. This statement appears in frontmatter of the teacher's edition:

In HBJ BOOKMARK, EAGLE EDITION, the basal vocabulary — the number of different words that appear in the Pupil's Edition — is realistic, and the rate of word recurrence is unusually high. A concentrated effort is made to keep the language in the Pupil's Edition as natural as possible. The controlled rate of word introduction, the frequent recurrence of words, and the natural language, combined with the close relationship between new words and known phonics elements, result in a treatment of vocabulary that is managed easily by most children. (Harcourt, Teacher's Edition)

Here is how Gerald McDermott begins his retelling of the Japanese folk tale he calls *The Stonecutter:*

Tasuko was a lowly stonecutter. Each day the sound of his hammer and chisel rang out as he chipped away at the foot of the mountain. He hewed the blocks of stone that formed the great temples and palaces.

He asked for nothing more than to work each day, and this pleased the spirit who lived in the mountains. (McDermott, 1975).

Here's the beginning of Harcourt's retelling of the same folk tale:

Once there was a strong man. Each morning he went to the mountains. There he dug up stones. He broke them into pebbles with a large steel hammer. He carried the pebbles to the village, where he sold them. (HBJ, Level 8, Grade 3)

Harcourt's editors do not seem to have been able to follow all of their control criteria and at the same time create a natural text. Meaning is also changed. In McDermott's telling the stonecutter's wishes to be transformed into more and more powerful things are heard and granted by the spirit of the mountains. In Harcourt's retelling he gets his wishes with no apparent help.

The claims of basal publishers that they draw on the rich literature for children that is available is certainly true. But it is also true that pupils will rarely meet the language of any children's author in a pure and unadapted form.

## So What Should We Do About It?

Some lovers of children's literature, when they see how the literature is changed in basal readers, have been tempted to say that it shouldn't be used at all in teaching children to read. That would mean using the synthetic and even less authentic texts exclusively. It would also mean delaying children's reading real literature until they already can read. And it would support the idea that learning the skills of reading can be separated from reading real authentic literature.

**107**

**Table 1: Revised, Synthetic and Authentic Texts**

| Level | Grade | Number of Texts | Revised or Abridged | | Synthetic or House Written | | Authentic | |
|---|---|---|---|---|---|---|---|---|
| **Ginn** | | | | | | | | |
| 2 | 1 | 7 | 1 | 14.29% | 6 | 85.71% | 0 | 0% |
| 3 | 1 | 10 | 0 | 0% | 9 | 90% | 1 | 10% |
| 4 | 1 | 11 | 2 | 18.18% | 8 | 72.73% | 1 | 9.09% |
| 5 | 1 Primer | 29 | 7 | 24.14% | 18 | 62.07% | 4 | 13.79% |
| 6 | 1 First | 27 | 9 | 33.33% | 16 | 59.26% | 2 | 7.41% |
| 10 | 3 Part 2 | 33 | 21 | 63.64% | 8 | 24.24% | 4 | 12.12% |
| 12 | 5 | 52 | 33 | 63.46% | 11 | 21.15% | 8 | 15.38% |
| **Holt** | | | | | | | | |
| 3 | 1 | 12 | 0 | 0% | 11 | 91.67% | 1 | 8.33% |
| 4 | 1 | 10 | 0 | 0% | 6 | 60% | 4 | 40% |
| 5 | 1 | 8 | 0 | 0% | 6 | 75% | 2 | 25% |
| 6 | 1 | 10 | 2 | 20% | 5 | 50% | 3 | 30% |
| 7 | 1 Primer | 21 | 5 | 23.81% | 9 | 42.86% | 7 | 33.33% |
| 8 | 1 First | 27 | 7 | 25.93% | 11 | 40.74% | 9 | 33.33% |
| 11 | 3 | 38 | 17 | 44.74% | 11 | 28.95% | 10 | 26.32% |
| 12 | 3 | 46 | 21 | 45.65% | 11 | 23.91% | 14 | 30.43% |
| 14 | 5 | 80 | 25 | 31.25% | 31 | 38.75 | 24 | 30% |

Many teachers are beginning to put away the basals, partially or completely, and build their own reading programs around literature. They use original books like *The One in the Middle is the Green Kangaroo*. The children read the book and respond to it in a variety of ways. The teacher doesn't need trivia questions to teach comprehension. The children are encouraged to relate the characters and the experiences they have in the story to their own experiences and attitudes. They have options, choosing which books they will read. The teacher supports their attempts to make sense of the book they've chosen, but they have ownership over their own reading.

Other teachers organize their classrooms around sets of children's books. Children choose which of several books they will read and join a group of five or six classmates who have also chosen that book. They share their reactions to the book and their own understandings of it. They compare their predictions and expectations of what will happen in the book.

Teachers of younger children make an easy transition from reading books to children to reading with them, perhaps in a "Big Book," an enlarged version of a favorite that several children can see and read together. They make available predictable sequences and events. They use the authentic language of songs, poems, and stories to build the reading ability of their pupils.

Ironically, all the tampering with authentic literature doesn't help kids learn to read. In fact, it gets in the way. What we now know is that authentic, sensible, and functional language is the easiest to read and to learn to read. When we tamper with narrative language, try to control the vocabulary, or tinker with texts to lower their readability levels, we make them less predictable, less cohesive, and less interesting. And that makes them harder to read.

This understanding that the children learn to read most easily by reading real stories, and not by being taught skills, is important. Some people, recognizing the value of literature in reading development but still believing that reading ability only results from skill lessons, have basalized children's books without the basals. They build sequences of lessons in which vocabulary drills, phonics exercises, and a multiplicity of single answer "comprehension" questions are woven around a popular children's book. Again, the book becomes a means of practicing skills, not an authentic experience in making sense of a real written story. Again, kids are led to believe that books exist primarily for reading instruction.

Teachers have known, intuitively, for a long time, that, just as kids learned to talk by talking, they learn to read by reading. Getting kids involved with real authentic children's books is the most important way teachers can support reading development. Halliday (1975) has helped us to understand that language is learned most easily when it serves a real function. Sharing narratives is a most important function of written language. In its broader sense, literature includes a full range of authentic language genre. So teachers can involve pupils in expository and informational reading. They can build a classroom library of authentic and unadapted fiction and non-fiction, of prose and poetry, of recreational and referential reading. There is much more that children can be reading if they are liberated from the contorted and constrained language of the basals. Whatever skills are involved in reading are learned best while trying to make sense of real language.

Teachers, like parents, can immerse their kids in a wonderful array of literature. And they can make sure that when children in their classrooms encounter Judy Blume for the first time, it's the real Judy Blume and not one contrived for a basal.

## References

*Basals*

Ginn Reading Program. (1985). Clymer, T., Indrasano, R., Johnson, D., Pearson, P.D., Venezky, R. Lexington, MA: Ginn and Co.

HBJ Bookmark Reading Program, Eagle Edition. (1983). Early, M., Cooper, E., Santeusanio, N., Fry, M., Harris, J. New York: Harcourt Brace Jovanovich.

Holt Basic Reading. (1986). Weiss, B., Everetts, E., Stever, L., Cruickshank, S., Hunt, L. New York: Holt.

Scott Foresman Focus. (1985). Allington, R., Cramer, R., Cunningham, P., Perez, G., Robinson, C., Tierney, R. Glenview, Ill.: Scott Foresman.

*Others*

Blume, J. (1981). *The one in the middle is the green kangaroo.* New York: Dell.

Goodman, K., Freeman, Y., Murphy, S., Shannon, P. (1987). *Report card on reading.* Urbana, Ill: NCTE.

Graham, G. (1978). *A present and historical analysis of basal reading series.* Unpublished doctoral dissertation, University of Virginia.

Halliday, M. (1975). *Learning how to mean.* London: Edward Arnold.

McDermott, G (1975). *The stone-cutter.* New York: Viking.

O'Dell, S. (1970). *Sing down the moon.* New York: Dell.

*Kenneth Goodman is a Professor at the University of Arizona and Co-director of the Program in Language and Literacy.*

# Digging Deeper in Literature

*Some things to do and think about the next time
real readers sit around and discuss real literature*

### BY CAROL OTIS HURST

One of the joys and frustrations of teaching is that we're never satisfied. We didn't like the hollow, made-for-easy-reading stories in the old basals. We wanted more and better ways to help children become lifetime readers. Whole language research cries out for drastic change in reading materials and the ways we use them. We want kids reading real literature, and most of us have made strides in that direction. We do author studies, webbing and themes, which push the basals back or even out. Many classrooms shout that reading of all sorts abounds here.

We use literature circles and other discussion formats in which real readers sit around and discuss real literature. It's the discussion part that's hard for some of us. We all agree that discussion is good, but what do we say after each person has given a thumbs up or thumbs down to a story?

In a desperate attempt to make those discussions meaningful, some of us turned to the basal reading format. We asked literal questions and got right or wrong answers—and knew that wasn't right either. Even open-ended questions often fell unanswered to the floor, or led only to an unfocused or boring discussion. Some teachers turned to resource books and sometimes to workbooks on literature for discussion topics, only to realize that they were in very real danger of ruining some wonderful books. What then can we discuss in these groups where everyone has read the same or related books?

**"Within the book."** Leland Jacobs has suggested that, during those discussions, we stay "within the book" as long as possible. What did you think about the book? Which characters did you trust, like, dislike, believe, disbelieve? What parts excited you, moved you to tears or laughter? He refers to such considerations as dealing with the verbal level of the story.

Stepping outside the story slightly, looking around it, dealing with it at the behavioral level, leads to another level of discussion. Dr. Jacobs' statement that "a story is a character coping in terms of a quest" can lead to some deeper analysis while staying within the confines of a book.

In most stories, including nonfiction biographies, one character (or more than one) is indeed on a quest. The outcomes vary.

> **"** . . . *what do we say after each person has given a thumbs up or thumbs down to a story?* **"**

| NAME OF CHARACTER | QUEST | INTERVENERS AND ABETTORS | OUTCOME |
|---|---|---|---|
| Charlotte | To save Wilbur's life | Fern<br>Mr. Arable<br>The Zuckermans<br>The fair<br>People's gullibility | Wilbur lives, Charlotte lays her egg sac and dies |
| Wilbur | to live | Fern<br>Mr. Arable<br>Charlotte<br>Templeton | Charlotte's words save Wilbur's life |
| Templeton | to eat | Lurvy<br>the fair<br>Charlotte | He gets lots to eat at the fair. |

***Diagramming a multi-quest story*** *like* Charlotte's Web *can facilitate discussion.*

**109**

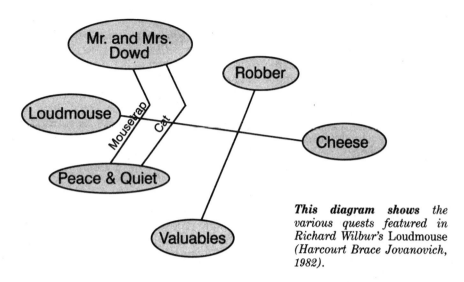

*This diagram shows the various quests featured in Richard Wilbur's* Loudmouse *(Harcourt Brace Jovanovich, 1982).*

Sometimes a character achieves the desired goal. Other times the character is thwarted by the actions of others. At still other times the character gets what he or she wanted but no longer wants it, or wants something and gets something else instead.

Some novels have several quests by different characters going on concurrently. Outlining or diagramming the multi-quest story can go a long way toward simplifying the plot so that it can be discussed.

Such outlining also works when setting up the plot for an original story. Decide who or what your main character could be and then what he or she could conceivably want, and you've got the beginning of a plot. Add characters and events to make the plot more interesting, and you could . . . But that's another story.

**Writer's viewpoint.** Stepping away from the plot of the book to get a different perspective, we can look at a book from a writer's viewpoint. We can ask ourselves such questions as: What did the author have to know in order to write this book? How might he or she have come to know this?

Reading *Julie of the Wolves* by Jean George (Harper & Row, 1972, ISBN 0-06-021944-0) leads us to care deeply for Julie and for those wonderful wolves. After wiping away the tears at the death of Amaroq, we can wonder about Julie's final decision about whether to go to San Francisco or Kapugen. We can each try to put ourselves

in her place and make our own decision about her decision.

Taking a more objective view of the book, we can find out more about wolves and then evaluate the book's reality. Would real wolves have taken in a human being? We are distancing ourselves slightly, but still within the framework of the story.

Then we can think about Jean George. How could anyone know that much about wolves, the tundra, the Eskimo culture? Now we're outside the book, looking in from the author's point of view.

It seems logical now to ask other questions: Why might the author have written this story? What is he or she trying to tell us about life or the world or people? Through such questions, we get to the author's purpose as a way of approaching the theme. When we get to that level which Dr. Jacobs calls "the transcendent level," we are looking beyond the story to its moral and spiritual considerations.

**Theme work.** It's difficult to get children to care about, much less identify or state a theme. The theme is deeper than the main idea which, in itself, is a real challenge for many readers.

In their book, *Bringing It All Together* (Heinemann, 1990, ISBN 0-435-08502-6), Terry D. Johnson and Daphne R. Louis work with the concept of author's purpose or theme, and state that while young children cannot articulate a theme after reading a book, they can recognize it as meaningful if it is stated for them. They can also find other books which seem to have the same theme. The authors then use the theme of "home is

*"One way to avoid the moralistic trap is to work with conflicting themes."*

Carol Hurst is a master storyteller and a children's literature consultant from Westfield, MA, and a Teaching Editor of *Teaching K-8*.

> 66 *The theme is deeper than the main idea which, in itself, is a real challenge for many readers.* 99

best" to outline a series of readings and discussions for early grade children.

Working with the author's purpose can take us perilously close to moralizing through literature, and that's a path that has, in the past, led to some of the worst in children's literature and teaching. So if we're going to work with children and theme, we need to avoid didactic and transparent works in which the moral takes over, even though these are the easiest for identifying theme.

In these books, the plot is merely a means of stating a moral: This book teaches that we should all share. That book teaches that it always pays to tell the truth. Such books are sermons, not stories—unless we're working with the genre of fable itself and that's another article (see "Teaching in the Library" in this issue).

**Conflicting themes.** One way to avoid the moralistic trap is to work with conflicting themes. To be sure, there are many books, particularly picture books and folk tales, in which the teller seems to be saying that home is best, but many other books seem to be saying, "It's a big, wide, wonderful world and you need to explore it." That, of course, is a theme which seems to be directly opposed to "home is best."

Try putting both statements at the top of a chart and ask the kids, as they read and listen to books and stories, to think which, if either, column would best fit a particular piece of writing.

Books such as Maurice Sendak's *Where the Wild Things Are* (Harper Jr Books, 1963, ISBN 0-06-025492-0) might fit in either category. Laura Ingalls Wilder's books surely celebrate home as the best place, no matter where it's currently located. Some old chestnuts like Marjorie Flack's *Story about Ping* (Viking, 1933, ISBN 0-670-67223-8) and Munro Leaf's *Story of Ferdinand* (Viking, 1936, ISBN 0-670-67424-9) are home-is-besters. Mary Ann Hoberman's *A House Is a House for Me* (Viking, 1978, ISBN 0-670-38016-4) practically shouts that theme.

Books with a wide-wonderful-world theme are also fairly easy to find. Vera Williams' *Stringbean's Trip to the Shining Sea* (Greenwillow, 1988, ISBN 0-688-07161-9) and her *Three Days on a River in a Red Canoe* (Greenwillow, 1981, ISBN 0-688-84307-7) seem to make that statement.

Other books are more subtle—Leo Lionni's *Tillie and the Wall* (Knopf, 1989, ISBN 0-06-024028-8), for instance.

There are other themes which seem to conflict with each other. Some stories seem to be saying, "One person can change the world"—for example, Seuss's *Yertle the Turtle* (Random House, 1958, ISBN 0-394-80087-7), in which the burp of a lowly turtle shakes the throne of a king, and Tomi Ungerer's *The Three Robbers* (Macmillan, 1962, ISBN 0-394-800-87), in which a child sees the fortune the robbers have amassed, asks, "What's it for?" and changes the three villains into heroes. Other books seem to imply the opposite: "We can only win if we all stick together." *Swimmy* by Leo Lionni (Pantheon, 1973, ISBN 0-394-82620-5) states that very strongly.

A related but slightly different set of conflicting themes are the ones that seem to say, "It's better to be part of a group" and those that proclaim, "We need nonconformists or loners in society."

Some books, particularly novels set in the Revolutionary War, Civil War and World War II periods, state that some things are worth fighting for, while others, particularly picture books, are saying just as clearly, "There's always an alternative to war." Louise Fitzhugh's *Bang, Bang, You're Dead* (Harper & Row, 1969, ISBN 0-06-021914-9) is an obvious though not subtle statement in that direction, but what about *Drummer Hoff* by Barbara and Ed Emberly (Simon and Schuster, 1974, ISBN 0-671-66745-9)? Is it anti-war or pro-war? I've never been sure.

Maybe it's best to stop with an enigmatic book. We don't want such discussion to degenerate into searches for the "correct" interpretation of a book. That's what killed literature for many readers years ago. Every book doesn't have a deep meaning, and even if a book does, there's no guarantee that you or any other reader have found its one and only theme.

What's the theme of *Julie and the Wolves*? Keep such discussions meaningful and open. Use the reader/teacher's light touch, steering the discussion only when necessary. Remember that Robert Frost, when told that his "Birches" was full of deep meaning, said something to the effect that he was surprised to hear that. He had thought it was about climbing birch trees. ↓

**Reprinted with permission of the publisher, Early Years, Inc., Norwalk, CT 06854. From the Aug./Sept. 1991 issue of *Teaching/ K-8.***

**111**

Donald H. Graves

# Trust the shadows

*Graves is Professor of Education and Director of The Writing Process Laboratory at the University of New Hampshire, Durham, New Hampshire. He is internationally known for his research on the teaching and learning of writing.*

A twin-engine Cessna crashed on a Saturday killing two persons several blocks from the school where I was studying the writing of 7-year-old children. On Monday I checked to see the effect of the crash on their topic choices.

The boys were agog with news. "There were ambulances, fire trucks, and I saw them take two bodies from the house." Another added, "My mother said that if the crash came when I went to catechism, I'd have been killed." Boys discussed and wrote about the event. Girls ignored it.

I had a hunch this difference in topic selection was worth pursuing. Besides, the itch to pursue it simply wouldn't go away. The problem was slightly off center of my main research question on children's composing during writing (Graves, 1973), yet I suspected that some child behaviors during writing were connected with their topic choices. Further reading into the development of sex-role differences showed marked patterns of territorial involvement in children's choices during play. I took a large piece of brown paper and made a bull's-eye with three concentric circles depicting three territories—home, school, and beyond—for classifying children's topic selections. One of the findings (Graves, 1973) showed that, of 120 pieces written by girls, only 8 fell in the territory beyond home and school, the very location of the plane crash.

That study was done 18 years ago, but since that time I've gradually come to trust questions that lurk in the shadows and make me wonder about children and the issues that surround their learning. I say gradually because I'm the type who enjoys a straight-ahead task whether in writing, teaching, or research. I state my objective, lay out the procedures, and plunge ahead to completion. High activity and determined purpose, however, tend to make me look for preconceived answers to my questions.

I'm beginning to slow down and keep the solution to my problems open longer. Although the problems are kept open, the work goes on, but in a different way. I write daily, toying with metaphors, allowing the intrusion of new ideas from the shadows. The writing is messy, first-draft-type composing. If I didn't write every day, however, I'd lose out on another essential element—off-task thinking. Composing continues in jottings on pads, when I'm running on the road or sitting in restaurants.

Daily composing cuts across all genres and types of problem solving. You will see in the three studies and one poem that follow that there is as much similarity in the thinking and writing of research problems as in the composing of a poem. The deliberate discipline of daily writing and off-task thinking regarding the same questions—What does this mean? What are the data? How do I write this?—are essential to all problem-solving acts.

## Decline in the teaching of writing

In 1976 I was in the midst of a study for the Ford Foundation (Graves, 1978) on the status of writing in U.S. education. I wished to get some inkling of the frequency of straight writing versus fill-in-the-blank writing. Since that time, the National Assessment of Education Progress has done some documenting of the incidence of writing from the reports of those taking the tests. At that time, however, there were no institutions taking surveys on the incidence of writing.

I remember jogging on a country road in Durham, New Hampshire. I had recently read an article in the *New York Times* about wastebasket research, that is, how business values could be understood by examining the contents of what was thrown away. In some cases, businesses hired sleuths to examine the garbage of competitors in order to understand the direction of their corporations. I knew at that time studying school wastebaskets was an impossible task. (It is, however, an intriguing area of research I'd like to examine someday.)

I began to examine the shadows more closely. Although I couldn't examine the waste flow from schools, perhaps incoming paper purchases might shed some light on the place of writing in school curricula. As a former school principal, I recalled speculating on teachers' values by the kinds of supplies they ordered for their classrooms. I asked Becky Rule, a colleague on the Ford study, to call major school supplyhouses to get a feel for paper orders over the previous 5 years. Our suspicions were starkly evident in the data. Orders for lined paper, which might have indicated more writing, were in sharp decline. Orders for duplicating paper, usually required for short answers (at best), were soaring.

## The purpose of research

In the winter of 1982 I was working hard on a final report for the National Institute of Education on our study of the composing processes of young children in Atkinson, New Hampshire (Graves, 1982). Our data were voluminous, and writing a final report was difficult. I remember analyzing the data on

---

*I'm beginning to slow down and keep the solution to my problems open longer.*

---

revision already published by Lucy Calkins (1980), a colleague on the study. I'd start where the data seemed to be "thickest." Her data showed quite clearly how children moved from small changes of a mechanical nature to seeing words as more temporary and to changing larger blocks of information. This final stage Calkins labeled as "interactive." She was also able to show how these children changed over time, as she gathered case study data over a 2-year period.

Although each child participating in a case study was able to keep the text open over a longer period of time than other children, during which the child being observed moved information back and forth, adding and deleting, each still had a highly individual way of working with his or her pieces. If all the children were different in their approach to revision, I wondered, then what kind of findings could come from the Atkinson study? For several months the problem perplexed me.

One day in March I happened to be chatting with my neighbor, Jim Pollard, a professor who specialized in fruit-tree management. Jim could look at a tree and discuss every anomaly of growth, disease, repair, and branching pattern. He was fascinated by the differences in the trees. But it struck me that Jim's knowledge of research in the field of pomology was so well developed, his understanding of possible similarities so codified, that he was able to see the differences more clearly than the lay person. Our short interchange gave me even more insight into the data on revision.

Lucy Calkins's (1980) data had indeed identified an important category in the interactive reviser. In that characteristic, all the children had something in common. Until we could see their similarities as revisers, we couldn't see the significance of their differences. All of the children in the "interacter" category revised differently: one revised in her head, another went through an enormous number of drafts, while another made changes through dialogue with other children. I think of those data when I read in language arts textbooks about *the* writing process.

---

*Case study work pushes beyond similarities to show the important differences that exist in all persons.*

---

Case study work pushes beyond similarities to show the important differences that exist in all persons. Not unlike a scanning electron microscope that magnifies a thousand-fold, case studies quickly reveal differences in children. I reasoned then that research has an important contribution to make to our understanding of children and their growth as learners, but our findings help us to see just how different one learner can be from another. Our openness in research to the amazing range of differences in learners structures the way in which we report our findings to teachers. In short, reporting details about child differences helps teachers to expect the inevitable differences among the children in their classrooms.

## Children's fiction

For years I've been bothered by the fiction children write. One child said, "Oh, when you write fiction, you can do anything you want because it isn't true." The quality of children's fiction I observed was consistent with that child's statement. Their writing was filled with high body counts, violence, war, unicorns, or insipid stories about Care Bears. That itch moved me to a study of children's fiction (Graves, 1989). I needed solid data to help me understand both children and fiction as a genre.

Before I began, I needed to get a sense of critical variables in the fiction genre. I needed to have a sense of play and discovery in searching for a critical place to begin. In this instance, as in many others, when trying to understand genres and writing in general, I turned to what professional writers have to say about writing. For years my colleague, Donald Murray, has maintained an 18-foot bookshelf on what professional writers have to say about all phases of the writing process. (He has recently classified and published the best of the quotes; Murray, 1990.)

A study of Murray's quote collection at the time of my study showed that "character is all." Almost without exception, professional writers cite the preeminence of character over plot; that is, events occur because of the nature of the characters involved. My study, therefore, focused on one question: How do children reveal characters in their fiction? I examined hundreds of pieces of fiction from each grade (1-6) in an elementary school where children read trade books and wrote large amounts of fiction. Some of the findings from the study follow:

● Characters are subordinate to plot. Characters largely exist so that certain things might happen in the story. "Let's have a murder. Who is going to be killed? Who will do it?" Children are fascinated by motion and action and often portray the exaggerated elements of what interests them.

● For the first 2 years of school, the characters in children's fiction are already known by the other children. That is, central characters are the writers themselves, other children in the room, or characters like Snoopy, He-Man, G.I. Joe, Ninja Turtles, and generic good guys/bad guys.

● A significant moment occurs when a child creates a *new character* with a name the other children don't know. "Who's that?" quickly follows. (New names begin toward the end of Grade 1, increase in Grade 3, and are a common occurrence in Grade 4.) Thus, a new name is the beginning of character development requiring the child to supply additional information about the "unknown" person.

● Physical descriptions of characters appear in Grade 3 with inner reflections of characters (i.e., characters responding inwardly to outward events) occurring in Grade 5. In all cases where characters demonstrated reflective qualities, the author was an extensive reader of fiction.

● Beginning in Grade 5, children enjoy creating characters much older than themselves, particularly those in the middle-teen years. These characters go out on dates, are concerned with wearing the latest attire, and drive automobiles.

Choosing characters for a focus in the research opened the door to seeing when other variables emerged: dialogue, character description, parallel reading habits, inner reflection, as well as the emergence of secondary characters. The study pointed out the need to help children have a sense of character development and a sense of plausibility in the stories they tell. Teachers need to show children how characters are created by demonstrating the process with their own writing as well as through classroom workshops in which students compose stories together and issues in plausibility can be debated (Graves, 1989).

This study of fiction began with an itch and a question: Why is children's fiction so poorly done? So much of conducting research requires us to place ourselves where good data will be found. In my research courses, I often say, "So much of gathering data is in knowing where to put your bucket in order to get worthwhile information." Just where to put the bucket didn't come until I could see an angle in Murray's quotes about the primacy of character. The breakthrough actually came from a collection of quotes Murray (1987) put together for a summer course in fiction. I remember reading a quote from Vincent McHugh (1950):

> From first to last, the novelist is concerned with character. In the novel, everything is character, just as everything is tone or process. Each event must be focused in human consciousness. Without someone to look at it, there is no landscape, no idea without someone to conceive it, and no passion without persons.

Fortunately, Murray had classified the nature of the quotes, and "character" was a category. Further investigation showed that, with rare exception, about 38 professional writers agreed with McHugh.

---

*This study of fiction began with an itch and a question: Why is children's fiction so poorly done?*

---

It took a long time to figure the best place to gather data. I read and took notes until the shadowy notion of exploring character came to me. In this instance, the contribution of professional writers, so seldom used as a source in conducting writing research, gave me the place to gather data effectively.

## Writing poetry

I find only small differences between my work in research and the writing of poetry, my favorite genre. Both require a strong selection of solid, specific data. In each case, I am often not aware of the meaning of the data at hand, and I must write, design, rewrite, abandon, and solve many problems en route. Above all, I have to trust the shadows of thought, look quickly at the periphery for solutions in design, structure, language, and, above all, meaning. I keep problems in poetry "open," sometimes for months and years.

Both poetry and my work in research are experiences in composing fiction. That is, both genres are my perceptions of the data. Furthermore, the reality of the event is more than just the information. I must do an interpretation of what I have seen, gathered, and experienced. I'll show what I mean through the composition of my most recent poem, "Interstate Highway 95."

---

*The driving force to writing poetry or research is that sense of wonder about what is just around the corner.*

---

I was driving north of Boston on Interstate 95 when I noticed a cloud of dust spurting from the edge of the southbound lane. Suddenly, a red Subaru headed crazily across the median, flipped several times, ejected a body, and stopped. I pulled over and raced across the highway, meeting two men carrying a person. She spoke. I couldn't believe that airborne body was still alive, and her first words perplexed me even more: "How am I going to get to Medford?" When I left the scene in the hands of the police and medics, the story, the ambiguity of the event, worked on me. I still had another 150 miles to drive alone on my journey. I was bursting with talk but had no one with whom to speak.

I knew a poem was brewing. In instances like the accident, poems usually occur. Something in the event bothered me. Writing would help me understand. The more complex the event, the more I use poetry to gain understanding. Continual revising in short space and working and reworking no more than 80 to 90 lines led to more discovery than when I later actually wrote an essay and straight narrative account of the event. Furthermore, if I write in a short space, I can think more intensely about the event than when I am not writing.

In poetry and in research, my first questions are the same: What is the question? What is this about? Then I ask: What are the details? What is the essential information? Both genres require specific information, as detailed as I can make it. I first wrote a rapid full account of the accident. I opened myself to the experience. I censored nothing in order to cast a first impression of the event.

Accident

Interstate 95 north,
Sweet Georgia Brown
and Canadian Brass
bounce a beat
from the deck,
two black strips
with green in between,
music and the open road.

Dirt spurts
like smoke,
a fountain of dust
like strafing bullets
chewing paths
on a country road;
from those plumes
a confusion
of red on green,
a veering Subaru,
hiccupping the median
then somersaulting
like an Olympian
in triple jump, once,
twice, and twice
but on cue
a body ejects
like Ringling
would be proud,
a long arch
to the ground;
I replay now
in slow motion,
the body racing
ahead of the car,
then bouncing
and halting to rest,
but the car
coming, rolling,
searching for the lost
master, ready
to crush the master.

I stop,
hit the flashers
race the highway,
sprint the median,
the car now an ugly
red beetle upside down,
the engine in fury
poops smoke, the wheels
race and paw the empty
air. Two men
cradle a young woman
racing from the car,
"might blow up,
get her out of here.
anyone else in there?
she's the only one."
"How can I get to Medford?"
asks the girl.

I wrote from pictures in my mind's eye, the pictures I'd replayed again and again from the poem. I told the story from the time I drove calmly north listening to music, to the woman's statement as she sat on the median strip. When I put words to paper, the images were clarified still further. Words do that. I don't know what I think until I see the words on the page, whether it is research or poetry.

The driving force to writing poetry or research is that sense of wonder about what is just around the corner. What will be discovered here in the data?

I continued to think about the poem when I wasn't writing. First, I realized I was too much in the poem. I had to edit myself out. I also needed much more economy. The accident happened quickly. If speed was to be felt, then the poem had to be shortened. As I pared away with the edits, the meaning became more and more clear to me. The final draft (at this time) is the following:

Interstate 95 North

A Subaru veers
the median,
a panic of red
on green, then vaults
an Olympic triple
somersault, once,
twice; a body ejects
a long, flopping arch
to the ground;
the body rolls
ahead of the car.

Now a sprawled
beetle on its back;
the engine exhausts
gusts of black smoke;
the wheels race
and whine the empty air.

Two men scoop the body
from the ground,
"might blow up,"
shouts one;
they race and cradle
the woman whose eyes blink
as if the light
is too much for her.
She asks, "How am I going
to get to Medford?"

For me, the last line had to carry the day. I suspected that the woman was uttering the very words I would have spoken in the same event. I am so goal-oriented that I could live through fire, flood, and pestilence, experience a delay, and still ask, "But how am I going to get to...?" Her message was so important that everything else, cute and clever though the lines may have been (and I edited out many favorite lines), had to be subordinate to the final statement. A long poem would detract from the final line.

This is a long way of saying that sometimes the shadows, the other details, ultimately must be *turned off*. After the long journey of listening, of allowing the shadows to enter and including detail, the truth of the matter came early and sat under my nose the entire time. At first I said "yes" to a lot of data before switching to many "no's" and nine drafts later arriving at the shorter version you have just read. Thus, my final "yes" to the shorter version is done more forcefully to myself and the reader because of the necessary "no's" I have done in the many deletions.

*I didn't begin to trust my own thinking in research or in poetry until I could link up several factors at one time: daily writing, a sense of play in the composing, and, above all, sustaining thought well beyond the actual composing on the page.*

The Ford study mentioned earlier was originally 130 pages in length. I cut the report to just under 30 pages. Whole chapters became single lines. I simply had to decide which data were essential and not tangle the reader's mind with other "interesting" facts about the national crisis in writing. I think the report's influence, as judged by the award it received from the National Council of Teachers of English, was due to the shortened, more penetrating version. If I had not allowed the more expanded version in early draft form, however, then some of the most important information, though contained in a few lines, might have been lost.

## Final reflection

Naturally, I wonder how I might have started trusting the shadows of thought much earlier. For most of my life, I worked hard to fit my responses into the preconceived slots required by my teachers. I probably had teachers who worked hard to get me to think for myself, but I was simply too caught up in the overall impact of the hurried school to respond to their efforts.

Throughout my school career and late into my dissertation, assignments assaulted me with such bewildering speed that my off-task thinking, as well as any original ideas in the shadows, were near nonexistent. "Get on with the job and get the job done," was my mental dictum. The Everest of requirements was simply too high for disengagement and reflection. The experience of drafting my way into thought, or toying with language and information under the guidance of a professional on a long-term assignment, was even more rare than the question of disengagement.

I didn't begin to trust my own thinking in research or in poetry until I could link up several factors at one time: daily writing, a sense of play in the composing, and, above all, sustaining thought well beyond the actual composing on the page.

### References

Calkins, L. (1980). Children's rewriting strategies. *Research in the Teaching of English, 14,* 331-341.

Graves, D. (1973). Sex differences in children's writing. *Elementary English, 30,* 1101-1106.

Graves, D. (1978). *Balance the basics: Let them write.* New York: Ford Foundation.

Graves, D. (1982). *A case study observing the development of primary children's composing, spelling, and motor behaviors during the writing process* (Report on NIE Grant No. G-78-0174). Washington, DC: National Institute of Education.

Graves, D. (1989). *Experiment with fiction.* Portsmouth, NH: Heinemann.

McHugh, V. (1950). *Primer of the novel.* New York: Random House.

Murray, D. (1987). Syllabus—Course in fiction. Durham, NH: University of New Hampshire.

Murray, D. (1990). *Shoptalk: Learning to write with writers.* Portsmouth, NH: Boynton Cook/Heinemann.

**Reprinted with permission of Don Graves and the International Reading Association.**

## Voices

When you feel you know how to teach a writing process workshop, watch out. When you feel it is easy to answer other people's questions about your teaching, watch out. When you feel others are wrong, wrong, wrong, watch out.

We need to watch out lest we lose the pioneer spirit which made this field great in the first place. We need to watch out lest we suffer hardening of the ideologies.

**Donald Murray
NCTE Conference, 1985**

**Reprinted with permission of Donald Murray.**

# Writing in Kindergarten

## Helping Parents Understand the Process

HOME SCHOOL
Strengthening The Connection

### Kathleen A. Dailey

As a parent, how would you react to this work from a kindergarten child? Would you respond in the following manner?

"I can't believe Miss Davis let Tommy bring home a paper with so many mistakes."

"Doesn't she take time to spell the words for the children?"

"Shouldn't Tommy learn to make the letters correctly first?"

"How will he learn to spell correctly if she lets him spell like that?"

"He doesn't even know how to read yet and they expect him to write!"

Many parents may have this initial reaction, especially if the teacher has not prepared the parents for such work. Research in homes and schools suggests that the writing process of the child can be enriched by communication between teachers and parents. When parents first encounter the idea of writing programs for kindergartners, they need to be educated about the program. The following research-based answers to some of the most common questions are helpful in

**Figure 1.** *The flowers are coming out of the ground.*

orienting kindergartners' parents to an early writing program.

### How does my child learn to read and write?

Literacy, the process of learning to read and write, begins at home long before children enter school (Ferreiro & Teberosky, 1982; Hall, 1987; Schickedanz, 1986). This process does not officially begin at a particular age; rather, it develops as children gain experience with language and print. The two processes, reading and writing, develop simultaneously.

A variety of activities, which can be a part of daily living in many homes, enhance literacy develop-

ment. Children learn purposes for reading and writing as the parent and child sing a lullaby, share a picture book, make a shopping list or write a telephone message. Many children *read* environmental print, such as the names on cereal boxes and restaurant signs. Likewise, children learn how a book *works* and realize that print conveys meaning as they partake in a variety of experiences with books. As 2-year-old Ryan sits propped on his mother's lap with a book, she points to the cat and says, "What's that?" "Ki-Ki," says Ryan. Young Ryan gathers meaning from the pictures and the dialogue with his mother. With increased book knowledge, he comes to understand that the black marks on the page tell a story as well as the pictures.

*Kathleen A. Dailey is Assistant Professor, Elementary Education Department, Edinboro University of Pennsylvania and Kindergarten Teacher, Miller Research Learning Center (campus laboratory school).*

At the same time, children begin to experiment with different forms of writing that meet their needs and interests. Children may begin to copy letters and words from books, to write lines of squiggle or letters or to ask an adult to make models of letters for them. Children may write the names of family members and spellings of common objects. Writing interests may further develop as children choose to write letters, send postcards to friends, cast their superhero as the main character of their story or write a poem based on a favorite story, such as *In a Dark, Dark Wood* (Melser & Cowley, 1980) (see Figure 2).

The kindergarten reading program should be an extension of reading and writing that began in the home. It should help young children draw upon their past experiences to increase their understanding of how reading and writing function for specific and meaningful purposes (Dyson, 1984; Hall, 1987; Teale, 1982; Teale & Sulzby, 1989).

## Do drawing and scribbling help my child learn how to write?

Children's first attempts at authorship are frequently accompanied by a drawing. Drawing is an integral part of the writing process because it is a way for children to plan and organize their written text (Dyson, 1988; Strickland & Morrow, 1989). A drawing can tell a story that written words cannot yet convey for the young child. Parents should accept their children's drawings and encourage them to talk about these drawings. Some researchers encourage parents and teachers to write down what children dictate so they can see their own speech put into words.

Young children will frequently scribble. Scribble drawing takes on a circular form. As children intend these marks to be writing, the scribbles take on a linear, controlled form. A page full of scribbles may be a letter to Grandma or a restaurant menu. When asked to *read* this message, the child may first glance at the picture then point to the scribbles as he or she relays the content of the written work. As

the child's print awareness increases, these scribbled marks become more refined and take on the characteristics of print (see Figures 3 & 4).

## How can I encourage my child to write at home?

Research indicates that children engage in literacy events more in the home than in school (Schickedanz & Sullivan, 1984). This evidence supports the importance of parents as writing models. Observational studies of young children reveal that adults involved in writing behaviors such as writing a letter, making a grocery list or writing a check are often a stimulus for a child's early attempts to write (Lamme, 1984; Schickedanz & Sullivan, 1984; Taylor, 1983). When children see adults writing for a variety of purposes, they discover ways in which writing is useful and meaningful.

Parents can create an environment that accepts and values writ-

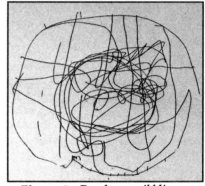

Figure 3. *Random scribbling*

Figure 2. *Poem based on the story, In a Dark, Dark Wood*
On a dark, dark path
In a dark, dark house
On a dark, dark stair
In a dark, dark room
Boo! Ha-ha-ha

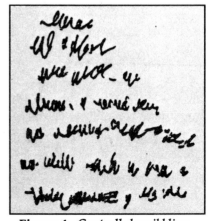

Figure 4. *Controlled scribbling*

ing by providing their children with many tools for writing. A variety of unlined paper and many different writing tools (markers, pencils, pens or chalk) are important materials for this craft. Children enjoy a variety of writing media. They may like the feel of writing letters or words in a tray of sand, pudding or jello. They may write using a computer or typewriter. Rich (1985) suggests using a "writing suitcase" as a portable writing station. The suitcase is filled with paper, markers, crayons, plastic letters and stencils. The child has access to the suitcase, is responsible for its contents and is free to add new items. The child is an active learner in the process. The writing that is produced is limited only by imagination.

**Aren't paper-and-pencil activities, like workbook pages, the best way of learning to read and write?** Children learn through direct participation in meaningful activities. When that learning is a complex process (like reading) rather than a skill (like tying shoes), it is even more important that the conditions of meaningful participation be met. Music is a good analogy. If we want young children to develop their musical abilities, we begin with enjoyment, not worksheets on musical notation. We accept their early efforts as well, realizing that the toddler who bounces in rhythm to a popular song may become a dancer or the child who pounds on a xylophone may play a musical instrument someday.

Reading programs that *teach* children to *read* and *write* through the use of dittos and workbook pages reflect practices that are developmentally inappropriate for young children (Elkind, 1986) for at least two reasons. First, the child's needs are not taken into consideration when the emphasis is on *every* child doing the same thing at the same time. Manuel has recognized the *M* at the beginning of his name and on the McDonald's sign since he was 3 years old. Manuel can write his own name and the word *MOM*. Manuel brings home a paper with neatly circled *M*s. As he hands the paper to his father, Manuel replies, "It was boring!" Molly completed the same paper yet is unable to tell you the letter name. The way and manner in which children learn varies for

## Table 1
### THE ASSOCIATION BETWEEN LANGUAGE DEVELOPMENT AND WRITING DEVELOPMENT

| Language | Writing | Spelling |
|---|---|---|
| Babbling | Random scribbling | |
| Holophrase—one word utterance is used to express a complete thought: "Mama" means "Mommy I want to get up." | | One letter spelling—one or two letters represent entire sentences or phrases: $H$ = This is my house. |
| Repetition | Controlled scribbling—the same forms or the same letters are repeated as the child progresses toward mastery of that form. | Writing the same letters or words in order to attain mastery |
| Expanded vocabulary of frequently used words | | Incorporation of conventional spellings with invented spellings |
| Grammatical rules are applied to speech. "I want up." replaces "Me up." | | Transitional spelling—using simple rules to spell |
| Overgeneralization—internalization of grammar rules, but applied to more cases than those in which they work: "He runned after me." | | Overgeneralization—reliance on rules applied in previous spellings, yielding errors due to inconsistencies of the language. "LETUS" (lettuce) |
| More precise speech | | More precise spelling |

Adapted from Lamme, 1984.

each individual. Approaches that may be effective for one child may be ineffective for the next.

Second, workbook writing directs the focus away from the child. "When worksheets and phonics lessons are given to young children all the initiative comes from the teacher. When this happens, teachers unintentionally prevent children from developing their own natural initiative" (Willert & Kamii, 1985). On the other hand, activities such as drawing and writing about a trip to the zoo, reading alphabet books and enjoying songs and fingerplays about sounds and letters allow children to take an active role in learning to read and write.

**I have difficulty figuring out what my child has written. How can I better understand what she writes?**
The writing of children develops in overlapping stages that parallel language development (Table 1).

As children make the transition from scribbling to more conventional forms of writing, they may represent their written work with a random ordering of letters such as

*mTEo* to represent house. This is followed by stages that reveal the child's understanding of letter-sound correspondence, which is a first step toward reading (Chomsky, 1971). These stages are referred to as "invented spelling" because children apply what they know about sounds and letters to their early writing. It is common, however, for children to be in several stages of spelling development at once and revert to earlier stages as they experiment with writing. The stages of invented spelling development are shown in Table 2.

These early attempts are systematic even though the spelling is unconventional (Richgels, 1987), as shown in the spelling of *monster*, *grass* and *class* (Table 2). This systematic process enables children to take control of their learning and become independent writers.

**Should I correct my child's written work?**
When a child says "ba" for bottle, parents understand what the child is trying to say and accept the pronunciation at the child's stage of development. Spelling develop-

ment should be treated similarly. Early writing contains many words spelled unconventionally because children experiment with written form at particular stages of development. Children need models who are supportive and patient. When Jane asks, "Mommy, do you spell *tree*, T-R-E?" her mother responds, "That's the way it sounds, but that's not the way it is spelled. It's *T-R-E-E*." This response tells children that there are conventional spellings, but we also accept the way they spell. Criticism of misspelled words makes children fearful of making mistakes. Under these conditions, research shows that they write less and less well, sticking with *safe* known words. What is worse, they learn to dislike writing because they see it as a test rather than as a means of creative expression.

Parents may help children sound out words or spell words for them, but at the same time provide materials that foster independence in writing. Picture dictionaries provide children with an early reference tool. Parents need to show children how the dictionary is set up and how to locate words using the alphabet and picture cues. Parents can help children compile their own personal dictionary of frequently used words, such as objects in the home or names of family members. A set of words on cards serves the same purpose (Ashton-Warner, 1965). An accompanying illustration may help the child use the word cards independently. Understanding spelling development and fostering independence in writing through positive and nurturing practices are essential to a child's healthy attitude toward writing.

**My child will write letters correctly one day and reverse them the next. Is that normal?**
When parents of young children see a backwards *S* or *2*, they often

## Table 2
### THE DEVELOPMENT OF INVENTED SPELLINGS

| Stage 1 | Use of initial consonant to represent an entire word | M for monster<br>G for grass<br>C for class |
|---------|------------------------------------------------------|-----------------------------------------------|
| Stage 2 | Initial and final consonants serve as word boundaries | MR<br>GS<br>CS |
| Stage 3 | Inclusion of medial consonant; awareness of blends; may divide blend | MSTR<br>GRS<br>CALS |
| Stage 4 | Initial, final and medial consonants and vowel place-holder. Vowel is incorrect | MESTR<br>GRES<br>CLES |
| Stage 5 | Conventional Spelling | MONSTER<br>GRASS<br>CLASS |

Adapted from: Gentry, 1981; Graves, 1983; Lamme, 1984 & Strickland & Morrow, 1989.

worry that their child has a learning disability. Actually, such reversals are very prevalent in kindergarten, 1st and 2nd grade. It is common for children to experiment with reversed writing. Sometimes letters are reversed; sometimes they are placed upside down. These characteristics, including a tendency to write in any direction, are all related (Schickedanz, 1986). Children need practice with directionality and the orientation of printed symbols. Until children have attained consistency in left-to-right and top-to-bottom orientation and formed a mental image of what the letter *b* looks like, for example, they may continue to reverse written symbols. "All exploration is perfectly normal; it is a healthy sign that children are investigating print, getting used to it and figuring out how it works" (Marzollo & Sulzby, 1988, p. 83). If a child consistently reverses written symbols beyond 2nd grade, a parent may want to seek advice. Generally, however, reversals are not a cause for concern at an early age.

**What should I look for in my child's writing program?**
"Everywhere I look, I see children's written work," comments a visitor to the kindergarten classroom. This atmosphere reflects one in which young writers have been experimenting with different types of print since their first day of school. Each time children sit down to write, they increase their knowledge of written form just through the act itself. At the writing center, children are working in their journals or writing a story. Writing, however, is not limited to one area of the room. In the block area, Erin made a sign that says *CASO* (castle). In the kitchen area, Patrick posted the special food for the day, *APLS* (apples). Meanwhile, the post office clerk is busy delivering letters addressed to Santa Claus (see Figure 5).

**Figure 5.** *Letter to Santa Claus*
*To Santa Claus*
*You are nice.*
*Get me a present.*
*I would like a Barbie.*
*I like you.*

Young children's writing, speaking and action are closely related. Early writing is not only a paper-and-pencil activity, but also a social process. In her observation of children, Dyson (1981) comments, "I saw no quiet, solemn-faced scholars, struggling to break into print. Rather, I saw (and heard) writers using both pencil and voice to make meaning on the empty page" (p. 777). In a writing environment one may observe children engaged in the following activities:

- Asking each other for help
  *How did you spell tyrannosaurus?*

- Planning and creating
  *I'm going to put brontosaurus in the water.*

- Rehearsing ideas
  *My brontosaurus will be eating plants.*

- Questioning each other about their products
  *What is your dinosaur doing?*

- Sharing and reading their work to each other
  *The Brotsrs is RunIng AWAW.* (*The brontosaurus is running away.*)

- Evaluating their work
  *That was a long sentence. I'll have to make more room on the paper next time.*
  (Adapted from Lamme, 1984)

In a quality kindergarten writing program, the child's teacher serves as model and facilitator of the writing process, providing the children with an environment rich in opportunities to use and create written materials (Rich, 1985). The teacher observes children write, confers with them and accepts their work. "Teachers who grow writers in their classrooms also regard pieces of writing as growing things to be nurtured rather than as objects to be repaired and fixed" (Bissex, 1981).

**What does the teacher do during the writing conference with my child?**
The writing conference serves as a personal and meaningful interaction between the child and the teacher; both are learners in the process. Early in the school year, Ms. Hart established a routine for writing conferences. She chose the couch area as a comfortable place where the children can share their written work. Chris knows that his conference with Ms. Hart is every Tuesday. As the other children in the class continue to write, Chris takes his folder, journal, personal dictionary and a pencil and sits with Ms. Hart on the couch. This time together provides Ms. Hart with insights into Chris's writing abilities.

Throughout the writing conference, Ms. Hart asks questions that guide the process (Table 3). This format eventually allows the children to go through the same process independently as they reflect on their own writing. She focuses on the child throughout the conference, allowing the child to take the lead. Through careful observation of written work, the teacher assesses what the child already knows about written language. She may notice, for example, that a child uses letter-sound correspondence correctly for *D* when writing *dog* (*DG*) but confuses *B* and *P* when spelling *boat* (PT). She may have the child write for her during the conference to observe the process firsthand. Ms. Hart keeps detailed records of the child's progress and makes teaching recommendations based on specific needs.

## Conclusion

Parents and teachers need to recognize that ". . . every child who can talk has the capacity to learn to write and also to seize upon its possibilities with enthusiasm" (Smith, 1981, p. 792). Parents and teachers have the responsibility to create an environment for children that develops confidence and success in writing. When parents and teachers understand the processes underlying writing development, they can help children participate in meaningful home and school activities that promote its growth. Thus, home and school partnerships built upon communication and understanding provide children with a firm foundation for successful writing experiences.

**Acknowledgment:** The author gratefully thanks Mary Renck Jalongo for her assistance in reviewing this article.

## References

Ashton-Warner, S. (1965). *Teacher*. NY: Simon and Schuster.

Bissex, G. (1981). Growing writers in classrooms. *Language Arts, 58*, 785-791.

Chomsky, C. (1971). Write first, read later. *Childhood Education, 47*, 296-299.

Dyson, A. H. (1981). Oral language: The rooting system for learning to write. *Language Arts, 58*, 776-791.

Dyson, A. H. (1984). N spell my grandmama: Fostering early thinking about print. *The Reading Teacher, 38*, 262-270.

Dyson, A. H. (1988). Appreciate the drawing and dictating of young children. *Young Children, 43*(3), 25-32.

Elkind, D. (1986). Formal education and early childhood education: An essential difference. *Phi Delta Kappan, 67*, 631-636.

Ferreiro, E., & Teberosky, A. (1982). *Literacy before schooling*. London: Heinemann.

Gentry, J. R. (1981). Learning to spell developmentally. *The Reading Teacher, 34*, 378-381.

Graves, D. (1983). *Writing: Teachers and children at work*. Portsmouth, NH: Heinemann.

Hall, N. (1987). *The emergence of literacy*. Portsmouth, NH: Heinemann.

Lamme, L. L. (1984). *Growing up writing*. Washington, DC: Acropolis.

Marzollo, J., & Sulzby, E. (1988). See Jane read! See Jane write! *Parents, 63*(7), 80-84.

Melser, J., & Cowley, J. (1980). *In a dark, dark wood*. San Diego, CA: The Wright Group.

Rich, S. J. (1985). The writing suitcase. *Young Children, 40*(5), 42-44.

Richgels, D. J. (1987). Experimental reading with invented spelling (ERIS): A preschool and kindergarten method. *The Reading Teacher, 40*, 522-529.

Schickedanz, J. (1986). *More than the ABC's: The early stages of reading and writing*. Washington, DC: National Association for the Education of Young Children.

Schickedanz, J. A., & Sullivan, M. (1984). Mom, what does U-F-F spell? *Language Arts, 61*, 7-17.

Smith, F. (1981). Myths of writing. *Language Arts, 58*, 792-798.

Strickland, D., & Morrow, L. M. (1989). Young children's early writing development. *The Reading Teacher, 42*, 426-427.

Taylor, D. (1983). *Family literacy—Young children learning to read and write*. Exeter, NH: Heinemann.

Teale, W. H. (1982). Toward a theory of how children learn to read and write naturally. *Language Arts, 59*, 555-570.

Teale, W. H., & Sulzby, E. (1989). Emergent literacy: New perspectives. In D. S. Strickland & L. M. Morrow (Eds.), *Emerging literacy: Young children learn to read and write* (pp. 1-15). Newark, DE: International Reading Association.

Willert, M. K., & Kamii, C. (1985). Reading in kindergarten. Direct vs. indirect teaching. *Young Children, 40*(4), 3-9.

### Table 3
### INAPPROPRIATE AND APPROPRIATE RESPONSES
### USED DURING WRITING CONFERENCES

| Inappropriate Responses | Appropriate Responses |
|---|---|
| "Allison, will you read this? I can't figure out what it says." | "What are you writing about Allison?" |
| "What is it?" | "Tell me about your picture." |
| "Can't you write about something else besides the zoo?" | "Do you like writing about the zoo?" |
| "Tomorrow, I think you should write about our field trip." | "What do you think you will write about next?" |
| "The next time I want you to figure out how to spell these words by yourself." | "Allison, how did you go about writing this?" |

Adapted from Graves, 1983.

**Reprinted by permission of Kathleen A. Dailey and the Association for Childhood Education International, 11501 Georgia Ave., Suite 315, Wheaton, MD. © 1991 by the Association.**

# "Stepping" into the Writing Process

## by Carol Peto-Ostberg

This article is a demonstration of reflective teaching. By watching, wondering, studying, and experimenting, Carol shows how she found a way to help children maintain a powerful engagement in expressive literacy activities while accommodating their physical and psychological development. Carol teaches Grade 1 at The Smith College Campus School, Prospect Street, Northampton, MA 01063.

---

"Well, the monster can't find any place that's good for him to live. See he's tried the ocean and the jungle...I want him to try one more place before he gets help. What would be good next?"

This is an example of peer conferencing in a first grade whole language classroom. Sean is in the process of writing the first draft of his creature fantasy story. It's going well. The students have been reading and comparing stories with creature characters that are non-animal, non-human products of an author's imagination. Now they're letting their own imaginations create the creature characters that are brought to life in their original stories. It is December, and this project is the first major story we've written in our classroom. It's far more successful than any December writing project I've initiated in past years. I'd like to share the reason for this with you.

I am a whole language teacher and I believe writing is a marvelous way for children to communicate important and creative thoughts. The structure of a whole language classroom provides a forum in which those thoughts are given time and value. Through the process of writing, children learn about the conventions of language while editing and publishing their writing in a final draft, and during conferences with peers and adults. The children write with invented spelling which means they write down the letters they believe stand for the sound they hear in a word if they do not know the standard spelling. Students initiated their writing experience using invented spelling in kindergarten. The process was always continued immediately in the first grade.

In past years, I began the first grade writing experience with daily writing in journals or in the form of stories. However, as time went on I began to observe that children became less invested in their daily writing. What was wrong? The children were given many opportunities to write for a wide variety of purposes, yet there was no inappropriate pressure to write. They verbally shared so many rich ideas. The children obviously had a lot to say. I thought about every aspect of the classroom and how I motivated writing.

During my evaluation process, our school began to examine its handwriting program. With this focus on the mechanics of writing, an important issue became clear. Despite the enthusiasm and desire the children had to tell their stories, for some the task of writing the letters that represented their words was impossibly tiring.

Our schools' consideration of fine motor and handwriting issues was motivated by the research of Mary Benbow, an occupational therapist who specializes in the field. The link between the muscles used in handwriting and actual letter formation is emerging as critical when planning a handwriting program in conjunction with a whole language program that incorporates writing process. Many children are using writing instruments at early ages at home and at school. Some are developing bad habits in their posture, body/paper positioning, and grip. Others have not developed the muscular maturity to manipulate a writing instrument. Our response to these issues was to develop a handwriting curriculum that includes a balance of muscle development activities and letter formation practice. We also decreased the writing expectation in kindergarten and beginning first grade for those children who need to develop writing muscles.

I began to consider ways of modifying the first-grade writing program. Dictation and paired writing were always available to children in my classroom to lessen the burden of writing. However, sometimes during those processes, the words on the page can be perceived by children as being owned by the individual who physically wrote them. That can be discouraging to young children who are so proud of every step they take towards autonomy. Dictation and paired-peer writing did not seem like sufficient alternatives to delaying the physical writing expectation in a whole language and process writing environment.

I certainly did not want to eliminate the writing process from my classroom. It's creative, it builds self-esteem, and it provides children with an opportunity to simultaneously own and share. An ideal solution would keep all the creative aspects of authorship and postpone the mechanics of writing. The children could still create, control, and share, yet not be discouraged by the written word.

The picture story format presented qualities that could answer some of the issues surrounding my writing program. This year the picture story was the first means offered to children through which they could express ideas. Those who strongly felt they wanted to write about their picture stories in invented spelling or through dictation were free to do so. However, the majority of children chose to orally communicate the ideas and stories that motivated their drawings. Children naturally moved from making single pictures to sequencing multiple pictures on one page, then verbally explaining the events. Sequenced pictures on one page evolved into sequencing individual picture pages. The children had wordless books available to them as motivating models.

For the next phase of the communicating process, I developed the conept of *Stepping Stories*. Four sequenced story pictures are placed on a *Stepping Story* mat, a large laminated rectangular paper about 7' x 3' and divided into a blank title block and four additional spaces. Each of the four additional spaces has a number, starting with 1, and two shoe sole outlines. A wooden block labeled "the beginning" holds down the large paper near the author/title area, and a block labeled "the end" holds down the other end of the paper near the fourth space. As the children take turns, their name and story title are written in the author/title space with an erasable overhead marker, and they place their sequenced pictures on the appropriately numbered spaces. They then step down the mat and tell their story, which is recorded on cassette tape. When the author concludes his or her story, the recording is stopped. Later, after all children in the small group have recorded, each child in the authors' group wears headphones, and the cassette of their sharing session is played. Each author stretches out their story when they hear their voice on the tape. The ideal group size for this activity is four or five. It is important for children to see each others' stories and their own during the listening session.

As children listen to their own voice, they get a *real* sense of their story. They hear elements of it in an objective way; the sequence of their story and how much detail they did or did not include. My experience with children and this technique has shown me that children, after listening, can appreciate and discuss their story more objectively than when they are in the reading or describing role. Also, waiting

The End

4

3

2

1

AUTHOR _____

TITLE _____

The Beginning

*Stepping Story Mat ©1992 Carol Peto-Ostberg*

a few days before listening to the tapes provides some distance for children. Events of the story are not fresh in the author's mind, and inconsistencies are more easily recognized. During the *Stepping Story* authoring process, children receive group feedback after the recording process and feedback from their own voice during the listening process.

Young authors are extremely proud of their *Stepping Stories* and tapes. They are a wonderful addition to the listening center. Children are fascinated by the sound of their own voices on the tapes. Compliments are regularly exchanged. That is where I see the most smiles also. Children beam as their stories live on in the classroom independently from print. They build their identity as authors and creative story tellers. The content and form of these stories are not limited by children's letter formation stamina. The format provides valuable sequencing and verbal communication experience while it retains the creative process so integral in the writing process. There is opportunity for peer interaction and revision while ownership of the story is never compromised.

By late November the group was enthusiastic about communicating stories, and some were ready for another means of telling their stories...the written word. The children had been developing and using invented spelling for other writing purposes in the classroom, linked with literature and math. Through this activity the group practiced writing down letters that stood for the sounds they heard in words. Writing activities ranged from labeling pictures drawn in response to literature experiences to describing the logic of patterning work done in math. While practicing the techniques or description and naming, the children were developing confidence in the communicative power of their written word. They were also cultivating a belief, through the use of their invented spelling and their *Stepping Stories*, that ideas are valuable and worthy of sharing. *Stepping Stories* offered the children the gifts of time and a creative forum; time to develop muscular maturity as writers and a forum in which they built confidence as individuals who have important stories and ideas to share.

*Stepping Stories* remain an author's option in the classroom throughout the year or as needed. Some children leave the format as soon as a writing option is available. Others remain with *Stepping Stories* until their confidence or muscular maturity dictates. There is always movement back and forth between the two means of expression. Some children take breaks from the challenge of getting it all down in print and let their ideas flow more freely on tape. Others simply enjoy stepping down those shoe prints or want to hear their voice on tape one more time.

As for Sean, the group suggested his monster try making his home in the desert. Sean incorporated their suggestion and went on to publish a written story that pleases him and those who read it. Maybe next time he'll make a *Stepping Story*. Regardless of the choice, the class is eager to begin the creative process again and again. Creating, sharing, shaping, and valuing ideas is what process language is all about. The "published" product can take many forms. I found that delaying writing expectations and simultaneously helping children develop their sense of story gives them greater success when they are ready to write with invented spelling, and greater comfort sharing ideas, because they have a choice about how their ideas will be communicated.

©1992
Carol Peto-Ostberg

**Reprinted with permission of Carol Peto-Ostberg. Article was originally printed in the *WLSIG Newsletter*, Vol. 5 No. 2, Spring 1992.**

# *Using the Write Approach to Reading*

## by Ellen Roberts

To some, it might seem a bit unusual, but to K.C. Heffernan Elementary School Principal David Taddeo of Marcellus, N.Y., log keeping and journal writing by second and third-graders "is just the way we teach reading here."

That way of teaching, part of the Reading/Writing Connection program, is one of several techniques that has won Heffernan, the Marcellus School District's kindergarten-through-third-grade building, designation as a "School That Works" from the New York Education Department.

Taddeo said the honor goes to schools that have used innovative programs and community resources to help pupils improve their skills.

The state recognized several key curriculum elements in the school's academic program, Taddeo said.

The Reading/Writing Connection was one.

In it, instead of reading only traditional textbooks, pupils in second and third grades read novels and trade books – what Taddeo calls "real literature."

Teachers then suggest topics pertaining to certain aspects of those stories – a particular character or scene or part of the plot — and pupils write brief log entries on the topics.

"What you get back is a higher level of thinking," Taddeo said, "and thinking increases reading comprehension."

In other kinds of classes such as music, the Reading-Writing Connection has students setting stories to music, or creating a story to go with a song.

Comprehension scores on pupils' Stanford Achievement Tests have risen dramatically, Taddeo said.

In 1983 the average Heffernan pupil ranked better than 61 percent of all who took the test; today, the average score is higher than 75 percent of the others.

A second part of the Reading/Writing Connection has pupils as young as kindergarten age writing and "publishing" books.

"The earlier you begin writing, the more successful you'll be at reading," Taddeo said.

Other programs recognized by the state include the Reading Enrichment Project, which uses parents as reading partners and the Early Intervention Reading Program.

Early Intervention matches first-graders who've experienced difficulty with reading with teachers — not their regular classroom teachers — for one-on-one tutoring. The two meet daily for about 30 minutes for 16 weeks.

The purpose of the sessions is to keep pupils from needing remedial reading classes in later grades, Taddeo said.

**From the April 30, 1992 edition of *The Post-Standard*, Syracuse, N.Y. Reprinted with permission.**

# Teach Skills *with a* Strategy

## By Regie Routman

**Is skills teaching appropriate in the whole language classroom?**

**Yes—if you teach strategically, says Regie Routman, a nationally recognized author, teacher, and expert on whole language instruction. In this article, excerpted from her latest book, INVITATIONS, Ms. Routman tells how you can teach skills strategically in your classroom.**

"I wonder if the kids are really learning anything." Teachers who make the transition from the basal to literature worry a lot about whether or not skills are being taught. Additionally, many teachers feel nervous that they are not teaching enough. We teachers feel guilty spending reading time reading, discussing, and enjoying the literature. We have spent years teaching reading using lots of skills sheets. Without worksheets, where you can "see" skills work, it's hard for teachers to trust that the skills are in the books and that learning is truly occurring. Many of us devise activities to be sure skills teaching occurs.

## UNDERSTANDING THE DIFFERENCE BETWEEN *SKILLS* AND *STRATEGIES*

While skills teaching is a necessary part of all good instruction, it is our beliefs about learning combined with our approach, method, context, and timing that determine whether or not we are teaching skills so that they later become useful strategies for the learner.

In discrete skills teaching, the teacher—or the publisher of a program—decides what the learner needs, and the skill is directly taught, often in a predetermined sequence, and then practiced in isolation. The skill, whether it includes word attack, alphabetizing, sequencing, or vocabulary acquisition, is directly taught with an emphasis on practice and automatic, correct responses. The teacher or program controls how much practice or how many exercises students need. Application of the skill to new, meaningful contexts rarely occurs.

In teaching for strategies, however, skills are taught in a broader context because the learner demonstrates a need for specific skills in the instructional/learning setting, perhaps in a guided reading group. The skill is taught because the learner genuinely needs to use it—or the teacher anticipates the

PHOTOGRAPHS BY DONNELLY MARKS/ILLUSTRATIONS BY BETH GLICK

learner's upcoming need to use the skill. The teacher guides the student to self-determine the generalization and think through possibilities in authentic contexts. While the teacher may question and suggest, it is the learner who is encouraged to make deductions and consciously apply what is learned from one context to another.

## From Skill to Strategy

A skill—no matter how well it has been taught—cannot be considered a strategy until the learner can use it purposefully and independently. Application of a skill to another context is far more likely to occur when the skill has been taught in a meaningful context that considers the needs of the learners. I have observed that teachers begin to focus on strategies when they begin to change the climate of their classrooms from teacher-dominated to student-centered and when they come to view reading and other language processes as constructive and interactive.

Applying the distinction between skill and strategy to the teaching of sight words, phonics, and vocabulary, we see clearly that merely teaching the skills in isolation and practicing on worksheets has no relation to meaningful teaching. While we may believe that a skill has been covered, until the learner can discover how to utilize the skill in varied reading and writing contexts, skills teaching is largely a waste of time. *The learner must know how and when to apply the skill; that is what elevates the skill to the strategy level.*

## Promoting Strategic Teaching

It has taken me many years to become convinced that all the skills are in the literature and that the literature itself can be used as a vehicle to teach skills strategically. Most of us initially need to see concrete evidence of skills teaching, and we use the literature to teach and practice the skills we believe

children need. Even then we must be careful that skills work does not interfere with enjoyment of the story and that our focus on skills results from a genuine need for meaning.

I have observed that after about five years or more, teachers seem to move away from practicing specific skills in literature to promoting strategies in the ongoing context of genuine reading and writing, as the need arises. By becoming careful observers of our students and practicing ongoing evaluation, we can determine what strategies students are using and not using. We need to give ourselves time for this transition. As our own learning theory develops, and as we begin to take ownership of our teaching and rely less on directed instructional programs, we have less of a need for a predetermined skills agenda. ⟶

# Self-Evaluation Checks in Teaching for Strategies

Because most of us have had training that emphasizes discrete skills teaching, heightened awareness is necessary to move toward teaching for strategies in reading.

✔ Is your language fostering meaning-based strategies and independence when a student can't read a word, or are you relying only on, "Look at the letters" and "What sounds do those letters make?"

✔ Are you using engaging books with predictable text that support the reader, or are your texts dull and sequentially based for skills?

✔ Are you guiding students to apply strategies, or are you teaching for mastery of skills?

✔ Are you giving students sufficient wait time and encouragement to figure out words and meanings on their own, or are you quick to supply the answer?

✔ Do other students know it is the reader's job to do the work and that they need to give the reader quiet wait time, or do students call out words?

✔ After students have one-to-one matching and some confidence as readers, are you introducing students to unfamiliar text to note what strategies they have under control, or are students reading only books they have already heard?

✔ Are you asking important questions that follow naturally from the text and encourage more than one possibility, or are you looking for only one "right" answer?

✔ Is vocabulary taught in context during and after reading, or are you introducing words in isolation before reading?

✔ Are follow-up activities leading to further enjoyment and engagement with the text or are they merely keeping students busy while others are in group?

Reprinted with permission from Regie Routman: *Invitations* (Heinemann Educational Books, Portsmouth, NH; 1991). Ms. Routman is a language arts resource teacher in Shaker Heights, Ohio. All artwork in this excerpt has been added by INSTRUCTOR.

# HOW TO TEACH PHONICS STRATEGICALLY

In meaningful phonics teaching, connections of sounds and letters are always made in real-life contexts. Beyond the book or story, we lead children to make connections in other contexts—signs, labels, charts, calendars, poems, and children's names.

Even with a natural approach to phonics, it is perfectly acceptable to call attention to sounds and words that we know students will need for reading and writing. In choosing Big Books to read, we are sensitive to the phonics and rhyming words that can be highlighted. For example, I have noticed that the Frank Asch books, some of which are available as Big Books, contain many examples of words with consonant digraphs. *Happy Birthday, Moon* (Prentice Hall, 1982) and *Mooncake* (Prentice Hall, 1983) have lots of words with *th* and *wh*.

Rather than telling students what the sounds and letters are, however, I have found that an inquiry method that has the children "discover" the sounds and rules works best for engaging students in meaningful phonetic associations. I might say, for example, "What do you notice about the words…?" "I see several words that begin with *th*. Who can point to one?" "Can you find any other words with the same sound?" This approach is in direct contrast to that of most commercial phonics programs which tell students the rule or generalization and then present practice examples as skills in isolation rather than in the context of meaningful, continuous text.

**FIGURE 1 — A PHONICS CHART IN FIRST GRADE**

## Making the Transition to More Meaningful Phonics Teaching

Most of us seem to find the transition from prescribed phonics in isolation to teaching meaningful phonics in the context of literature very difficult and slow-going. It may be reassuring to know that most teachers are struggling with making phonics teaching more relevant and applicable to reading and writing. I believe it is critical to remember that before we can change our teaching, we have to carefully re-examine our beliefs in the light of current research and learning theory.

Susan Mears has been a first-grade teacher for eight years. In talking about phonics, she describes herself as "struggling awfully" despite the fact that she had done much reading and thinking about phonics teaching:

**"I did more phonics in context this year, noting beginning and ending sounds and digraphs in chart poems and Big Books. The kids really like the big charts we made, where they could add their own words, but I am still struggling to find a balance in teaching phonics. I find myself feeling pressure from some of the second grade teachers who expect kids to arrive with solid word attack skills. Also, I feel guilty for not giving spelling tests. When I'm teaching all the phonics sounds, I feel as though I'm teaching spelling, too. I still teach phonics separately even though I don't see kids transferring the skills. I notice that every time I pull a sound out of context, two or three kids give me an example of a word that doesn't fit the rule at all. I'm still not comfortable with the way I handle phonics."**

Colleen Thompson has been teaching first grade for two years. After a series of workshops on whole language, she began to question the traditional workbook approach to phonics teaching:

**"I have continued to teach phonics lessons through the workbooks, but I now see that the kids don't transfer that phonics to their reading. I had five kids who learned to read who never did catch on to phonics. I still use the workbooks, but I'm trying to use context more. If I can feel comfortable teaching phonics in context, I'd rather go that way. I saw this year that all the sounds are in the literature books. Next year I plan to spend most of reading time reading. I see I have to work with the parents, too. They use only "sounding out" when working with their kids. If the child can't read the word in isolation, parents think the child is not reading and has just used memorization. I need to make them aware of the other cuing systems."**

Opportunities for ongoing phonics teaching and evaluation arise daily in the following contexts:

◆ **Shared reading**
◆ **Shared writing**
◆ **Writing aloud**
◆ **Self-selected writing**
◆ **Guided reading**

Within these contexts, there is nothing wrong with direct, explicit teaching of phonics as long as it is done strategically. Words can be taken out of context as long as they are put back into context before moving on.

## Phonics Charts

Making enlarged phonics charts is perfectly appropriate in the whole language classroom. The order of sounds taught and the words used as examples are determined by the teacher and children, as the need arises in the context of reading and writing. This is very different from the use of traditional phonics charts that emphasize rules and use a prescribed sequence and fixed set of words.

For example, after *Who's in the Shed?* (Parkes, 1986) had been enjoyed over and over again during shared book experiences in a first-grade class, I demonstrated for the teacher how the *sh* sound could be reinforced through the book. I asked the children, "Who can find a word that begins with *sh* (I made the sound) on this page?" ( Figure 1 )

A child was then invited to come up and point to a word. As the child pointed to *sheep* and read it, I used a sliding mask to blend the word parts and highlight the *sh* and the whole word. I then wrote the word on our new *sh* chart, stretching out the sounds and verbalizing as I wrote it. In the same manner, children found *shed* and *she* on that page and subsequent pages, and those words were added to our chart.

It has worked well to tell children, "When you find a word as you are reading, come up and put it here on the chart." Limiting the words to books helps keep the spelling on the charts fairly accurate (we also tell children to write in pencil) and keeps the children from calling out scores of words. Children easily and excitedly work together to fill up our charts, and they develop increasing phonetic awareness and knowledge in the process. Phonics charts are posted in the room for children to add to and refer to. Separate sheets can be hole-punched and put together for easy referral and organization in a large, spiral-bound chart tablet (24 by 16 inches). In the kindergarten classroom, phonics charts may be made with pictures from magazines, with the word written next to each picture.

## Personal Phonics Booklets

Some kindergarten and first-grade teachers also have students keep

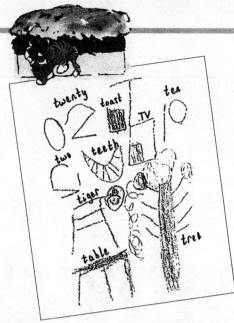

**FIGURE 2 — A PAGE FROM A KINDERGARTNER'S PERSONAL PHONICS BOOKLET**

their own sound and letter books in which students draw or paste in pictures to represent sounds for letters (figure 2). Sometimes these books are also used to practice handwriting after the teacher has students write optional "tongue twisters" (figure 3).

Some first-grade teachers have students keep lists of words that students notice from their reading to go along with particular letter-sound combinations. Students can always read these words before they examine them phonetically. These booklets serve as personal phonics charts.

Such individual phonics books are appropriate as long as they are a very minor part of the total reading program and students have some ownership over what goes into them. I have noticed that teachers tend to move away from these booklets once they are convinced that children are learning phonics in the normal course of daily reading and writing. One teacher said, "I did the booklets because I needed to see the evidence that phonics was being taught."

## Phonics: A Suggested Teaching Order

While there is no predetermined order for teaching letter-sound relationships, the following suggested sequence may be helpful when the teacher is trying to decide where to place emphasis first in the early grades. This order is based on my own observations working with young children.

◆ **Beginning consonants**
◆ **Ending consonants**
◆ **Consonant digraphs** (sh, th, ch, wh)
◆ **Medial consonants**
◆ **Consonant blends**
◆ **Long vowels**
◆ **Short vowels**

Instruction should always have meaning for the child and not just follow a prescribed sequence.

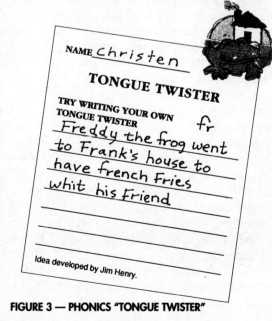

NAME *Christen*

**TONGUE TWISTER**

**TRY WRITING YOUR OWN TONGUE TWISTER**

*fr*
*Freddy the frog went to Frank's house to have french Fries whit his Friend*

Idea developed by Jim Henry.

**FIGURE 3 — PHONICS "TONGUE TWISTER"**

In determining what letter-sound relationships to highlight, we need to be constantly observant of children's needs and be flexible in our teaching. For example, word endings, especially *-ing*, are often needed early in writing and should be taught as the need arises. It will also be necessary to do repeated demonstrations, individually and in small groups.

Demonstrations of how we are teaching phonics need to occur with parents, too. For parents to understand the meaningful teaching of phonics, we need to educate them about the current research and how we are applying it to the classroom. When parents see that phonics is still being taught and are shown the how and why, they are very supportive. ■

Steven A. Stahl _____

# Saying the "p" word: Nine guidelines for exemplary phonics instruction

*Stahl is an associate professor at the University of Georgia in Athens, Georgia. He has written widely in the area of beginning reading instruction.*

Phonics, like beauty, is in the eye of the beholder. For many people, "phonics" implies stacks of worksheets, with bored children mindlessly filling in the blanks. For some people, "phonics" implies children barking at print, often in unison, meaningless strings of letter sounds to be blended into words. For some people, "phonics" implies lists of skills that must be mastered, each with its own criterion-referenced test, which must be passed or the teacher is "in for it." For some people, "phonics" somehow contrasts with "meaning," implying that concentrating on phonics means that one must ignore the meaning of the text. For others, "phonics" is the solution to the reading problem, as Flesch (1955) argued and others have concurred (see Republican Party National Steering Committee, 1990), that if we just teach children the sounds of the letters, all else will fall into place.

Because "phonics" can be so many things, some people treat it as a dirty word, others as the salvation of reading. It is neither. With these strong feelings, though, extreme views have been allowed to predominate, seemingly forcing out any middle position that allows for the importance of systematic attention to decoding in the context of a program stressing comprehension and interpretation of quality literature and expository text. The truth is that some attention to the relationships between spelling patterns and their pronunciations is characteristic of all types of reading programs, including whole language. As Newman and Church (1990) explain:

> No one can read without taking into account the graphophonemic cues of written language. As readers all of us use information about the way words are written to help us make sense of what we're reading.... Whole language teachers do teach phonics but not as something separate from actual reading and writing.... Readers use graphophonic cues; whole language teachers help students orchestrate their use for reading and writing. (p. 20-21)

"Phonics" merely refers to various approaches designed to teach children about the orthographic code of the language and the relationships of spelling patterns to sound patterns. These approaches can range from direct instruction approaches through instruction that is embedded in the reading of literature. There is no requirement that phonics instruction use worksheets, that it involve having children bark at print, that it be taught as a set of discrete skills mastered in isolation, or that it preclude paying attention to the meaning of texts.

In this article, I want to discuss some principles about what effective phonics instruction should contain and describe some successful programs that meet these criteria.

## Why teach phonics at all?

The reading field has been racked by vociferous debates about the importance of teaching phonics, when it is to be taught, and how it is to be taught. The interested reader can get a flavor of this debate by reviewing such sources as Adams (1990), Chall (1983a, 1989), Carbo (1988), and so on. To rehash these arguments would not be useful.

The fact is that all students, regardless of the type of instruction they receive, learn about letter-sound correspondences as part of learning to read. There are a number of models of children's initial word learning showing similar stages of development (e.g., Chall, 1983b; Frith, 1985; Lomax & McGee, 1987; McCormick & Mason, 1986). Frith, for example, suggests that children go through

three stages as they learn about words. The first stage is *logographic* in which words are learned as whole units, sometimes embedded in a logo, such as a stop sign. This is followed by an *alphabetic* stage, in which use children use individual letters and sounds to identify words. The last stage is *orthographic* in which

*Some attention to the relationships between spelling patterns and their pronunciations is characteristic of all types of reading programs, including whole language.*

children begin to see patterns in words, and use these patterns to identify words without sounding them out. One can see children go through these stages and begin to see words orthographically by the end of the first grade. Following the orthographic stage children grow in their ability to recognize words automatically, without having to think consciously about word structure or spelling patterns.

These stages in the development of word recognition take place while children are learning about how print functions (what a written "word" is, directionality, punctuation, etc.), that it can signify meanings, about the nature of stories, and all of the other learnings that go on in emergent literacy (see Teale, 1987). Learning about words goes hand in hand with other learnings about reading and writing.

*Letter-sound instruction makes no sense to a child who does not have an overall conception of what reading is about.*

All children appear to go through these stages on their way to becoming successful readers. Some will learn to decode on their own, without any instruction. Others will need some degree of instruction, ranging from some pointing out of common spelling patterns to intense and systematic instruction to help them through the alphabetic and orthographic stages. I want to outline some components of what exemplary instruction might look like. These components could be found in classrooms based on the shared reading of literature, as in a whole language philosophy, or in classrooms in which the basal reader is used as the core text.

### Exemplary phonics instruction...

1. *Builds on a child's rich concepts about how print functions.* The major source of the debates on phonics is whether one should go from part to whole (begin by teaching letters and sounds and blend those into words) or from whole to part (begin with words and analyze those into letters). Actually, there should

be no debate. Letter-sound instruction makes no sense to a child who does not have an overall conception of what reading is about, how print functions, what stories are, and so on, so it must build on a child's concept of the whole process of reading.

A good analogy is baseball. For a person learning to play baseball, batting practice is an important part of learning how to play the game. However, imagine a person who has never seen a baseball game. Making that person do nothing but batting practice may lead to the misconception that baseball is about standing at the plate and repeatedly swinging at the ball. That person would miss the purpose of baseball and would think it a boring way to spend an afternoon.

Adams (1990) points out that children from homes that are successful in preparing children for literacy have a rich idea of what "reading" is before they get to school. They are read to, play with letters on the refrigerator door, discuss print with their parents, and so on. Other children may have had only minimal or no exposure to print prior to school. The differences may add up to 1,000 hours or more of exposure to print.

For the child who has had that 1,000 hours or more, phonics instruction is grounded in his or her experiences with words. Such a child may not need extensive phonics instruction. Good phonics instruction should help make sense of patterns noticed within words. Just "mentioning" the patterns might suffice. However, for the child with little or no exposure, phonics instruction would be an abstract and artificial task until the child has additional meaningful encounters with print.

To develop this base of experience with reading, one might begin reading in kindergarten with activities such as sharing books with children, writing down their dictated stories, and engaging them in authentic reading and writing tasks. Predictable books work especially well for beginning word recognition (Bridge, Winograd, & Haley, 1983). Stahl and Miller (1989) found that whole language programs appeared to work effectively in kindergarten. Their effectiveness, however, diminished in first grade, where more structured, code-emphasis approaches seemed to produce better results. In short, children benefited from the experiences with reading that a whole language program gives early on, but, once they had that exposure, they benefit from more systematic study.

2. *Builds on a foundation of phonemic awareness.* Phonemic awareness is not phonics. Phonemic awareness is awareness of sounds in *spoken* words; phonics is the relation between letters and sounds in *written* words. Phonemic awareness is an important precursor to success in reading. One study (Juel, 1988) found that children who were in the bottom fourth of their group in phonemic awareness in first grade remained in the bottom fourth of their class in reading four years later.

An example is Heather, a child I saw in our clinic. As part of an overall reading assessment, I gave Heather a task involving removing a phoneme from a spoken word. For example, I had Heather say *meat* and then repeat it without saying the /m/ sound (*eat*). When Heather said *chicken* after some hesitation, I was taken aback. When I had her say *coat* with the /k/ sound, she said *jacket.* Looking over the tasks we did together, it appeared that she viewed words only in terms of their meaning. For her, a little less than *meat* was *chicken,* a little less than *coat* was *jacket.*

For most communication, focusing on meaning is necessary. But for learning to read, especially learning about sound-symbol relationships, it is desirable to view words in terms of the sounds they contain. Only by understanding that spoken words contain phonemes can one learn the relationships between letters and sounds. The alternative is learning each word as a logograph, as in Chinese. This is possible, up to a certain limit, but does not use the alphabetic nature of our language to its best advantage.

Heather was a bright child, and this was her only difficulty, but she was having specific difficulties learning to decode. Other children like Heather, or children with more complex difficulties, are going to have similar problems. We worked for a short period of time on teaching her to reflect on sounds in spoken words, and, with about 6 weeks of instruction, she took off and became an excellent reader. The moral is that phonemic awareness is easily taught, but absence of it leads to reading difficulties.

3. *Is clear and direct.* Good teachers explain what they mean very clearly. Yet, some

phonics instruction seems to be excessively ambiguous.

Some of this ambiguity comes from trying to solve the problem of pronouncing single phonemes. One cannot pronounce the sounds represented by many of the consonants in isolation. For example, the sound made by *b* cannot be spoken by itself, without adding a vowel (such as /buh/).

To avoid having the teacher add the vowel to the consonant sound, however, some basals have come up with some terribly circuitous routes. For example, a phonics lesson from a current basal program begins with a teacher presenting a picture of a key word, such as *bear*, pronouncing the key word and two or three words with a shared phonic element (such as *boat, ball*, and *bed*). The teacher is to point out that the sound at the beginning of each is spelled with a *B*. The teacher might then say some other words and ask if they, too, have the same sound. Next, written words are introduced and may be read by the whole class or by individuals. After this brief lesson, students might complete two worksheets, which both involve circling pictures of items that start with *b* and one which includes copying upper- and lowercase *b*'s.

In this lesson, (a) nowhere is the teacher supposed to attempt to say what sound the *b* is supposed to represent and (b) nowhere is the teacher directed to tell the children that these relationships have anything to do with reading words in text. For a child with little phonemic awareness, the instructions, which require that the child segment the initial phoneme from a word, would be very confusing. Children such as Heather view the word *bear* not as a combination of sounds or letters, but identical to its meaning. For that child, the question of what *bear* begins with does not make any sense, because it is seen as a whole meaning unit, not as a series of sounds that has a beginning and an end.

Some of this confusion could be alleviated if the teacher dealt with written words. A more direct approach is to show the word *bear*, in the context of a story or in isolation, and pointing out that it begins with the letter *b*, and that the letter *b* makes the /b/ sound. This approach goes right to the basic concept, that a letter in a word represents a particular phoneme, involving fewer extraneous concepts. Going the other direction, showing the letter *b* and then showing words such as *bear* that begin with that letter, would also be clear. Each of these should be followed having children practice reading *words* that contain the letter *b*, rather than pictures. Children learn to read by reading words, in stories or in lists. This can be done in small groups or with pairs of children reading with each other independently. Circling pictures, coloring, cutting, and pasting, and so on wastes a lot of time.

4. *Is integrated into a total reading program*. Phonics instruction, no matter how useful it is, should never dominate reading instruction. I know of no research to guide us in deciding how much time should be spent on decoding instruction, but my rule of thumb is that at least half of the time devoted to reading (and probably more) should be spent reading connected text—stories, poems, plays, trade books, and so on. No more than 25% of the time (and possibly less) should be spent on phonics instruction and practice.

Unfortunately, I have seen too many schools in which one day the members of the reading group do the green pages (the skills instruction), the next day they read the story, and the third day they do the blue pages. The result is that, on most days, children are not reading text. Certainly, in these classes, children are going to view "reading" as filling out workbook pages, since this is what they do most of the time. Instead, they should read some text daily, preferably a complete story, with phonics instruction integrated into the text reading.

In many basals, the patterns taught in the phonics lessons appear infrequently in the text, leading students to believe that phonics is somehow unrelated to the task of reading (Adams, 1990). What is taught should be directly usable in children's reading. Juel and Roper/Schneider (1985) found that children were better able to use their phonics knowledge, for both decoding and comprehension, when the texts they read contained a higher percentage of words that conformed to the patterns they were taught. It is best to teach elements that can be used with stories the children are going to read. Teachers using a basal might rearrange the phonics lessons so that a more appropriate element is taught with each story.

Teachers using trade books might choose elements from the books they plan to use, and either preteach them or integrate the instruction into the lesson. A good procedure for doing this is described by Trachtenburg (1990). She suggests beginning by reading a quality children's story (such as *Angus and the Cat*, cited in Trachtenburg, 1990), providing instruction in a high utility phonic element appearing in that story (short *a* in this case), and using that element to help read another book (such as *The Cat in the Hat* or *Who Took the Farmer's Hat?*). Trachtenburg (1990) provides a list of trade books that contain high percentages of common phonic elements.

Reading Recovery is another example of how phonics instruction can be integrated into a total reading program. Reading Recovery lessons differ depending on the child's needs, but a typical lesson begins with the rereading of a familiar book, followed by the taking of a "running record" on a book introduced the previous session (see Pinnell, Fried, & Estice, 1990, for details). The phonics instruction occurs in the middle of the lesson and could involve directed work in phonemic awareness, letter-sound correspondences using children's spelling or magnetic letters, or even lists of words. The teacher chooses a pattern with which the child had difficulty. The "phonics" instruction is a relatively small component of the total Reading Recovery program, but it is an important one.

5. *Focuses on reading words, not learning rules*. When competent adults read, they do not refer to a set of rules that they store in their heads. Instead, as Adams (1990) points out, they recognize new words by comparing them or spelling patterns within them to words they already know. When an unknown word such as *Minatory* is encountered, it is not read by figuring out whether the first syllable is open or closed. Instead most people that I have asked usually say the first syllable says /min/ as in *minute* or *miniature*, comparing it to a pattern in a word they already know how to pronounce. Effective decoders see words not in terms of phonics rules, but in terms of patterns of letters that are used to aid in identification.

Effective phonics instruction helps children do this, by first drawing their attention to the order of letters in words, forcing them to examine common patterns in English through sounding out words, and showing similarities between words. As an interim step, rules can be useful in helping children see patterns. Some rules, such as the silent *e* rule, point out common patterns in English. However, rules are not useful enough to be taught as absolutes. Clymer (1963) found that only 45% of the commonly taught phonics rules worked as much as 75% of the time.

A good guideline might be that rules might be pointed out, as a way of highlighting a particular spelling pattern, but children should not be asked to memorize or recite them. And, when rules are pointed out, they should be discussed as tentative, with exceptions given at the same time as conforming patterns. Finally, only rules with reasonable utility should be used. Teaching children that *ough* has six sounds is a waste of everyone's time.

6. *May include onsets and rimes*. An alternative to teaching rules is using onsets and rimes. Treiman (1985) has found that breaking down syllables into onsets (or the part of the syllable before the vowel) and rimes (the part from the vowel onward) is useful to describe how we process syllables in oral language. Teaching onsets and rimes may be useful in written language as well.

Adams (1990) points out that letter-sound correspondences are more stable when one looks at rimes than when letters are looked at in isolation. For example, *ea* taken alone is thought of as irregular. However, it is very regular in all rimes, except *-ead* (bead vs. bread), *-eaf* (sheaf vs. deaf), and *-ear* (hear vs. bear). Then rime *-ean*, for example, nearly always has the long *e* sound. Of the 286 phonograms that appear in primary grade texts, 95% of them were pronounced the same in every word in which they appeared (Adams, 1990).

In addition, nearly 500 words can be derived from the following 37 rimes:

| | | | | | |
|---|---|---|---|---|---|
| -ack | -ain | -ake | -ale | -all | -ame |
| -an | -ank | -ap | -ash | -at | -ate |
| -aw | -ay | -eat | -ell | -est | -ice |
| -ick | -ide | -ight | -ill | -in | -ine |
| -ing | -ink | -ip | -ir | -ock | -oke |
| -op | -or | -ore | -uck | -ug | -ump |
| -unk | | | | | |

Rime-based instruction is used in a number of successful reading programs. In one such program, children are taught to compare an unknown word to already known words and to use context to confirm their predictions (Gaskins et al., 1988). For example, when encountering *wheat* in a sentence, such as *The little red hen gathered the wheat*, a student might be taught to compare it to *meat* and say "If m-e-a-t is *meat* then this is *wheat*." The student would then cross-check the pronunciation by seeing if *wheat* made sense in the sentence. This approach is comprehension oriented in that students are focused on the comprehension of sentences and stories, but it does teach decoding effectively (see also Cunningham, 1991).

7. *May include invented spelling practice*. It has been suggested that when children work out their invented spellings, they are learning phonic principles, but learning them "naturally." For this reason, many whole language advocates suggest that practice in writing with invented spelling might be a good substitute for direct phonics instruction. Practice with invented spelling does improve children's awareness of phonemes, which, as discussed earlier, is an important precursor to learning to decode.

However, there is very little research on the effects of invented spelling. That research is positive, but I know of only one study that directly addresses the question. Clarke (1989) found that children who were encouraged to invent spelling and given additional time for writing journals were significantly better at decoding and comprehension than children in a traditional spelling program. However, the classes she studied used a synthetic phonics program as their core reading program. These results may not transfer to a whole language program or even to a more eclectic basal program. An evaluation of the Writing-to-Read program, a computer-based program incorporating writing, found that it had little effect on children's reading abilities (Slavin, 1991).

We need not wait for the research needed to evaluate the use of invented spelling. Writing stories and journal entries using invented spelling does not seem to hurt one's reading or spelling abilities and may help them, and it certainly improves children's writing.

8. *Develops independent word recognition strategies, focusing attention on the internal structure of words*. The object of phonics instruction is to get children to notice orthographic patterns in words and to use those patterns to recognize words. Effective strategies,

whether they involve having a child sound a word out letter by letter, find a word that shares the same rime as an unknown word, or spell out the word through invented or practiced spelling, all force the child to look closely at patterns in words. It is through the learning of these patterns that children learn to recognize words efficiently.

Good phonics instruction should help children through the stages described earlier as quickly as possible. Beginning with bookhandling experiences, story book reading and "Big Books," and other features of a whole language kindergarten support children at the logographic stage. Frith (1985) suggests that writing and spelling may aid in the development of alphabetic knowledge. This can be built upon with some direct instruction of letters and sounds, and showing students how to use that knowledge to unlock words in text. Sounding words out also forces children to examine the internal structure of words, as does rime-based instruction. These can help children make the transition to the orthographic stage. In the next stage, the child develops automatic word recognition skills, or the ability to recognize words without conscious attention.

---

*The purpose of phonics instruction is not that children learn to sound out words.*

---

9. *Develops automatic word recognition skills so that students can devote their attention to comprehension, not words.* The purpose of phonics instruction is *not* that children learn to sound out words. The purpose is that they learn to recognize words, quickly and automatically, so that they can turn their attention to comprehension of the text. If children are devoting too much energy sounding out words, they will not be able to direct enough of their attention to comprehension (Samuels, 1988).

We know that children develop automatic word recognition skills through practicing reading words. We know that reading words in context does improve children's recognition of words, an improvement which transfers to improved comprehension. There is some question about whether reading words in isolation necessarily results in improved comprehension. Fleisher, Jenkins, and Pany (1979-1980) found that increasing word recognition speed in isolation did not result in improved comprehension; Blanchard (1981) found that it did. Either way, there is ample evidence that practice reading words in text, either repeated readings of the same text (Samuels, 1988) or just reading of connected text in general (Taylor & Nosbush, 1983), improves children's comprehension.

Good phonics instruction is also over relatively quickly. Anderson, Hiebert, Wilkinson, and Scott (1985) recommends that phonics instruction be completed by the end of the second grade. This may even be too long. Stretching phonics instruction out too long, or spending time on teaching the arcane aspects of phonics—the schwa, the silent *k*, assigning accent to polysyllabic words—is at best a waste of time. Once a child begins to use orthographic patterns in recognizing words and recognizes words at an easy, fluent pace, it is time to move away from phonics instruction and to spend even more time reading and writing text.

## The "politics" of phonics

Given that all children do need to learn about the relationships between spelling patterns and pronunciations on route to becoming a successful reader, why all the fuss about phonics?

Part of the reason is that there is confusion about what phonics instruction is. A teacher pointing out the "short *a*" words during the reading of a Big Book in a whole language classroom is doing something different from a teacher telling her class that the short sound of the letter *a* is /a/ and having them blend in unison 12 words that contain that sound, yet both might be effective phonics instruction. The differences are not only in practice but in philosophy.

In discussions on this issue, the philosophical differences seem to predominate.

These exaggerated differences often find people arguing that "phonics" proponents oppose the use of literature and writing in the primary grades, which is clearly false, or that "whole language" people oppose any sort of direct teaching, also clearly false. The truth is that there are commonalities that can be found in effective practices of widely differing philosophies, some of which are reflected in the nine guidelines discussed here.

In this article, I have proposed some characteristics of exemplary phonics instruction. Such instruction is very different from what I see in many classrooms. But because phonics is often taught badly is no reason to stop attempting to teach it well. Quality phonics instruction should be a part of a reading program, integrated and relevant to the reading and writing of actual texts, based on and building upon children's experiences with texts. Such phonics instruction can and should be built into all beginning reading programs.

## References

Adams, M.J. (1990). *Beginning to read: Thinking and learning about print.* Cambridge, MA: M.I.T. Press.

Anderson, R.C., Hiebert, E.F., Wilkinson, I.A.G., & Scott, J. (1985). *Becoming a nation of readers* . Champaign, IL: National Academy of Education and Center for the Study of Reading.

Blanchard, J.S. (1981). A comprehension strategy for disabled readers in the middle school. *Journal of Reading, 24,* 331-336.

Bridge, C.A., Winograd, P.N., & Haley, D. (1983). Using predictable materials vs. preprimers to teach beginning sight words. *The Reading Teacher, 36,* 884-891.

Carbo, M. (1988). Debunking the great phonics myth. *Phi Delta Kappan, 70,* 226-240.

Chall, J.S. (1983a). *Learning to read: The great debate* (revised, with a new foreword). New York, NY: McGraw-Hill.

Chall, J.S., (1983b). *Stages of reading development.* New York: McGraw-Hill.

Chall, J.S. (1989). Learning to read: The great debate twenty years later. A response to "Debunking the great phonics myth." *Phi Delta Kappan, 71,* 521-538.

Clarke, L.K. (1989). Encouraging invented spelling in first graders' writing: Effects on learning to spell and read. *Research in the Teaching of English, 22,* 281-309.

Clymer, T. (1963). The utility of phonic generalizations in the primary grades. *The Reading Teacher, 16,* 252-258.

Cunningham, P.M. (1991). *Phonics they use.* New York: HarperCollins.

Fleisher, L.S., Jenkins, J.R., & Pany, D. (1979-1980). Effects on poor readers' comprehension of training in rapid decoding. *Reading Research Quarterly, 15,* 30-48.

Flesch, R. (1955). *Why Johnny can't read.* New York: Harper & Row.

Frith, U. (1985). Beneath the surface of developmental dyslexia. In K.E. Patterson, K.C. Marshall, & M. Coltheart (Eds.), *Surface dyslexia: Neuropsychological and cognitive studies of phonological reading.* Hillsdale, NJ: Erlbaum.

Gaskins, I.W., Downer, M.A., Anderson, R.C., Cunningham, P.M., Gaskins, R.W., Schommer, M., & The Teachers of Benchmark School. (1988). A metacognitive approach to phonics: Using what you know to decode what you don't know. *Remedial and Special Education, 9,* 36-41.

Juel, C. (1988). Learning to read and write: A longitudinal study of fifty-four children from first through fourth grade. *Journal of Educational Psychology, 80,* 437-447.

Juel, C., & Roper/Schneider, D. (1985). The influence of basal readers on first grade reading. *Reading Research Quarterly, 20,* 134-152.

Lomax, R.G., & McGee, L.M. (1987). Young children's concepts about print and reading: Toward a model of reading acquisition. *Reading Research Quarterly, 22,* 237-256.

McCormick, C.E., & Mason, J.M. (1986). Intervention procedures for increasing preschool children's interest in and knowledge about reading. In W.H. Teale & E. Sulzby (Eds.), *Emergent literacy: Writing and reading* (pp. 90-115). Norwood, NJ: Ablex.

Newman, J.M., & Church, S.M. (1990). Commentary: Myths of whole language. *The Reading Teacher, 44,* 20-27.

Pinnell, G.S., Fried, M.D., & Estice, R.M. (1990). Reading Recovery: Learning how to make a difference. *The Reading Teacher, 43,* 282-295.

Republican Party National Steering Committee. (1990). *Position paper on teaching children to read.* Washington, DC: Author.

Samuels, S.J. (1988). Decoding and automaticity: Helping poor readers become automatic at word recognition. *The Reading Teacher, 41,* 756-760.

Slavin, R.E. (1991). Reading effects of IBM's "Writing to Read" program: A review of evaluations. *Educational Evaluation and Policy Analysis, 13,* 1-11.

Stahl, S.A., & Miller, P.D. (1989). Whole language and language experience approaches for beginning reading: A quantitative research synthesis. *Review of Educational Research, 59,* 87-116.

Taylor, B.M., & Nosbush, L. (1983). Oral reading for meaning: A tecnhique for improving word identification skills. *The Reading Teacher, 37,* 234-237.

Teale, W.H. (1987). Emergent literacy: Reading and writing development in early childhood. In J.E. Readence & R.S. Baldwin (Ed.), *Research in literacy: Merging perspectives, Thirty-sixth yearbook of the National Reading Conference* (pp. 45-74). Rochester, NY: National Reading Conference.

Trachtenburg, P. (1990). Using children's literature to enhance phonics instruction. *The Reading Teacher, 43,* 648-653.

Treiman, R. (1985). Onsets and rimes as units of spoken syllables: Evidence from children. *Journal of Experimental Child Psychology, 39,* 161-181.

James Flood
Diane Lapp, Sharon Flood, Greta Nagel

# Am I allowed to group? Using flexible patterns for effective instruction

*At San Diego State University, James Flood and Lapp are professors, Sharon Flood is an instructor, and Nagel is a doctoral student. All four work closely with classroom teachers throughout San Diego County, California.*

Classroom reading instruction in the U.S. has been characterized by "ability groups"—instructional groups consisting of children sorted out by their teachers' assessments of their reading achievement—since World War I (Barr, 1989). However, a great deal of research conducted during the past two decades has concluded that ability grouping can create serious problems for students that are social in nature, but cognitive in effect (Allington, 1980; Barr, 1989; Hiebert, 1983; Indrisano & Parratore, 1991). Consequently, recent state and national guidelines have advocated a movement away from ability grouping to an implementation of flexible grouping alternatives (California State Department of Education, 1987a).

Despite such explicit suggestions calling for the implementation of flexible grouping, many misinterpretations have arisen. For example, Lapp and Flood (1992) observed a prevailing misunderstanding among several teachers that "whole language" instruction necessitated "whole class" instruction. While some educators look at whole class groups as the single alternative to the "old" ability groups, others have espoused collaborative peer groups as the preferred alternative (Schell & Rouch, 1988). Still others cling to ability groups as the only effective way to teach reading. As recently as 1990, in a study of 100 teachers, Nagel, Flood, and Lapp found that 44% still perceived ability groups as "the best way to teach."

The purposes of this article are threefold: (a) an examination of historical perspectives and contemporary research on grouping, focusing specifically on research findings about ability grouping; (b) an investigation of the alternatives to ability grouping; and (c) a model of what flexible grouping patterns look like in the classroom.

## Historical perspectives and contemporary research

Various sorts of instructional groups have been considered good and effective at different times throughout the history of reading instruction. Multigrade classrooms gave way to school organizations with one grade per room. Students were often further grouped into levels of ability by classroom. Ability groups became the predominant means of arranging children within classrooms during World War I, along with the advent of IQ tests and achievement tests (Barr, 1989).

Groups that were good for organizing schools or classrooms were not necessarily good for the children, but opinions have varied over the years. In the 1940s, ability groups were seen as good for "slow" children, but bad for "bright" ones (Otto, 1950). Later, authorities declared ability groups to be necessary for "gifted children;" some educational leaders still promote this view (Feldhusen, 1990).

Ability groups have, in spite of any controversy, remained the primary grouping strategy through the 1980s. Studies of elementary ability groups have used a wide variety of methodological approaches and have produced mixed results (Barr, 1989), particularly in analyses that involve short-term observations. However, the research appears to support the notion that ability groups are negative for students in the low groups because the process of grouping in this way labels and sorts them into indelible hierarchies or "castes" (Allington, 1980). Starting in the first grade, students do not escape their placement; they receive differentiated treatment over the years that puts them further and further behind their peers (Hallinan, 1984; Shannon, 1985).

Some of the negative effects of ability grouping include the differences in the amount of silent reading time that children are allotted (Allington, 1980). Low group readers read more words out loud, they are expected to do more drill work in skill materials, they have less exposure to works of literature, and they do far less silent reading than children assigned to high groups (Cook-Gumperz, Simons, & Gumperz, 1981). Further, students in low groups are asked questions that do not expect them to use high levels of thinking (Shake & Allington, 1985).

Situations within low groups shape behavior in negative ways; the amount of teachers' controlling talk is much higher and their expectations for behavior are far lower than their expectations for high group children (Schell & Rouch, 1988). In addition, student attentiveness is less in lower groups (Allington, 1980). In studies focused upon first-grade students, the gaps between ability groups widen during the school years (Weinstein, 1976), because more teacher management and distractions interrupt low groups (Eder, 1981) and lower groups spend less time on meaning-related activities than on decoding words (Hiebert, 1983).

Despite the differences in instruction that occur for groups at various levels, there are also interesting similarities that Barr (1989) observes. For example, she found that both low and high groups read the same materials and participated in many of the same activities at different times throughout the school year. The pacing of specific lessons is not necessarily slower for lower groups; as a matter of fact, when low groups get to a story they may complete it faster than the group that read it several months before.

## Alternatives to ability grouping

If static ability groups are not necessarily wise practice, the alternatives need to be examined. Many teachers, aware of the negative research on ability grouping, often ask, "How can I instruct in heterogeneous groups when I know my students have vastly different needs?" For example, at the beginning of the first grade, teachers often have students who are unable to identify the entire alphabet or to read and write any words in the same classroom with students who are quite able to read and write "real" texts.

Teachers wonder how they can use whole group instruction to meet the needs of each student. They are right to wonder. The use of flexible grouping patterns can serve a wide variety of roles as alternatives to ability grouping.

## What are effective groups?

Effective groups are groups in which teachers use a variety of grouping patterns to enhance student learning. Many educators have suggested alternatives to ability grouping using a variety of grouping patterns. The patterns that are suggested include: working individually, working in cooperative groups, working in pairs or small groups to develop questions, meeting in small groups to read to each other, reading aloud to the teacher on an individualized basis, and listening as a whole group to a read-aloud piece of literature and working individually. (Au, 1991; California State Department of Education, 1987a, 1987b; Cunningham, Hall, & Defee, 1991).

The most appropriate grouping pattern for each instructional experience can only be determined by analyzing student strengths and needs and matching this information with the choices available to the teacher and student. There must be a successful interaction of three sets of variables to ensure student success: (a) choosing the most appropriate basis for grouping, (b) choosing the most effective format, and (c) choosing the most appropriate materials.

## Variables in using flexible grouping patterns

There are many ways to implement flexible grouping. Groups may vary in terms of why they are established and who they will contain, how large they will be, and what materials will be used, but they should always encourage interactions among students as well as between the teacher and students. Teachers can provide scaffolding (appropriate instructional assistance) in a variety of settings.

The chart in Figure 1 delineates three interactive sets of variables that play key roles in instructional decision making.

---

### Figure 1
### Flexible grouping variables

Possible bases for grouping learners

Skills development
Interest
Work habits
Prior knowledge (content)
Prior knowledge (strategies)
Task/activity
Social
Random
Students' choice

Possible formats for groups

| Composition: | Leadership: |
|---|---|
| Individuals | Teacher-led |
| Dyads | Student-led |
| Small groups (3-4) | Cooperative |
| Larger groups (7-10) | |
| Half-class | |
| Whole group | |

Possible materials for groups

Same material for all groups
Different levels of material with similar theme
Different themes within a topic
Different topics

---

*Bases for grouping*

The first category for consideration involves 9 bases for grouping:

(1) Sometimes certain students (including the whole class) have a need for direct instruction in a *skill* that relates to a particular lesson.

(2) Students who share the same *interest* may be placed together (or spread to serve as motivators within separate groups).

(3) The quality of their *work habits* may place students into heterogeneous groups, often because of the modeling provided by some students.

(4) Knowledge of *content* may put children in a group together (or have them spread as experts among several groups).

(5) Knowledge of *strategies* can put certain children in discussion or problem-solving groups because of the modeling they provide.

(6) The *task/activity* criterion may dictate that certain children work together because they succeed best through certain kinds of projects.

(7) *Social* reasons may help place leaders (or followers, talkers) in certain groups.

(8) Sometimes *random* selection techniques (such as numbering off and putting all of the "ones" in one group) are the most useful procedures.

(9) Finally, encouraging *student choice* may be the best basis for forming some types of learning groups.

*Formats for grouping*

The next group of variables includes possible formats for groups. Although teachers usually interact with students in all situations, they need not always be in directive positions. As indicated in the chart above, groups may vary by their dimensions and then also vary as to their types of leadership.

The six usual sizes of groups include: (1) *individuals,* (2) *dyads* (pairs), (3) *small* groups of 3 or 4, (4) *large* groups of from 7 to 10, (5) *half-class* groups of 15 or so, and (6) *whole* (total class) groups.

The three usual types of leadership include: (1) teacher-led, (2) student-led, and (3) cooperative groups in which the leadership responsibilities are shared among students or between teacher and students.

*Materials for grouping*

The other major category of variables involves the materials to be used by groups:

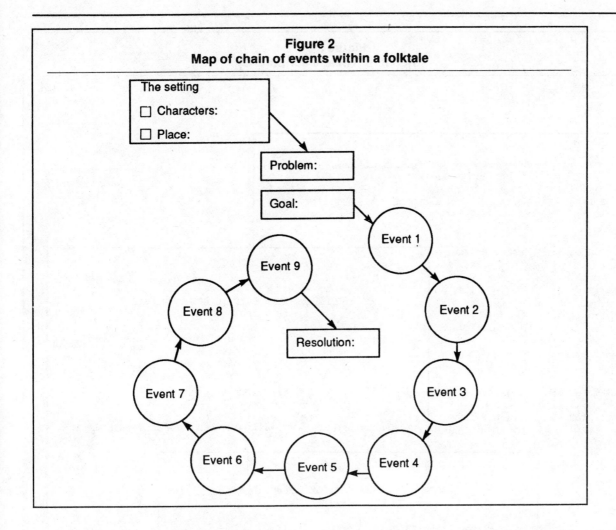

**Figure 2**
**Map of chain of events within a folktale**

(1) The *same material* for all groups is appropriate in many situations because identical material is often required of all students, as in reading core literature selections.

(2) *Different levels* (types) of similar material may be appropriate when students can learn the same concepts, but may benefit from the support of easier readability or from reading about the subject in their first language.

(3) *Different themes* within a topic may be appropriate, as in learning about the different states of someone's life, or analyzing the different characters of a story.

(4) Having materials that represent *different topics* may be appropriate when individual interests are taken into consideration.

## A model of using flexible grouping patterns

Flexible grouping practices can enhance the teaching and learning of reading. Through flexible grouping, each child's needs can be met and each child can develop an understanding of the relations among the language arts.

In the following lesson, in which children read *Why Mosquitoes Buzz in People's Ears,* five different grouping patterns were used and instruction in each of the language arts was emphasized at various stages of the lesson. This lesson was conducted with a heterogeneously grouped third-grade class in a magnet school in San Diego. The 30 children in the class represented a rich mix of ethnic, cultural and linguistic backgrounds and a wide range of reading and writing abilities.

As we explain the way we taught the lesson, we will also explain our decisions for selecting and forming the groups that we used. Many grouping patterns could have been used, and we do not want to suggest that our patterns are either the only ones or the best. The best pattern for you is the one that will best meet your needs and the individual needs of each of your students.

**Figure 3**
**Readers' Theatre scripts**

Readers' Theatre for <u>Poor Old Lady</u>
Author unknown

Chacters:      Narrator 1      Narrator 4      Narrator 7
               Narrator 2      Narrator 5      Narrator 8
               Narrator 3      Narrator 6

Narrator 1:    Poor old lady, sh
               I don't know why

Narrator 2:    Poor old lady, I

Narrator 3:    Poor old lady, sh
               It squirmed and

Narrator 1:    She swallowed the
               I don't know why

Narrator 2:    Poor  old lady, I

Narrator 4:    Poor old lady, sh
               How absurd! she

Readers' Theatre for
<u>Why Mosquitoes Buzz in People's Ears</u>
by Verna Aardema

Chacters:    Narrator 1   Iguana     Rabbit   Mother Owl
             Narrator 2   Mosquito   Monkey   King Lion
                          Python     Crow

Narrator 1:  One morning a mosquito saw an iguana drinking
             at a waterhole.  The mosquito said ...

Mosquito:    Iguana, you will never believe what I saw yesterday.

Readers' Theatre for <u>A Fly Went By</u>
by Mike McClintock

Chacters:    Narrator 1    Frog    Cow
             Narrator 2    Cat     Fox
             Fly           Dog     Man
             Boy           Pig     Sheep

Narrator 1:  I sat by the lake.  I looked at the sky, and
             as I looked, a fly went by.

Narrator 2:  A fly went by.  He said ...

Fly:         "Oh, dear!"

Narrator 2:  I saw him shake.  He shook with fear

Narrator 1:  And when I saw that fly go past, I asked him
             why he went so fast.  I asked him why he
             shook with fear.  I asked him why he said ...

Fly:         "Oh, dear!"

Step 1: Preparing. As we prepared the children for *Why Mosquitoes Buzz in People's Ears,* we explained to them that this is an African folktale in which events are explained as a chain—as one event occurs it causes another event to happen. Many different aspects of *Why Mosquitoes Buzz in People's Ears* and folktales could be selected for emphasis. For the sake of this lesson, we chose to emphasize an appreciation of the folktale focusing on the "event chain," which explains why mosquitoes buzz in people's ears. We stacked eight books in a row, slightly separating each from the ones next to it. Then we asked the children what would happen if we pushed the first book into the second book. We told them that we could tell the tale of "Why the Last Book Fell" by explaining a chain of events.

Step 2: Reading. We read the folktale aloud to the entire class and discussed the chain of events that led to an understanding of why mosquitoes buzz in people's ears.

Step 3: Explaining. We explained to the children the concept that stories have structures that advance the plot.

Step 4: Assisting/coaching. We assisted/coached the children in completing a map (Figure 2). This further developed their understanding of the structure of a chain of events within a folktale.

Step 5: Explaining. We explained to the children the idea that many folktales have a structure like this. We introduced the concept of Readers' Theatre (for a discussion of Readers' Theatre, see Ratliff, 1980), by explaining to them that they would have the opportunity to perform a Readers' Theatre of a "chain" folktale for the entire class. We showed them the three prepared scripts: *Why Mosquitoes Buzz in People's Ears, Poor Old Lady,* and *A Fly Went By.* The examples in Figure 3 show the first several lines of each of the Readers' Theatre scripts.

Step 6: Assisting. We let the children choose one of the three scripts and assigned them to that group. We asked them to prepare their role, which we assigned to them. We took their reading ability into consideration as we assigned the roles. We asked them to read the entire script together before they started practicing their own parts. We assisted them as they read the script, helping them to develop an overall comprehension of the story.

Step 7: Performing. When they were

ready, we asked the children to perform their Readers' Theatre for the entire class.

Step 8: Explaining. We explained to the children that they would be writing their own "chain" folktale. We prepared them for this writing activity by showing them more models of folktales that use this structure.

Step 9: Assisting/coaching. We assigned each child to a heterogeneous writing group of 7-10 students, ensuring that each group consisted of some proficient writers and some novice writers. We explained that each child would write and illustrate one page of the book. Although they were working on their own page, we assisted/coached them as they composed a whole "chain" folktale which explained a phenomenon. Together they composed, drafted, and revised their folktale before they began the final production (writing and illustrating) of their own page.

Step 10: Sharing. When all the pages were completed, the children bound their books into a whole to be read to the entire class. Samples from a completed tale by one group of third graders are presented in Figure 4. The two pages are the first and last pages of "How Roses Got Their Thorns." Eight children told how a weed and a rose were once great friends, but at a tea party with other roses and weeds, they all got to talking about who was the best rose or weed. The argument ended the party. They were all very angry and they fought with one another. The weeds beat the roses down. A fairy had to come to help them stand again, but they were full of holes. The fairy gave the roses "pointy things" to fill their holes and protect them so they would never have to be hurt again.

The chart in Figure 5 illustrates the effective use of flexible grouping that took place during this lesson.

## A final note

Although ability groups have been the preferred instructional format for the teaching of reading in the past, growing evidence has shown that the exclusive use of ability groups for language arts instruction can have a deleterious effect on student learning, particularly for those children assigned to the lowest groups. The alternative to this practice, as proposed here, is the use of flexible grouping patterns. Its practice is based on the theory

**Figure 4**
**Sample tale completed by third graders**

First Page of Story

Last Page of Story

## Figure 5
## Flexible grouping patterns used in the lesson
### *Why Mosquitoes Buzz in People's Ears*

| Step | Teacher activity | Student activity | Basis | Format | Materials |
|------|------------------|------------------|-------|--------|-----------|
| 1 | Preparing for reading | Listening, interacting | Task/activity | Whole group | Same text |
| 2 | Reading the folktale | Listening to text | Task/activity | Whole group | Same text |
| 3 | Explaining story mapping | Listening, questioning | Task/activity | Whole group | Same text |
| 4 | Assisting, coaching map work | Completing story map | Task/activity | Individual | Same text |
| 5 | Explaining Readers' Theatre | Listening | Task/activity | Whole group | Same text |
| 6 | Assisting in preparing Readers' Theatre | Practicing Readers' Theatre | Student choice | Larger groups (7-10) | Different scripts |
| 7 | Listening to performance | Performing Readers' Theatre | Student choice | Larger groups | Different scripts |
| 8 | Explaining how to write a folktale | Listening, interacting | Task/activity | Whole group | Different scripts |
| 9 | Assisting, coaching folktale writing | Writing folktales | Work habits/interest | Cooperative small group | Different (their own) scripts |
| 10 | Sharing | Sharing folktales | Work habits | Dyads | Different folktales |

that every instructional episode demands careful attention to matching students' needs with the most appropriate group experience (including group composition, grouping format, and instructional materials).

Because the use of alternative, flexible groups is relatively new, more research will need to be conducted to further clarify its relative strengths and weaknesses. It is evident that flexible grouping holds promise for the future in classrooms that will, more and more, serve widely diverse needs.

### References

Allington, R.L. (1980). Poor readers don't get to read much in reading groups. *Language Arts, 57,* 872-876.

Au, K. (1991, April). A special issue on organizing for instruction. *The Reading Teacher, 44,* 534.

Barr, R. (1989). The social organization of literacy instruction. In *Cognitive and social perspectives for literacy research and instruction: The thirty-eighth yearbook of The National Reading Conference.* Chicago: The National Reading Conference.

California State Department of Education. (1987a). *English-language arts framework for California public schools.* Sacramento, CA: Author.

California State Department of Education. (1987b). *English-language arts model curriculum guide, K-8.* Sacramento, CA: Author.

Cook-Gumperz, J., Simons, H., & Gumperz, J. (1981). *School/home ethnography report.* NIE Grant No. G-78-0082.

Cunningham, P., Hall, D., & Defee, M. (1991). Non-ability grouped, multilevel instruction: A year in a first grade classroom. *The Reading Teacher, 44,* 566-571.

Eder, D. (1981). Ability grouping as a self-fulfilling prophecy: A micro-analysis of teacher-student interaction. *Sociology of Education, 54,* 151-162.

Feldhusen, J. (1990, October). Issue: Should gifted students be educated outside the regular classroom? *ASCD Update, 32,* 7.

Hallinan, M. (1984). Summary and implications. In P.L. Peterson, L.C. Wilkinson, & M. Hallinan, (Eds.), *The social context of instruction: Group organization and group processes.* Orlando, FL: Academic Press.

Hiebert, E. (1983). An examination of ability grouping for reading instruction. *Reading Research Quarterly, 18,* 231-255.

Indrisano, R., & Parratore, J.R. (1991). Classroom contexts for literacy learning. In J. Flood, J. Jensen, D. Lapp, & J. Squire (Eds.), *Handbook of research on teaching the English language arts.* New York: Macmillan.

Lapp, D., & Flood, J. (1992). *Teaching reading to every child,* 3rd ed. New York: Macmillan.

Nagel, G., Flood, J., & Lapp, D. (1990, November). *California dreaming? *Literature-based English-language arts.* A presentation at the National Reading Conference, Miami, FL.

National Governors' Association. (1990). *Report on education.*

Otto, H.J. (1950). Elementary education III organization and administration. In W.S. Monroe (Ed.), *Encyclopedia of educational research* (pp. 376-388). New York: Macmillan.

Ratliff, G. (1980). *Readers' theatre: The theatrical approach to teaching literature.* Montclair, NJ: Montclair State College.

Schell, L.L., & Rouch, R.L. (1988). The low reading group: An instructional and social dilemma. *Journal of Reading Education, 14,* 18-23.

Shake, M., & Allington, R. (1985). Where do teachers' questions come from? *The Reading Teacher, 38,* 432-437.

Shannon, P. (1985). Reading instruction and social class. *Language Arts, 62,* 604-613.

Weinstein, R. (1976). Reading group membership in first grade: Teacher behaviors and pupil experience over time. *Journal of Educational Psychology, 68,* 103-116.

**Reprinted with permission of James Flood and the International Reading Association.**

## Voices

Here's an irony. Proponents of both whole language and phonics want children to read and write easily, accurately and joyfully. Yet language — terminology and labels — is driving many intelligent benevolent people apart. The ongoing (never-ending?) debate over the teaching of reading and writing has led to confrontations and extreme positions, instead of united action in behalf of our children. How and whether students read and write will have a major impact on all our futures. The goal is too important to be compromised by factionalism. We need to move from rival turf to common ground.

*Priscilla Vail*
**Common Ground: Whole Language and Phonics Working Together**

Camille L.Z. Blachowicz
John J. Lee

# Vocabulary development in the whole literacy classroom

*Blachowicz is Professor of Education at the National College of Education of National-Louis University in Evanston, Illinois. Lee is Assistant Superintendent for Instruction at Northbrook/ Glenview School District No. 30 in Northbrook, Illinois.*

Currently there is an active and productive dialogue about what constitutes appropriate literacy instruction (e.g., Aaron, Chall, Durkin, Goodman, & Strickland, 1990; Hoffman, 1989) which is resulting in attempts to structure more holistic literacy instructional approaches. These approaches are many and varied and include programs such as whole language programs, literature-based instruction, and content reading programs. At the same time, teachers and researchers are rethinking many of the components of traditional instruction, such as that of vocabulary instruction (Baumann & Kameenui, 1991; Beck & McKeown, 1991; Nagy & Herman, 1987) in the light of these new perspectives.

How to use the information generated by these dialogues to make sensible change while continuing to offer effective instruction is every teacher's challenge. One way to approach this task is to extract shared principles from different proposals for change and to test them in instruction. The first purpose of this article is to describe three characteristics of what will be termed whole literacy instruction, an umbrella term used for current holistic trends in literacy instruction. The second goal will be to relate these characteristics to current perspectives on vocabulary instruction. Included are examples designed by middle-grade teachers who were interested in using these ideas to shape classroom instruction.

## Defining whole literacy instruction

Though not exhaustive, there are three characteristics we believe to be essential to whole literacy instruction and relevant to making sense of current perspectives on vocabulary instruction.

1. *Time is spent on real reading*. Both early and more recent research emphasize that instructional time is often squandered on isolated drill, management, and other activities of questionable instructional effectiveness (Fisher et al., 1980). A significant trend in whole literacy instruction has been toward allocating more in-school time to the reading and writing of longer, natural texts. This is a

**Any instructional tasks surrounding authentic reading must engage learners in active, meaningful ways.**

general recommendation in the literature from educators whose theoretical perspectives might place them at different spots along the whole literacy continuum (Durkin, 1987; Smith, 1982) and is consistent with classroom initiatives calling for literature-based curricula.

2. *Learners are actively engaged with meaningful, language-rich tasks.* Any instructional tasks surrounding authentic reading must engage learners in active, meaningful ways. Whether the task is student initiated, teacher directed, or cooperatively defined, it is a task that makes sense to all involved and is one in which students are personally involved. This occurs when students read and respond, write and share, as active participants, rather

than passive receivers of information.

3. *Problem-solving strategies are utilized and developed.* Whole literacy instruction emphasizes the development of student problem-solving strategies and metacognition within the context of larger communicative tasks, such as predictive reading or process writing. Specific instruction is given when it is needed to accomplish the larger task. Further, the instruction is scaffolded to promote the development of the student's own problem-solving abilities. The teacher can help a student develop a personal question, provide clues or models for its solution, and help the student consolidate new processes or knowledge for future learning (Pearson & Gallagher, 1983).

A good metaphor for this characteristic is

**150**　　　　　　　　　　　　　　　　　　　　　　　　**Vocabulary development**

that provided by learning a sport, for example, tennis. A general ability to play tennis is best developed by game play, but it is sometimes helpful to have an expert help you locate a problem to take you aside and show you how to hit a more effective backhand, for example. However, such instruction is truly helpful only when the expert gets you right back into a game where you can try out new instruction integrated into a real game situation.

## Whole literacy and vocabulary development

These three characteristics—emphasizing real reading in classrooms, engaging learners in active ways in instruction, and developing independent problem-solving strategies—are hallmarks of current best practice in literacy instruction (Alvermann & Moore, 1991; Pearson & Fielding, 1991; Sulzby & Teale, 1991). Further, these same three assumptions are also critical to understanding current perspectives on vocabulary instruction.

*Wide reading is agreed to be an important contributor to general vocabulary development.*

Wide reading is agreed to be an important contributor to general vocabulary development by researchers and theorists who might disagree on the shape of appropriate school vocabulary instruction (cf. Baumann & Kameenui, 1991; Beck & McKeown, 1991; Nagy, 1988). Knowledge of a word is not an all-or-nothing proposition, like a light switch that is in an "off" or "on" position. A better metaphor is that of a light *dimmer* switch that gradually supplies an increasingly richer supply of light. Learners move from not knowing a word, to being somewhat acquainted with it, to a deeper, richer, more flexible word knowledge that they can use in many modalities of expression (Carey, 1978; Dale, 1965). Repeated encounters with a word, in oral and written language, provide experiences with and clues to the word's meaning that accrue over time and help build and change our mental structures for the word's meaning (Eller, Pappas, & Brown, 1988; Nagy, 1988; Vosniadou & Ortony, 1983).

Wide reading also helps readers develop and retain meaningful personal contexts for words (Whittelsea, 1987). For example, the word *wardrobe* becomes meaningful in *The Lion, the Witch and the Wardrobe* (Lewis, 1950) in a way it never could in its dictionary definition or in an isolated sentence. Specific events in the novel help the learner note that a wardrobe is a piece of furniture that can be located in a bedroom, that has a front door, and that is big enough to walk through; it is a term that is critical to the setting and action of this novel. The setting, problems, and actions of stories; the structure and content of exposition; and the imagery and affective appeal of literature all provide situational contexts to build and retain word knowledge.

The principles of effective vocabulary learning are also consistent with the remaining two assumptions of whole literacy instruction: active engagement with meaningful, language-rich tasks and the development of problem-solving strategies. Surveys of effective instruction conclude that vocabulary must be learned in meaningful contexts with wide reading, that the learner must be active in solving the problem of a word's meanings, and that meaning-focused use and manipulation of the word in many modalities give the learner ownership of the new terms (Beck, Perfetti, & McKeown, 1982; Mezynski, 1983; Nagy, 1988; Stahl & Fairbanks, 1986).

## The need for vocabulary instruction

Though it is clear that wide reading provides students with many rich and meaningful contexts for word learning, there is still a place for vocabulary instruction. Contextual reading does not automatically result in word learning (Jenkins, Stein, & Wysocki, 1984), nor does context always give clear clues to word meaning (Schatz & Baldwin, 1986). Small instructional interventions, such as priming students to notice new words, can increase the likelihood that students will learn from context (Elley, 1989; Jenkins et al., 1984). This may be of special importance for readers who begin school knowing fewer school-type words (Becker, 1977) and those who have limited networks of meaning for the words that are familiar to them (Graves & Slater, 1987).

Poorer readers know less about fewer words than do more able readers, and poor readers are frequently unmotivated or unable to do the amount of contextual reading required to extend their vocabularies. Further, McKeown (1985) found that disabled readers lagged behind able readers in the use of strategies that allow readers to gain new word meanings from context. Research suggests that judicious attention to vocabulary can build knowledge of specific vocabulary and can have a positive, though modest, impact on comprehension. Specifically, interventions that call for deeper, more meaningful uses of words result in learning that is more durable and that affects comprehension (Mezynski, 1983; Stahl & Fairbanks, 1986). This deeper processing can be achieved through discussion (Stahl & Vancil, 1986), by establishing rich semantic networks (Beck et al., 1982), through mapping of semantic features (Johnson, Toms-Bronowski, & Pittleman, 1982), and from examination of context and production of new uses (Gipe, 1979). Engagement can also be brought about by playful activities such as word collection contests (Beck et al., 1982) and dramatization (Duffelmeyer, 1980). All of these studies provide useful insights for generating guidelines for classroom instruction. But what should the shape of vocabulary instruction be like to concur with the research, the needs of the students, and the other assumptions of whole literacy instruction?

## Guidelines for classroom vocabulary instruction

Based on the preceding insights, the following guidelines for vocabulary instruction in the whole literacy classroom can be drawn:

1. *Choose all vocabulary for instruction from contextual reading to be done in the classroom, both literary and content material.* By focusing on words that students will encounter within the regular curriculum, the teacher integrates vocabulary instruction with wider areas of learning to emphasize word meanings as they relate to reading comprehension.

2. *Use maps or organizers of the reading material to help identify the words for study, in contrast to more traditional frequency-based selection processes.* If words are important in explaining, summarizing, using, or responding to the material, they are appropriate for consideration. For example, for the book *No One Is Going to Nashville* (Jukes, 1983) used in a fourth-grade classroom, the teacher chose the vocabulary from a map she constructed (see Figure 1).

3. *Plan prereading knowledge activation activities for the selection or chapter.* Where appropriate, use vocabulary in this process, being sure to highlight the focal terms by having the students, at the minimum, see and hear the words before reading (Elley, 1989). For *No One Is Going to Nashville*, the teacher decided to focus on the concept *stepmother* (in this story the stepmother aids her stepchild). The teacher used a technique called "Connect-2" (Blachowicz, 1985) where the students made prereading predictive connections among the vocabulary words centered around *stepmother* (see Figure 2). This also set the purpose for reading which was to focus on finding out what the stepmother was like and to evaluate the students' predictions about how the words might be connected.

Alternatively, if the teacher felt many of the important words were familiar to her class, the teacher might have chosen to place the words on the board, pronounce them with the students, ask them to watch for the words as they read, and then discuss them after reading as needed.

4. *Involve vocabulary in postreading discussion.* If vocabulary is chosen properly, it is difficult *not* to use it in postreading discussion. The italicized words in Figure 1 naturally emerge in retellings, question responses, or other comprehension activities. For example, when asked to summarize *No One Is Going to Nashville*, a fourth grader responded with the following:

> Sonia wanted to be a *veterinarian* and loved animals. Max was her *stray* dog and she wanted to keep Max. Her dad didn't like animals as much 'cuz they always *abused* him. He wanted to send Max to the dog *pound*. Her *stepmother* helped her dad make the *decision* to let her keep Max.

As is frequently the case when words are chosen to reflect the story line in narratives or key concepts in expository text, students must use them when responding after reading.

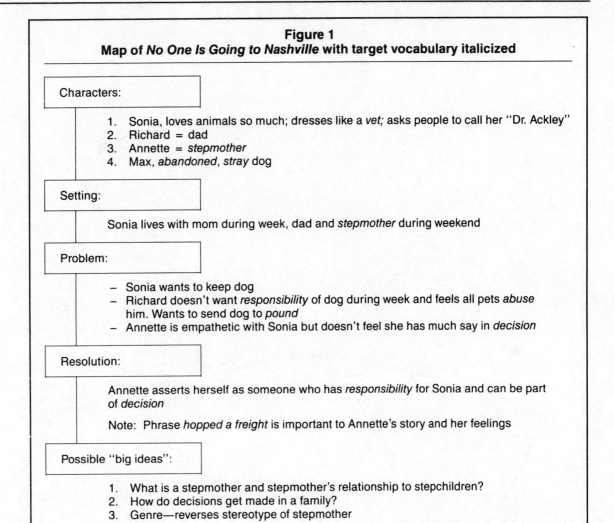

**Figure 1**
**Map of *No One Is Going to Nashville* with target vocabulary italicized**

**Characters:**

1. Sonia, loves animals so much; dresses like a *vet;* asks people to call her "Dr. Ackley"
2. Richard = dad
3. Annette = *stepmother*
4. Max, *abandoned, stray* dog

**Setting:**

Sonia lives with mom during week, dad and *stepmother* during weekend

**Problem:**

– Sonia wants to keep dog
– Richard doesn't want *responsibility* of dog during week and feels all pets *abuse* him. Wants to send dog to *pound*
– Annette is empathetic with Sonia but doesn't feel she has much say in *decision*

**Resolution:**

Annette asserts herself as someone who has *responsibility* for Sonia and can be part of *decision*

Note: Phrase *hopped a freight* is important to Annette's story and her feelings

**Possible "big ideas":**

1. What is a stepmother and stepmother's relationship to stepchildren?
2. How do decisions get made in a family?
3. Genre—reverses stereotype of stepmother

Another teacher planned postreading questions using the vocabulary. She asked: "Who was the *stray*? Why wouldn't Sonia want Max to go to the *pound*? Would Sonia be a good *vet*?" In asking students to answer specific questions using these words, she could assess their knowledge of the words, ask them to go back to the text to gather clues, or provide more direct instruction.

5. *Use contextual reinspection and semantic manipulation for words that are still unclear after reading and discussion.* Research has suggested that most vocabulary instruction occurs before reading, with little attention to vocabulary after reading (Blachowicz, 1986). Since whole literacy classrooms focus on developing *students'* problem-solving abilities, it is necessary that postreading time be allocated to help students locate information to flesh out their knowledge of words and experiment with using words in situations where they receive feedback on their attempts.

Many ways of further analyzing the vocabulary are possible. For example, the teacher who did the Connect-2 chart returned to the words *stray, pound,* and *vet* after reading. She asked the students if they knew what the words meant and had them locate and read text sections which gave clues to their meanings. For the word *pound,* the students located the following sentences in the text and extracted some information:

Richard wanted to send Max to the pound.
(*pound* is a place)

"We'll keep the dog as long as the pound would..."
(*pound* keeps animals)

Richard called the pound. They only kept dogs 5 days.
(*pound* only keeps animals 5 days)

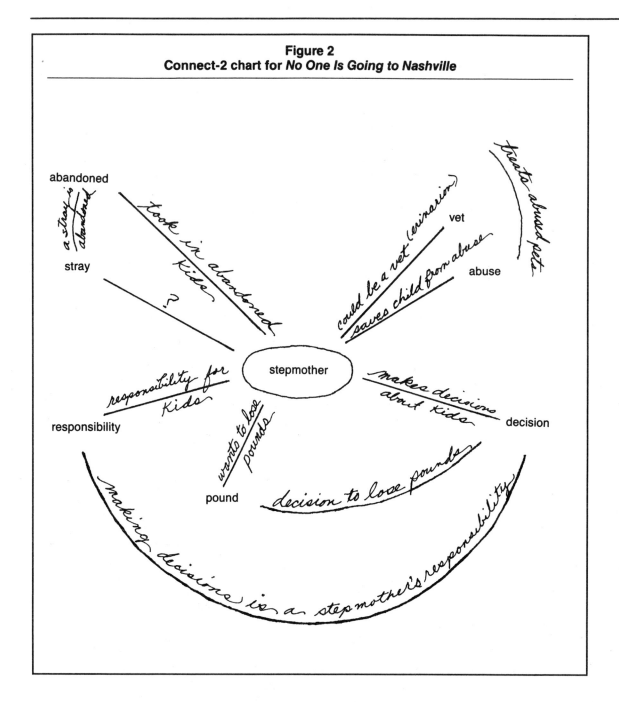

**Figure 2**
**Connect-2 chart for *No One Is Going to Nashville***

From these examples, the teacher had the students conclude that the pound is a place that keeps unwanted animals but only for a limited time. They then discussed why this was so distressful to Sonia.

Alternatively, the teacher could pose, or have students pose, a series of questions that would have the readers respond on the basis of their understanding of the semantic features of the word. For example, a teacher might ask, "Does a pound need walls? Explain. Would a dog want to go to the pound? Explain."

6. *Use vocabulary in an integrated way.* By this point in the lesson, the readers would have seen, heard, read, and used the vocabulary in many ways. If needed, further response activities could also require use of the words in retelling, response, artistic, dramatic, or aesthetic ways. Because the selection integrates what would otherwise be a somewhat unrelated set of words, a teacher might let the use of the words emerge in response activities. For example, one teacher's group dramatized the selection. Some of the

vocabulary was utilized in the character descriptions; other vocabulary emerged in dialogue, such as when Richard, the father, explains: "Those animals all *abuse* me. One bit my foot. The other tore up my best slippers. They know I am afraid of them and they take advantage of me, especially that *stray*, Max."

Another teacher had students do the illustrations to the book in their own style, writing descriptive phrases labeling each. A third teacher had students rewrite the ending when the *decision* was made in a different way. In each of these extensions, words were used in new, student-created contexts, all of which were related to the selection.

## A final word

Teachers employing appropriate vocabulary instructional techniques select words from contextual reading situations and involve the students in some or all of the steps in problem solving. They require that the students activate what they know about the vocabulary; make predictions about how words will be used; gather data; and later reformulate, refine, or clarify what they know about a term. In some instances, this process is modeled by the teacher; in other instances, the teacher provides explicit instruction in the process. Providing readers broad, rich experiences with words within a framework of contextual reading, discussion, and response is the goal of vocabulary instruction in a whole literacy classroom.

**References**

Aaron, I.E., Chall, J.S., Durkin, D., Goodman, K., & Strickland, D.S. (1990). The past, present, and future of literacy education: Comments from a panel of distinguished educators, Parts I and II. *The Reading Teacher, 43,* 302-311, 370-380.

Alvermann, D.E., & Moore, D.W. (1991). Secondary school reading. In R. Barr, M. Kamil, P. Mosenthal, & P.D. Pearson (Eds.), *Handbook of reading research: Vol. II* (pp. 951-983). White Plains, NY: Longman.

Baumann, J.F., & Kameenui, E.J. (1991). Research on vocabulary instruction: Ode to Voltaire. In J. Flood, J.M. Jensen, D. Lapp, & J.R. Squire (Eds.), *Handbook on teaching the English language arts* (pp. 604-632). New York: Macmillan.

Beck, I., & McKeown, M. (1991). Conditions of vocabulary acquisition. In R. Barr, M. Kamil, P. Mosenthal, & P.D. Pearson (Eds.), *Handbook of reading research: Vol. II* (pp. 789-814). White Plains, NY: Longman.

Beck, I., Perfetti, C., & McKeown, M. (1982). Effects of long term vocabulary instruction on lexical access and reading comprehension. *Journal of Educational Psychology, 74,* 506-521.

Becker, W.C. (1977). Teaching reading and language to the disadvantaged—What we have learned from field research. *Harvard Educational Review, 47,* 518-543.

Blachowicz, C.L.Z. (1985). Vocabulary development and reading: From research to instruction. *The Reading Teacher, 38,* 876-881.

Blachowicz, C.L.Z. (1986). Making connections: Alternatives to the vocabulary notebook. *Journal of Reading, 29,* 643-649.

Carey, S. (1978). Semantic development: The state of the art. In E. Warner & L.R. Gleitman (Eds.), *Language acquisition: The state of the art* (pp. 345-489). Cambridge, England: Cambridge University Press.

Dale, E. (1965). Vocabulary measurement: Techniques and major findings. *Elementary English, 42,* 895-901, 948.

Duffelmeyer, F.A. (1980). The influence of experience-based vocabulary instruction on learning word meanings. *The Reading Teacher, 34,* 35-40.

Durkin, D. (1987). *Teaching young children to read* (3rd ed.). Boston: Allyn and Bacon.

Eller, R.G., Pappas, C.C., & Brown, E. (1988). The lexical development of kindergarteners: Learning from written context. *Journal of Reading Behavior, 20,* 5-24.

Elley, W.B. (1989). Vocabulary acquisition from listening to stories. *Reading Research Quarterly, 24,* 174-187.

Fisher, C., Berliner, D., Filby, N., Marliave, R., Cahen, L., & Dishaw, M. (1980). Teaching behaviors, academic learning time, and student achievement: An overview. In C. Denham & A. Lieberman (Eds.), *Time to learn.* Washington, DC: National Institute of Education.

Gipe, J. (1979). Investigating techniques for teaching new word meanings. *Reading Research Quarterly, 14,* 624-644.

Graves, M.F., & Slater, W.H. (April 1987). *The development of reading vocabularies of rural disadvantaged students, inner-city disadvantaged students, and middle-class suburban students.* Paper presented at the meeting of the American Educational Research Association, Washington, D.C.

Hoffman, J.V. (Ed.). (1989). Whole language [Special issue]. *Elementary School Journal, 90*(2).

Jenkins, J.R., Stein, M.L., & Wysocki, K. (1984). Learning vocabulary through reading. *American Educational Research Journal, 21,* 667-687.

Johnson, D., Toms-Bronowski, S., & Pittleman, S.D. (1982). *An investigation of the effectiveness of semantic mapping and semantic feature analysis with intermediate grade level students* (Program Rep. No. 83-3). Madison, WI: Wisconsin Center for Education Research, University of Wisconsin.

Jukes, M. (1983). *No one is going to Nashville.* New York: Knopf.

Lewis, C.S. (1950). *The lion, the witch and the wardrobe.* New York: Macmillan.

McKeown, M.G. (1985). The acquisition of word meaning from context by children of high and low ability. *Reading Research Quarterly, 20,* 482-496.

Mezynski, K. (1983). Issues concerning the acquisition of knowledge: Effects of vocabulary training on reading comprehension. *Review of Educational Research, 53,* 253-279.

Nagy, E. (1988). *Teaching vocabulary to improve reading comprehension.* Newark, DE: International Reading Association.

Nagy, W.E., & Herman, P. (1987). Breadth and depth of vocabulary knowledge: Implications for acquisition and instruction. In M. McKeown & M. Curtis (Eds.), *The nature of vocabulary acquisition* (pp. 19-36). Hillsdale, NJ: Erlbaum.

Pearson, P.D., & Fielding, L. (1991). Comprehension instruction. In R. Barr, M. Kamil, P. Mosenthal, & P.D.

Pearson (Eds.), *Handbook of reading research: Vol. II* (pp. 815-860). White Plains, NY: Longman.

Pearson, P.D., & Gallagher, M.C. (1983). The instruction of reading comprehension. *Contemporary Educational Psychology, 8,* 317-344.

Schatz, E.K., & Baldwin, R.S. (1986). Context clues are unreliable predictors of word meanings. *Reading Research Quarterly, 21,* 439-453.

Smith, F. (1982). *Understanding reading* (3rd ed.). New York: Holt, Rinehart & Winston.

Stahl, S., & Fairbanks, M. (1986). The effects of vocabulary instruction: A model-based meta-analysis. *Review of Educational Research, 56,* 72-110.

Stahl, S., & Vancil, S. (1986). Discussion is what makes semantic maps work in vocabulary instruction. *The Reading Teacher, 40,* 62-67.

Sulzby, E., & Teale, W. (1991). Emergent literacy. In R. Barr, M. Kamil, P. Mosenthal, & P.D. Pearson (Eds.), *Handbook of reading research: Vol. II* (pp. 727-758). White Plains, NY: Longman.

Vosniadou, S., & Ortony, A. (1983). The influence of analogy in children's acquisition of new information from text: An exploratory study. In J. Niles (Ed.), *Searches for meaning in reading/language processing and instruction* (pp. 27-39). Rochester, NY: National Reading Conference.

Whittelsea, B.W. (1987). Preservation of specific experience in the representation of general knowledge. *Journal of Experimental Psychology: Learning, Memory and Cognition, 13*(1), 3-17.

**Reprinted with permission of Camille L. Z. Blachowicz and the International Reading Association.**

## Voices

Becoming a whole language teacher is no easy journey. There is no blue-print, recipe, or formula for success. There are few shortcuts and no ready solutions, and each teacher's route is slightly different. There is no best class to take or classroom to visit to get all the answers. There is not even a commonly understood definition, for whole language is a philosophy, a way of thinking. Becoming a whole language teacher is more about learning than it is about teaching. It is more about asking questions than it is about finding answers. Most of all it is about making a profound philosophical shift in beliefs about learning and teaching. It is a highly personal, intellectual, and thoughtful endeavor.

*Regie Routman*
Invitations

**Reprinted with permission from Regie Routman: Invitations (Heinemann Educational Books, Portsmouth, NH, 1991).**

# The Arts and Whole Language

*"Schools that have adopted a whole language philosophy demonstrate an abundance of well-crafted art forms."*

BY MARYANN AND GARY MANNING

A Mozart violin sonata is playing softly in the classroom. Van Gogh, Picasso and Faith Ringgold prints are on the wall interspersed with students' art work. The poetic works of Shel Silverstein, Eloise Greenfield, Karla Kuskin, Myra Cohn Livingston and class members are also on display. A small group of students is viewing a video of "The Tales of Beatrix Potter" featuring dancers of the London Royal Ballet Company. In the hall outside the room, several students are creating a mime presentation for the spring festival.

You may have already decided that this is an alternative school for the fine arts.

***Drumsticks*** *and cymbals can be used to express some ideas.*

Wrong! It's a whole language classroom. The teacher's beliefs aren't just about reading and writing; they're reflected in the integrated curriculum. She knows that the arts help develop students' imagination and capacity to view the world through alternative means of expression. She believes that it's possible for students to experience a rich arts curriculum and, at the same time, engage in language learning.

Whole language teachers are joining teachers who have always emphasized the arts. These teachers believe that every student needs access to all of the arts because the arts enhance our humanity. They also believe that students should know their artistic heritage and learn to appreciate the diversity of cultural expression.

**Traditional forms.** The art forms used in whole language classrooms are the traditional ones: dance, drama, drawing, graphics, literature, music, painting, photography, poetry, pottery, sculpture and writing.

The manner in which the students experience the arts has changed considerably since we first taught many years ago. Instead of 45-minute periods devoted to painting or to writing a poem, students now experience the arts throughout the entire day. Students are immersed in the study of themes. As they acquire new knowledge, they express what they have learned. Instead of writing a report about Abraham Lincoln, they might reenact a scene from a Lincoln biography.

Maryann and Gary Manning are on the faculty of the School of Education, The University of Alabama at Birmingham, and are Teaching Editors of *Teaching K-8*.

***In many classrooms,*** *art projects provide a means to explore other curriculum areas.*

Whole language teachers know the interrelatedness between teaching and the arts. In *Writing: Teachers and Children at Work* (Heinemann, 1983), Donald Graves discusses writing and teaching. He explains that you can't separate the two. The teacher of writing understands the art of teaching and at the same time is a writer, showing students a writer in action.

It's difficult to imagine someone who is not a pianist, teaching a student to play the piano. Likewise, a teacher who is not a writer will meet with frustration and little success in teaching writing.

Whole language teachers know that all forms of expression are developmental. In drawing, students progress from making a few lines to drawing a rough rectangle and ultimately to creating an approximation of a house. As dancers practice, they improve their technique. Students become more fluent and expressive as they develop as writers.

The creative process is similar in all art forms. In writing, students go through the process of rehearsing, drafting, revising and ultimately publishing and celebrating. Teachers value each student's uniqueness and use anecdotes about artists to help each student develop his or her voice and personal style. Beatrix Potter's voice and style of writing, for instance, was uniquely hers. She created her illustrations and story of Peter Rabbit by using her life experiences at Hilltop Farm.

Since there are skills and techniques to be learned in each art form, art educators are voicing concern that these skills may not be taught in an integrated curriculum.

Beth McDavid, Elementary Director of the National Art Education Association,

teaches art at Tarrant Elementary School in Tarrant, Alabama. Beth is enthusiastic about what is happening in the whole language classrooms in her school, but she says, "Instruction in the arts should be used to facilitate and enrich the teaching of other subject matter. The arts must maintain their integrity in the curriculum and be taught for their own sake rather than serve exclusively as aids to instruction in other disciplines. The use of the arts as an instrument for the teaching of nonartistic content should in no way diminish the time or effort devoted to the teaching of each of the arts as distinct academic disciplines in their own right."

**Abundance of forms.** We appreciate Beth's concern. However, the whole language teachers we know do teach skills and techniques. When they integrate social studies, science and other content areas through thematic units, their students' skills in the arts develop as they create and express their new knowledge. In fact, the integrated

*"In fact, the integrated curriculum actually increases the teaching of the arts."*

***Not only*** *is this child learning to express herself through dance, but she's also developing technique while she learns.*

curriculum actually increases the teaching of the arts. Schools that have adopted a whole language philosophy demonstrate an abundance of well-crafted forms.

Borton Primary School, a whole language school in Tucson, Arizona, for example, bursts with an abundance of the arts. Principal Bob Wortman and his teachers are active participants with the students. The halls are alive with murals, sculptures and mosaics. There's a large collection of art prints classified by period and culture in the multipurpose room. Students can check out and take home collections of materials about

**"**Whole lan-
guage teachers
know the inter-
relatedness
between teaching
and the arts.**"**

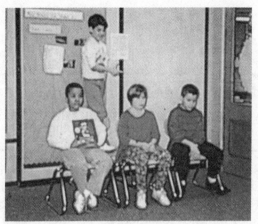

*Often, dramatizing* an oral or written report
increases the report's effectiveness.

composers and artists.

An individual teacher can have a powerful impact on his or her students. Our own
daughter, for instance, had a year-long, in-
depth art experience provided by her second
grade teacher. The arts were emphasized in
every theme and she provided instruction of
art skills and techniques. Marilee and her
classmates left second grade with a rich
appreciation for and understanding of the
arts. They also knew they were artists.

The arts, through the integrated curriculum, can be emphasized in numerous ways.
Here are some things you can do that will
help your students develop a greater understanding of the arts:

**Many art forms.** Too often, giving an oral
report and writing a report are the only
choices given to students. Drawing, painting, sculpting, photographing, dancing,
singing and creative writing are all alternatives students can use to express their ideas.
For instance, a student can communicate
knowledge about the movement of clouds
through many art forms, including dance,
poetry or painting.

**School galleries.** School corridors and
classrooms can be changed into galleries by
displaying art prints, poetry and art objects.
Prints found in museum stores and similar
places are affordable substitutes for original
works of art. Many teachers save art from
calendars and laminate them for long-term
use. When children's writing and art are
also displayed, the students join the ranks
of other artists.

**Field trips.** When students become artists,
field trips become visits to hallowed places.
Back in the classroom, teachers highlight
the artists whose work they viewed and talk
about the processes the artists went
through in creating their work.

**Invited artists.** Just as teachers invite published authors into the classroom to talk
about how they write, they can invite artists
from all fields to discuss the processes they
use. It's important for students to learn that
authors may produce many drafts of a book
before they reach a final draft. It's also
helpful for students to know that a painter
may proceed through several "drafts."
Moreover, children learn that writers and
painters may have an attic full of unfinished
or unpublished pieces.

**Artist studies.** Many students study the
lives and works of authors. Some teachers
also conduct studies of artists in all fields.
Children who listen to Mozart's early violin
sonatas also learn that he wrote sonatas
before he was ten years old.

**Picture books.** When teachers focus on
illustrations while reading picture books,
the books are often viewed as works of art.
Students become acquainted with authors
and illustrators such as Ashley Bryan, Anita
and Arnold Lobel, Leonard Everett Fisher
and Tomie de Paola.

**Art specialists.** The in-depth training and
expertise of specialists in art education play
an important role in ensuring that students
acquire the necessary skills, techniques and
development in the areas of art criticism,
art history and aesthetics. Beth McDavid
puts it this way: "When students have instruction in the arts and then participate in
integrated instruction, they bring the additional strength of knowledge in the arts. If
the arts are to enrich other disciplines, then
a strong knowledge base in the arts can only
strengthen the learning process."

In conclusion, when students in whole language classrooms share information about
content through various art forms, their
knowledge of the content is extended and
clarified. Through the integrated curriculum, art education will reach new
heights. ↓

**Reprinted with permission of the publisher, Early Years, Inc., Norwalk, CT 06854. From the March 1992
issue of** *Teaching! K-8.*

# Passion - Impaired

## by Ginny Stiles

I came across a phrase in an article I was reading the other day. The phrase was "passion-impaired," and the author used it to describe burned-out middle-aged men who prefer boredom because it is safer than passion and intensity.

The phrase has been circling around my brain ever since because it's the perfect adjective for something I've experienced but could never quite describe. It is a state of being I have seen in far too many of the children I deal with. And these are not high school or junior high school kids but 4- and 5-year olds.

Nothing is sadder than 5-year-olds who think they have already seen and done it all: Children who talk of nothing but Nintendo and Teenage Mutant Ninja Turtles but have no idea how a bird intricately builds its nest or where the sun goes when it isn't shining — and who aren't interested in knowing.

Of course, it isn't their fault that they are passion-impaired. Two-thirds of them come from stressed-out families that can barely get them to school in clean clothes. And I live in a nice rural area in Wisconsin, not the inner city. I can only imagine what inner-city teachers must see every day.

It's my job to find the passion, to open eyes and weave a web of intrigue and surprise. This has never taken more skill and energy than today. Indeed, some teachers themselves have be-

> **"It's my job to find the passion, to open eyes and weave a web of intrigue and surprise."**

come passion-impaired due to years of relentless failure to reach many students and the failure of families to support learning and schooling. They become that English teacher who has used the same blue-purple dittos for 30 years or that social studies teacher who assigns pages 415 through 420 the fourth week of every February.

So it is that passion-impaired adults sire passion-impaired offspring taught by passion-impaired teachers. Mediocrity conspires to perpetuate itself.

But the worst thing we can do is admit defeat and give in to the boring, non-creative approach to life. We must surround ourselves with other passionate people because passion is catching. We must keep trying to let students catch it from us. Children bred in front of the television have never felt the warmth of the earth against their backs on a star-lit August night, examined a locust under a magnifying glass, watched blue and red blend together as purple, or seen a kitten born. We mustn't give up. We must insist on a life lived — with passion.

*Ginny Stiles teaches kindergarten at Reek Elementary School, Lake Geneva, WI. Reprinted with permission.*

Photo by Deborah Sumner

Teachers must share a passion for life with their students.

# Sleeping Beauty, Sleeping Beauty, Sleeping Beauty, Etc.

Here is a story you have probably heard 100 times. It is a familiar old tale that happened perhaps 100 years ago.

Now, once upon a time, there was a king, Hedrund, and his queen, Huddern. As time passed, as many as 100 months, Hedrund and Huddern wished they had a child.

"What will we do?" they asked 100 times.

One day it was 100 degrees in the shade, and the queen, Huddern, was bathing in a pool 100 feet wide. (It was a very big pool.)

Suddenly 100 frogs appeared before the queen and told her that she would have a child.

"Oh, boy," said Queen Huddern. She told King Hedrund, but they had a daughter instead.

The king was so happy he clapped 100 times and planned a big party. He invited 100 friends and relatives. What a wonderful party it would be. He also invited 100 fairy women. When the king did this he had made a big, big mistake because there really were 101 fairy women. I can tell you for sure that the one fairy woman who was left out was very angry indeed. In fact, she was as angry as 100 barbarians. She was so angry that her temperature went up to 100 degrees.

At the party, 99 of the invited fairy women presented the very lovely and beautiful Princess Hurdned with their gifts.

All of a sudden the castle door flew open, and it felt like the wind was blowing 100 miles per hour. The old fairy woman who had not been invited, entered the castle.

Everyone froze in terror at the very sight of her horridness. She was more horrible than anything they had ever seen. She was even more horrible than 100 ugly warts.

The ugly old fairy woman told King Hedrund 100 times that he was a mean, old, nasty person. (That hurt his feelings.)

She also said, "Your beautiful, lovely, radiant daughter, Princess Hurdned, will prick her finger on a spinning wheel and drop dead." With that the old fairy woman spun around 100 times and fled the castle.

Upon hearing this news the king and queen were very concerned.

The 100th fairy woman still had to present her gift. She had 100 ideas on what gift would be best. Finally, she decided to help King Hedrund and Queen Huddern. The 100th fairy said, "Your daughter will not die, but she will sleep for 100 years."

Alas it happened, and the Princess Hurdned fell fast asleep, as did everyone in the realm. (Now there's a 100 dollar word.)

As time went on, 100 thorny rose bushes grew about the castle walls, and they grew 100 feet high, completely covering the castle. From time to time 100 different princes tried to free Princess Hurdned, but they were turned away or died in the rose thorns.

One day, the most dashing and handsome prince for 100 miles around appeared outside the castle. Oh, how handsome he was!

The roses were so enchanted by the prince, whose name was Dedhurn, that they opened a path for him.

He found the Princess Hurdned and was overwhelmed by her glorious beauty. She was more beautiful than 100 white swans, or 100 cupcakes, or 100 peanut butter sandwiches.

When Prince Dedhurn moved close enough, he gave the princess 100 kisses. Of course, she woke up immediately and was struck by how handsome the prince was and this made her shiver like 100 ice cubes and made her very happy. Everyone else in the realm woke up with the princess.

They all yawned 100 times and stretched 100 times. Even the dogs barked and wagged their tails 100 times. This made a lot of noise throughout the countryside (perhaps as loud as 100 decibels).

The handsome Prince Dedhurn and beautiful Princess Hurdned made plans for their wedding right away, and they told King Hedrund and Queen Huddern 100 times how happy they were.

The prince and princess were married, and as a gift they were showered with 100 balloons.

This truly is the end.

# The Mad Scientist

Easily thought up by:
Ha! Ha!
Susan Benjamin, Dick Tabor and Dave Bailey

Characters:
Narrator, Mad Scientist, Author, Illustrator, Editor, Publisher, Librarian, Book Tree

| | |
|---|---|
| **Narrator** | Once upon a time, in a scientific laboratory far, far away, there lived a mad scientist named Professor Shovel T. Digindirt. The professor had been working on a secret potion for years and years. |
| **Professor** | Ha, ha, ha! My secret potion is nearly complete. I, Professor Shovel T. Dingindirt, have discovered the secret formul for growing a book tree. I will be rich, rich, rich! |
| **Narrator** | Professor Digindirt goes to a giant plant pot in the center of his laboratory. |
| **Professor** | All I need to do is water this plant with my secret formula and poof! I'll have the world's first and only book tree! |
| **Narrator** | But wait Professor Digindirt, what is in your secret formula for growing a book tree? |
| **Professor** | I will only tell you the secret formula if you promise never to tell a soul. |
| **Narrator** | Well, kids, shall we keep the professor's secret? |
| **Kids** | Yes! |
| **Narrator** | All right Professor, we promise. |
| **Professor** | Okie-dokie, then here I go! The first item in my secret book tree potion is a writer — an author with a good idea, an idea for a wonderful story. |
| **Narrator** | Yes Professor. What is first, boys and girls? |
| **Kids** | An author! |
| **Professor** | Second — my secret book tree potion will need words — words that tell a story. |
| **Narrator** | Yes professor — and what comes next kids? |
| **Kids** | Words! |
| **Professor** | Third — my secret potion requires an illustrator an artist who will bring the story to life for all to see and enjoy. |

# and The Book Tree

| | |
|---|---|
| **Narrator** | And what is needed for the formula, kids? |
| **Kids** | An illustrator. |
| **Professor** | But in order to put all of the story ideas into neat and clean order, the formul needs an editor as well! |
| **Narrator** | What did the professor say we needed, kids? |
| **Kids** | An editor. |
| **Professor** | And don't forget the publisher, someone to print the story into a beautiful book to keep forever. |
| **Narrator** | Ah, yes.  A publisher.  What was that word, kids? |
| **Kids** | A publisher. |
| **Narrator** | But professor — where do all of those beautiful published books go? |
| **Professor** | What?  Have you never heard of a library?  A place to care for all of those beautiful books where kids like you can read and share adventures day by day! |
| **Narrator** | Where do we keep the books kids? |
| **Kids** | A library. |
| **Professor** | And now to try out my secret book tree potion. |
| **Narrator** | Hey, kids — let's help the professor.  Everybody count one, two, three — and say Presto! |
| | The professor puts the magic potion and a book tree grows up in the giant plant pot. |
| | The tree sings a special song about reading, and the narrator invites several children to come and select a book from its branches. |

# TEACHING
# WITH
# THEMES

## LEVEL: Pre-First

**September**
  All About Me
  Our School Community (Town, etc.)
  Transportation and Bus Safety

**October**
  Apples
  Night — Monsters (include feelings)
  Pumpkins — Halloween

**November**
  Quilts and Colors
  Native Americans
  Thanksgiving

**December**
  Fairy Tales
  Holiday Traditions/Beliefs

**January**
  Seasons — Calendar — Resolutions
  Bears
  Circus
  Oceans and Fish

**February**
  Space — Stars — Planets and much more!
  Careers
  Animals in Winter

**March**
  Exotic Animals
  Green Things
  Eggs — Rabbits
  Government

**April**
  Pets
  Environment
  Plants — Farms
  Nutrition — Food

**May**
  Dinosaurs
  Insects
  Neighbors Around the World
  Maps

**June**
  Birds
  Cartoons — Animation — Puppets
  Saying Good-bye

---

### EXTRA IDEAS
**Just For The Fun Of It!**

**Secret Circle Game** — Teacher or students print a secret message about someone in the class on a piece of paper. Pass paper around the circle of students until a special signal is given. Whoever has the secret gets to read it — with help if needed.

**Chalk the Sidewalk** — Use large sidewalk chalk to make drawings depicting thematic unit of the week. Inventive spelling labels are great, too.

**Presto-Chango Game** —Use hats from a story box. As the story is read, teacher says "presto-chango" every once in a while. When this happens, students pass their hat to the person sitting next to them.

---

Susan Benjamin

# INTEGRATING THE CURRICULUM THROUGH THEMES

**Sample Thematic Unit — Grades Pre-1. Integrated activities across the curriculum areas of art, science, math, literature, and social studies.**

## Theme — *NATIVE AMERICANS*

The Native American unit is best suited for use in the classroom during the fall. The basic aim of the unit is to create a viable, working knowledge of the life-style, culture and beliefs of the people embracing the culture today. Some activities to be included are:

### ART
• Construct an author study of the books by Paul Goble. Use the illustrations found in these books as a starting point for students to create their own artwork.
• Make clay pottery.

### SCIENCE
• Read aloud together the book entitled *Brother Eagle, Sister Sky*. Discuss the Native American love of the land and the belief that land can be cared for and passed on from one generation to the next but cannot be owned.
• Take a nature collection walk.

### MATH
• Play the Native American game of three cups with a stone under one. Mix them up and have students guess where the stone is.
• Graph types of homes — teepee, longhouse, hogan, etc., found in stories and research materials.

### SOCIAL STUDIES
• Read aloud *The Encounter* by Jane Yolen to the class. Discuss the way in which Native Americans might have looked at the explorers who first came to the shores of the Americas long ago.
• Visit the library and collect books which depict the different types of dwellings typical of Native American tribes of the past. Compare these with dwellings found on reservations today. Make dioramas of dwellings if desired.
• Study recipes from Native American tribes of your specific geographic area. Cook some of the foods for a class "tasting" party.
• Study the Native American game of lacrosse. Invite lacrosse players or coaches to visit the classroom to teach the basics of the game. Write to the National Lacrosse Foundation for books depicting the stories of animals and explaining how the game of lacrosse began.

### BIBLIOGRAPHY
*Long Failed Bear*, legends to read aloud — Natalia Belting
*Golden Book of Indian Stamps*, sign language, masks, lacrosse, etc. — Sonia Bleeker
*The Popcorn Book* — Tomie dePaola
*American Indian Reference Books for Children and Young Adults* — Barbara J. Kuipers
*Translator's Son* — Joseph Bruchac
*Children of the First People* — Dorothy Haegert

## Theme — *BEARS*
Time: Two Weeks

### ART
• Make construction paper teddy bears with movable arms and legs, using brass fasteners to attach appendages.
• Cut out magazine photos of bears and make collages.
• Make fuzzy bears with googly eyes out of brown pompoms from a craft store.
• Make construction paper bear hats for students to wear.
• Make a forest of bears created by the children from scraps of construction paper and cloth.

### SCIENCE
• View the Kodak Wildlife Video cassettes on polar and grizzly bears.
• Visit a zoo to observe bears first hand, or invite a bear expert to visit the classroom.
• Study the different kinds of bears and what they eat.

### MATH
• Make a graph of the different kinds of bears and allow students to vote for their favorites.
• Make a graph of the foods bears eat and allow children to vote for their favorite after tasting the foods.
• Use Teddy Grahams cookies, Berry Bears fruit bits,

Grahammy Bears cookies, etc. to sort, count, graph, eat and make fluff and cereal type designs.

## SOCIAL STUDIES/COOKING
• Hold a Teddy bear tea party where students bring in their favorite Teddy bears. Eat honey, jam, crackers, etc. Give award ribbons or necklaces to each bear and owner.

## BIBLIOGRAPHY
*Berenstein Bears Series* — Stan and Jan Berenstein
*Buzzy Bear Series* — Dorothy Marino
*Little Bear Series* — Else H. Minarik
*Little Bear Series* — Janice
*The Bashful Bear* — Earle Goodenow
*Walt Disney's Bear Country* — Jane Watson
*The Mighty Bears* — Robert McClurg
*The Giant Panda Book* — Anthony Hiss
*Brown Bear, Brown Bear* — Scholastic, Inc.

## Theme — *FAIRY TALES*
Time: Two Weeks

### ART
• Make and or collect costumes to act out favorite fairy tales. Video same to be taken home and watched.
• Build a dragon out of paper mache.
• Build castles out of blocks, legos, and old painted refrigerator boxes.
• Make puppets using old socks, bags, paper mache, etc., and create fairy tale puppet shows.
• Paint murals of favorite fairy tale stories.
• Do body tracings and turn them into favorite fairy tale characters.

### SCIENCE
• Study legends like the Loch Ness monster and Big Foot. Compare them to scientific findings.

### MATH
• Make graphs of fairy tales heroes, and villains and allow children to vote for their favorites on each.
• Allow children to interview teachers, staff and students in the school regarding their favorite fairytales, heroes, and villains. Publish results in paper form or on the loudspeaker.

### SOCIAL STUDIES/COOKING
• Make dragon stew after reading the book by the same name.
• Hold a dragon stew costume party — parents may come in costume as well.
• Hold a fairy tale costume parade day for the whole school.
• Make circles of construction paper with favorite fairy tale tiles and pictures on them to use as body parts for a giant dragon on the wall.
• Act out fairy tale stories with costumes and video same.

### BIBLIOGRAPHY
**Big Book** Series of Fairy Tales — *Cinderella, Sleeping Beauty, Alice in Wonderland, Snow White, Little Red Riding Hood, Hansel and Gretel.* Stoneway Books — PO Box 548, Southeaster, PA 19399, Ottenheimer Publishers, Inc.

## Theme — *READING AROUND THE WORLD*

The Reading Around the World unit combines the study of geography and cultural differences with literature. The unit begins with a letter sent home to parents enlisting their helping as reading partners for their youngsters. Parents as Reading Partners (PARP) originated from the New York State Education Department. This unit is very exciting to do as a whole school project. It was carried out by both the Marcellus and Skaneateles (New York) Elementary Schools in 1992.

### ACTIVITIES
• Each classroom selects a country to study during the Read Around the World theme. The students make a large flag from that country to hang by their classroom door, plus a "Welcome to _____" banner.
• The class uses a globe, maps, etc., to locate and study the geographical aspects of their country.
• The class is divided into cooperative learning groups in order to create projects (dioramas, costumes, travel posters, food, money, language, government, etc.) on their country.
• The class creates salt and flour maps of the country being studied.
• Students visit the library to select books to be read in class and at home with their parents. The reading may be documented on postcards made from Xerox copy machines. The postcards are hung around the flag mounted above the classroom door.

**Sample postcard**

| _____Class |
| --- |
| Book Title_____ |
| Author _____ |
| Student _____ |

- As a finale celebration, the classes may create a display for other classes to visit. Passports made from folded oaktag may be given to all students in the school. As they visit classroom displays, the students receive a special stamp from the "country" they have just visited. The passports might look like the diagram below.

| Read Around The World ⊕ Passport | Name _____ Birth Place _____ _____ Age _____ Class _____ |
|---|---|

*Street Rhymes Around the World* by Jane Yolen is a wonderful source of rhymes in English and other languages.

## Theme — A CHILD'S GARDEN OF VERSES

The Child's Garden of Verses unit comes from a whole school reading project done in the Marcellus Central School, Marcellus, N.Y. It involves parents and children in reading together with a special emphasis on poetry.

This unit is great fun and helps to create both a love of poetry and a basic knowledge of the germination process.

The unit begins with a letter sent home to parents from the school telling about the Parents as Reading Partners program.

Children create a huge construction paper flower for their classroom door, with a poem printed in the center. As children read books, poetry, etc., with a partner at home, they bring construction paper petals to school to hang around the flower on their classroom door. The petals look like the diagram below:

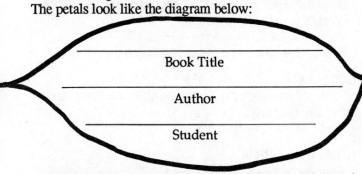

Some activities to be included in the Child's Garden of Verses theme are:

- Invite local poets, gardeners, college mascots (especially those shaped like vegetables and fruits) to come share their expertise with the class.
- Have a poet in residence for one week to work on poetry writing with classroom groups.
- Plan a garden party and have students and teachers wear their best clothes. Bring in a blanket to sit on and collect healthy snacks (raisins, juice, carrot sticks, etc.) for a party. Many grocery stores will donate items.
- Plant seeds in the classroom and conduct experiments based on the growing process.

## Theme — APPLES AND SEASONS

Time:  One or Two Weeks

### ART
- Apple people made of red construction paper with legs folded as if for a fan — made of green paper.
- Large construction paper tree with cut out apples on it for display — each apple having one student's picture on it.
- Apple people made of construction paper — each apple person representing a different career — e.g., doctor apple, teacher apple, etc.
- Apple trees made of construction paper with fluff for glue and red cinnamon candies for apples.

### SCIENCE
- Plant apple seeds and chart growth.
- Visit an apple farm and observe kinds of trees, varieties of apples, and cider making process.
- Discuss and study the role of honey bees in the growth of apple trees.

### MATH
- Cut up apples and estimate the number of seeds.  Count and graph same.
- Ask students to bring in different kinds of apples to graph, cut up and make into something good to eat.

### SOCIAL STUDIES
- Study the story of Johnny Appleseed and act out the story as a class play.  Video tape the play to send home with one child at a time.

### COOKING
- Apple cooking can be done every day if the students bring in lots of apples.  Applesauce, apple pie, apple fritters, muffins, cookies and cake are just a few ideas. Invite parents to help cook for a special apple day celebration. Everyone in the area of your room will want to do some taste testing.

**BIBLIOGRAPHY**
*Apple Tree* — Peter Parnell
*Johnny Appleseed* — Steven Kellogg
*One Apple Up On Top* — Dr. Seuss

These are just a beginning when it comes to apple books! You will find tons of your own for sure! *The Ten Apples Up On Top* book by Dr. Seuss lends itself beautifully to work on counting, one-to-one correspondence, etc. It is fund to make the book into a flannel board story.

## Theme — *NIGHT*

Time: One Week

### ART
• Night sky pictures with black paper and stars made of white paint or glue on tin foil, etc.
• Owl drawings or construction paper owls cut out and displayed on a tree on the wall.
• Monster under the bed costumes or murals made and or painted by the children.
• Murals of magazine photos depicting animals who come out at night.

### SCIENCE
• Invite a zoo keeper or veterinarian to visit and bring in an owl or other night animal for observation.
• Study about different night animals and allow students to work in pairs making posters and short reports on the animals for display.
• Study how the length of day and night change as the seasons change.

### MATH
• Make a graph of night animals and allow students to vote for their favorite. Compare columns, find the winner, etc.
• Use a box of Lucky Charms cereal in groups of three or four children. Give each group a pile of cereal to separate into sets (e.g., moons, stars, etc.), then graph the number of each item on a floor graph. Divide the items evenly with the group, then have an eating party.

### SOCIAL STUDIES/LITERATURE
• Read a series of night stories based on a monster theme or on a theme of night lore. Use the stories as a basis for discussion and art work on dreams, fears of the dark, etc.

### BIBLIOGRAPHY
*Boris and the Monsters* — Elaine MacMann
*Maggie and the Monster* — Elizabeth Winthrop
*Sleepy Dog* — Harriet Ziefert
*The How and Why Wonder Book of the Moon* — Felix Sutton
*MoonGame* — Frank Asch
*Owl Moon* — Jane Yolen
*Snowy the Barn Owl* — Jane Burton
*How the Rabbit Stole the Moon* — Louise Moeri
*There's One in Every Bunch* — Robert West
*Goodnight Moon* — Margaret Wise Brown

## Theme — *OCEANS AND FISH*

Time: One or Two Weeks

### ART
• Make large, painted cut outs of marine life such as sharks, whales, etc. Display same in the hallway.
• Make murals of cut out magazine photos of sea life to display on classroom walls.
• Make construction paper fish, seaweed, etc., and lightly iron same between two pieces of waxed paper.
• Use shoe boxes to make displays of scenes from the ocean. Use seashells to make designs — glue same to construction paper.

### SCIENCE
• View the Kodak Wildlife Series video tapes on sea life.
• Make short reports on differing sea life to display in the hallway with large painted cut outs.
• Visit an aquarium or a zoo to view sea life.
• Keep a little booklet with colored in pictures of all of the creatures observed.
• Make a classroom aquarium.
• Bring in and compare seashell collections.

### MATH
• Use seashell collections to count, sort into sets and graph.
• Play the Go Fish card game.
• Make fish shaped cards with numerals on the back — a double set may be used for playing concentration.

### SOCIAL STUDIES
• Invite an expert in the area of oceanography or sea life to come in to speak to the class.
• View Walt Disney's movie — *The Little Mermaid* — create a class skit based on the movie.

### COOKING
• Cook different types of seafood and have a "try it and see" sample party.
• Visit a seafood restaurant.

### BIBLIOGRAPHY
*Life in the Sea* — Gwynne Vevers
*Oceans* — Katherine J. Carter
*Exploring Under the Sea* — Sam Hinton

"Learning to read and to write ought to be one of the most joyful and successful of human undertakings."

"Children learn to listen and to speak in an unbreakable unity of function."[1] Reading and writing are two sides of an integrated learning process. We approach these skills together — and term them literacy learning. Reading is a developmental process starting early in childhood and continuing throughout life.

The essence of reading is to gain meaning from text, and children learn to read by reading. Therefore we teach reading strategies through quality children's literature, rich in human meaning. The joy of reading a novel is superior to using a commercial series for language learning.

The essence of writing is to communicate ideas in written form. Techniques of grammar and spelling are taught after children experience the thrill of expressing themselves in writing. We believe phonics skills need to be taught in order for children to spell correctly and we incorporate these skills as the child is ready.

"Children taught in this way take pride in their work, take pride in themselves, and take joy in communicating from their own writing and reading."[2]

1. Don Holdaway, *The Foundations of Literacy* (Sydney, Australia: Ashton Scholastic, 1979).

2. Marlene J. McCracken and Robert A. McCracken, *Reading, Writing, and Language, A Practical Guide for Primary Teachers* (Winnipeg, Canada: Peguis Publishers Limited, 1979) Foreword, viii.

# 3 Cue Systems

| Meaning |
| --- |
| (semantic) |

| Structure |
| --- |
| (grammar/syntax) |

| Visual |
| --- |
| (shapes • sounds • graphophonic) |

| | MONDAY Miss Minor | TUESDAY ART Ms. Robinson | WEDNESDAY GYM Miss Taylor | THURSDAY MEETING Moe | FRIDAY GYM Miss Taylor |
| --- | --- | --- | --- | --- | --- |
| 9:00- 9:40 | | ART Ms. Robinson | GYM Miss Taylor | MEETING Moe | GYM Miss Taylor |
| 9:40- 10:15 | OPENING | | SHARING | | CALENDAR |
| 10:15- 10:30 | | | SNACK | | |
| 10:30- 10:45 | NOISY OR SILENT READING | | RECESS- IN AUTUMN | REST OF YEAR | |
| 10:45- 11:45 | | | WRITING | | |
| 11:45- 12:10 | | | LUNCH | | |
| 12:15- 12:40 | | | RECESS | | * DUTY |
| 12:40- 2:05 | | INTEGRATED DAY WHOLE LANGUAGE wed ½ group libary(?) gym share writing | | | |
| 2:05- 2:40 | | | PLAY childs choice | | |
| 2:40- | EARLY BUS! | Share outcome | of "Play". | | Readiness Schedule J.Buros |
| 3:00- | EVERYONE LEAVES | To go HOME. | | | |
| | MONDAY | TUESDAY | WEDNESDAY | THURSDAY | FRIDAY |

Jay Buros

# WHOLE LANGUAGE

1. WARM-UP
   - Songs
   - Poems
   - Nursery Rhymes
   - Jingles
   - Cheers

2. OLD STORY
   - Have a child choose the story

3. NEW STORY
   - a. Big Book
   - b. Good literature on opaque projector or overhead
   - c. Student made Big Book
   - d. Teacher published Big Book
   - e. Song/Poem, chant on chart paper

4. OUTPUT/DEMONSTRATIONS — Student participation in relationship to new story
   1. Wall Chart
   2. Student made, published Big Book
   3. Student made small books (copy of large book)
   4. Murals
   5. Puppets
      - hand (made out of socks)
      - popsicle stick
   6. Flannel board characters and magnetic board characters
   7. Play of story
   8. Innovation of new story (Creating a new story together — probably after it has been read 8-10 times)
   9. Mobile of all the characters in the story
   10. Personal writing about the story — mine and the children's
   11. Field trips to make story come alive
   12. Invite people — to make story come alive (example: teddy bear collector to talk with children)
   13. Share book with a larger audience

# Whole Language Block

| Monday | Tuesday | Wednesday | Thursday | Friday |
|---|---|---|---|---|
| | ← | Warm-up → | | |
| | ← | Children choose "old" story → | | |
| | ← | New story — song — poem — rhyme Teacher's choice from observation of children → | | |
| | ← | Demonstration by teacher — Output by children → | | |

Jay Buros

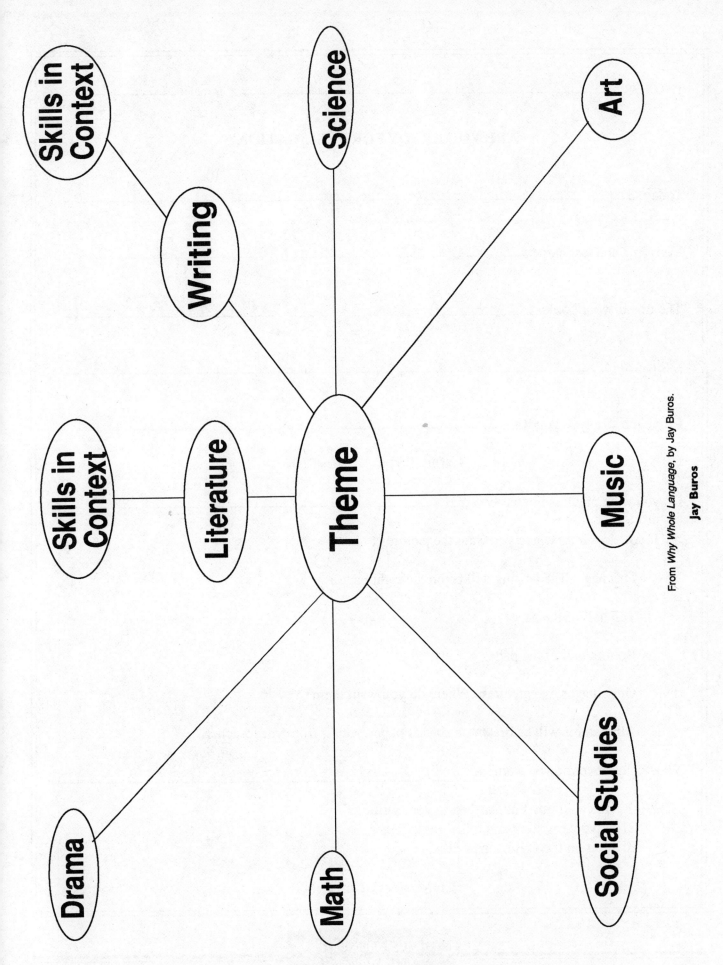

From *Why Whole Language*, by Jay Buros.

**Jay Buros**

173

TEACHER: _____ Grade: _____

## ARE YOU READY FOR PUBLICATION?

Today's Date: _____

Your first and last name: _____

The title of your book: _____

Dedicated to: _____

Circle the size type you want. _____

## Large Type     Small Type

Do you want pictures in your book? _____

    If you do, circle where you want the pictures to be.

        Left page (The writing will be on the right page.)

        Top half of the page.

        Bottom half of the page.

        Only one or two pictures...Where do you want them?

        All pictures will be drawn on special paper. Get it from your teacher.

What color cover do you want? _____

NOW: 1. Attach **About The Author** to your writing.
       2. Clip your writing and this form together.
       3. Put it on the **manuscript** desk.

## CONGRATULATIONS!

# BIBLIOGRAPHY. . . BEARS!
## Compiled by Jay Buros

** A to Z Subject Access to Children's Picture Books. by Caroline Lima, Bowker Co.

* Asch, Frank. *Happy Birthday Moon, Mooncake*. Prentice Hall.
* Berenstein, Stan & Jan. *Bears in the Night, The Bike Ride*. Random House.
  Brustlein, Janice. *Little Bears Pancake Party*. Lothrop, Lee & Shepard.
  Carlstrom, Nancy. *Jesse Bear, What Will You Wear?*
  Cauley, Lorinda. *Bryan, Goldilocks and the Three Bears*. Putnam's Sons.
  Craft, Ruth. *The Winter Bear*. Atheneum.
* Dabcovich, Lydia. *Sleepy Bear*. Dutton.
  Douglas, Barbara. *Good As New*. Lothrop, Lee & Shepard Co., NY.
  DuBois, William. *Bear Party*. Viking.
* Duvoisin, Roger. *Snowy and Woody*. Knopf.
* Flack, Marjorie. *Ask Mr. Bear*. Puffin.
* Freeman, Don. *Beady Bear, Corduroy*. Puffin.
  Galdone, Paul. *The Three Bears*. Seabury.
  Ginsburg, Mirra. *Two Greedy Bears*. Macmillan.
* Kennedy, Jimmy. *The Teddy Bears' Picnic*.
* Kraus, Robert. *Three Friends*. Windmill Books.
  Kuratomi, Chizuko. *Mr. Bear Goes to Sea*. Judson.
* Martin, Bill. *Brown Bear, Brown Bear, What Do You See?* HRW Press.
* Waber, Bernard. *Ira Sleeps Over*.
* Wahl, Jan. *Humphrey's Bear*.
* Ward, Lynn. *The Biggest Bear*.
  Yolen, Jane. *The Three Bears Rhyme Book*. HBJ.

## CHARTS

Teddy Bear, teddy bear, turn around. Teddy Bear, teddy bear, touch the ground.
Teddy Bear, teddy bear, go upstairs. Teddy Bear, teddy bear, say your prayers.
Teddy Bear, teddy bear, turn out the light. Teddy Bear, teddy bear, say goodnight,
"Goodnight!"

One little, two little, three little Teddy bears, four little, five little, six little Teddy bears, seven little, eight little, nine little Teddy bears, ten little Teddy bears and _____.

**ME AND MY TEDDY BEAR**
Me and my Teddy bear
Have no worries have no cares.
Me and my Teddy bear
Just _____ and _____ all day.
    (play)           (play)

**BEARS ARE SLEEPING** (Sung to "Frere Jacques" from More Piggyback Songs)
Bears are sleeping, bears are sleeping. In their dens, in their dens.
Soon it will be spring, soon it will be spring. Wake up bears, wake up bears!

**TEDDY BEAR SONG** (Sung to: Mary Had A Little Lamb from More Piggyback Songs)
 (child's name)  has a Teddy bear, Teddy bear, Teddy bear.
_____ has a Teddy bear. It's  (brown)  and  (furry)  all over.

**I'M GOING ON A BEAR HUNT**

_____ Observation

_____ Date

I looked at: _____

A picture of what I saw:

Here are things I noticed: _____

_____

_____

_____

Jay Buros

① (The Dream)

② If you achieved it how would you know?

A.

B.

C.

D.

E.

F.

Benchmarks (back plan — include span of time)

④

⑤ Methods you will try. "Be flexible."

Jay Buros

③ Where are you today? (in each area listed under ②)

A.

B.

C.

D.

E.

F.

# Why Whole Language

## By Jay Buros

What do you want children to accomplish by the end of the year?

# Using Themes to Plan the Day

Theme _____ Date _____

|  |  |
|------|----------|
| 8:00 - 8:10 | **Opening** |
| 8:10 - 8:20 | **DOL** |
| 8:20 - 8:35 | **Poem or song** |
| 8:35 - 8:50 | **English/reading skill mini-lesson** |
| 8:50 - 9:05 | **Penmanship** |
| 9:05 - 9:30 | **Teacher reads to class** |
| 9:30 - 10:00 | **Conference groups** • Listening station • Journals • Read and Share • Conference |
| 10:00 - 10:15 | **Spelling** |
| 10:10 - 10:25 | **Writing mini-lesson** |
| 10:25 - 10:50 | **Writing workshop** |
| 10:50 - 11:00 | **Writer's share time** |
| 11:00 - 11:35 | **Center/group work time** |
| 11:35 - 12:05 | **Lunch** |
| 12:05 - 12:20 | **Recess** |
| 12:20 - 1:05 | **Math** |
| 1:05 - 1:45 | **Social studies** |
| 1:45 - 2:30 | **Planning** |
| 2:30 - 2:40 | **Read to class** |
| 2:40 - 2:45 | **Dismissal** |

## Conference Record Sheet

| Date | | | | | | | Material Read |
|------|---|---|---|---|---|---|---|
| Conference | 1 | 2 | 3 | 4 | 5 | 6 | 4 Terrific |
| Fluency | | | | | | | 3 Good |
| Expression | | | | | | | 2 OK |
| Word Recognition | | | | | | | 1 Poor Try |
| Word Attack Skills | | | | | | | 0 Not Done |
| Comprehension | | | | | | | |

**Observations/Recommendations:**

# Thematic Units

- **Example**

- **How to plan**

- **Parental involvement**

- **Reading, writing, publishing**

- **Assessment**

# How to Plan a Thematic Unit

1. Choose a theme.

2. Make a list of books that fit your theme.

3. Make a list of read-aloud books for the theme.

4. Choose one book or story for total class instruction.

5. Make your plans for the whole group selection:

    a. select skills

    b. include objectives for content areas

    c. provide activities for assessment

6. Choose three or four books for small group instruction.

7. Make plans for small groups:

    a. discussion questions

    b. group activities or projects

8. Plan for individual reading projects.

9. List culminating activities for groups.

10. List possible enrichment activities.

11. List materials that go with theme — filmstrips, videos, music, software, etc.

# Webbing Topic Ideas

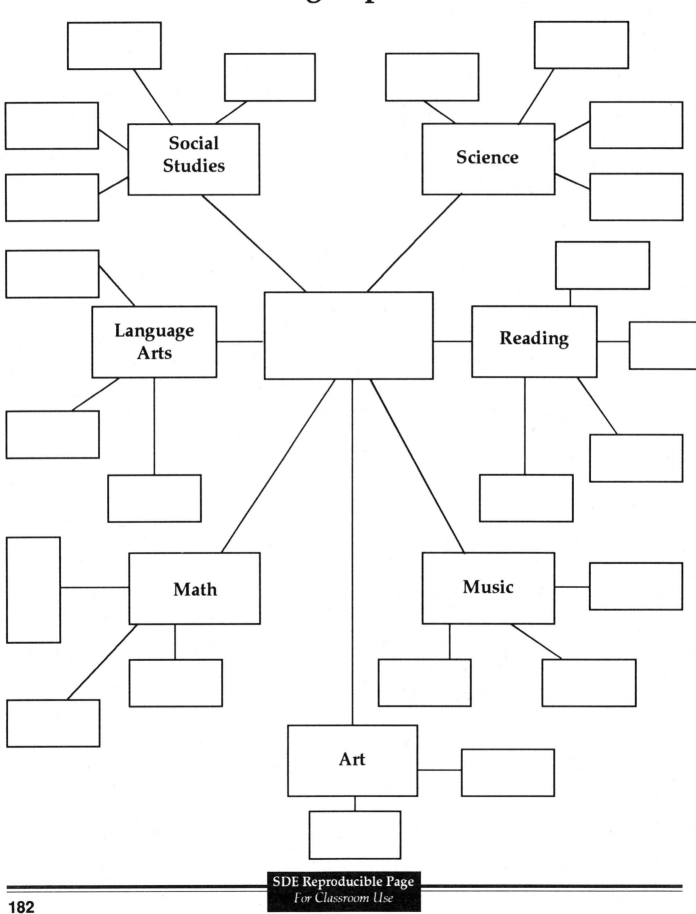

Linda Carpenter

# STORY MAP

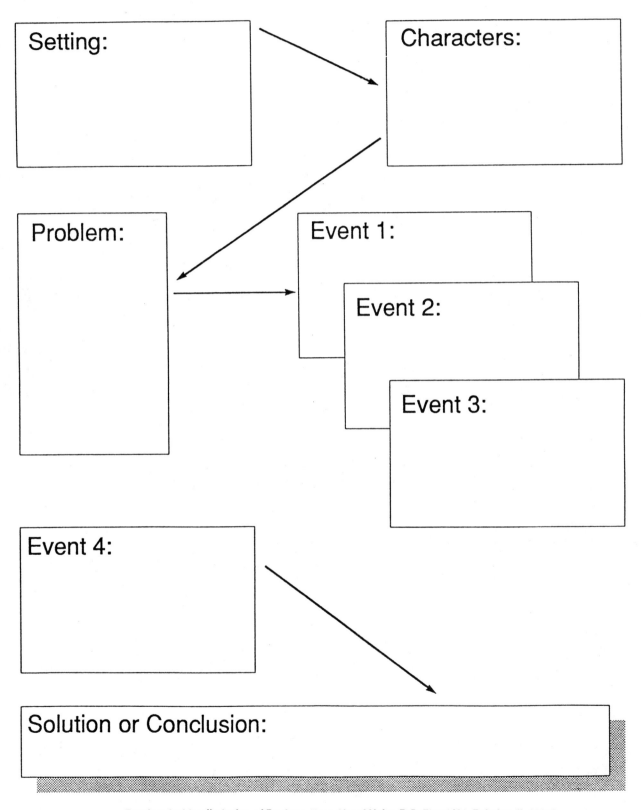

Setting:

Characters:

Problem:

Event 1:

Event 2:

Event 3:

Event 4:

Solution or Conclusion:

Reprinted with permission of Dr. Anne Troy, Novel Units, P.O. Box 1461, Palatine, IL 60078

# VENN DIAGRAM

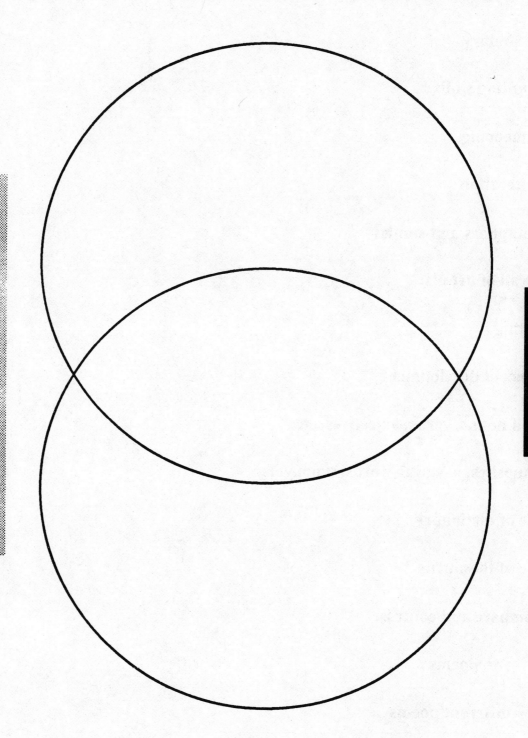

# Use a Poem to Teach

• **Memory skills**

• **Vocabulary**

• **Counting skills**

• **Sequencing**

• **Alliteration**

• **Metaphors and similes**

• **Recall of details**

• **Setting**

• **Concept development**

• **Find nouns, verbs, adjectives, etc.**

• **Opposites, rhyming words, synonyms**

• **Use of dictionary**

• **Use of thesaurus**

• **Compare and contrast**

    **two poems**

    **different poems**

    **characters**

    **Linda Carpenter**

# Daily Schedule

| Time | Activity | |
|---|---|---|
| 8:50 | Welcome | Get Organized |
| 9:00 | Creative writing/Independent Study | |
| 9:20 | Group Time — Plannning the Day, Current Events | |
| 9:30 | Super Readers | |
| 9:40 | Literature Block | |
| 10:00 | Recess/Snack | |
| 10:15 | Guided Writing | |
| 10:30 | Language Arts | |

| Mini Groups by Interest | Independent Reading Centers<br>Buddy Reading | Literature Extenstion<br>Reenforcement |
|---|---|---|

| Time | Activity | |
|---|---|---|
| 11:30 | Story, Songs, Sharing | |
| 11:45 | Lunch & Recess | |
| 12:15 | Read Aloud | |
| 12:30 | Math | |
| 1:00 | Thematic — Social Studies & Science | |
| 2:00 | Art | Music | P.E. |
| 2:30 | Centers | |
| 3:00 | Clean Up, Story, Songs, Discuss the Day, Plan for Tomorrow | |
| 3:20 | | |

# WHOLE LANGUAGE — THE COMPLETE CYCLE

By Kathryn L. Cloonan

## *WHOLE LANGUAGE STEPS*

1. Share a Piece of Literature...

    Story — oral as well as written.

    Song

    Flip Chart

    String Story

    Big Book

    Flannel Board Story

    Student Made Book

2. Personalize It        READ IT!

3. Put It Into Print      READ IT!

4. Model It           READ IT!

5. Make a Big Book     READ IT!

6. Expand It — Recreate It

    Mini Books

    Puppets

    Bulletin Board Stories

    Mobiles

    Wall Stories

    Overhead Transparency Stories

    Tutorette Stories

    Masks, Plays, Etc.

    Innovations

7. Make The Writing Connection

    Slot Stories

    Signs

    Posters

    Letters to a Character in the Story

    Letter to the Author

    "News" Article

    Adding Another Chapter

        Different Ending, etc.

    Writing Their Own Stories

# WHOLE LANGUAGE AT HOME

## *MAKING A READING AND WRITING CONNECTION FUN!*

1. Encourage reading, writing, listening and discussing ideas at home.

2. Develop confidence and self-esteem by encouragement and praise.

3. Surround your whole family with a variety of types of literature: magazines, newspapers, encyclopedias, books.

4. Be a model — show your family you read for your own enjoyment.

5. Read to your family — no matter how old they are, they will still enjoy hearing a story.

**When Reading With Your Children...**

6. Keep it fun and stress free.

7. Read your children's favorite over and over if they ask — you are allowing them to hear the "music or rhythm" of the story called the story structure.

8. Stop before a predictable word and let your child fill in the word — you are giving him an opportunity to use the pictures and the sense of the story as strategies for reading.

9. Encourage your child to read along with you — it's good rehearsal before he tries it on his own.

**When Your Child Is Reading To You...**

10. Let your child decide on the book she/he wants to read to you.

11. Remember that even reading pictures is reading.

12. Overlook mistakes — he is still getting good practice on all the words he is reading correctly — and feeling successful, too.

13. Tell your child the word he is having trouble with — he learns from hearing the correct word and seeing it at the same time.

14. When helping your child figure out a word...
    a. Just point to the words and give him an opportunity to self-correct.
    b. Ask him what word would make sense.
    c. Point to the beginning letter and see if he can think of a word that begins with this letter sound and also makes sense.
    d. If your child has tried and can't figure it out, tell him the word.

15. Encourage your child to make a writing connection...
    a. Add a new ending to the story.
    b. Write a letter to the author.
    c. Write an "ad" telling friends at school about the book.
    d. Write to one of the characters in the story, i.e., Dear Big Bad Wolf,...
    e. Write his or her own story.

# MAKING THE WRITING CONNECTION

By Kathryn L. Cloonan

## HOW TO ENCOURAGE YOUR CHILDREN'S WRITING

### HAVE A WRITING ENVIRONMENT...

1. Make available easy access to paper — different sizes, colors, and shapes, too.

2. Make available easy access to markers, crayons, pencils and pencil sharpeners.

3. Have a message board or chalk board where children see the importance of writing by giving and receiving messages.

4. Model — write notes, have a special writing time when everyone writes.

5. Look for any excuse to encourage writing. Have your child: write to Grandmother, write Mom a note, make a list of chores he's done, keep a photo album and write a little bit about his favorite pictures.

6. Treat any creative attempt as special.

7. Have correct spellings around for the child to refer to — label things in the home, label drawers in his bedroom.

8. Have your child draw a picture and write about it.

9. Listen to your child read his writing.

10. Use "Post-it" paper to write what the child was trying to say on the back.

Kathryn L. Cloonan

# WHAT DO YOU SAY WHEN

**YOUR CHILD SAYS:**                                    **YOU SAY:**

"I don't know how...."                                  *"Do the best you can..."*

"How do you spell..."                                   *"Use your inventive spelling."*

                                                        *"Sound it out and write down some clues."*

                                                        *"Don't worry about correct spelling...*
                                                        *just get those great ideas down first."*

"I don't know how to use inventive spelling..."         *"What are you trying to say?"*
                                                        *"What sounds do you hear?"*

"What does this say?"                                    *"What do you want it to say?"*
(When they show you their inventive spelling.)

"Does this really spell..."                             *"It's close.  Remember the neat thing about*
                                                        *inventive spelling is you're always right."*

"Can you read this?"                                    *"You're giving me lots of clues.*
                                                        *Read it to me won't you?"*
                                                        (Point out a good clue.)

# Writing the Right Way!

| Benefits | Process | Purpose |
|---|---|---|

### Writing

**Benefits:**
Encourages self-expression

Makes letter-sound connections

Builds fluency in ideas

**Purpose:**
Getting great ideas down on paper

### Conference I

**Benefits:**
Makes the connection between their ideas and the printed word

Supports inventive spelling/ corrective spelling

**Purpose:**
Communicating ideas

Learning new skills in
- phonics
- decoding skills
- grammar
- spelling
- punctuation
- sight words

### Conference II

**Benefits:**
Builds self-confidence by acceptance

Enhances creativity

Increases communication skills through making choices and decisions

**Purpose:**
Creating, planning, and expressing ideas for a finished product

### Publishing

**Benefits:**
Encourages further efforts
Builds self-respect and self-concept

**Purpose:**
Modeling correct spelling, punctuation, sentence formation, and publishing

### Illustrating

**Benefits:**
Builds the connection between print and ideas

Encourages sight vocabulary

**Purpose:**
Increasing comprehension

Encouraging creativity

### Reading

**Benefits:**
Builds sight vocabulary

Enhances decoding strategies

Builds reading fluency

Encourages a love for reading and writing

**Purpose:**
Building sight vocabulary

Decoding through meaningful context and phonetic clues

### Celebrating

# Celebrating with an Authors' Tea

Encourages a love for reading and writing

Enhances acceptance of others

Increases awareness of "presenting" to others

Enriches sight vocabulary

Builds a collection of readable materials

Encourages learning more about a subject

Builds self-confidence

Enriches organizational and planning skills

Models respect and love for literature

Gives *all* children an arena for success

Offers a completed reading and writing cycle that is relevant to children

Kathryn L. Cloonan

## AUTHOR'S PLANNING PAGE

Name: _____

Title: _____

Dedicated to: _____

Because: _____

About - Me - The Author: _____

_____

_____

I would like my book:

      Handwritten      _____

           or

      Typed           _____

I would like the words this size:

# VERY LARGE      LARGE      SMALL

I would like the color of the cover to be: _____

1. I have chosen my paper: _____

2. I have talked with my Publisher: _____

3. I have a picture of me: _____

4. I have done my illustrations: _____

5. My book is all put together: _____

**I DID IT!!!**

Kathryn L. Cloonan

# R.E.A.L. Reading
# for
# Upper Grades

## I. Share a Piece of Literature

### A. Book Groups
Students choose book group to be in

### B. Author's Study
Class is reading a variety of same author's work

### C. Story Types

Mysteries

Fables, Myths

Nursery rhymes

Folklore

Folk songs

Fantasy

Science fiction

Nonfiction

Humor

### D. Thematic Units

Space

Insects

Ocean

Pets

Dinosaurs

### E. Historical Collections

Pilgrims,

Civil War

Settlement of state

Kathryn L. Cloonan

# SING ME A STORY — READ ME A SONG

### INTEGRATING MUSIC INTO THE WHOLE LANGUAGE CLASSROOM
#### By Kathryn L. Cloonan

## PURPOSE

1. Instill a love for reading and music.
2. Make use of simple, delightful materials that have rhythm, rhyme, repetition.
3. To give children early successes in reading.
4. Give children an opportunity to make the connection between print and what they say and sing.
5. Build sight vocabulary by frequently seeing words in meaningful, predictable context.
6. Enrich decoding/reading skills through meaningful print.

## STEPS

SHARE IT — Sing Lots of Songs Often
PRINT IT — Print a Favorite on Chart Paper
ILLUSTRATE IT — Make a Big Book, Make Mini Books
READ IT — Let the Children Read It

## RESOURCES

**Record and Tapes**
*Sing Me a Story, Read Me A Song,* Kathryn Cloonan
*Whole Language Holidays — Stories, Chants and Songs,* Kathryn Cloonan
*Peter, Paul and Mommy,* Peter, Paul and Mary
*Elephant Show Record,* Sharon, Lois and Bram
*Special Delivery,* Fred Penner
*The Cat Came Back,* Fred Penner
*Learning Basic Skills Through Music,* Hap Palmer
*We All Live Together,* Volumes 1, 2, 3 & 4, Greg Scelse and Steve Millang
*Doing the Dinosaur Rock,* Diane Butchelor
*You'll Sing a Song and I'll Sing a Song,* Ella Jenkins
*Singable Songs for the Very Young,* Raffi
*More Singable Songs for the Very Young,* Raffi

**Resource Books**
*A Song Is a Rainbow,* Patty Zeittin. Scott Foresman and Co., 1982
Piggyback Books
*Sing Me a Story, Read Me a Song, Book I,* Kathryn Cloonan. Rhythm & Reading Resources, 1991.
*Sing Me a Story, Read Me a Song, Book II,* Kathryn Cloonan, 1991.

## SONGS

**WE HAVE A FRIEND**
We have a friend and
her name is Amy
Amy is her name
Hello, Amy-Hello, Amy
Hello, Amy
We're so glad you're here.
Innovation:
    Change names of children

**TWINKLE TWINKLE LITTLE STAR**
Twinkle, twinkle little star
How I wonder what you are.
Up above the world so high.
Like a diamond in the sky.
Twinkle, twinkle little star
How I wonder what you are.

**HICKORY, DICKORY DOCK**
Hickory, Dickory Dock
The mouse ran up the clock
The clock struck one
The mouse ran down
Hickory, Dickory Dock
Innovations:
    The clock struck 2, 3, 4, etc.

**BAA, BAA, BLACK SHEEP**
Baa, Baa Black Sheep
Have you any wool?
Yes sir, yes sir three bags full.

One for my master
One for the dame
One for the little boy
that lives down the lane.

Baa, Baa, Black Sheep
Have you any wool?
Yes sir, yes sir three bags full.
Innovation:
    Color Words
    Baa, Baa, Purple sheep, etc.

**BINGO**
There was a farmer
Had a dog and Bingo was his name-o.
B I N G O
B I N G O
B I N G O
And Bingo was his name-o.

**TEN LITTLE INDIANS**
One little, two little, three little Indians
Four little, five little, six little Indians
Seven little, eight little, nine little Indians.
Ten little Indian boys.
Ten little, nine little, eight little Indians.
Seven little, six little, five little Indians.
Four little, three little, two little Indians.
One little Indian boy.
Innovations: Change with theme or holiday — pumpkins, Christmas trees

**ON A SPIDER'S WEB**
One elephant went out to play
On a spider's web one day.
He had such enormous fun
He asked another elephant to come.

Two elephants went out to play
On a spider's web one day.
They had such enormous fun
They asked another elephant to come.

Three elephants, four elephants,
Five elephants, six elephants,
Seven elephants, eight elephants,
Nine elephants................

Ten elephants went out to play
They had such enormous fun
They asked everyone to come.
Innovations: Change with theme or holidays — black cat, Christmas elf, leprechaun, dinosaur, Panda bear, etc.

**FIVE SPECKLED FROGS**
Five green and speckled frogs
Sat on a speckled log
Eating the most delicious bugs.
    YUM!    YUM!
One jumped into the pool
where it was nice and cool
Then there were four green speckled frogs.
Four...etc., Three...etc.,
Two...etc., One...etc.
Then there were NO green speckled frogs.

## THE WHEELS ON THE BUS
The wheels on the bus go
       round and round
       round and round
       round and round
The wheels on the bus go
       round and round
All through the town.
Innovations:
1. doors...open and shut
2. children...up and down
3. wipers...swish, swish, swish
4. babies...wah, wah, wah
5. snakes...Sss, Sss, Sss
6. bears...growl, growl, growl, etc.

## I KNOW AN OLD LADY
I know an old lady who swallowed a fly
I don't know why she swallowed a fly...
perhaps she'll die.

I know an old lady who swallowed a
    spider
(that wiggled and jiggled and tickled
    inside her)
She swallowed the spider to catch the fly
But I don't know why she swallowed a
    fly
perhaps she'll die.

I know an old lady who swallowed a
    bird
She swallowed the bird to catch the
    spider
(that wiggled and jiggled and tickled
    inside her)
She swallowed the spider to catch the fly
But I don't know why she swallowed a
    fly
perhaps she'll die.

I know an old lady who swallowed a cat
She swallowed the cat to catch the bird
She swallowed the bird to catch the
    spider
(that wiggled and jiggled and tickled
    inside her)
She swallowed the spider to catch the fly
But I don't know why she swallowed
    the fly
perhaps she'll die.

I know an old lady who swallowed a dog
She swallowed the dog to catch the cat
She swallowed the cat to catch the bird
She swallowed the bird to catch the
    spider
(that wiggled and jiggled and tickled
    inside her)
She swallowed the spider to catch the fly
But I don't know why she swallowed
    the fly
perhaps she'll die.

I know an old lady who swallowed a goat
She swallowed the goat to catch the dog
She swallowed the dog to catch the cat
She swallowed the cat to catch the bird

She swallowed the bird to catch the
    spider
(that wiggled and jiggled and tickled
    inside her)
She swallowed the spider to catch the fly
But I don't know why she swallowed
    the fly
perhaps she'll die.

I know an old lady who swallowed a
    horse
She's Full, of course!
Innovations: Change the animals she
    swallowed

## TEN IN THE BED
There were ten in the bed
And the little one said,
"Roll over, Roll over"
So they all rolled over and one fell out
       And they gave a little scream
       And they gave a little shout

Please remember to tie a knot in your
    pajamas
Single beds were only made for
1,2,3,4,5,6,7,8,
Nine in the bed etc.
Eight etc., Seven etc.
Six-five-four-three-two...etc.
One in the bed and the little one said,
"I've got the whole mattress to myself"
(repeat last line three more times)
       GOOD-NIGHT!

## LITTLE COTTAGE IN THE WOODS
"Little cottage in the woods" (Touch
fingertips of both hands together to
form a triangle shape for the house.)
"Little man by the window stood."
(Form "glasses" shapes with forefinger
and thumb of each hand making a
circle — put hands up to eyes in that
shape, against face.) "Saw a rabbit
hopping by" (Make rabbit "ears" by
two fingers held up on one hand and
"hop" them about.) "Frightened as
could be." (Arms held crossed across
chest, "shake" in mock fear.) "Help me,
help me, help me, he said." (Raise arms
overhead and down several times.)
"Before the hunter shoots me dead:
(Form "guns" with forefingers and
"shoot.") "Come, little rabbit, come
inside" (Beckon with hand.) "And
happy we will be." (Stroke the back of
one hand with the other as though
tenderly petting a rabbit.)

## LITTLE SKUNK
Oh! I stuck my head in a little skunk's
hole — and the little skunk said, "God
bless your soul." Take it out! Take it
out! Take it out! Remove it! But I didn't
take it out and the little skunk said, "If
you don't take it out you'll wish you

had." Take it out! Take it out! Take it
out! Psssss — I removed it.

## MICHAEL FINNAGIN
There once was a man named Michael
    Finnagin
He had whiskers on his chin-a-gain
The wind came along and blew them
    in-again
Poor old Michael Finnagin...begin-
    again.

There once was a man named Michael
    Finnagin
He went fishing with a pin-again
Caught a whale that pulled him in-
    again
Poor old Michael Finnagin...begin-
    again.

There once was a man named Michael
    Finnagin
He was fat and then grew thin-again
Ate so much he had to begin again
Poor old Michael Finnagin...begin-
    again.

## TINY TIM
I had a little turtle,
His name was Tiny Tim
I put him in the bathtub
To see if he could swim.
He drank up all the water.
He ate up all the soap.
And now he's home sick in bed
With a bubble in his throat.

## THE ANTS GO MARCHING
The ants go marching one by one
Hurrah! Hurrah!
The ants go marching one by one
Hurrah! Hurrah!
The ants go marching one by one
the little one stops to suck his thumb
And they all go marching down —
into the ground — to get out — of the
    rain —
BOOM, BOOM, BOOM, BOOM,
BOOM, BOOM, BOOM, BOOM
two by two.....tie his shoe
three by three.....climb a tree
four by four.....shut the door
five by five.....jump and dive
six by six.....pick up sticks
seven by seven.....wave to heaven
eight by eight.....climb the gate
nine by nine.....look behind
ten by ten.....pat a hen

## GOOD-BYE
We have a friend and her name is Amy.
Amy is her name. Good-bye, Amy,
    good-bye Amy
Good-bye, Amy, we'll see you
    tomorrow.
Innovation: Change names of children.

Kathryn L. Cloonan

# A TEDDY BEAR'S MERRY CHRISTMAS

Teddy Bear, Teddy Bear
Touch your knee.

Teddy Bear,
Teddy Bear
Trim the tree.

Teddy Bear,
Teddy Bear
Touch your wrist.

Teddy Bear,
Teddy Bear
Make your list.

Teddy Bear,
Teddy Bear
Touch your feet.

Teddy Bear,
Teddy Bear
Eat, Eat, Eat!

Teddy Bear,
Teddy Bear
Touch your toe.

Teddy Bear,
Teddy Bear
It's Mistletoe!!!

Kathryn L. Cloonan

# SCHEDULING

## Daily Schedule

| | |
|---|---|
| 9:00-9:40 | Special |
| 9:40-10:00 | Circle: news and poems |
| 10:00-10:10 | Snack |
| 10:10-10:20 | Focus of the morning |
| 10:20-11:00 | Language activity based on focus. |
| 11:00-11:40 | Math |
| 11:40-12:40 | Lunch, recess |
| 12:40-1:10 | Sharing, read aloud |
| 1:10-2:15 | Reading/writing/sharing |
| 2:15-2:50 | Continuation of reading/writing, activity or free time |

## What I Wanted to see:

*Nurturing, caring environment*

1. Teacher a coach rather than dictator.

2. Children feel safe and can take chances.

3. Children have choices and learn to take control of their learning.

4. Teach $500 concepts rather than "cover" the curriculum.

5. Each child has a positive self image and is proud of his/her activities.

6. Children are learning through doing.

7. Each child has the feeling that he/she is a reader and writer.

## What do I want to happen? How can I foster that in my room?

1. Coach, not direct
   a. my desk not the focus
   b. children's areas most attractive
2. Kids have control
   a. materials available
   b. books available
   c. workspace for individuals, pairs and groups
   d. booklists, book report forms, observation sheets and paper available
   e. room for children to move around easily
3. Children's positive self image
   a. places to display kids' work
   b. child able to be self-sufficient
4. Room run easily with little effort
   a. ease of movement
   b. transitions
   c. materials I need ready to go and moveable

# CHARACTER WEB

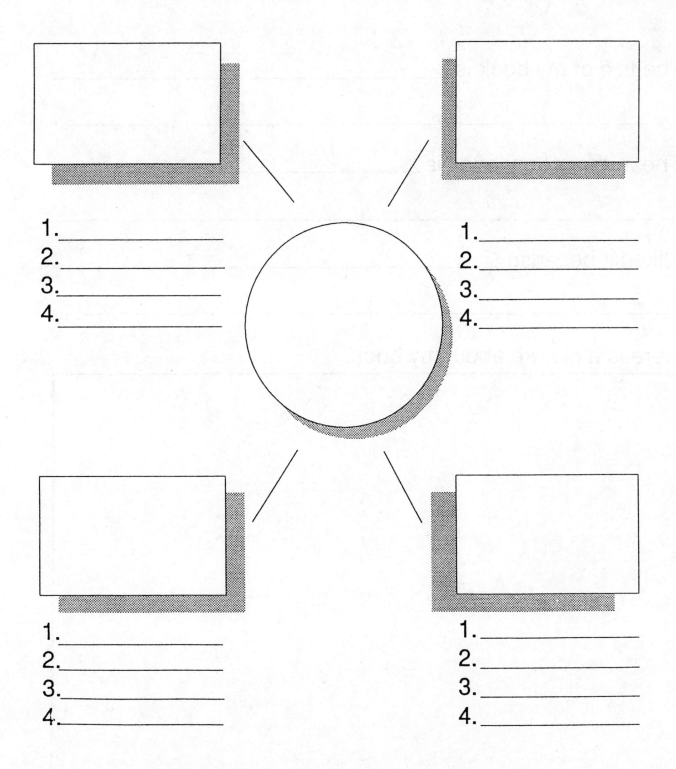

1._____
2._____
3._____
4._____

1._____
2._____
3._____
4._____

1._____
2._____
3._____
4._____

1._____
2._____
3._____
4._____

Reprinted with permission of Dr. Anne Troy, Novel Units, P.O. Box 1461, Palatine, IL 60078

My name is _____.

The date is _____.

The title of my book is _____

_____.

The author of my book is _____

_____.

I liked it because _____

_____.

Here is a picture about my book.

```
┌─────────────────────────────────────────┐
│                                         │
│                                         │
│                                         │
│                                         │
│                                         │
│                                         │
│                                         │
│                                         │
│                                         │
│                                         │
└─────────────────────────────────────────┘
```

Name _____ Date _____

Title: _____

Author: _____

Illustrator: _____

Who was in this book? _____

_____

What did they do? _____

_____

Where did they do it? _____

_____

When did they do it? _____

_____

How did you like this book? _____

_____

**Ann Lessard**

# My Weekly Reading Log

by Ann Lessard

My name: _____ The date: _____

## Monday

1. _____

2. _____

3. _____

alone?_____

with partner? _____

## Tuesday

1. _____

2. _____

3. _____

alone?_____

with partner?_____

## Wednesday

1. _____

2. _____

3. _____

alone? _____

with partner?_____

## Thursday

1. _____

2. _____

3. _____

alone? _____

with partner?_____

## Friday

1. _____

2. _____

3. _____

alone?_____

with partner?_____

## How did you do?

HOME
Strengthening
The Connection
SCHOOL

Dear _____,

You're invited to my Authors' Tea

on _____ at _____. I'll be

reading my new book.

I need to bring _____.

Love,

_____

# Guided Reading

1. Select material at correct instructional level.

2. High level of interest.

3. Prepare for reading.

4. Read the text.

5. Subsequent discussion and questions.

6. Integrate story with own experience.

7. Critical thinking.

8. Determine need for group teaching.

9. Follow-up.

10. Sharing.

# Steps for Individualized Reading

1. Establish management, expectations.

2. Appropriate time frame, materials.

3. Whole group session.

4. Children choose materials.

5. Reading log.

6. Silent reading.

7. Conferencing.

8. Follow-up.

9. Whole group closure.

# BOOK TALK

I. Introduction

Tell title, author, publishing company, category.

II. Support

Discuss beginning of book, main characters, main action of book.

III. Conclusion

Conclude report. Do not reveal ending in case others want to read it.

IV. Evaluate

Evaluate and give recommendation to others.

V. Project

Show visual and explain relevance to book.

Time allotted for book talk _____

Required this year:

Book talks_____

Written reports _____

Name:_____ September – June, 19_____

# BOOK LIST

| Title | Author | Start | End | Report |
|---|---|---|---|---|
| 1. | | | | |
| 2. | | | | |
| 3. | | | | |
| 4. | | | | |
| 5. | | | | |
| 6. | | | | |
| 7. | | | | |
| 8. | | | | |
| 9. | | | | |
| 10. | | | | |
| 11. | | | | |
| 12. | | | | |
| 13. | | | | |
| 14. | | | | |
| 15. | | | | |
| 16. | | | | |
| 17. | | | | |
| 18. | | | | |
| 19. | | | | |
| 20. | | | | |

Jean Mann

# Independent Reading Book List

Name:

| Date | Title | Author | # pages | E,M,C |
|------|-------|--------|---------|-------|
|      |       |        |         |       |
|      |       |        |         |       |
|      |       |        |         |       |
|      |       |        |         |       |
|      |       |        |         |       |
|      |       |        |         |       |
|      |       |        |         |       |
|      |       |        |         |       |
|      |       |        |         |       |
|      |       |        |         |       |
|      |       |        |         |       |
|      |       |        |         |       |

# Imagery: 5 Senses Web

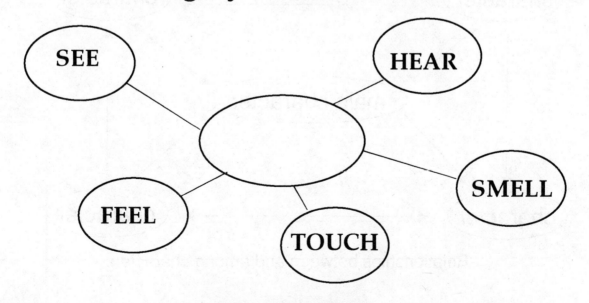

# What a Character!

Authors use various ways to reveal a character's personality:

1. What the author says about the character.

2. What the character does or says.

3. What other characters reveal about the character.

4. How other characters act toward the character.

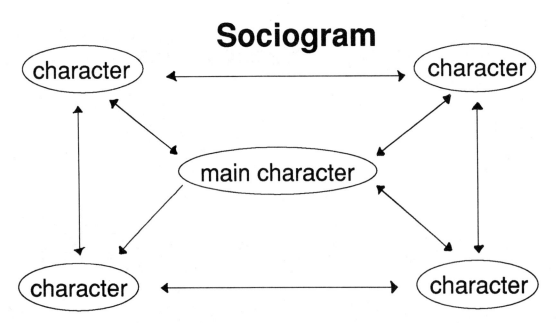

## Sociogram

Relationships between and among characters

# WANTED

Name:

Height:

Hair:

Eyes:

Likes to:

# Character Web
## *Great Gray Owl* by Orin Cochrane

BEAUTIFUL

WISE

DEADLY

MIGHTY

KIND

POWERFUL

# Character Chart
## *Good Dog Carl* by Alexandra Day

| | | | | | | |
|---|---|---|---|---|---|---|
| **Clever** | ● | | | | | **Not Clever** |
| **Happy** | | | ● | | | **Unhappy** |
| **Friendly** | ● | | | | | **Unfriendly** |
| **Careful** | | | | ● | | **Careless** |
| **Loving** | ● | | | | | **Unloving** |
| | | | | | | |

**Jean Mann**

# CHARACTER ANALYSIS CHART

**Character Trait**     **Evidence**     **How Trait is Revealed**

# Pop-up Books

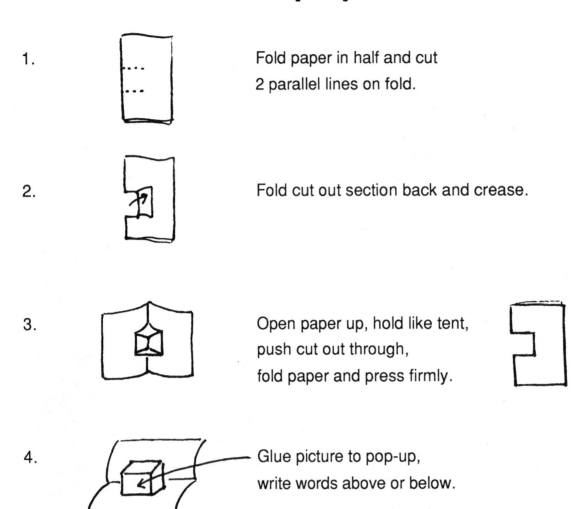

1.   Fold paper in half and cut
     2 parallel lines on fold.

2.   Fold cut out section back and crease.

3.   Open paper up, hold like tent,
     push cut out through,
     fold paper and press firmly.

4.   Glue picture to pop-up,
     write words above or below.

5.   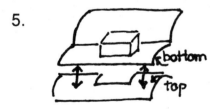 To connect pages of book,
     glue bottom of first page
     to top of second page.
     Continue in same manner.

6.    To make a cage, simply cut strips
     in cut out section as shown.

For more ideas on pop-up books, see *How to Make Pop-ups* by Joan Irvine.
Published by Beech Tree Books.

**Jean Mann**

# TRIARAMA

1. Fold a square piece of paper diagonally both ways.

2. Make a cut ½-way up one fold.

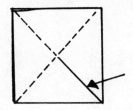

3. Fold ½ of cut section under other cut section.

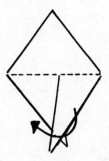

4. Attach together with glue, staple, or clip. This will form a half shell.

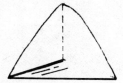

# DIAMANTE

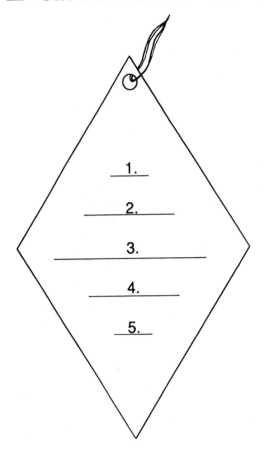

Line 1:   subject

Line 2:   2 adjectives to describe subject

Line 3:   3 participles

Line 4:   2 adjectives describing how writer feels about subject

Line 5:   noun re-naming subject

Jean Mann

# Suggested Materials for Writing

Organize a writing center or area where materials are available at all times for children to use. Separate materials in different containers to make it easy for children to choose what is appropriate for them.

A.  **Writing utensils (vary sizes to accommodate different fine motor abilities)**
pencils
pens
colored pencils
crayons
markers
crayons, paints, brushes
(try covering coffee cans with wall paper and separate utensils in them)

B.  **Paper (use different sizes, weight, color)**
lined
unlined
story-book
drawing
stationery
graph
computer

C.  **Organizing writing**
folders (manila, duo-tang) for keeping current work in
folders for permanent work
dish tubs for younger children (put student's name on front; paper, utensils in tub)
corrugated cardboard boxes (to store past work)
plastic milk crates for folders
box for "finished papers"

D.  **Additional supplies at hand**
stapler
staple remover
erasers
rulers
scissors
glue
tape
paper clips
paper punches
paper fasteners
date stamp and pad

E.  **Other**
tape recorder
typewriter/computer
dictionaries
reference books

---

# Conferencing Techniques in Writing

1. CONTENT

2. EXPAND

3. FOCUS

4. SHOW, DON'T TELL

5. SEQUENCE

6. LEADS

7. CONCLUSIONS

In Conjunction with Content

8. REVISION

9. SKILLS

10. EDITING

Jean Mann

# Daily Schedule

8:00 - 8:10    D.E.A.R. Time

8:10 - 9:10    **Reading Activities**

---

**Sample 1**

| 8:10 - | 8:25 | Big Book |
| 8:25 - | 8:40 | Poetry |
| 8:40 - | 9:10 | Basal story |

9:10 - 9:40    **Writing Activities**

**Sample 1**

| 9:10 - | 9:30 | Individual small books |
| 9:30 - | 9:40 | Journals |

9:40 - 10:10    Physical education, library or music

10:10 - 11:00    Morning assignments (English, spelling, math)

11:00 - 11:25    Lunch

11:25 - 12:25    Complete assignments/center time

12:25 - 12:45    Read aloud

12:45 - 1:30    Science, social studies, health

1:30 - 1:40    Clean-up/dismissal

**Reading Activities**

D.E.A.R. time = 10 minutes
Big Book, poetry, or author/theme of the week = 15 minutes
Basal story, book set, or reader's choice = 30 minutes

---

**Sample 2**

Author/theme of the week
Book set
Poetry

**Sample 2**

Whole-class book
Short stuff

---

**Sample 3**

| 8:10 - | 8:40 | Reader's Choice |
| 8:40 - | 8:55 | Big Book |
| 8:55 - | 9:10 | Author/theme of the week |

**Sample 3**

Writers' workshop
Book commercials

**Writing Activities**

Journals, short stuff, book commercials = 10 minutes
Individual small books, whole-class books, writers' workshop = 20 minutes

Pam Haack

Student Name _____

Grade: _____     Year: _____

| Date | Title | Author | Response | I read this book to myself | I shared this book out loud |
|------|-------|--------|----------|----------------------------|-----------------------------|
|      |       |        |          |                            |                             |
|      |       |        |          |                            |                             |
|      |       |        |          |                            |                             |
|      |       |        |          |                            |                             |
|      |       |        |          |                            |                             |
|      |       |        |          |                            |                             |
|      |       |        |          |                            |                             |
|      |       |        |          |                            |                             |
|      |       |        |          |                            |                             |
|      |       |        |          |                            |                             |
|      |       |        |          |                            |                             |
|      |       |        |          |                            |                             |
|      |       |        |          |                            |                             |
|      |       |        |          |                            |                             |
|      |       |        |          |                            |                             |

# TASK SHEET/PROGRESS REPORT

Name: _____

Week: _____

Behavior: _____

Parent Signature: _____

E = excellent          S = satisfactory          N = needs improvement          Red zone = unacceptable behavior

|  | Mon | Tue | Wed | Thurs | Fri |
|---|---|---|---|---|---|
| Reading |  |  |  |  |  |
| Handwriting |  |  |  |  |  |
| Spelling |  |  |  |  |  |
| English |  |  |  |  |  |
| Math |  |  |  |  |  |

# Over in the Meadow
## (a traditional rhyme)

Over in the meadow, in the sand in the sun
Lived an old mother turtle and her little turtle one.
"Dig," said the mother.
"I dig," said the one.
So they dug all day in the sand in the sun.
Over in the meadow where the stream runs blue
Lived an old mother fish and her little fishes two.
"Swim," said the mother.
"We swim," said the two.
So they swam all day where the stream runs blue.

# Hey There Neighbor

Hey there neighbor, what do you say?
It's gonna be a beautiful day.
Clap your hands and boogie on down.
Give 'em a bump and pass it around.

# Good Morning

Good Morning, how are you?
It's so nice to see you.
So sing and be happy,
That we're all back together again.

Here's_____ , and _____
and _____ , and _____ .
There's_____ , and _____
And we're all back together again.

# Hey Joe

Hi. My name is Joe.
And I work at the Donut Factory.
I've got a wife, a dog, and a family.

One day my boss came to me.
He said, "Hey Joe, are you busy?"
I said, "No." "Then work with your right hand."

left hand
right foot
left foot
head

# Sample Daily Schedule

| | |
|---|---|
| 7:50-9:40 | Whole Language* |
| 9:40-10:10 | Resource (Music, Library, PE) |
| 10:10-10:52 | Math |
| 10:52-11:17 | Lunch |
| 11:17-11:40 | Recess/Bathroom/Water |
| 11:40-12:00 | Read-Aloud |
| 12:00-12:45 | Lessons: Handwriting, Spelling, English, Skills |
| 12:45-1:25 | Science, Social Studies, Health, Computers, Art |
| 1:25-1:40 | Records |

*Detail of Whole Language time:

| | |
|---|---|
| 7:50-8:00 | D.E.A.R. (Drop Everything and Read) |
| 8:00-9:10 | Reading (Journals T, Th — Short Stuff W) |
| 9:10-9:40 | Poetry/Writing |

# Daily Reading/Writing Schedule

This schedule consists of a 1 hour and 50 minute block of time, which can be rearranged according to teacher preference.

Activities listed next to the letter **A** equal a 30 minute block of time.

| | | |
|---|---|---|
| **B** | = | 30 minutes |
| **C** | = | 15 minutes |
| **D** | = | 10 minutes |

D.E.A.R. Time (Drop Everything And Read) is included in the daily schedule constantly and equals a 10 minute block of time.

| Reading Activities | Writing Activities | Reading Activities | Writing Activities |
|---|---|---|---|
| A — book sets | B — individual small books | C — big book | D — journals |
| A — basal story | B — whole class big book | C — poetry | D — short stuff |
| A — reading by choice | B — writers' workshop | C — author of the week | D — book commercials |

To "build" your own schedule, choose: 1A, 1B, 2Cs, 1D, and include 10 minutes of D.E.A.R. time.

| EXAMPLE 1 | EXAMPLE 2 |
|---|---|
| **D.E.A.R. time (10 min.)** | **D.E.A.R. time (10 min.)** |
| C — author of the week (15 min.) | D — journals (10 min.) |
| A — book sets (30 min.) | C — big book (15 min.) |
| C — poetry (15 min.) | A — reading by choice (30 min.) |
| B — individual small books (30 min.) | B — writers' workshop (30 min.) |
| D — short stuff (10 min.) | C — author of the week (15 min.) |
| = 1 hour, 50 minutes | = 1 hour, 50 minutes |

# Write on Target Handout

## Five Day Schedule
## for Writing Individual Small Books

**Day 1 — Format:**

Familiarize your students with a format found in a predictable book or a familiar poem, such as "The House That Jack Built" or "Roses are red, violets are blue..."

Begin brainstorming substitutions for these formats out loud in class and on the board (for your visual learners).

**Day 2 — "Sloppy Copies":**

Continue brainstorming and have students begin writing their ideas down in rough drafts, or "sloppy copies," while you circulate and conference with children about their content, word choice, audience, punctuation, and spelling.

**Day 3 — Begin Final Copies:**

When students feel that their stories are ready to publish, they may begin transferring their ideas to their final copy. We make final copies by stapling ditto paper inside a piece of 9x12 folded construction paper to form a small booklet. Students begin with the cover, title, copyright and dedication page.

**Day 4 — Complete Final Copies:**

Students continue transferring ideas from the rough draft copies to the booklets.

**Day 5 — Sharing:**

Allow students to read their completed books aloud to your class and to other classes in your school. Then the students will enjoy taking the books home and sharing them with their familes.

Cynthia Merrilees

# Classroom Smorgasbord

## Ideas That Make School Fun

### Resource List

All the records and tapes used in this workshop can be obtained
by ordering through the Educational Record Center.

Educational Record Center, Inc.
3233 Burnt Miller Dr., Suite 100
Wilmington, NC 28403-2655
Toll Free: 1-800-438-1637

| Catalog Number | Title |
| --- | --- |
| 1KB 8102 | *Singable Songs for the Very Young* by Raffi |
| 1KB 8116 | *Raffi's Christmas Album* by Raffi |
| 1YT 31 | *We All Live Together Vol. 1-4* by Greg & Steve |
| 1YT 35 | *On the Move with Greg and Steve* by Greg & Steve |
| 1EL 7902 | *Smorgasbord* by Sharon, Lois & Bram |
| 1RS 1329 | *Rosenshontz Tickles You* by Rosenshontz |
| 1RC 410C | *Collections* by Fred Penner |
| F190 | *Really Rosie* by Carole King |

CHILDREN MAY
FORGET WHAT YOU SAY,
BUT
THEY'LL NEVER
FORGET HOW YOU MAKE
THEM FEEL.

---

Cynthia Merrilees

# The "Working Calendar"

## ROUNDING

**10 /120**

*(day of month and day of the year)*

## EQUATIONS

⑦

## MONEY

| 7¢ | $7 |
|----|-----|
| ⑤ | $5 |
| ① | $1 |
| ① | $1 |

## MEASUREMENT *(Yard Stick)*

1 2 3 4 5 6 7 •

## Number Line *(Days Of School Year)*

120  121  122  123

### *Calendar*   *(patterns)*

### MARCH

| | | 1 ▲ | 2 ▲ | 3 ● | 4 ▲ | 5 ▲ |
|---|---|---|---|---|---|---|
| 6 ● | ⑦ | 8 | 9 | 10 | 11 | 12 |
| 13 | 14 | 15 | 16 | 17 | 18 | 19 |
| 20 | 21 | 22 | 23 | 24 | 25 | 26 |
| 27 | 28 | 29 | 30 | 31 | | |

## TALLY

卌 II

## TIME

**7:00**

### Yesterday was: Sunday
### Today is: Monday
### Tomorrow will be: Tuesday

16
15
14
13
12
11
10
9
8
7
6
5
4
3
2
1

## Place Value *(Days of School Year)*

Hundreds   Tens   Ones

Cynthia Merrilees

# Math Songs

Five little speckled frogs, sitting on a hollow log, eating delicious bugs.  One jumped into the pool, where it was nice and cool, now there are four little speckled frogs.

Four little speckled frogs, etc.

Five little monkeys, jumping on the bed, one fell off and bumped his head. Mama called the doctor and the doctor said, "No more monkeys jumping on the bed!"

Four little monkeys, etc.

One little monkey, jumping on the bed, one fell off and bumped his head. Mama called the doctor and the doctor said, "Put those monkeys back to bed!"

There were ten in the bed, and the little one said,, "Roll over, roll over!"  So they all rolled over, and one fell out.

There were nine in the bed, etc.

## Mad Minute Math

Name: _____     Number Correct: _____

| | | | | | |
|---|---|---|---|---|---|
| 8<br>x 2 | 8<br>x 8 | 9<br>x 8 | 8<br>x 1 | 4<br>x 8 | 5<br>x 8 |
| 0<br>x 8 | 9<br>x 8 | 7<br>x 8 | 8<br>x 1 | 8<br>x 2 | 8<br>x 6 |
| 4<br>x 8 | 8<br>x 3 | 7<br>x 8 | 8<br>x 8 | 9<br>x 8 | 3<br>x 8 |
| 8<br>x 1 | 8<br>x 2 | 9<br>x 8 | 8<br>x 7 | 5<br>x 8 | 8<br>x 6 |
| 8<br>x 5 | 8<br>x 3 | 8<br>x 8 | 7<br>x 8 | 9<br>x 8 | 8<br>x 2 |

Cynthia Merrilees

_____'s Spelling List

_____'s Spelling List

_____'s Spelling List

1.
2.
3.
4.
5.
6.
7.
9.
10.

1.
2.
3.
4.
5.
6.
7.
9.
10.

# Spelling Study Sheet

Name_____

Lesson_____

1._____  11._____
2._____  12._____
3._____  13._____
4._____  14._____
5._____  15._____
6._____  16._____
7._____  17._____
8._____  18._____
9._____  19._____
10._____  20._____

# Dictation Sentences

1._____
2._____
3._____

Cynthia Merrilees

# Teachers

Teachers show respect for children's ideas, feelings, and actions.

Teachers recognize and consider children's home environments and cultural uniquenesses in planning curriculum.

Teachers use evaluation to gain information and apply it in seeking better ways of encouraging and providing for children's learning.

Teachers' expectations affect students' achievements and attitudes.

Teachers are knowledgeable of the process by which children learn best.

Teachers provide activities based upon children's interests and developmental levels.

Teachers model language and an enthusiasm for learning.

Teachers provide an accepting, non-threatening climate for the development of literacy.

Teachers provide an exciting, literate environment which fosters independent learners.

Teachers share children's strengths and needs with parents, and actively encourage parent participation in their children's learning.

Teachers are active learners and see the classroom as an opportunity for their personal growth and change. Their classrooms reflect this.

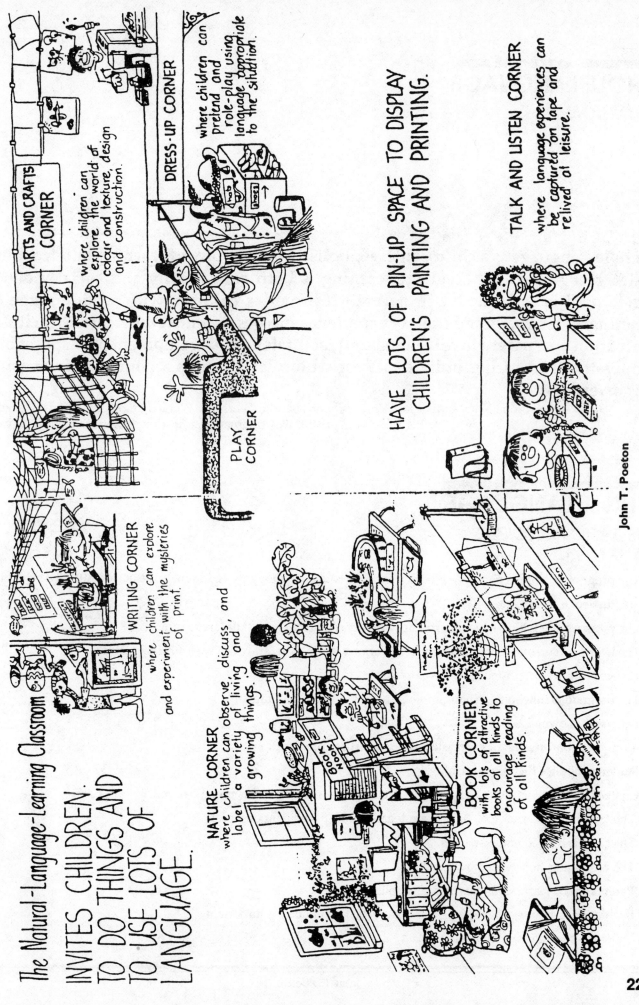

The Natural-Language-Learning Classroom

INVITES CHILDREN
TO DO THINGS AND
TO USE LOTS OF
LANGUAGE.

ARTS AND CRAFTS CORNER
where children can explore the world of colour and texture, design and construction.

DRESS-UP CORNER
where children can pretend and role-play using language appropriate to the situation.

PLAY CORNER

WRITING CORNER
where children can explore and experiment with the mysteries of print.

NATURE CORNER
where children can observe, discuss, and label a variety of living and growing things.

BOOK CORNER
with lots of attractive books of all kinds to encourage reading of all kinds.

HAVE LOTS OF PIN-UP SPACE TO DISPLAY CHILDREN'S PAINTING AND PRINTING.

TALK AND LISTEN CORNER
where language experiences can be captured on tape and relived at leisure.

John T. Poeton

229

# WHOLE LANGUAGE
## DEFINITION

Whole Language is a child-centered, holistic philosophy of learning and teaching which recognizes that language learning is both contextually and socially determined, and is constructive in nature. It provides children with a wide range of meaningful language and literary experiences across the entire curriculum, includes evaluation and parent involvement and facilitates the development of responsible, cooperative and caring individuals for whom language is a source of increasing empowerment.

From: Norma Mikleson, University of Victoria, Centre for Whole Language, Victoria, Canada
Presentation April 30, 1989 International Reading Association, New Orleans

# WHOLE LANGUAGE
## THE BASIC PRINCIPLES

1. The program is child-centered — it begins with the language, thoughts and knowledge of the child. The child is the curricular informant.

2. The program is not hierarchial or arbitrarily sequenced. However, skills are taught.

3. The learner is surrounded with language at various levels. Literature is a basis for the program.

4. Choice is allowed. Autonomy is developed.

5. The program is functional. Thoughtful use of language is encouraged.

6. Language is owned, social.

7. Multiple opportunities for expression and support are provided.

8. Students monitor their own learning.

9. Content subjects continue to be taught — but language in all its forms is emphasized.

10. The teacher is a learner too. S/he is a researcher — a participant observer.

11. The child is trusted and respected.

12. The program is holistic and integrated.

13. Parents are co-learners, co-teachers, and colleagues.

14. Evaluation is an integral on-going component. Self-evaluation is important.

15. There is a strong research base.

John T. Poeton

# COMPONENTS OF A WHOLE LANGUAGE PROGRAM

**A Balanced WHOLE LANGUAGE Program
Should Include The Following Components:**

Reading to Children

Shared Book Experience

Uninterrupted Sustained Silent Reading (USSR)

Guided Reading

Individualized Reading

Language Experience

Children's Writing

Modelled Writing

Sharing Time

Content Area: Reading, Writing, Talking, Listening

Evaluation and Assessment Procedures Including:

Logs, Portfolios, Self-Evaluation

and Kid Watching

*Revised by: John Thomas Poeton*

# Directed Reading and Guided Reading

In recent articles pertaining to reading there has been much made of a new term called "guided reading." Here are some comparisons between guided reading and a term which has been a part of pre-service reading instruction since 1960 — directed reading.

| Directed | Guided |
|---|---|
| *The focus is on:* | |
| author's meaning and it is often found in the teacher's guide | reader constructs own meaning |
| literal questions often based on content and recall | reading strategies, process |
| prepared script, teacher professional plan | interactive responsive to the learner |
| answer questions after reading | making predictions before reading |
| follow-up enrichment activities | "preparing the soil" dialogue interaction before reading |
| the text at hand | the learner as a life long reader |

*Developed by Mike Hagan of San Jose, California with a group of teachers.*
*Reprinted with permission of Mike Hagan.*

John Poeton

# Reading Strategies

| Date | observer | Name | self-assessed |
|------|----------|------|---------------|
| | | Reading is supposed to make sense. When it doesn't make sense any more I need to stop and find out why. | |
| | | Think about what you already know about the topic. You probably know some of the things the author knows. | |
| | | Try to guess what will happen next. Do this often while reading, and check your guesses now and then to see if they were right. | |
| | | Skip a word if it's too hard. Read ahead to figure out what's happening. The whole story is more important than a few of the words. | |
| | | Look at the pictures for information. | |
| | | When something doesn't make sense, go back and read it again. Learn how to fix your own mistakes. | |
| | | Reading is just like talking. Think about the way English works. | |
| | | Try to read several words together sometimes, like "Once upon a time." | |
| | | Sound it out. Think about what you know about letter names and sounds. | |
| | | Read different things different ways. Sometimes readers skip through a piece, sometimes they read from the beginning. Use the table of contents. | |
| | | Try to imagine what the character or the place looks like. Try to make a movie in your head. | |

(A reading strategy is signed and dated when it is observed being used consistently. A strategy is self-assessed when a child is aware of using it.)

Reprinted with permission of Mike Hagan

**John Poeton**

# Literature Study

Name _____  Date _____

During the week of _____ I agree to read the book entitled:

_____

This book has a total of _____ pages.  I will pace myself according to the schedule below:

| Mon | Tue | Wed | Thu | Fri | Sat | Sun |
|-----|-----|-----|-----|-----|-----|-----|
|     |     |     |     |     |     |     |

I kept closely to my planned schedule.       YES ☐       NO ☐

I finished the book on time.       YES ☐       NO ☐

I did not finish my book.  I am on page _____ .

Child's Signature _____

Teacher's Signature _____

Parent's Signature _____

Next book proposed _____

Next literature study date _____

# Teaching Approaches in a Balanced Reading Programme

| Approach | Advantages | Limitations |
|---|---|---|
| *Reading to Children* | Familiarises children with the language and conventions of books. Helps children discover that books are worthwhile. | May reflect the teacher's interests rather than children's preferences. Does not allow for children to process print independently. |
| *Language Experience* | Child centred. Makes the connection between spoken and written forms of language. Offers familiar language. Provides meaningful text. Encourages memory for text. | Restricted to the child's spoken language. Does not give experience with book language. |
| *Shared Reading* | Offers rich book language, new vocabulary, and growing familiarity with conventions of written language. As with reading to children, gives access to interesting, lively literature that may be beyond children's present reading capabilities. | Some children may develop a memory for text, with little other basis for self-correction strategies. |
| *Guided Reading* | Deepens understandings of the text. Presents many opportunities for specific teaching as difficulties arise. Encourages silent reading. | Choice of text depends on the teacher's assessment of group capabilities and interests. |
| *Independent Reading* | Caters for individual abilities, interests. Opportunities to practise self-monitoring on real reading. | Children may choose books that are too difficult. Children may limit their choice to the same type of material. |
| *Writing* | Writing involves continuous reading. It develops understandings about visual cueing systems, e.g., grapho-phonic relationships, punctuation and other conventions. Semantic and syntactic prediction is high, increasing attention to checking and confirming. The child uses background knowledge and experience to compose meaningful text. See also Language Experience. | The child's imagination and knowledge are not enriched by the contents of good books, and by the range of forms and styles of book language. See also Language Experience. |

From *Reading in Junior Classes* (1985) Wellington: Ministry of Education of New Zealand. Distributed in the U.S. by Richard C. Owen Publishers, Inc., 135 Katonah Ave., Katonah, NY 10536. Reprinted with permission.

# Potential Literature Discussion Responses

Student _____  Date ___ Grade ___ Literature

| Use of Resources for Meaning Construction | Relationships Focus: Outward | Connections Focus: Inward | Transactions | Discussion |
| --- | --- | --- | --- | --- |
| Uses information from other than book sources | Addresses social issues | Forms new understandings from interaction with text | Recognizes relationships of story and life themes | Promotes action |
| Uses reference material | Addresses previous readings by other authors | Moves into the world of the text | Examines story in light of self as audience | Identifies with characters |
| Frames questions to get information | Addresses previous readings by same author | Shares personal and emotional connections | Sees plot developing | Addresses the reading |
| Rereads to focus on important details and concepts needed to make sense | Addresses life experiences appropriate to text and readers | Shares a point of view (own, character's, family's, group's, etc.) | Draws from story traits of characters | Retells for own purpose (parts like/don't like, not understood, to prove something) |
| Demands meaning by using prior knowlege | Addresses ideas of others | Shares information from text | Discusses setting within context of story (e.g., mood) | Initiates related discussion |

John T. Poeton

# VERMONT WRITING SURVEY

The conclusions that follow concerning the teaching of writing are the result of information gathered from questionnaires and interviews with students, teachers and parents involved in the Vermont Writing Project 1979-1982.

1. Teachers who write with their students and share their writing with their students experience more success than teachers who do not.

2. Teachers need to provide ample opportunity for their student writers to confer with them and their peers as a given piece of writing develops.

3. Daily writing is important.

4. Teachers should provide opportunities for students to read their writing aloud.

5. Teachers should allow time for students to discuss their writing in the context of the writing process so that they can come to an understanding of themselves as writers.

6. Teachers should encourage students to see themselves as writers of reading and not writers of writing and should point out the difference to students.

7. Teachers should not create problems by making an unnecessary distinction between writing that is "creative" and all other types of writing (by implication "non-creative" writing).

8. Teachers who have their students maintain writing folders have a distinct advantage in that their students are able to follow their own development as writers and to feel some sense of achievement.

9. Teachers should recognize that writing provides a very useful function in establishing a sense of community within a group of students.

10. Teachers who use a workshop format and actively conference with their students are more instructive and have a greater effect on the development of students as writers than teachers who spend much time and effort grading papers.

11. Teachers of writing believe that writing is a useful and unique mode of learning and, therefore, is helpful in teaching the content areas.

# A portfolio approach to classroom reading assessment: The whys, whats, and hows

Sheila Valencia, University of Washington

## Why do we need portfolios?

Developing artists rely on portfolios to demonstrate their skills and achievements. Within the portfolio, they include samples of their work that exemplify the depth and breadth of their expertise. They may include many different indicators: work in a variety of media to demonstrate their versatility, several works on one particular subject to demonstrate their refined skill and sophistication, and work collected over time to exemplify their growth as artists. With such rich sources of information, it is easier for the critics and the teachers, and most importantly, artists themselves, to understand the development of expertise and to plan the experiences that will encourage additional progress and showcase achievements. A portfolio approach to the assessment of reading assumes the position that developing readers deserve no less.

A portfolio approach to reading assessment has great intuitive appeal: It resonates with our desire to capture and capitalize on the best each student has to offer; it encourages us to use many different ways to evaluate learning; and it has an integrity and validity that no other type of assessment offers. In addition to its intuitive appeal, there are theoretical and pragmatic reasons for a portfolio approach to reading assessment that are summarized in four guiding principles drawn from both research and instructional practices.

1. Sound assessment is anchored in authenticity—authenticity of tasks, texts, and contexts. Good assessment should grow out of authentic reading instruction and reading tasks. Students read a variety of authentic texts in class

and in life; thus, they should be presented with that same diversity of texts during assessment. Students read for a variety of purposes; therefore, they should be presented with various purposes for reading during assessment. Reading assessment must mirror our understanding of reading as an interactive process. Any assessment must consider not only how the reader, the text, and the context influence reading but how they interact and impact the construction of meaning.

Further, because the assessment activities resemble actual classroom and life reading tasks, they can be integrated into ongoing classroom life and instruction. Teachers and students do not have to take time away from real reading for assessment. Real reading is *used* as an assessment opportunity.

Finally, the principle of authenticity insures that we assess the orchestration, integration, and application of skills in meaningful contexts. We cannot become lost in the mire of subskill assessment because assessment of such isolated skills would not resemble authentic reading.

2. Assessment must be a continuous, on-going process; it must chronicle development. This is the difference between simply assessing the outcome of learning (the product) and assessing the process of learning over time. When we are positioned to observe and collect information continuously, we send a message to students, parents, and administrators that learning is never completed; instead, it is always evolving, growing, and changing.

3. Because reading is a complex and multifaceted process, valid reading assessment must be multidimen-

sional—committed to sampling a wide range of cognitive processes, affective responses, and literacy activities. In addition to assessing across a range of texts and purposes, we need to consider other important dimensions of reading such as interest and motivation, voluntary reading, and metacognitive knowledge and strategies. If we simply model our assessments on existing reading tests, we accept a constrained definition of reading and ignore many of the aspects that we value and teach.

4. Assessment must provide for active, collaborative reflection by both teacher and student. Historically, teachers and students have viewed assessment as something that must be done to appease others, something to be done for them rather than something to be done for ourselves. Instead, assessment must be viewed as a process within our control that helps us evaluate how well we have learned and what we need to learn next.

As teachers, assessment helps us evaluate our own teaching effectiveness and helps us with our instructional decisions. Similarly, assessment activities in which students are engaged in evaluating their own learning help them reflect on and understand their own strengths and needs, and it instills responsibility for their own learning. It is when students and teachers are collaboratively involved in assessment that the greatest benefit is achieved. Collaborative assessment strengthens the bond between student and teacher and establishes them as partners in learning. Collaboration precipitates meaningful dialogue about the criteria and process we use in evaluation and provides an important model for students as they become self-evaluators.

These four guiding principles provide a powerful rationale for proposing a portfolio approach. No single test, single observation, or single piece of student work could possibly capture the authentic, continuous, multidimensional, interactive requirement of sound assessment.

## What do portfolios look like?

Our rationale for portfolios helps us construct a picture of what such an approach to assessment might look like. Physically, it is larger and more elaborate than a report card. Practically, it must be smaller and more focused than a steamer trunk filled with accumulated artifacts. It is more like a large expandable file folder that holds (a) samples of the student's work selected by the teacher or the student, (b) the teacher's observational notes, (c) the student's own periodic self-evaluations, and (d) progress notes contributed by the student and teacher collaboratively. The range of items to include in a portfolio is almost limitless but may include written responses to reading, reading logs, selected daily work, pieces of writing at various stages of completion, classroom tests, checklists, unit projects, and audio or video tapes, to name a few. The key is to ensure a *variety* of types of indicators of learning so that teachers, parents, students, and administrators can build a complete picture of the student's development.

Logically, portfolios should be kept in a spot in the classroom that is easily accessible to students and teachers. Unlike the secretive grade book or the untouchable permanent records stored in the office, these are working folders. Their location must invite students and teachers to contribute to them on an ongoing basis and to reflect on their contents to plan the next learning steps.

## How is a portfolio organized?

There is little doubt that portfolios can be messy business. However, many teachers and school districts committed to more valid and useful as-

sessment procedures are beginning to give portfolios a try. Because the exact nature of the portfolio will vary depending on the curriculum goals and the students, it is difficult to prescribe exactly what should be included and how and when it should be evaluated. But it *is* possible to think of some organizational strategies that might make a portfolio more useful and more manageable.

*Planning for a portfolio.* First, it is important to be *selective* about what should be included in the portfolio. Since the decision about what to assess must grow out of curricular and instructional priorities, the critical step is to determine, as a school, grade level, district, or state, the key goals of instruction. Goals of instruction are broad, not overly specific-isolated skills or individual lesson objectives. For example, goals might involve understanding the author's message, learning new information from expository texts, summarizing the plot of a story, using word identification skills flexibly to construct meaning, reading fluently, or exhibiting an interest and desire to read. If the goals of instruction are not specified, portfolios have the potential to become unfocused holding files for odds and ends, or worse, a place to collect more isolated skills tests.

Second, it is helpful to think about what you do *instructionally* to help students progress toward those goals and how you and the students determine progress. This step will help you to identify some of the content and format of the assessment activities. One way to approach this task is to examine existing evaluation strategies and to decide the areas that are being assessed adequately and those that need to be added, adapted, or expanded. There is no need to start from scratch because many good instructional activities currently used in classrooms would be appropriate for portfolios. For example, many teachers use story maps as part of their instruction on understanding story structure. The very same technique could be used to assess students' plot knowledge after they have completed a story. No special test would be required; no special text or passage would be assigned; yet, we would as-

sess an important goal of instruction.

*What goes into a portfolio.* After planning the focus of the portfolio, it is helpful to organize the contents in two layers: (a) the actual evidence, or raw data, that is included in the portfolio, and (b) a summary sheet or organizing framework to help synthesize that information. Including the first layer enables teachers to examine students' actual work and progress notes rather than relying simply on a number or grade. Including the summary sheet forces teachers to synthesize the information in a way that helps them make decisions and communicate with parents and administrators.

*Managing the contents of a portfolio.* In many ways, a portfolio approach to assessment mirrors what good teachers have been doing intuitively for years. The difference is that now we acknowledge the importance and value of alternative forms of assessment. However, if we are not careful, portfolio information will remain only in the classroom, failing to inform others who are involved with decision making. That is why we must deliberately plan to make portfolio assessments accessible to administrators and parents.

While the flexibility of the portfolio is one of its greatest assets, it may also be one of its greatest problems. One reason this type of classroom assessment has not been more popular is the concern about unreliability, inconsistency, and inequity across classrooms, schools, and districts. However there are several mechanisms to protect against this criticism. First, by engaging in discussions about the goals and priorities for instruction and assessment, we can build a common understanding of expectations and criteria. Second, by assessing in an ongoing way, we collect several indicators for any particular goal; generally, the more measures one has, the greater the reliability of the conclusions or decisions one makes.

A third way to attend to consistency is to include two levels of assessment evidence—required evidence and supporting evidence. The required evidence enables us to look systematically across students as well as within each student. This provides the kind of evidence that administrators desire and expect, thus enhancing the likelihood that they will use the portfolio in *their* decision making. These assessments might be particular activities, checklists, or projects (or a list from which to choose), which are tied to identified goals and included in the portfolios of all students at a grade level. They might be fairly structured (e.g., an emergent literacy checklist; a reading log) or more flexible (e.g., students select their best piece of writing to include every six weeks; an audio tape of a student reading a favorite passage recorded at the beginning and end of the school year).

Supporting evidence is additional documentation of learning to include in the portfolio. The evidence may be selected independently or collaboratively by the student and the teacher. It may be the result of a spontaneous activity (e.g., a letter to an author of a favorite book), or it may be carefully planned (e.g., a semantic map completed before and after reading an informational selection). Supporting evidence is critical to building a *complete* picture of a student's literacy abilities because it adds the depth and variety typically missing in traditional assessments. It provides the opportunity for teachers and students to take advantage of the uniqueness of each classroom and each student by encouraging the inclusion of a variety of indicators of learning.

*Using the portfolio for classroom decision-making.* A portfolio can be used at planning time for periodic review and reflection of its contents. The teacher and student might plan to collaboratively visit the portfolio every several weeks; in addition, the students might plan to visit it at other times individually or with a friend. During the collaborative visits, the teacher and student might discuss progress, add written notes, and plan for the inclusion of other pieces. At the end of the school year, they might collectively decide which pieces will remain in the portfolio for the next year and which are ready to go home. In addition, portfolios are a valuable source of information during conferences with parents and administrators. While parents might be interested in the raw data, the actual evidence of learning, principals or superintendents might be interested in the condensed information found on the summary sheet. In either case, the assessments would reflect more authentic, continuous information than ever before available.

The intrapersonal and interpersonal dialogue that results from visits to the portfolio is a critical component of both assessment and instruction. And as a way of encouraging and monitoring the use of the portfolio, everyone might be asked to initial and date each visit. This is a sure way to remind us that portfolio evaluation is intended to be used.

## Summary

In the coming months and years, there are sure to be many very different, perhaps conflicting, iterations of a portfolio approach to reading assessment. The real value of a portfolio does not lie in its physical appearance, location, or organization; rather, it is in the mindset that it instills in students and teachers. Portfolios represent a philosophy that demands that we view assessment as an integral part of our instruction, providing a process for teachers and students to use to guide learning. It is an expanded definition of assessment in which a wide variety of indicators of learning are gathered across many situations before, during, and after instruction. It is a philosophy that honors both the process and the products of learning as well as the active participation of the teacher and the students in their own evaluation and growth.

**For additional information on portfolios see the following:**

Au, K.H., Scheu, J.A., Arakaki, A.J., & Herman, P.A. (in press). Assessment and accountability in a whole literacy curriculum. *The Reading Teacher.*

Lucas, C.K. (1988). Toward ecological evaluation, part one and part two. *The Quarterly of the National Writing Project and the Center for the Study of Writing, 10*(1), 1-7; *10*(2), 4-10.

Valencia, S.W., McGinley, W., & Pearson, P.D. (in press). Assessing reading and writing: Building a more complete picture. In G. Duffy (Ed.), *Reading in the middle school.* Newark, DE: International Reading Association.

Wolf, D.P. (1989). Portfolio assessment: Sampling student work. *Educational Leadership, 46* (7), 4-10.

---

Assessment is a column dealing with all forms of the measurement and evaluation of children's literacy abilities. Send questions, comments, or suggestions about the column to **John J. Pikulski, Department of Educational Development, University of Delaware, Newark, DE 19716, USA.**

---

**Reprinted with permission of Sheila Valencia and the International Reading Association.**

Lynn K. Rhodes
Sally Nathenson-Mejia

# Anecdotal records: A powerful tool for ongoing literacy assessment

*Rhodes and Nathenson-Mejia are faculty members in the Language, Literacy, and Culture program at the University of Colorado at Denver where they work with teachers on issues of classroom assessment.*

A great deal of attention is being paid to the assessment of process in addition to product in reading and writing. Observing the process a student uses provides the teacher with a window or view on how students arrive at products (i.e., a piece of writing or an answer to a comprehension question). This allows the teacher to make good decisions about how she or he might assist during the process or restructure the process in order to best support more effective use of strategies and students' development as readers and writers. Anecdotal records can be written about products or can include information about both process and product. As process assessment, resulting from observation, anecdotal records can be particularly telling.

Observations of students in the process of everyday reading and writing allow teachers to see for themselves the reading and writing and problem-solving strategies students use and their responses to reading and writing. Genishi and Dyson (1984), Jaggar (1985), Pinnell (1985), Y. Goodman (1985), Galindo (1989), and others discuss the need to observe children while they are involved in language use. Goodman notes:

> Evaluation provides the most significant information if it occurs continuously and simultaneously with the experiences in which the learning is taking place.... Teachers who observe the development of language and knowledge in children in different settings become aware of important milestones in children's development that tests cannot reveal. (Goodman, 1985, p. 10)

When teachers have developed a firm knowledge base that they can rely on in observations of students' reading and writing, they usually prefer recording their observations in anecdotal form. This is because the open-ended nature of anecdotal records allows teachers to record the rich detail available in most observations of literacy processes and products. The open-ended nature of anecdotal record taking also allows teachers to determine what details are important to record given the situation in which the student is reading/writing, previous assessment data, and the instructional goals the teacher and student have established. In other words, what is focused on and recorded depends upon the teacher, the student, and the context, not on the predetermined items on a checklist.

Taken regularly, anecdotal notes become not only a vehicle for planning instruction and documenting progress, but also a story about an individual. The definition of an anecdote is "a short narrative (or story) concerning a particular incident or event of an interesting or amusing nature" (*The Random House Dictionary of the English Language*, 1966). A story is "a way of knowing and remembering information—a shape or pattern into which information can be arranged.... [Story] restructures experiences for the purpose of 'saving' them" (Livo, 1986, p. 5). Anecdotes about events in the reading/writing life of a student tell an ongoing story about how that child responds to the classroom's literacy environment and instruction. Since stories are how we make sense of much of our world, anecdotal records can be a vehicle for helping us make sense of what students do as readers and writers. In addition, teachers find that telling the story accumulated in anecdotal records is a natural and easy way to impart information about students' literacy progress to parents and others who care for the children.

In short, anecdotal records are widely acknowledged as being a powerful classroom tool for ongoing literacy assessment (Bird, 1989; Cartwright & Cartwright, 1974; Morrissey, 1989; Thorndike & Hagen, 1977). In this article we will provide information about techniques for collecting and analyzing anecdotal records. In addition, we will review uses of anecdotal records including planning for instruction, informing parents and students, and generating new assessment questions.

## Techniques for writing anecdotal records

Reflecting about techniques for writing anecdotal records can positively affect both the content of the records as well as the ease with which they are recorded. Thorndike and Hagen (1977) suggest guidelines for the content of anecdotal records that teachers may find helpful:

1. Describe a specific event or product.
2. Report rather than evaluate or interpret.
3. Relate the material to other facts that are known about the child.

We have found these points particularly helpful if teachers feel that the content of their previous anecdotal records has not been useful to them. Below we have included an example of an anecdotal record for a first grader, Eleanor. Note how Eleanor's teacher uses detailed description to record how Eleanor is starting to understand sound/letter relationships but is still confused about word boundaries and sentences.

Eleanor
STRDAIPADENBSNO
(Yesterday I played in the snow)
STRDA = yesterday
I = I
PAD = played
EN = in
B = the (said "du" and thought she was writing "D")
SNO = snow
Showed her how to stretch her words out like a rubberband—doing it almost on own by SNO. E does have a fairly good grasp of sound/letter relationships. However, has a hard time isolating words and tracking words in sentences in her mind. That may hold up progress for awhile. Asked her—at end—what she did in writing today that she hadn't done in previous writing. She said, "I listened to sounds." Told her to do it in her writing again tomorrow.

*Taken regularly, anecdotal notes become not only a vehicle for planning instruction and documenting progress, but also a story about an individual.*

Instead of recording the descriptive detail found in Eleanor's anecdotal note, the teacher might have written, "Eleanor sounded out words in writing for the first time today and will continue to need lots of help to do so." A general conclusion such as this is not as useful to instructional planning or to documenting progress as the detailed description in the note written by Eleanor's teacher. However, we believe that Thorndike and Hagen's points should be treated as guidelines, not as strict rules. We find that it is sometimes helpful to evaluate or interpret what has been observed.

*Anecdotes about events in the reading/writing life of a student tell an ongoing story about how that child responds to the classroom's literacy environment and instruction. Since stories are how we make sense of much of our world, anecdotal records can be a vehicle for helping us make sense of what students do as readers and writers. In addition, teachers find that telling the story accumulated in anecdotal records is a natural and easy way to impart information about students' literacy progress to parents and others who care for the children.*

For example, read the sample anecdotal record below written about Katie, a fourth grader.

### Katie

I asked if I could read more of the poetry book she had written at home over the last two years. (She had read selected poems to her classmates earlier.) She showed me a poem she didn't want to read to the class "because they wouldn't understand." (It's quite serious and deep.) Poetry doesn't look like poetry though she reads it as poetry—could use a formatting lesson.

The teacher's comment, "could use a formatting lesson," in Katie's note provides useful evaluation and interpretation as long as it is supported by a description of the event or product itself. The comment "Poetry doesn't look like poetry though she reads it as poetry," is the description that supports the interpretive comment.

Observational guides can be valuable complements to anecdotal recording because they serve to remind teachers what might be observed. If teachers find an observation guide helpful, they may want to post for themselves a list of the kinds of observations that might be recorded anecdotally. The table illustrates such a guide resulting from teachers' brainstorming. The list is displayed in a place in the classroom where the teachers can easily consult it, especially when they feel they need to improve the content of their notes.

In addition to increasing the content value of anecdotal notes, teachers also are concerned about increasing the ease with which anecdotal notes can be recorded. In part, ease of recording emanates from the classroom environment the teacher has established. Classroom routines that encourage students to be increasingly independent and responsible as readers and writers enable teachers to more easily record anecdotal records than classrooms in which literacy tasks are more teacher directed. Once students are familiar with and secure about the structure and behaviors demanded in routines such as Sustained Silent Reading, Author's Circle, Literature Circles, Writers' Workshop, and Readers' Workshop, teachers can find the time to work with and record observations of individuals or groups.

In addition to encouraging student independence and responsibility in literacy situations, it is easier to write anecdotal notes as teachers discover recording techniques that fit their styles and busy classroom lives. It is useful to carry a clipboard to a variety of classroom settings, using such complementary recording tools as sticky notes to transfer information to a notebook sectioned off by students' names. Teachers can take notes on a prearranged list of children each day, labeling sticky notes with the date and the names of students to be observed. This technique makes it possible to take notes on every child a minimum of once a week in each curricular area in which notes are taken. Students can keep records too. Following a conference, the teacher might ask the student to record a summary statement of what they worked on together, what the student learned, or what the student still had questions about or wanted help with. Students can use sticky notes too so that their notes may be placed in the notebook along with the teacher's notes.

Teachers can take notes on groups as well as on individuals. For example, in working with a group of Chapter 1 students, one teacher noted that all five students were having difficulty putting the information they were gathering from books into their own words as they took notes. Instead of writing the same information five times, she wrote it once and put the note in a spot in her notebook reserved for notes about the group. When a note is taken in a group, but applies only to

selected students in the group, the note can be photocopied for the file of each student to whom it applies.

## Analyzing anecdotal records

Good techniques for recording anecdotal notes must be matched with good techniques for analyzing those notes if the potential for anecdotal records is to be realized. Effective analysis techniques include making inferences from the notes, looking for developmental trends or patterns within individuals and across children, identifying both strengths and weaknesses in learning and teaching, and making time for analysis.

*Making inferences.* Teachers continually make inferences about students' reading and writing on the basis of observations. Looking back at the sample anecdotal record on Eleanor, you can see that Eleanor's teacher made one of her inferences explicit: "E does have a fairly good grasp of sound/letter relationships." Because the teacher observed that Eleanor was able to consistently produce letters that matched the sounds she heard, she was able to infer that Eleanor had developed knowledge of sound/letter relationships.

Katie's teacher doesn't explicitly infer anything in the first anecdotal record but it is

---

### Teacher-generated observation guide

- functions served in reading/writing
- engagement in reading/writing
- what appears to impact engagement in reading/writing
- what aspects of text student attends to
- interactions with others over reading/writing
- interactions with materials
- insightful or interesting things students say
- hypotheses students are trying out in reading/writing
- misconceptions students have
- miscues students make while reading
- changes students make in writing
- how students use text before, during, and after reading
- how a lesson affects students' reading/writing
- comparisons between what students say and what they do
- plans students make and whether/how plans are amended
- how, where, and with whom students work
- what students are interested in
- what students say they want to work on in their reading/writing
- what students say about reading/writing done outside of school
- how students generate and solve problems in reading/writing
- ideas for reading/writing lessons and materials
- how students "symbol weave" (use multiple symbolic forms)
- how students theorize or talk about reading/writing
- how one reading/writing event relates to another
- how students use a variety of resources in reading/writing

---

possible for us to hypothesize that Katie may think she is different from many of her classmates with regard to what she thinks and writes. An analysis of other anecdotal records on Katie may lead the teacher to uncover a pattern in Katie's responses that confirms her hypothesis.

*Identifying patterns.* Patterns of behavior can be uncovered for individuals and groups by reading and rereading anecdotal records looking for similarities and differences. For example, the following two notes were taken during a reading period in a second-grade classroom in which the majority of the students elect to read in pairs or small groups. What pattern of behavior do you see?

> Brooke & Larry reading a Nate the Great story together—switching off at each paragraph. Brooke jumps in to correct Larry or give him a word at the slightest hesitation.

> Aaron & Shawn reading—switching off after every 2 pgs. Shawn loves the story—keeps telling Aaron the next part will be funny & chuckling as he reads aloud. Shawn is the leader in this situation. He interrupts with immediate help when Aaron hesitates with a word.

In recording and reviewing these notes, the teacher noticed that she had observed the same problem in both pairs of readers: one reader would take over the responsibility for working out words from the other reader. Since she had notes on only two pairs of students, however, the teacher interviewed the class the next day, focusing on what they did to help classmates who encountered difficult words to find out whether the pattern she had uncovered in these two situations was a more general problem. Differing patterns in language use, both oral and written, can be seen through regular anecdotal record keeping.

To illustrate with another example, a second-grade teacher, one of our practicum students, was concerned about Raul, who was new to the United States. She felt he was gaining more control over written and oral English, but she had nothing to document his progress. Moreover, she did not want to push him too hard if he wasn't ready, or cause him to lag behind. The following are excerpts from anecdotal records Sally took as the practicum supervisor while observing Raul working with his peers, none of whom spoke his native Spanish. These notes demonstrate not only his interaction with print, but also his use of oral language.

> The boys begin reading through the questions. Raul looks at the book and says, "Que es esto?" (What is this?). No one answers him.

> They are sitting next to a chart that has all their names on it. They proceed to copy each others' names from the chart. Raul says to the group, "You can get my name from the chart."

> T [the teacher] comes over to see what they are doing. She asks which question they are on. Raul replies, "Where do they live? Water." T reminds them to write the answer in the appropriate square.

Using these and other notes, the teacher was able to see patterns in Raul's use of language on two levels, interacting with print, and interacting with peers. Getting no response when he initiated interaction in Spanish, Raul proceeded to use English to read from the chart, read from the book, speak to his classmates, and respond to his teacher. Together the teacher and Sally were able to plan for how his use of English could continue to be encouraged in context-laden situations without worrying about pushing him too fast.

*Identifying strengths and weaknesses.* Anecdotal records can be analyzed for both strengths and weaknesses in students' reading and writing. Katie's anecdotal record, which we discussed already, reveals that she writes poetry for herself outside of school and that she has a sense of audience. These are strengths. The record also reveals an area in which Katie can grow—formatting the poetry she writes. A look back at Eleanor's note also reveals strengths and weaknesses. For example, the teacher discovered that Eleanor has graphophonic knowledge not previously revealed in her writing and that she could verbalize what she learned during the conference with the teacher. The teacher also discovered that Eleanor had previously been using random strings of letters in her writing because she had such difficulty tracking words in sentences in her mind.

*Finding time for analysis.* Finally, just as it is important to find time to *record* anecdotal records, it is important to find time to *analyze* anecdotal records. Some analysis occurs concurrently with recording anecdotal notes and is recorded along with a description of the event that was observed. However, other analysis follows the recording of notes. We recommend that teachers try two things to make time for such analysis. First, use the start of each instructional planning period for an analysis of anecdotal records for individuals and groups. This will serve to focus planning time so that it may be used more efficiently. Second, if teachers meet on a regular basis with other teachers, analyzing anecdotal records can be a fruitful part of the meeting. For example, if a classroom teacher and Chapter 1 teacher both take anecdotal records on the same child, they can analyze both sets of notes together by comparing individual notes and looking for shared patterns and trends. If a group of teachers from the same grade level meets regularly, an analysis of one another's notes may uncover a great deal to talk about, including how best to adapt teaching to students' needs.

## Uses of anecdotal records

Analysis of anecdotal records allows teachers to find patterns of success and difficulty for both individuals and groups of students. Students who have a need for particular information or for particular kinds of reading and writing opportunities can be grouped together and provided with the information or opportunities meeting their needs. In addition to instructional planning, the records also can be used to inform students and parents about progress and the value of various instructional and learning contexts. Finally, anecdotal records can help teachers generate new assessment questions.

*Instructional planning.* To extend what Genishi and Dyson say about oral language to written language (1984), anecdotal records on children's social behaviors and responses to written language can help teachers plan stimulating situations for the reluctant as well as the enthusiastic reader/writer. Using the set of anecdotal notes taken in the second-grade classroom during buddy reading discussed previously, we will show how the earlier analysis we provided can lead naturally to an instructional plan.

To review, the teacher noted that students in the buddy reading activity were taking reading responsibility away from their classmates when they hesitated or showed any sign of difficulty with reading words. When she interviewed the class the next day to glean more information about why this happened, she found that few students knew any options for helping partners with difficult words except to tell them the words. These assessment data helped the teacher plan lessons to demonstrate

how to help readers retain responsibility for figuring out difficult words. For example, she talked to the children about the strategies she used with them—providing plenty of wait time, suggesting that they read on, suggesting that they reread, and so on. Then she demonstrated each of these strategies with a child and made a list of the strategies for the children to refer to. Finally, she ended the next several reading sessions early so that the children could share with her and each other the strategies they used to successfully figure out their own words and to assist peers in figuring out words they didn't know. The children also shared problems they encountered and talked about how to solve them.

*Analysis of anecdotal records allows teachers to find patterns of success and difficulty for both individuals and groups of students.*

During the week the class focused on improving their strategies, the teacher observed pairs as they read, provided individual coaching for some, recorded more anecdotal notes, and used the notes to couch her lessons in detailed examples. In short, though the original anecdotal records and class interview were the basis of her first lesson, the anecdotal notes taken *after* the lessons began became equally important in planning ongoing instruction to further develop the students' strategies and understanding.

*Informing.* In addition to using anecdotal records for planning ongoing instruction, teachers also may use them to periodically inform others, including the students themselves, about students' strengths, weaknesses, and progress. Reviewing anecdotal records with students helps them see the growth they have made as readers and writers, and helps them gain a sense of progress over time and learn to pinpoint where improvements need to be made. To illustrate, one Chapter 1 teacher who involved students in generating instructional goals claimed that the process of writing anecdotal records affected the students' attention to the goals they had set: "The children seem to get more focused faster since I started carrying a clipboard and taking notes. It seems to remind them about the goals they decided to work on."

Anecdotal records also can help teachers create support systems for students outside the classroom. Report cards, parent conferences, and staffings are all situations in which instructional planning can take place on the basis of the teacher's analysis of anecdotal records. Specific examples pulled from anecdotal records help parents or other school personnel see the child in the same way as the teacher who has collected the anecdotal records. They can augment the home or test information provided by others and provide clues about what contexts are and are not supportive of the child's learning in school.

*Generating new questions.* Analyzing anecdotal records and using them to plan instruction encourages teachers to generate new questions that lead full circle to further assessment of students and of teaching itself. One teacher commented, "As I review kids' notes, sometimes even as I write them, I realize what else I need to find out." Bird (1989) commented that anecdotal records "not only guide [a teacher] in her instructional decision making but also provide her with a frequent opportunity for self-evaluation, enabling her to assess her role as a teacher" (p. 21).

We agree, and find that the use of anecdotal records to inform instruction helps teachers become more aware of how their instruction is interpreted by students. Teachers are able to see how they can influence students' interactions with each other as well as with books and other materials through specific instructional practices. To illustrate, below are some assessment questions generated by the teacher who recorded the anecdotal notes on pairs of students who were reading together in her classroom:

• What effect will the planned lessons have on students' interactions over words during reading?

• What other interactions do students have with each other over *ideas* in the story when they read together? (Her notes about Shawn led her to wonder this.)

• Do different pairings during reading make a difference in how readers interact with each other? What kinds of pairings are optimal?

• In what other situations is Shawn a leader? What can be done to further encourage that side of him?

The teacher has come full circle. Her original anecdotal notes were analyzed and used to plan instruction. But the notes also led to more focused assessment of individuals as well as assessment of a wider range of students and incidents. Her analysis and instructional planning led her to consider new assessment questions, questions not only about the students' reading but also about the effect of her teaching on their reading. For this teacher and for others who have realized the potential of anecdotal records, these "stories" are the basis from which they assess both their students' learning and their own teaching.

## Conclusion

Anecdotal records are a powerful tool for collecting information on an ongoing basis during reading and writing and for evaluating the products of instruction. Keeping anecdotal records on a regular basis can enhance a teacher's classroom observation skills. Teachers report that they see and hear with more clarity when using anecdotal records, by focusing more intensively on how children say things and how they interact with each other.

Anecdotal records are advantageous not only for planning instruction but for keeping others informed of children's progress in reading and writing and for focusing future assessment. When teachers discover the value of anecdotal records and figure out techniques to embed them in classroom literacy events and planning, anecdotal record keeping becomes a natural and important part of teaching and learning.

**References**

Bird, L.B. (1989). The art of teaching: Evaluation and revision. In K. Goodman, Y. Goodman, & W. Hood (Eds.), *The whole language evaluation book* (pp. 15-24). Portsmouth, NH: Heinemann.

Cartwright, C.A., & Cartwright, G.P. (1974). *Developing observational skills*. New York: McGraw-Hill.

Galindo, R. (1989). "Asi no se pone, Sí" (That's not how you write, "sí"). In K. Goodman, Y. Goodman, & W. Hood (Eds.), *The whole language evaluation book* (pp. 15-24). Portsmouth, NH: Heinemann.

Genishi, C., & Dyson, A.H. (1984). *Language assessment in the early years*. Norwood, NJ: Ablex.

Goodman, Y. (1985). Kidwatching. In A. Jaggar & M.T. Smith-Burke (Eds.), *Observing the language learner*. Newark, DE: International Reading Association.

Jaggar, A. (1985). On observing the language learner: Introduction and overview. In A. Jaggar & M.T. Smith-Burke (Eds.), *Observing the language learner* (pp. 1-7). Newark, DE: International Reading Association.

Livo, N. (1986). *Storytelling: Process and practice.* Littleton, CO: Libraries Unlimited.

Morrissey, M. (1989). When "shut up" is a sign of growth. In K. Goodman, Y. Goodman, & W. Hood (Eds.), *The whole language evaluation book* (pp. 85-97). Portsmouth, NH: Heinemann.

Pinnell, G.S. (1985). Ways to look at the functions of children's language. In A. Jaggar & M.T. Smith-Burke (Eds.), *Observing the language learner* (pp. 57-72). Newark, DE: International Reading Association.

*The Random House Dictionary of the English Language.* (1966). New York: Random House.

Thorndike, R.L., & Hagen, E.P. (1977). *Measurement and evaluation in psychology and education* (4th ed.). New York: John Wiley and Sons.

**Reprinted with permission of Lynn K. Rhodes and the International Reading Association.**

## Voices

I t is our goal to spread the enthusiasm and love we have found in sharing books with our children. We were already dedicated teachers, but now our days are filled with magic—

- the magic in a child's eyes when she finishes her first "whole" book.
- the magic hug from the "class toughie" when a touching novel is finished.
- the magic you feel when a child tells you his mom cried when he read her a book for the first time.
- the magic sound of your whole class laughing at something you just read together.
- the magic you feel when your students beg for more reading time.

*Cindy Merrilees and Pam Haack*
**Ten Ways to Become a Better Reader**

Reprinted with permission of Modern Curriculum Press.

# WHOLE  CATALOG

### Kindergarten Clinic

# Anatomy of Assessment

By MARY BETH SPANN

Report cards don't look like they used to for kindergarten, first-, and second-grade students at Bennington Elementary School in Bennington, Nebraska. This year, their teachers are leaving the old report cards behind in favor of annotated portfolios—large envelopes chock-full of student work, and checklists that sketch academic profiles of the children who produce this work.

By most schools' standards, Bennington's assessment approach is a progressive and dynamic complement to a child-centered program. Still, Bennington kindergarten teacher Susan Johnston, is not satisfied. "Our school has spent the past ten years trying to make the K–2 classrooms developmentally appropriate. I know tinkering with the assessment process will take time, too, but I'm impatient for the right tools to be in place now."

### ASSESSMENT OVERHAUL

With the support of their administration, Johnston and her colleagues gradually revamped their assessment system. "We don't have it perfect yet, but we're still working on it together," says Johnston

"*Together* is the operative word here," says Ann Lessard, a consultant with the Society for Developmental Education in Peterborough, New Hampshire, an organization that sponsors workshops on whole language, literature-based programs, and self-esteem. Lessard believes that teachers must first work together with each other, and then together with parents and children to develop a responsible, accurate program of assessment. In her work with teachers and schools, she stresses the need for patience and persistence when overhauling a report card system. "Such important change," she says "is rarely snag-free."

Johnston and her colleagues know the

feeling. In their attempt to move away from the old report card, they worked hard to devise a new checklist system covering all areas of the curriculum. Unlike the old report cards that focused on isolated skills such as "Child can identify alphabet letters," the new checklists included items such as, "Child uses pictures as cues."

"Despite all our work and good intentions, the checklist system didn't work the way we hoped it would," says Johnston. "Instead of viewing the checked items as a list of what the child could do, we worried that parents would focus on items that weren't checked and on what the child couldn't do. Now we're toying with the idea of putting the checklists into a computer database where we can just select and print items specific to each child's level of progress."

### STUDENT PARTICIPATION

In addition to modifying the checklist system, Johnston also wants her school to move in the direction of including children more actively in parent/teacher conferences. This and other trends, such as conferencing before school opens and scheduling school time for home visits, says Lessard, mean a greater commitment of time on the part of the teacher and the school. They also require administrative support to work effectively.

But perhaps most important, these kinds of changes need to be reflected in the day-to-day classroom. Allowing children to be privy to what and how they learn

is in itself a multidimensional process that begins with ongoing, informal classroom conferences and observations, explains Lessard. "When you peek over a young writer's shoulder and say, 'Look how many capital letters you included here!' and then show the child an earlier writing sample where the skill was not evident, the child can see his or her own progress. When you allow children to select their own best work for inclusion in portfolios, you are infusing assessment with elements of respect, trust, and choice."

### REPORT CARD ADD-ONS

What if your school still has an old-fashioned report card in place? Lessard recommends that you "begin augmenting your current system with an annotated developmental overview of each child or the class—assemble portfolios for each child. Give yourself permission to use class time to 'kid watch' and to jot down observations. Ask parents to write down and share their own viewpoints, opinions, and expectations regarding their children." In this way, she says, "you can take baby steps toward shaping an assessment process that will be as creative and exciting as the children you teach."

### FOR FURTHER READING

• *Put Portfolios to the Test*, INSTRUCTOR (August, 1990). A how-to guide to assembling and using portfolios as an assessment tool in the classroom.

• *Portfolio Assessment in the Reading/Writing Classroom* by Robert J. Tierney (Christopher-Gordon Publishers, 1991). A comprehensive look at the hows and whys of establishing and implementing a portfolio-assessment process.

• *The Assessment and Evaluation in Whole Language Programs* by William Harp (Christopher-Gordon Publishers, 1991). Evaluates assessment tools past and present, and offers a vision of responsible, effective assessment for the future.

*MARY BETH SPANN is a kindergarten teacher in the North Shore School District in Sea Cliff, New York.*

# Tests, Independence and Whole Language

*Standardized tests often do more harm than good, but is there an alternative? Here's what a noted New Zealand educator has to say*

BY BRIAN CUTTING

Why should children fail? Is it their fault, or does it have more to do with the educational system?

It would seem difficult to blame the children themselves. After all, most of them learn to talk, with all of language's complexities, well before they go to school (even though their learning continues for some years after that). Why is this learning so successful? Why do children learn to talk so naturally, and with apparent ease? These are some of the contributing factors:

• No one expects children to fail—not the children themselves, not their parents, not even the politicians and administrators concerned with education policy.

• Children are responsible for much of their own learning. Parents don't teach them every day. There's no manual for learning to talk which says: *Step one, tongue movements; Step two, consonants; Step three, vowels.* If such manuals did exist, children would certainly be less successful.

• Children practice for a long time. In fact, we're happy to let them take up to three years before some concern is voiced. And we're tolerant and full of praise for their "mistakes," not even seeing them as mistakes, but (especially at the beginning stages of learning) delighting in their attempts to say words.

• There are no tests of talking. Everyone recognizes that children will learn different things, at different rates and in different ways. There are no tests, because children *do* learn to talk.

But imagine what would happen if someone decided that tests of talking were essential. A test would be designed, and talkers tested. For some children, the test items would be easy. These children would be ahead of the test. For some, the test items would match what they know—their stage of development. They would be fine. For others, the test items would be beyond their present competence. They, on the basis of the test, would fail.

What would happen to these failed talkers? Using the model given by learning to read, there would be remedial type classes where the children could practice all the things they didn't know. There would be exercises designed to improve their ability to pass the test, rather than on learning to talk (which the children were doing quite happily until they, and their parents, found out that they couldn't). These would be artificial exercises which someone had identified as important elements in the "learning-to-talk" process.

Even the most elegant of standardized tests of "talking" would show that some children were good (passed) and some children were bad (failed). In fact, there would be an outcry if such a test were given, because of the huge number of children who would be placed behind their more successful peers and who would be removed to attend specially funded "talking" programs.

If we really wanted to make learning to talk a non-success story, the easiest way would be to design tests that would set a standard which all children would be

Brian Cutting is Educational Director of Wendy Pye Limited, an international publishing consultant and book publisher based in Auckland, New Zealand.

*Assessment, first hand and one-on-one, as Brian Cutting checks out a wonderful tiger.*

the children end up in special education classes?

There has to be a better way and there is. The focus on independent learning implies that the focus should be on independent evaluation as well.

This personal assessment of individual learning is not haphazard or random. (Whole language is not "airy-fairy" and neither is whole language evaluation.) It is systematic, regular and thorough. It can be used by teachers to help individual children learn more effectively about reading. (Is this book too difficult? Which books would help most?)

This kind of assessment caters to children's individual needs, while providing teachers with the feedback needed to help their children become independent. It helps teachers learn about reading and changes their ways of thinking about *how* children learn to read. Evaluation should not be viewed as an isolated chore necessary to give a child some grade, but rather as a natural part of the daily class program—a part that is vital for successful teaching and learning.

**Proving failure.** The whole point of learning is to be independent. Independence can never be achieved if children have been turned away from learning by repeated failure, no matter how lofty the goals of the original program. It always amazes me that we have to prove failure over and over again. Most adults couldn't face such a system, so why do so many adults seem to support such a system for children, even when they're aware of its consequences?

The recorded observations of reading behavior provide all the information needed to show parents that their children are making progress. They also allow teachers to show parents how they can help their children at home.

Is it too heretical then to ask if we need the tests, the workbooks and the reading materials associated with them? Is it so difficult to replace them with alternative methods of assessment which place the emphasis on individuals and observations?

By the way, I wonder whether the basal workbook test system survives not because of its educational value (which is a proven failure for so many children). I wonder whether it owes its resilience to administrators who don't really trust their teachers to

> **❝** *The focus on independent learning implies that the focus should be on independent evaluation as well.* **❞**

expected to reach. We all know that such procedures would be futile for children learning to talk. So why do we use similar procedures for children learning to read and write?

Apart from learning to talk, children have learned many things successfully. It's worthwhile asking how they learned to do all these things. Not from following a manual. Not from learning to do all the parts before trying the whole. Not from artificial exercises divorced from real contexts. And not from tests, which supposedly identify what children know and don't know about a task. (Unfortunately, tests don't free learners; they constrain learning to what test developers believe to be important.)

**Dismal cycle.** We can't treat children as if some will be winners and others failures, because gradually the children who fail (when they really thought they were doing quite well) will begin to associate learning with failure. After repeated failure, they'll see school as futile. Worse, they'll begin to see themselves as hopeless. They and their parents never question what the test is testing or how how well it tests. Why would any education system fail children in this way, almost guaranteeing that five-year-olds will become habitual failures, doomed to a dismal cycle of practice-test-remediation until provide effective learning through alternative models of learning like whole language.

**The upper grades.** There is often an assumption that real learning starts after children move on from the lower grades, that more formal education and evaluation procedures now become essential. No more play! Down to work! Well, such a system may work for the successes of the school system, but for those already disillusioned by repeated failure, more of the same will hardly prove to be the panacea they seek. Why continue a cycle of failure?

If the differences between children entering school are great, so are the differences between children entering a class at the beginning of the year. The implication for teachers is that, just as in the lower grades, independent learning should be the focus of classroom practice. It follows that evaluation should be as individualized as possible. Children's learning can't be constrained by the uniformity that testing brings. The emphasis on individuals and independent learning means that teachers have created classrooms where diversity is recognized and can exist.

If learning in the upper primary and middle school years is to change, teachers and children must be allowed independence from a set, inflexible program of teaching and testing. The principles of whole language learning can help teachers to provide more enjoyable and successful learning for all their children. And, the same principles which guided evaluation in the lower grades should guide evaluation for older children.

A balanced approach to evaluation should continue, with emphasis placed on observations, listening to children read, individual responses of various kinds, the children's own evaluation of their learning. Tests just don't give the feedback needed for self-evaluation of learning. They only give feedback on success or failure.

**Worthwhile system.** Listening to children read (running records, miscue analysis) is essential. You cannot find out what your children really know about reading without doing this. No test can do it more effectively, so it's worthwhile to organize a system where you listen to children read on a regular basis.

There's no reason why you shouldn't extend the "listening" with an individual conference, getting children to read both orally and silently, and then questioning them to find out how to help them understand more (about both the book and the reading process itself).

Also, there's no reason why these individual conferences should not be in the form of informal prose inventories, both published and those made up by you. All you need to make your own inventories are books with a developmental, gradual sequence of difficulty. The information collected can be stored in cumulative records, which will provide all the valid evidence needed by the school and parents about a child's progress.

The responses children make about their learning is one of the most valuable ways of evaluating their learning. If they can read a book and successfully turn it into a play, they have demonstrated their understanding of it. As they read independently, they can construct responses of many kinds to show how well they have understood what they read—information which is not available through other means.

If national comparisons need to be made, the standardized tests used should correlate with the teaching practice and assessment used in schools. Otherwise, the mismatch will guarantee failure for many learners.

It's difficult being a whole language teacher. You often have to work in a system which subverts your beliefs. You integrate language arts and then unravel the strands, teaching and testing tenses of verbs. You teach reading using whole contexts and marvelous materials, and you do worksheets on phonics because that is what will be tested. You evaluate learning by running records and observations (and even some diagnostic tests), only to have a standardized test tell you and your children—children you know are learning to read well, especially in terms of their competence—that they really are failures.

It's hard, but teachers and the parents of the children they teach must look for alternative ways of evaluating language learning, ways that move away from the tests and classroom practices that guarantee, for too many children, failure in school. ✿

*I would like to gratefully acknowledge the contribution to this article made by Jill Eggleton, author of* Whole Language Evaluation *(available through The Wright Group).*

> **"***It always amazes me that we have to prove failure over and over again.***"**

# The Whole Language Newsletter for Parents

ANTHONY D. FREDERICKS

Assistant Professor of Education • York College • York, PA

VOL. 1, NO. 3 FEBRUARY 1992

## Evaluation

Depending on where you live, you may be locked in winter's icy grip or braving cold winds sweeping down from the north. The season may be chilly, but there are probably a lot of "hot" ideas taking place in your child's classroom.

As your child participates in *whole language* activities in the classroom, you're probably concerned about how he or she is being evaluated. Your child's teacher may have told you about some of the ways in which students are being assessed in reading and language arts.

For many of us raised on a diet of chapter tests and midterm exams during our school years, some of the evaluation procedures used today may not be all that familiar. You may hear terms such as "holistic evaluation," "portfolio assessment," "kidwatching" or "observational checklists." No doubt you're confused by some of these terms and by some of the ways your child is being graded in reading and language arts. Let's see if we can clear away the confusion by considering some of the major questions parents are asking about whole language evaluation.

### What is portfolio assessment?
Artists use portfolios to present their best work to a gallery or a collector for review. In the classroom, a portfolio is a collection of evidence used by both the teacher and the student to monitor the intellectual growth of the student as well as the student's progress toward identified goals. In short, a portfolio is a sampling of student work which both documents and shows evidence of the student's growth.

The items included in a portfolio are often selected by the student in collaboration with the teacher, although some may be selected solely by the student and others may be placed in the portfolio by the teacher. The portfolio itself may be a file folder, a box in the classroom, or an elaborate notebook. Whatever it is, it provides the student, the teacher, the principal and *you* with a multidimensional record of how your child is progressing.

A portfolio is a much better record of student progress, simply because it contains many different kinds of evidence, has both depth and breadth, and shows evidence of growth not measured by typical formal tests.

### Why isn't my child taking more graded tests?
Standardized tests and teacher-prepared tests can be valuable elements in the evaluation of student performance. But, as we've discovered, they're not the only forms of evaluation. For example, a test cannot always measure a student's attitude towards reading and/or language arts; a test cannot show how a student progresses in writing from one week to the next; a test cannot chronicle the variety of books read over an extended period of time.

### How is my child being graded in reading and/or language arts?
For those of us from "the old school," evaluation meant studying a lot of facts and then taking a written test on that information. Today, we're learning that evaluation doesn't have to be the scores earned on a series of exams; rather, evaluation can be more meaningful to the teacher and more useful to the child if it includes a number of tasks. In other words, evaluation that is broad-based and all-inclusive is more indicative of a child's work than is a handful of chapter tests, worksheets and standardized tests at the end of the year.

As a result, your child's teacher looks at many different forms of performance: writing samples, observation notes by the teacher, self-evaluation checklists prepared by the student, progress sheets, projects completed, daily work, reading logs, audio/video tapes and response journals. What makes this form of evaluation different is that many different performance measures are taken into account, not simply a relatively few tests scattered throughout the year.

### How does the teacher know if my child is doing well?
Most teachers have goals for both the class as a whole and for individual students. Those goals are "markers" by which progress can be evaluated. As students make progress towards those goals, evidence of that progress can be included in a portfolio. By using many different measures,

the teacher is able to determine more accurately if an individual student is progressing toward established goals.

Effective evaluation is continuous and daily. It also involves the student and teacher working together to insure that progress is being made towards established goals.

### How does my child compare with other students in the class?

Even though many students are completing identical assignments, they may tackle those assignments in different ways. The object is not to have everybody finish a task in exactly the same way, but to have students make progress within that task in keeping with their academic potential. In other words, your child's teacher is much more interested in the *processes* your child uses to achieve success than the *products* obtained at the end of an assignment.

How your child thinks, the methods used to work through an assignment, and the procedures involved in learning new ideas are all important in academic work. As a result, your child will not be compared with other children in the class as much as he or she will be compared with his or her own potential and progress towards established goals. Portfolio assessment, for example, is individualistic and represents how one student is progressing. It does not compare a student with other students, but allows a student to share (with the teacher and parents) in how he or she is attaining the goals established for him or her.

### Things You Can Do

Here are some things you can do that will give you "inside information" on your child's progress in reading and/or language arts. They'll also help you monitor your child's educational progress, provide your child's teacher with necessary data, and give your youngster some information that will be useful in self-evaluation.

- Be sure to share the goals and expectations you have for your child with your child's teacher. This should be done on a regular basis. It's important that teachers and parents work together to ensure the academic success of each student. Your child's teacher needs to know what you expect of your child as much as your child needs to know.
- Provide your child's teacher with feedback on homework assignments. If you think an assignment was too difficult or too easy, attach a brief note to the assignment and have your child take it to school. Explain why you believe the assignment was not in keeping with your child's ability.
- Ask your child's teacher if you can provide a biweekly or monthly summary sheet on which you can record some observations about your child's growth in reading. Your child's teacher may be interested to learn about the number of books read at home, letters or messages your child writes, number of visits to the public library, or other literacy-related activities accomplished.
- Try to visit your child's classroom occasionally throughout the school year. Find out what's happening in the reading/language arts program. Observe your child as well as other children to learn about the different activities being pursued. Talk to your child's teacher to learn about upcoming projects.
- Talk with your child about his or her perceptions of the progress made in reading and/or language arts. How does your child feel about the classroom activities in reading and/or language arts? Is your child satisfied with his or her performance or progress? What can be done to improve performance? In other words, give your child opportunities to engage in some self-evaluation, too.

### Recommended Reading

The following books will provide you with valuable information on how you can become an "activist" for your child in a whole language classroom. Besides offering you some guidelines on the nature of evaluation, these books will give you ideas that will help you support your child's literacy education for a long time.

Baghban, Marcia. *Our Daughter Learns to Read and Write*. International Reading Association, Newark, DE, 1985. The literacy growth and development of one youngster provides parents with many lessons about how children can and do learn.

Butler, Dorothy and Clay, Marie. *Reading Begins at Home*. Heinemann, Portsmouth, NH, 1987. This book shows how children can have meaningful and long-lasting relationships with books and reading, and how developing literacy can become a family venture.

Fredericks, Anthony D. *Social Studies Through Children's Literature*. Teacher Ideas Press, Englewood, CO, 1991. An introduction to the integration of children's literature and whole language concepts into the elementary curriculum—specifically social studies.

### Books for Children

It's important for students to do some self-evaluation every so often so that they have a personal stake in their own educational progress. Here are children's books on "self" you may wish to share with your youngster.

Baehr, Patricia. *School Isn't Fair*. Four Winds, New York, NY, 1989. The self-concept of a four-year-old is very low until he's recognized for a particular skill.

Wilhelm, Hans. *Let's Be Friends Again*. Crown, New York, NY, 1986. Sibling rivalry is the issue here, but this book is also about the importance of forgiving.

# WORKING WITH PARENTS

# Involving parents in the assessment process

Anthony D. Fredericks, York College

Timothy V. Rasinski, Kent State University

Involving parents throughout the reading curriculum is one of the most productive, effective ways to enhance children's literacy development. When parents are provided with opportunities to take a sincere, active role in their child's reading growth, reading performance escalates; in addition, pupils' attitudes toward reading improve. Research has convincingly demonstrated that parent involvement can dramatically affect the total reading development of every child.

We believe that parents should be more than passive participants in reading curricula; they should be invited to participate in all aspects of the classroom reading program. Such parent participation assumes a commitment on the part of the classroom teacher to provide parents with opportunities to interact with their children in meaningful, relevant activities.

At the 1990 IRA Convention in Atlanta, Georgia, we saw considerable interest in various literacy assessment procedures. Teachers with a whole language orientation to literacy instruction were eager for ideas and procedures that would make the assessment process purposeful. For example, many educators were looking for assessment procedures that would move assessment beyond norm- or criterion-referenced tools and focus more on an evaluation of processes involved in meaningful, functional reading.

To that end, we believe that parents can and should play a significant role in the assessment process. Any teacher who has attempted to explain standardized test scores to parents at conference time knows the frustration parents feel about their child's per-

formance in reading. Flood and Lapp (1989) note that parents often read more into a single test score than educators do. What often ensues during discussions of test scores is a great deal of misunderstanding between teachers and parents about the actual progress students are making in reading.

Parents' participation in evaluating their children's growth can help to eliminate many misconceptions and misinterpretations that may occur during parent-teacher conferences or at report card time. Moreover, it helps give parents direction in aiding their children's literacy development. We do not mean to imply that parents should take on all or even the major responsibilities of evaluating progress in reading; rather, parents can make a positive contribution to assessment and thus develop a healthy regard for the process and their children's progress.

Inviting parents to take an active role in assessing individual literacy growth is predicated on three interdependent principles:

1. *Involving parents in the assessment process must be an integral part of that program.* By this we mean that the assessment process should be a natural extension of the reading program and not portrayed as an "add-on" to the curriculum.

2. *Parent assessment procedures must be conducted comprehensively.* That is, the information garnered from all assessment measures must be taken from all aspects of the reading curriculum. Purposeful assessment is not a single activity done once or twice during the year, but an activity that is addressed on a regular basis and is pertinent to the direction of that pro-

gram. Parents need to understand that assessment can and will lead to sound curricular decisions.

3. *Parents' involvement in assessment should be approached systematically.* Parents cannot be expected to assess and monitor their children's reading development without sufficient time or training. Getting them involved and keeping them involved are important to the success of the assessment process.

An effective parental assessment program does not happen overnight; but by the same token it need not be an elaborate or confusing array of tasks that overwhelms parents, either. Nevertheless, when parents take part in observing and assessing their children's literacy development, they will be taking an active role in the reading program; they will have first-hand knowledge about their children's personal progress throughout that program. Regular opportunities to monitor and assess reading growth provide parents with a better understanding of the demands of effective reading instruction. Such opportunities also allow them to develop an appreciation of reading consistent with the goals of the reading program.

Following are six ideas for teachers who want parents to become active partners in the assessment process.

1. Early in the school year, provide a means for parents to state individual expectations for their child. You might ask what kind of progress individual parents like to see. Record parents' responses to these queries and refer to them on a regular basis.

2. Ask parents to help design an evaluation instrument that rates home

assignments. Develop a brief questionnaire that can be attached to each homework assignment on which parents can indicate such factors as (a) the difficulty level of the assignment, (b) how well their child understood the assignment or the procedures, (c) the appropriateness of the assignment, or (d) suggestions for improvement.

3. Provide parents with a weekly or biweekly summary sheet on which they can record their own observations about their child's reading growth. You may want to prepare some questions ahead of time such as: What were some positive things you noted in your child's reading this past week? What were some negative events? Keep a record of these sheets and refer to them regularly in home telephone calls or face-to-face conferences.

4. Develop a series of simple "question sheets" for parents to complete frequently. Each sheet would be designed to elicit parents' questions about the progress of their child; a space should be included for your responses.

5. Ask parents to compose frequently lists of things their children have learned in reading. Also, direct parents to provide information on lessons or parts of lessons that their children did not understand. Ask that these be submitted at intervals throughout the year and take time to discuss them with parents.

6. Provide opportunities for parents to visit classrooms and observe the reading program in action. Afterward, ask them to evaluate their child's performance in that class and elicit their perceptions about their child's strengths or weaknesses. Record these parental observations and keep them in a portfolio for sharing later in the year.

Two of the must useful parental assessment tools are an attitudinal scale and an observation guide (see Figures 1 and 2). These two instruments, if used thoughout the year, can provide teachers and parents with a host of relevant information through which joint decisions can be made concerning children's reading progress. More im-

portant, however, is "the inside look" these instruments provide parents into salient aspects of literacy growth, giving them an opportunity to take an active role in the assessment procedure. This new role results in a deeper appreciation for the demands of reading instruction and a personal awareness of each stage of their child's growth. Moreover, it establishes important bonds that should exist between home and school.

Parental assessment procedures can become an important component of the reading program. Not only does the assessment process allow parents to take an active role in the reading curriculum, it also gives them valuable data beyond standardized test scores that help them understand the whole reading process.

One school that has begun to actively solicit the involvement of parents in assessing students' literacy growth is the Escondido Elementary School in Stanford, California. According to principal Julie Ryan, "Pro-

**Figure 1**
**Attitudinal scale for parents**

Child's name: _____ Date: _____
Please indicate your observation of your child's reading growth since the last report. Feel free to comment where appropriate.

A = Strongly agree
B = Agree
C = Disagree
D = Strongly disagree

My child:                                                                Comments
1.  Understands more of what he/she reads        A    B    C    D
2.  Enjoys being read to by family members       A    B    C    D
3.  Finds time for quiet reading at home          A    B    C    D
4.  Sometimes guesses at words, but they usually make sense    A    B    C    D
5.  Can provide a summary of stories read         A    B    C    D
6.  Has a good attitude about reading             A    B    C    D
7.  Enjoys reading to family members              A    B    C    D
8.  Would like to get more books                  A    B    C    D
9.  Chooses to write about stories read           A    B    C    D
10. Is able to complete homework assignments      A    B    C    D

Strengths I see: _____
_____

Areas that need improvement: _____
_____

Concerns or questions I have: _____
_____

## Figure 2
## Observation guide for parents

Child's name: _____

Date of last report: _____ Today's date: _____

The skills and attitudes you observed in your child on the last report have been recorded in the first column. Please place a check (✓) next to those items in the second column that you have observed in your child since the last report.

My child:

_____  _____  1.  Reads from a wide variety of materials such as books, magazines, newspapers, etc.

_____  _____  2.  Takes time during each day to read in a quiet place

_____  _____  3.  Talks with family members about the things he/she is reading

_____  _____  4.  Finds reading to be an exciting way to learn about the world

_____  _____  5.  Brings home books and other reading materials from the school or public library

_____  _____  6.  Seems to understand more of what he/she reads at home

_____  _____  7.  Tries to discover new words and uses them in his/her conversations

_____  _____  8.  Seems to have developed higher-level thinking skills

_____  _____  9.  Uses study skills (e.g. notetaking, organizing time, etc.) regularly

_____  _____  10. Has shown improvement in his/her reading ability since the last report

My child would be a better reader if: _____
_____
_____

My child's greatest strength in reading is: _____
_____
_____

By the next report my child should learn: _____
_____
_____
_____

_____
Signature

cedures which provide parents with active opportunities to take part in the assessment process not only arouse parents' awareness of critical issues in literacy acquisition, but also provide both teachers and parents with valuable information prior to the fall and spring conferences."

Escondido School is located on the Stanford University campus and, as such, has a significant number of students entering and exiting during the school year. Principal Ryan and her staff have designed several assessment forms for children at different grade levels. These forms are sent home prior to the start of school or prior to parent-teacher conferences. As a result, parents take an active role in observing and becoming aware of those behaviors that contribute most to growth in reading and language arts.

The forms Escondido School uses are important for both teachers and parents. Not only do the data provide teachers with important information upon which to make instructional decisions, parents and teachers begin to communicate in positive ways about the literacy activities necessary for individual children. Just as important, the forms will be used to chart progress between parent-teacher conferences to determine the nature and direction of each child's reading development.

The staff at Escondido School feels that these assessment tools are a positive way for parents and educators to share knowledge. As Ryan points out, "Parents are a child's first teacher—and we need to validate that. We hope our assessment forms will allow parents to use information gained at home to work with teachers in designing specific and purposeful reading plans." In

short, the staff at Escondido Elementary School believes that informal parental assessment should be a significant part of the entire school program and serves as a foundation for good home-school relationships.

In summary, involving parents in the assessment process does not mean turning them into psychometricians, but rather provides them with opportunities to monitor and supervise the literacy growth of their own children. Such a process requires regular contacts between parents and students and allows parents to understand more fully the entire reading program. Communication bonds are established that lead to a greater understanding between educators and parents—an understanding that can have a significant impact in the lives of all students. Shared assessment processes hold the potential for close and positive relationships—certainly a laudable goal for any effective outreach program.

*Note: Readers interested in obtaining copies of the forms used at Escondido School can send a self-addressed, stamped envelope to Julie S. Ryan, Principal, Escondido Elementary* School, 890 Escondido Road, Stanford, CA 94305, USA, or call (415) 856-1337.

**Reference**
Flood, J., & Lapp, D. (1989). Reporting reading progress: A comparison portfolio for parents. *The Reading Teacher, 42,* 508-514.

Working with Parents is a column dealing with ways in which teachers might involve parents more in the learning of literacy abilities in school and at home. Send questions, comments, or suggestions about the column to **Anthony D. Fredericks, Department of Education, York College, York, PA 17403, USA.**

# The Search for a Custom Kindergarten Portfolio

### by Ginny Stiles

1. **Writing Samples.** Formal — dictated sentences and "write-me-all-the-words-you-know" lists, and informal — daily journals, self-written books/stories or just for fun writing including invented spelling.

2. **Alphabet/phonics Assessments.** My favorite is an adaptation of Marie Clay's three-part assessment.

3. **Print Concepts Assessment.** My favorite is one which utilizes a simple format that allows me to check off concepts demonstrated by the child, such as: left to right sweep; recognition of word, letter and sentence; use of punctuation; knowledge of title and author; finding the beginning and ending letter in a word, etc. I use an actual book during the test.

4. **Drawings.** I prefer the simple Draw-A-Person request since it allows some comparison. I do not try to interpret technical information from the drawing such as a trained psychologist might do. I assess it informally for improvement over the year.

5. **Word Lists.** With children who are in emergent levels of reading you may wish to either develop your own word lists based on key words being used in the classroom or you may want a more formal list of commonly used words to see how the child is beginning to try to figure out words. I like to tape children and listen to this later. Consult your local reading specialist for help.

6. **Developmental Skills Checklist.** Kindergarten teachers have always used this well. They assess whether the child knows common colors, shapes, alphabet song, has pencil grip, is left/right handed, knows birthday and age, etc. These are useful determiners of growth and skills. If the report card already covers these then a copy will suffice.

7. **Syntax Assessment.** A quick check of whether a child is able to find a word in a short sentence that you read together is helpful to discover if a child is able to use the syntax of the actual sentence as a clue to word reading. Example: *The man is running.* You and the child read this together twice. Then ask if s/he will circle the word "man" in the sentence. Watching how s/he finds this (or doesn't) is very useful. Murphy-Durell Pre-Reading Phonics Inventory has one of these printed, but you could devise 10 sentences of two to five words and do just as well.

8. **Mathematics.** Math Their Way and similar approaches have proven to match the thematic and whole language philosophies well. These programs often come with suggestions on evaluation. Children are asked to count objects, estimate, print numerals and perform some addition and subtraction tasks. Especially in curriculums where children will go from one program to another it is important that first grade teachers be appraised of the method used to teach the children. Unfamiliarity with workbooks will certainly affect first grade performance if workbooks are highly used there.

**Resources**
Clay, Marie. *The Early Detection of Reading Difficulties,* Portsmouth, NH: Heinemann, 1985.
Eggleton, Jill. *Whole Language: Reading, Writing and Spelling.* Bothell, WA: The Wright Group, 1990.
Fisher, Bobbi. *Joyful Learning.* Portsmouth, NH: Heinemann, 1991. (especially recommended for kindergarten teachers)
Routman, Regie. *Invitations.* Portsmouth, NH: Heinemann, 1991.
Schroeder, LaVern. "Custom Tailoring in Whole Language Evaluation." *The Wisconsin State Reading Association Journal,* fall 1990.
Wisconsin State Reading Association, "Toward an Ecological Assessment of Reading Progress," 1990.

**Kathryn C. Heffernan Elementary School**
**Pre-First Grade Conference Report**

Name _____ Date _____

## Social Interaction

- Works and plays well with others
- Initiates activities
- Considers others' viewpoints and feelings
- Uses a variety of strategies to resolve conflicts
- Controls impulses
- Is cooperative
- Is dependable

## Mathematics

- Counts by ones to _____
- Counts sets of objects to _____
- Recognizes numerals 0-10
- Copies numerals 0-10
- Uses mathematics manipulatives correctly
- Copies a simple pattern
- Participates in calendar activities
- Participates in graphing activities

## Work Habits

- Knows and participates in room routines:
  - meetings
  - games
  - quiet time
  - clean up
- Makes appropriate choices in room
- Works independently
- Works cooperatively in:
  - peer groups
  - large groups
  - small groups
- Stays with an activity for an appropriate amount of time
- Listens attentively in groups:
  - large
  - small
- Uses materials and equipment appropriately

## Language Arts

**Speech and language**
Talks fluently in groups:
- large groups
- small groups

Uses language appropriate to situation

**Basic Writing**
Write or attempts to write:
- labels
- pictures
- sentences

**Spelling Skills**
Prephonemic spelling (no concept of word, few sound/symbol associations)

Phonemic speller (uses initial and final consonants, word concept established)

Transitional speller (uses growing list of correctly spelled sight words)

**Basic Reading Skills**
Reads on a daily basis:
- morning message
- familiar names and words
- own writing

Relies on memory for reading

Uses pictures to tell a story

Uses sound/symbol cues to read a story

Library/reading books

Knows _____ lower case letters

Knows _____ capital letters

## Academic Readiness

- Recognizes first name
- Recognizes last name
- Copies first name
- Copies last name
- Writes first name independently
- Writes last name independently
- Holds pencil appropriately for writing
- Holds book appropriately for reading
- Willing to try a new or unfamiliar task

## Concepts About Print

Can Identify:
- Beginning of book
- End of book
- Title
- Top/bottom of book
- Left to right page sequence

**Comments:**

Parent(s) Signature _____

Teacher's Signature _____

**Susan Benjamin**

259

## READING: READINESS LEVEL

**Vocabulary**:
Reads by sight:
Own name in print
A personal sight vocabulary (high interest)
20 words from the basic sight vocabulary

**Word Meaning:**
Understands **beginning** and **end** in relation to:
print
speech
When listening, predicts:
outcome
vocabulary, word, rhyme

**Comprehension**:
Knows that:
reading makes sense
print represents the sounds of the language
Has a reading attitude.
Listens well to stories.
Has a desire to read:
Looks at books on his/her own
Is interested in words and symbols.

**Auditory:**
Identifies:
beginning sounds
ending sounds
rhymes
Discriminates the major consonant sounds.

**Visual:**
Has correct directional habits:
looks at books from front to back
looks at books from left page to right page
begins left top
proceeds left to right
proceeds top to bottom
Identifies:
word
letter

**Auditory/Visual:**
Matches spoken and printed words when some
one reads
Knows most letter names:
upper case
lower case

**Oral Reading:**
Attacks words using context and initial letter
checked by sense

## WRITING: READINESS

**Fluency:**
Writes independently
Has confidence as a writer

**Composition:**
Expresses thoughts in writing
Writes telling sentences
Talks about what he/she has written
Revises one or more words during conferences

**Mechanics:**
Capitalizes:
First name and initial of last name
I

**Handwriting**
Tries to make recognizable letters

**Spelling:**
Own first name
Uses major consonants: b, d, j, k, l, m, n, p, s, t, z
for the beginnings of words

### SPEAKING

Expresses his/her needs

Asks questions

Responds appropriately to questions

Maintains the subject line in conversation

Shares experiences in a group

Uses complete sentences

Uses specific vocabulary for objects

(book, puzzle, scissors)

Jay Buros

# First Grade Sight Words
## Peterborough Elementary School

| | | | | |
|---|---|---|---|---|
| the | be | which | into | now |
| of | this | she | time | find |
| and | have | do | has | long |
| a | from | how | look | down |
| to | or | their | two | day |
| in | one | if | more | did |
| is | had | will | write | get |
| you | by | up | go | come |
| that | words | other | see | made |
| it | but | about | number | may |
| he | not | out | no | part |
| was | what | many | way | |
| for | all | then | could | |
| on | were | them | people | |
| are | we | these | my | |
| as | when | so | than | |
| with | your | some | first | |
| his | can | her | water | |
| they | said | would | been | |
| I | there | make | called | |
| at | use | like | who | |
| | an | him | oil | |
| | each | | its | |

# FIRST GRADE—READING SKILLS

### Developed by First Grade Team at the
### Peterborough Elementary School, Peterborough, NH

**VOCABULARY:**

Quickly reads 200 words on basic sight vocabulary list

Recognizes words with upper or lower case letters

    at beginning

**WORD ANALYSIS:**

Reads words with:

    Suffixes: -s, -ed, -ing, -er, -'s

    Prefixes: a-, (away) be-

    Contractions: -n't, -'ll

    Abbreviations: Mr. & Mrs.

Reads simple compound words

Attacks words using context focused upon initial consonant

    or blend & checked by sense & final letters

Knows symbol/sound associations for:

All consonants in initial, final & medial

    positions except soft c & g

Consonant blends, bl, fl, pl, sl, br, cr, dr,

    fr, gr, tr, str, sm, sn, sw, pr, cl, gl, tw, sp, spr

Consonant digraphs: ch, sh, th

Substitutes initial consonants or blends with these rhyming groups:

    at, an, and, ake, ay, all, et, en, ell, et, ill, ing, ight, ot, own, un, y

Auditory discrimination of vowel-sounds

Understands that final <u>e</u> is silent

**COMPREHENSION**

Follows single printed directions

Verifies a statement

Draws conclusions from facts

Retells events in sequence

**ORAL READING:**

Reads with:

    Correct phrasing

    Attends to simple punctuation

**SILENT READING:**

Reads with understanding

Reads for a sustained period

# FIRST GRADE—WRITING SKILLS

Developed by First Grade Team at the
Peterborough Elementary School, Peterborough, NH

**FLUENCY:**

Writes an average of 40 words during a day
(fluctuation from day to day is expected)

The student has confidence as a writer.

**COMPOSITION:**

Writes five or more related sentences using
sight vocabulary & invented spelling

Reads what s/he has written

Revises one or more words through addition or elimination

**MECHANICS:**

Capitalizes:

First & last names of own name

I

Names of persons

**HANDWRITING:**

Writes on lined paper

Writes alphabet in upper and lower case most of the time

**SPELLING**

Own first & last name

Uses beginning & ending consonants to spell words

Uses invented spelling

Spells correctly one-third of Grade 1 & 2
Competency Spelling List in writings

**SPEAKING:**

Expresses his/her needs

Asks questions

Responds appropriately to questions

Maintains the subject line in conversation

Shares experiences in a group

Uses complete sentences

Retells a story to include sequence, characters and pertinent facts

Extends vocabulary

Tells personal information

Uses specific vocabulary for objects (table, book, pencil)

**LISTENING:**

Listens to peers & adults

Follows directions

**Month of** _____

## Writing

fluency _____
composition _____
capitals _____
punctuation _____
handwriting _____
spelling _____

Child's name _____

## Reading

sight words _____
word analysis _____
comprehension _____
verifies _____
draws conclusions _____
sequences _____
oral _____ silent _____

---

**Month of** _____

## Writing

fluency _____
composition _____
capitals _____
punctuation _____
handwriting _____
spelling _____

Child's name _____

## Reading

sight words _____
word analysis _____
comprehension _____
verifies _____
draws conclusions _____
sequences _____
oral _____ silent _____

---

**Month of** _____

## Writing

fluency _____
composition _____
capitals _____
punctuation _____
handwriting _____
spelling _____

Child's name _____

## Reading

sight words _____
word analysis _____
comprehension _____
verifies _____
draws conclusions _____
sequences _____
oral _____ silent _____

---

**Month of** _____

## Writing

fluency _____
composition _____
capitals _____
punctuation _____
handwriting _____
spelling _____

Child's name _____

## Reading

sight words _____
word analysis _____
comprehension _____
verifies _____
draws conclusions _____
sequences _____
oral _____ silent _____

**Created by Ann Lessard**

# EVALUATION

## EVALUATION SHOULD:

- be ongoing and integrated, built into the daily process
- give a child positive feedback
- make self-evaluation valuable; a child knows best about him/ or herself
- represent individual growth
- emphasize change, progress, growth
- encourage independence in the learner and the teacher
- be innovative, creative, dynamic
- be able to be modified and changed according to the individual or situation
- be consistent with language development: reading for meaning, writing for communication
- be holistic, not fragment language
- be "user" friendly
- be natural, in context
- not be judgmental
- be useful
- value what people know and make a bridge between what they know and don't know

## Ways to evaluate — Things to observe

Levels box
Sight words
Observe during S.S.R., work time

### Things to observe

Do they:

look at pictures or print?

choose familiar or unfamiliar?

choose to read during free time?

follow written directions?

finish what they start?

make good or bad choices, books or activities?

share books with others?

look for same title, author, subject, illustrator?

get books from the library?

enjoy reading?

use multiple strategies to figure out words?

proofread their work?

read aloud with expression?

respond in sharing groups?

interact with books?

self-initiate projects?

read outside of school?

Are they:

overwhelmed by print? Still look at pictures?

independent?

peer teachers?

critical thinkers?

**Sandy Cook**

# ASSESSING PROGRESS

## FIRST GRADE

### Midyear Expectations

**Reading:**
- Can see him/herself as a reader
- Reads 50 sight words
- Sustains reading for 15 minutes
- Fluent at third pre-primer
- Uses picture and beginning sound cues
- Can focus and participate in shared reading and discussion for 10 minutes
- Can generally retell a story
- Can draw a picture about a book read

**Writing:**
- Writes for 15-20 minutes at a sitting
- Gaining confidence as a writer
- Writes two related thoughts
- Can read back what he/she has written during the process
- Uses inventive spelling
- Has concept of word; leaves spaces between words
- Shares writing willingly

### Third Term Expectations

**Reading:**
- Knows 75 sight words
- Reads 15-20 minutes on his/her own
- Uses picture cues, beginning and ending sounds
- Can skip unknown words and go on
- Can focus and participate in shared reading and discussion for 15 minutes
- Can retell a story with details
- Can write a sentence about what he/she has read

**Writing:**
- Writes for 20-30 words at a sitting
- Writes three or four sentences that are related
- Reads what he/she has written after a period of time
- Uses inventive spelling, beginning and ending sounds and some sight words
- Begins to use punctuation
- Writes 15-20 minutes at a sitting
- Begins to revise after teacher conference

### End of Year Expectations

**Reading:**
- Fluent at 1.9 level test
- Knows 100 sight words
- Sustains 20 minutes reading on his/her own
- Uses picture; beginning and ending sound cues
- Can skip unkown word and go on, can reread for meaning
- Realizes that print constructs meaning
- Can focus and participate in shared reading and discussion for 20-25 minutes
- Can retell a story with details
- Can write about his/her reading

**Writing:**
- Writes for 40 words at a sitting
- Writes four or five sentences
- Can read back own writing
- Uses inventive spelling, beginning and ending sounds, and some sight words
- Begins to use capital letters
- Begins to use classroom units as ideas for writing
- Begins to use punctuation
- Can revise a few words after a teacher conference

# SECOND GRADE

|  | First Term | | | Third Term | |
|---|---|---|---|---|---|
|  | Sept. | Oct. | Nov. | Sept. | March |
| Writing Samples (words written in ½ hr.) | ___ | ___ | ___ | ___ | ___ |
|     Average for class | ___ | ___ | ___ | ___ | ___ |
| Percentage of words correctly spelled in writing samples. | ___ | ___ | ___ | ___ | ___ |
| Spelling test — approximate grade equivalents (Morrison McCall) | ___ | ___ | ___ | ___ | ___ |
| Class Average on Morrison McCall | ___ | ___ | ___ | ___ | ___ |

## First Term Profile

**Social:**
> takes turns and listens to others
> listens and focuses in group discussion
>     (15-20 minutes)

**Reading:**
> knows about 125 sight words
> reads on own for 20 minutes
> uses picture clues plus beginning/ending sounds
> can skip unknown word and go back
> can retell a story read with some details
> can focus and participate in shared reading
> can write two or three sentences about a book s/he's read

**Writing:**
> writes 40-50 words daily
> can write four or five related sentences
> can read what s/he's written
> uses invented spelling with correct beg/ending
>     and vowel sound
> is using capital at beginning for names and self;
>     periods at end
> can write for 20-25 minutes
> beginning to add or delete words

## Third Term Profile

**Social:**
> takes turns and listens to others
> listens and focuses in group discussions
>     for 15-20 minutes

**Reading:**
> knows about 200 sight words
> reads on own for 20 minutes
> uses picture clues plus beginning/ending sounds
> can skip unknown word and go back
> can retell a story read s/he's read with some details
> can focus and participate in shared reading
> can write two/three sentences about a book
>     s/he's read

**Writing:**
> writes 60-70 words daily
> can write four or five related sentences
> can read what s/he's written
> uses invented spelling with correct beg/ending
>     and vowel sound
> is using capital at beginning of name and self;
>     periods at end
> writes for 30-35 minutes
> begins to add/delete words for clearer menaing

# Second Grade Sight Words
## Peterborough Elementary School

In addition to the words listed in grade 1, students will be able to correctly spell the following:

| | | | |
|---|---|---|---|
| over | say | see | try |
| new | great | put | kind |
| sound | where | end | hand |
| take | help | does | picture |
| only | through | another | again |
| little | much | well | change |
| work | before | large | off |
| know | line | must | play |
| place | right | big | spell |
| years | too | even | air |
| live | means | such | away |
| me | old | because | animals |
| back | any | turned | house |
| give | same | here | point |
| most | tell | why | page |
| very | boy | asked | letters |
| after | following | went | mother |
| things | came | men | answer |
| our | want | read | found |
| just | show | need | study |
| name | also | land | still |
| good | around | different | learn |
| sentence | form | home | should |
| man | three | us | American |
| think | small | move | world |

Ann Lessard

# Developing Writing Fluency

## Kindergarten → First Grade

**Yes, I can ...**                                   Dates checked

| | | | | |
|---|---|---|---|---|
| Draw picture and tell about it. | | | | |
| Draw picture and write random marks. | | | | |
| Draw picture and write letters. | | | | |
| Begin to leave spaces. | | | | |
| Write the first letters in words. | | | | |
| Write the first and last letters in words. | | | | |
| Write some middle letters. | | | | |
| Write some whole words. | | | | |
| Use a period. | | | | |
| Use capital letters correctly. | | | | |
| Write sentences. | | | | |

## Second Grade

**Yes, I can ...**                                   Dates checked

| | | | | |
|---|---|---|---|---|
| Use capital letters at beginning. | | | | |
| Put periods at end. | | | | |
| Use a capital I for myself. | | | | |
| Write two sentences that go together. | | | | |
| Write three sentences the go together. | | | | |
| Spell sight words correctly. | | | | |
| Use spelling dictionary to correct words. | | | | |
| Can change or add words to make meaning clearer. | | | | |
| Can write four or more sentences that go together. | | | | |

# PROGRESS REPORT

**Grades 1-3**
**PROGRESS REPORT**
**CLAY COUNTY SCHOOLS**
**FLORIDA**
19 ____ - 19 ____

## TO PARENTS AND GUARDIANS:

The purpose of this report is to inform you of your child's progress. Your child is evaluated according to his/her individual development. We believe a cooperative home/school relationship enhances educatinal progress. You are welcome to contact your child's teacher for additional information.

Name: ____
Teacher: ____
School: ____
Grade: ____

## MARKING KEY

E = Excellent Progress
S = Satisfactory Progress
I = Improvement Shown
N = Needs Improvement
* = Grade earned through Exceptional Student Education program

+ = Strong Development
✓ = Appropriate Development
– = Weak Development
☒ = Not Evaluated

| ATTENDANCE | 1 | 2 | 3 | 4 | Total |
|---|---|---|---|---|---|
| Days present | | | | | |
| Days absent | | | | | |
| Days tardy | | | | | |
| Irregular attendance affects progress (✓) | | | | | |

## LANGUAGE ARTS

| | | | | |
|---|---|---|---|---|
| Reads for pleasure and/or information | | | | |
| Understands material read | | | | |
| Expresses meaning through writing | | | | |
| Applies language skills orally and in writing | | | | |
| Puts forth effort | | | | |

**Meets grade level expectations**
✓ = yes    x = no

## MATHEMATICS

| | | | | |
|---|---|---|---|---|
| Understands concepts | | | | |
| Knows basic facts | | | | |
| Computes accurately | | | | |
| Applies problem solving skills | | | | |
| Puts forth effort | | | | |

**Meets grade level expectations**
✓ = yes    x = no

## PERSONAL DEVELOPMENT AND STUDY HABITS SKILLS

| | 1 | 2 | 3 | 4 |
|---|---|---|---|---|
| Follows school rules | | | | |
| Demonstrates self-discipline | | | | |
| Respects rights of others | | | | |
| Listens and follows directions | | | | |
| Completes classwork on time | | | | |
| Completes homework on time | | | | |
| Works cooperatively with others | | | | |
| Writes legibly | | | | |

## SOCIAL STUDIES

| | | | | |
|---|---|---|---|---|
| Puts forth effort | | | | |

## SCIENCE/HEALTH

| | | | | |
|---|---|---|---|---|
| Puts forth effort | | | | |

## SPECIAL AREAS

| | 1 | 2 | 3 | 4 |
|---|---|---|---|---|
| **MUSIC** | | | | |
| Conduct | | | | |
| **PHYSICAL EDUCATION** | | | | |
| Conduct | | | | |
| **ART** | | | | |
| Conduct | | | | |

Cynthia Merrilees

# Evaluation
# A Portfolio Approach

## I. Reading Literacy

Awareness — checklist

Activity — Booklog

Analysis of strategies

PLUS

**Comprehension**

a. written
b. oral
c. illustrations
d. cloze

**Expansion Activities**

## II. Writing and Spelling

Awareness — checklist

Activity — writing folder

Analysis of strategies

PLUS

**Publishing projects**

## III. Self-evaluation

# Making Sense of Assessment

## Types of Authentic Assessment

- **Portfolio**

- **Anecdotal Records**

- **Reading Logs**

- **Comprehension Matrix**

- **Discussion Record**

- **Performance Samples**

- **Outcome Checklist**

## Roles in Evaluation

- **Teacher**

- **Student**

- **Parent**

# Language Assessment Sheet

**Name** _____      **Valid Dates** _____

**Indicators of Development**
Key: + = consistently, * = sometimes, N = not yet

*Speaking and Listening*

Communicates clearly with others

Uses expanded vocabulary

Repeats nursery rhymes, songs, chants

Dictates stories, ideas, sentences

Listens to others

Talks about reading and writing

*Reading*

Interested in reading materials

Joins in shared reading activities

Understands story line (plot)

Retells story in sequence

Pretend or memory reads

Recognizes some sight words

Derives meaning from text

Has knowledge about letters

Uses environmental print

*Writing*

Interested in writing (print)

Pretend writes (scribble)

Spends time writing

Uses invented spelling

      random letters

      representation letters

      phonetic spelling

        conventional spelling/high frequency words

Uses writing to communicate

Uses literary structures

*Social*

Shares with others

Works cooperatively with others

Respects authority/peers

Remains on task

Listens and shares ideas with others

*Developed by Elizabeth Lolli*

## Central Academy Individual Education Plan

| Academic Goals | Assessment Instruments | Effective Dates | Date Tested | Mastery Level |
|---|---|---|---|---|
| Math | | | | |
| | | | | |
| | | | | |
| | | | | |
| | | | | |
| | | | | |
| Reading | | | | |
| | | | | |
| | | | | |
| | | | | |
| | | | | |
| English/Grammar | | | | |
| | | | | |
| | | | | |
| | | | | |

# Middletown Ohio City Schools
# Central Academy Nongraded
# Together Everyone Achieves More

School Year 19__ - 19__

Grading Period _____

Date of Birth
_____

Days Absent _____
Days Tardy _____
Total Absence _____
Total Tardies _____

Student Name
_____

Teacher Name/Level
_____

_____

Parent Signature

_____

*Developed by Elizabeth Lolli, Central Academy/Nongraded.*

# INDEPENDENT READING RECORDS AND EVALUATIONS

A. Children's Independent Reading Log

| Date | Title | Author | Opinion (Easy — E; Medium — M; Hard — H) |
|------|-------|--------|-------------------------------------------|

B. Reading Journals (Following independent silent reading)

1. Journals for written summary of material read during s.r. (list date, title, author)

2. Journals of blank pages for non-readers who will summarize their book in picture form.

3. Journals for specific information requested by teacher.

   Examples: Who is the most important character in the book?
   What is the story about?
   How did the story end?
   How did you feel while reading the story?

C. Teacher's conference log (individual conferences take place during s.r. time)

| Student | Date | Title | Author |
|---------|------|-------|--------|

1. Questions: ex.  Who are some of the characters?
   What is the story about?
   Where does it take place?
   What did you like best about the story?

2. Oral Reading by student: small passage chosen in advance. If non-reader, explanation of chosen picture in book.

3. Independent incidental instruction on any skill or concept that may be needed at that moment. (Ex. explanation of vocabulary word or specific skill within a word that child is struggling with)

D. Student vocabulary list. List of words with meaning and context which child would like to make his/her own.

E. Sharing Time

1. Group or whole class discussions and sharing of books.

2. Group activities, drama, projects, as follow-up to books.

3. Audience reading.

# Independent Reading Conference Records

Name:                                              Date:
Title:                                             Author:
BME

Characters:

Setting:

Main idea:

Ending:

Feelings:

Specific questions:

Liked/disliked:

Vocabulary:

Skills:

Strategies:

Conventions:

Oral reading:

General comments:

# Writing Group Conference

Name:                                              Date:

Topic:

Comments:

Questions:

# Sample use of folder for record-keeping

Books_____(name)_____
has written

1. My cabin   9-16

2. My New House   10-5  Ⓟ

3. Louisiana   10-21

4. Thanksgiving dinner   11-16

**Front Cover**

Spelling/Vocabulary

too            Christmas

to             Louisiana

two            ocean

**Back Cover**

Topics_____(name)_____
knows much about

1. skiing
2. whales
3. drawing
4. playing piano

**Inside Left**

Topic list

1. my cabin
2. skiing
3. Louisiana
4. new house
5. poodle

Attach to inside
of folder

Things_____(name)_____
knows

capitals
periods
quotation marks
ai

**Inside Right**

Jean Mann

# Writing —
## Sample teacher's conference record

Child's name      Kevin

| Date | Title | Skills used correctly | Skills taught |
|------|-------|----------------------|---------------|
| 1-19 | "ski getaway" | Quotes<br>Apostrophes on possessives<br>Edited for spelling,<br>   checked circled words. | capitals for<br>   Title words<br>work on<br>   paragraphs |
| 1-25 | "Future"<br>(poem) | Rhyming words at<br>ends of 2nd and 4th | stanzas |

# Sample Record-keeping for Writing Conferences
## — Status of Class —

| week of_____ | Monday | Tuesday | Wednesday | Thursday | Friday |
|---|---|---|---|---|---|
| Andy | "White Tail Deer" | | "The War" | c.c.+ "The War" good info spaces | "The War" P |
| Nathaniel | "The Swamp" | "The Swamp" e.c. "ed" [2 subjects] | "The Swamp" caps/periods P | "Abominable Snowman" | g.c. ! |
| Lara | "Apple Bear In The Snow s.c. vowels aio | "Skiing" | "Gina Coming Over" | | To be published |
| Julie | "Ice Cream" (Flavors) | "Colors" (Picture book) | "Hearts" | "Rainbows" | "Ice Cream" c.c. |
| Trevor | "The Cabin" | | "The Cabin" s.c. silent "e" ai (main) quotes | Skiing | g.c. |
| Amanda | "Julie Going To My House" c.c.+ good content | "Everything In The World" | | | |

concepts written in <u>black</u> are concepts taught during conference

concepts written in <u>blue</u> show that a child is using a concept previously taught, but inconsistently

concepts written in <u>red</u> are mastered and used consistently

## Suggested Symbols:

| | | | |
|---|---|---|---|
| cc | content conference | EV | evaluation conference |
| sc | skills conference | 1D | first draft |
| ec | editing conference | 2D | second draft |
| gc | group conference | P | publish |

**Jean Mann**
**(Adapted with permission from Paula Fleming)**

# Meaning-Based Evaluation

**Portfolio evidence might include:**

- self-assessment
- samples of student writing, in many subject areas:
  rough drafts, journals, reading logs, research reports
- lists of books read and pieces published
- checklists, strategies, skills, genres
- home surveys, parent conferences
- teacher observations, anecdotes, notes
- audiotape, videotape
- interviews, conferences with learner
- running records, miscue analysis
- scores, standardized test results, progress report forms

**Portfolio evaluation should be:**

| | |
|---|---|
| **ongoing** | updated regularly |
| **instructive** | provide insights into instructional strategies, the responsibility of the teacher |
| **manageable** | easy to implement |
| **informative** | provide information on progress to student, parents, teachers, administrators |
| **evolving** | subject to revision, re-thinking |
| **comprehensive** | describe a range of attitudes, understandings, and behaviors |
| **selective** | based on evaluation priorities, regularly revised |
| **collaborative** | items are included during teacher/student conferences |
| **articulated** | provide useful information to successive teachers |
| **individualized** | based on goals set by the learner, with focus on self-evaluation |
| **supportive** | positive, based on what student can do rather than deficit model |
| **consistent** | reflective of the learning theory upon which the classroom environment is based |

# Questions for Early Readers

## Assessment and Evaluation

1. Does the learner show an interest in books?

2. Does the learner show an interest in words?

3. Can the learner tell a familiar story?

4. Can the learner make up a story that has appropriate story structure?

5. Can the learner find and point to individual words on a page?

6. Does the learner turn or try to turn the pages at the appropriate time when a story is being read aloud?

7. Does the learner comment about books read?

8. Does the learner reread favorite books?

9. Is the learner aware that s/he can make meaning through print?

10. Does the learner compare books, authors, illustrators?

11. Does the learner love favorite books?

12. Does the learner ask questions about print?

13. Can the learner find favorite books on a bookshelf?

14. Does the learner recall details from stories?

15. Does the learner self-correct reading and/or writing?

16. Does the learner choose to read or write during independent practice time or free choice time?

17. Does the learner notice words or symbols in the environment?

18. Does the learner predict outcomes in stories or story segments?

These are a few questions which may be a part of a literacy evaluation procedure for young learners? Please add other questions you would use and let me know about them.

# Observing the Inefficient Reader's Use of the Three Cueing Systems

1.  When it appears that the beginning reader perceives the decoding process as one of producing sounds for letters and blending the sounds together, then he may perform this process as an end in itself and show no behavior which indicates that he is aware that decoding is the use of various clues to process language into meaning.

    Therefore, when observing an inefficient reader, watch his behavior to infer what his understanding of the decoding process is.

    Is he aware that the passage should have meaning for him? What kinds of clues does he use to arrive at the meaning: semantic, syntactic, phonetic? Does he depend on one type of clue to the virtual exclusion of others?

2.  The reader who understands that reading should make sense to him is likely to demonstrate the use of context clues, i.e., he will take risks and make predictions about unknown words and guess what they might be. Therefore, when observing an inefficient reader, watch for his risk-taking behaviors in dealing with words he is trying to decode. Do his guesses have some amount of semantic and syntactic acceptability? Does he try to answer comprehension questions on the basis of his experiences when he hasn't gotten the information from the passage?

3.  The reader who understands that reading is processing language will sacrifice accuracy in decoding in order to get the meaning of a selection. Therefore, when an inefficient reader makes substitutions, insertions, and omissions, check his comprehension on those parts of the passage to attempt to determine what meaning he was after, i.e., since he couldn't cope with what was printed in the passage, what meaning did he try to force into it? Did he try to make it make sense to him? Do his errors indicate his attempts to process language into meaning? Does he show the flexibility to sacrifice oral reading accuracy for the meaning?

    When the inefficient reader arrives at an interpretation of a passage which is markedly different from the range of possible interpretations, it may be an indication of insufficient experiential background for the passage. Conversely, it is important to be aware that the reader who arrives at a possible interpretation does so in part because of his experiential background.

    When the inefficient reader has not been sufficiently reinforced as a user of (oral) language, his self-concept as a reader suffers. Therefore, when observing an inefficient reader, attempt to ascertain whether his attitude is positive or negative toward himself as a user of language. Does he let his current difficulties with the reading act intimidate him, or does he perform in the security that he has mastered oral language and is currently working through some impasses with written language?

**John Poeton**

# Mastery of Narrative/Expository

Student Name _____

## Narrative

Date  Observer

| | |
|---|---|

**PRESCHOOL**

tells a simple story

listens to a story

engages in dramatic play

identifies who/what in a story

moral of story

**KINDERGARTEN/FIRST**

has concept of plot (beginning, middle, end)

author's craft (as listener)

describes setting

has concept of setting

has concept of character (major/minor)

concept of theme

**SECOND/THIRD**

author's craft (as reader — character motivation, reader response, purpose)

compares/contrasts characters

knows relationship of setting to plot

visualizes setting

analyzes and extends a theme

recognizes complex plots

uses cause and effect

**FOURTH/FIFTH**

character dynamics/personification

author's craft (as writer)

reconstructs a setting

episodic analysis (rising/falling action)

## Expository

date  observer

| | |
|---|---|

takes part in large group investigation

creates a picture that informs

differentiates between fiction/non-fiction

presents an informative piece

uses a variety of sources

uses conventions (table of contents, title page, bibliography)

finds author's voice

Understands appropriate resource and format

organizes and interprets information

understands forms of expository

identifies author's purpose

John Poeton

## Reading/Writing/Learning Self-Evaluation Form

This self-evaluation form is designed for teachers involved in the Reading/Writing/Learning Staff Development Project Coordinated by the Elementary Reading and Language Development Department of the Orange County Public School, Orlando, Florida.

| | Implemented | Goal for next year |
|---|---|---|
| **Classroom environment** | | |
| I increased print in the environment | _____ | _____ |
| I increased shared decision making | _____ | _____ |
| I provided a risk-free environment | _____ | _____ |
| I increased the variety of genre and levels of difficulty of the books in the library corner | _____ | _____ |
| **Schedule** | | |
| I refined the schedule to provide adequate time daily for children to read and write | _____ | _____ |
| **Teachers as learners** | | |
| I read professionally | _____ | _____ |
| I read for pleasure | _____ | _____ |
| I read new children's books | _____ | _____ |
| I wrote with students for authentic purposes | _____ | _____ |
| **Readers' workshop** | | |
| I provided a predictable structure | _____ | _____ |
| I conducted minilessons | _____ | _____ |
| I provided a block of time daily for self-selected and self-paced reading | _____ | _____ |
| I held literature discussion groups | _____ | _____ |
| I conferred with individual students | _____ | _____ |
| I provided opportunities for children to respond to reading | _____ | _____ |
| **Reading aloud** | | |
| I read aloud to students | _____ | _____ |
| **Sharing** | | |
| I conducted shared reading (big books, charts, multiple copies) | _____ | _____ |
| **Guided reading** | | |
| I met with small group for guided reading sessions | _____ | _____ |
| **Comprehension** | | |
| I activated children's prior knowledge | _____ | _____ |
| I modeled strategies good readers use | _____ | _____ |
| I provided opportunities to integrate new knowledge (summarize, evaluate, synthesize) | _____ | _____ |
| **Writers' workshop** | | |
| I provided a predictable structure | _____ | _____ |
| I conducted minilessons | _____ | _____ |
| I provided a block of time for independent writing (student-selected topics) | _____ | _____ |
| I conferred with individual students | _____ | _____ |
| I provided opportunities for students to share their writing | _____ | _____ |
| **Assessment** | | |
| I gathered data for students' portfolio | _____ | _____ |
| I analyzed writing samples | _____ | _____ |
| I took anecdotal records | _____ | _____ |
| I used running records to evaluate miscues and strategies | _____ | _____ |
| I made instructional decisions based on the data collected | _____ | _____ |
| **Communication with parents** | | |
| I reported student progress through use of portfolios | _____ | _____ |
| I established a method for sharing information | _____ | _____ |

*From "Changing Reading and Writing Programs through Staff Development" by Janet Speer Johnson and Sue Le Master Wilder. The article appeared in The Reading Teacher, April 1992.*

MaryEllen Vogt

# An observation guide for supervisors and administrators: Moving toward integrated reading/language arts instruction

*Vogt, past president of the California Reading Association and a former curriculum director and district reading resource teacher, is currently an assistant professor in the Graduate School of Education, California State University, Long Beach, California.*

Since the publication of *Becoming A Nation of Readers* (Anderson, Hiebert, Scott, & Wilkinson, 1985), teachers have been moving gradually toward a new, meaning-focused way of teaching children to read and write. To facilitate this change in language arts instruction, supervisors of reading and building principals are also changing the way they support, assist, observe, and supervise teachers.

The purpose of this article is: (a) to briefly examine the characteristics of and roles assumed by supervisors and administrators who promote and support change, specifically in the area of reading/language arts; and (b) to provide questions designed to guide supervisors' and administrators' observations of reading and writing lessons and enable them to assist teachers who are working toward integrated reading/language arts programs.

## Characteristics of supervisors and administrators who support change

Recent research findings (Fullan, 1985; Hord & Goldstein, 1982; Paulu, 1989; Vanderpool, 1990; Venezky & Winfield, 1979) indicate that despite differing personal characteristics, leadership styles, and behaviors, those leaders who have been most successful in implementing positive changes in schools are individuals who:

● bring focus to the change process by tailoring their reform efforts to their particular schools;

● maintain open communication with their students, faculty, staff, parents, and community policy-makers, primarily by listening and providing opportunities to share;

● encourage, support, and provide adequate and ongoing staff development for everyone involved in the change process, including themselves;

● form instructional leadership teams that are involved in the collaborative planning of objectives and decision making;

● know how to get things done even when resources are limited;

● articulate a comprehensive educational plan for change, rather than taking a piecemeal approach;

● create an atmosphere within the school where ideas flourish and where risk-taking and initiative are rewarded; and

● understand and communicate the fact that change cannot and does not take place overnight, and that the role of the facilitator is ongoing (Binkley, 1989; Bozik, 1989; Erickson, 1990; Havelock, 1973; Paulu, 1989; Ridley, 1990; Vanderpool, 1990).

In sum, what appears to be an important characteristic of educational change agents is their ability to exercise their leadership responsibilities within an environment that has been prepared for change.

## Guiding change in reading/language arts instruction

To enable schools to move toward integrated reading/language arts instruction, effective supervisors and administrators should be first and foremost open to new philosophies and approaches to literacy instruction, such as whole language and literature-based reading. Largely, this is due to the belief that reading and writing instruction should focus on strategic reading, building language development, sharing meaning through oral and written communication, and "unlimited individual horizons" (Vujea, 1990, p. 161).

Second, these administrators, along with teachers, parents, and children, are working collaboratively to plan, solve problems, and negotiate ways to bring about change (Erickson, 1990).

Third, supervisors and administrators who are change agents are knowledgeable and understand current reading research and its translation into practice.

Fourth, supervisors and administrators who effect change in reading/language arts instruction accept and encourage teachers' need for varying amounts of transition time as they learn how to integrate the language arts.

Fifth, supervisors and administrators who effect change commit to not only providing a nurturing environment for change but also provide the personnel, resources, and funding to support change efforts.

*To enable schools to move toward integrated reading/language arts instruction, effective supervisors and administrators should be first and foremost open to new philosophies and approaches to literacy instruction, such as whole language and literature-based reading.*

Finally, it appears that administrative leaders of reading/language arts reform are willing to revise their thinking about the supervision and evaluation of teachers. Supervisors and administrators are recognizing that a seven-step daily lesson plan may not be appro-

---

## Observation guide used to develop an integrated reading/language arts program

**Reading**

In this classroom, is the teacher:
- modeling and sharing his/her own joy of reading?
- recommending books of interest to students?
- providing a variety of literature genres (e.g., short stories, novels, poetry, biographies, essays, informational books, magazines, etc.)?
- providing time for daily, self-selected silent reading?
- reading aloud to students on a daily basis?
- requiring a minimum of oral reading practice by the students (and providing silent practice before any oral reading)?
- incorporating thematic units in language arts instruction?
- providing skills (e.g., phonics) instruction for those needing it, not in isolation but within meaningful contexts?
- utilizing a variety of grouping strategies for instruction (e.g., whole class, flexible small groups, partners, cooperative learning groups)?
- providing opportunities for students to read independently and work individually on some tasks?
- utilizing strategies that promote discussion, divergent thinking, and multiple responses?
- assigning reading tasks that promote collaboration and cooperation among students?
- planning reading tasks and strategies that activate and utilize students' prior knowledge before, during, and after reading?
- asking questions that encourage and promote dialogue, inquiry, and critique?
- encouraging a variety of responses to literature and to questions that are asked about the literature?
- collecting portfolio assessment data that is authentic in nature (e.g., transcribed, taped, or analyzed retelling) and selected for inclusion by the student and teacher so that the student, parents, and teacher all are involved in assessing progress?
- using portfolio data to guide instructional decisions and individual instruction?

**Writing**

In this classroom, is the teacher:
- modeling and sharing his/her own joy of writing?
- modeling and teaching the stages of the writing process (prewriting, drafting, sharing, revising, editing, publishing)?
- assigning daily writing for a variety of purposes to a variety of audiences?
- encouraging divergent, creative thinking through writing assignments?
- encouraging students to use their writing as a natural response to literature?
- incorporating invented ("temporary") spelling strategies for beginning readers/writers?
- encouraging more mature writers to attempt invented spellings when composing, then assisting them with checking for correct spellings during editing?
- regularly conferring with each student about his/her writing?
- responding to student writing with helpful suggestions, thoughtful comments, and very little "red-marking"?
- promoting student self-assessment and peer conferences for the revision and editing stages?
- displaying and publishing student writing?
- collecting portfolio assessment data that is authentic in nature (e.g., samples of writing in various stages and journal entries) and selected for inclusion by the student and teacher so that the student, parents, and teacher all are involved in assessing progress?
- using portfolio data to guide instructional decisions and individual instruction?

**Listening**

In this classroom, is the teacher:
- promoting listening as a means of learning?
- providing opportunities for students to hear other students' responses to the literature they have read?
- providing a variety of listening experiences for differing purposes (e.g., "sharing" time, reports, Readers Theatre, students' rehearsed oral reading, etc.)?
- reading aloud to students from narrative and expository text and from poetry selections?
- providing discussion opportunities for students to collaborate, cooperate, and compromise?
- promoting social skills through listening (e.g., providing and maintaining eye contact, paraphrasing to demonstrate understanding, and summarizing what was heard)?

**Speaking**

In this classroom, is the teacher:
- providing daily opportunities for structured oral language development (e.g., choral reading, speeches, drama, "sharing" time, oral reports, debates, discussion)?
- modeling and teaching correct language usage?
- teaching students to facilitate group discussion?

---

**Observation guide used to develop an integrated reading/language arts program (continued)**

- modeling and teaching language for a variety of purposes (e.g., informing, persuading, sharing feelings, evaluating, imagining, predicting)?
- using literature and student writing as a source for oral language development?

**General**
In this classroom, is the teacher:
- actively observing and noting or recording students' responses and participation during reading/language arts instruction?
- enabling all children to make choices about what they read and write?
- resisting labeling students in terms of ability or achievement?
- communicating to parents the tenets of integrated reading/language arts instruction?
- encouraging parents to read to their children, discuss literature with them, and support and encourage their children's reading and writing progress?
- providing a structured reading environment where opinion, creative thought, and sharing of ideas are valued?
- celebrating literacy and learning on a daily basis?
- participating in staff development activities and then attempting to implement newly learned ideas?

---

priate for literature-based instruction, when an entire language arts block for one day may be used just for activating and utilizing students' prior knowledge while moving them into a piece of literature. Likewise, observation procedures such as recording "time-on-task" need to be redefined; active discussions among small group members, quiet reflection, and silent reading may have replaced worksheets and other seatwork that formerly provided data for recording minutes on task.

In order to guide the supervisor or administrator as he/she visits with and observes teachers in transition, both the supervisor or administrator and the teacher need to be familiar with the characteristics or elements of effective reading/language arts programs and watch for these elements. For example, one element of an integrated program would be daily time for students' self-selected reading and writing activities. Obviously, not all elements may be present in every observed lesson, but as teachers work to integrate their reading/language arts programs, ideally more elements should become a part of the instruction. By occasionally checking to see if the elements are present, teachers, supervisors, and administrators can work together to facilitate the change process. The following section of this article outlines questions that highlight the elements present in effective reading/language arts programs.

## Observation guide: Integrated reading/language arts instruction

To assist teachers, supervisors, and administrators in determining which elements should be present in integrated reading/language arts programs, a list of questions was developed into an observation guide; these questions are based on current research and practice (California State Department of Education, 1987; Cullinan, 1987; Goodman, 1986; Macon, Bewell, & Vogt, 1989; Vogt, 1989). It is important to note two things about this guide: (a) the questions included in the guide presume a degree of acceptance of the whole language philosophy as well as a basic understanding of integrated teaching methods, and (b) the questions are separated into discrete categories of the language processes; they are grouped this way merely for clarity and focus. However, observers know that these are not discrete processes and one should observe several elements from several categories intertwined and occurring at the same time.

Focusing on the questions will enable teachers to gradually implement elements that should result in an integrated reading/language arts program. *Integration* necessarily suggests that instruction in the language processes of reading, writing, listening, and speaking should not be separated. It is believed that integrated teaching contributes to the interdependence of the processes because growth in one appears to result in growth in the others (Pearson, 1990).

After teachers, supervisors, and administrators discuss the questions included in the observation guide and after teachers have become comfortable implementing some of the elements, supervisors and administrators may use the guide as a focus for observing classroom lessons. For example, prior to observing a teacher's lesson the administrator and teacher could meet together and jointly decide which elements may be displayed during the reading/language arts lesson. This discussion should serve as a learning and sharing experience, making the teacher and administrator comfortable with the observation process and the outcomes of the observation. Further, the teacher could request that the administrator observe particular elements that he/she is working to implement and that may be observed during a particular lesson. The administrator may then note those elements and perhaps any that have been agreed upon but are not evident.

After the conference, the teacher may choose to supplement what was/was not observed using the observation guide by collecting and compiling weekly letters written to parents, lists of stories or books that have been read aloud to children, or student work from a thematic, literature-based unit. Jointly, the teacher and supervisor or administrator could then discuss and list other elements on the observation guide that appear in these documents; then elements that teachers would like to gradually implement could be discussed. With this type of sharing and by focusing on specific program elements, teachers will feel successful and have the opportunity to reflect and expand on their own understanding of integrated teaching.

The most important point to remember is that the questions are meant as guides for support, assistance, and encouragement during a time of change. Obviously, as our understanding of the language processes and of teaching changes, so too might the questions on the observation guide. The successful use of this guide, of course, is predicated upon adequate staff development, a district or school philosophy which is congruent with integrated teaching, and open communication between administrators and teachers.

## Conclusion

I hope these questions will be helpful in facilitating the change process many teachers are engaged in as they work toward a more integrated reading/language arts program. However, change will not take place if we simply make a checklist of "things to do" in the classroom without reflecting on what we do each day, how children learn, and how schools change.

Critically needed in schools everywhere are staff development opportunities for teachers, administrators, parents, and school board members; these staff development sessions need to be practical, yet grounded in current theory and research. Further, teachers need the chance to observe and interact with each other as they work toward making changes in their instruction. Administrative support in the form of released time would allow teachers to observe mentors who are modeling innovative instructional strategies. This is just one way of providing invaluable assistance.

School and classroom libraries should be stocked sufficiently with a variety of quality literature so that teachers may build thematic units and, more important, provide children with opportunities to read self-selected books and stories. If a basal reading series is adopted, teachers and administrators must be selective to ensure that all students are provided with materials that enhance their reading experiences. Assessment instruments should be developed to more closely reflect meaningful reading and writing behaviors (e.g., portfolio assessment).

Finally, as educators we must recognize and trust that the changes we are making, if based upon a solid research foundation, will represent a true shift in perspective and practice, not just another pendulum swing (Slavin, 1989). We do not have time to "wait this one out," yet we also do not have to make changes all at once. As teachers we can collaboratively and gradually implement changes in the way we teach reading/language arts. As supervisors and administrators we can recognize and accept our role as catalysts for change. To facilitate change we need to build an educational environment where (a) new ideas are listened to, (b) change is supported and assisted through positive supervision, and (c) we model for children, parents, and teachers elements of integrated reading/language arts instruction. In so doing, perhaps the reform efforts of today will become the "traditional way" of teaching reading and writing tomorrow.

### References

Anderson, R.C., Hiebert, E.H., Scott, J.A., & Wilkinson, I.A.G. (1985). *Becoming a nation of readers: The report of the commission on reading.* Washington, DC: U.S. Department of Education.

Binkley, M. (Ed.) (1989). *Becoming a nation of readers: What principals can do*. Office of Educational Research and Improvement, U.S. Department of Education, National Association of Elementary School Principals. Boston: Houghton Mifflin.

Bozik, M.L. (1989). Ten ways that principals can promote effective communication. *Principal, 69*(1), 34-36.

California State Department of Education. (1987). *The English-language arts framework*. Sacramento, CA: Author.

Cullinan, B. (Ed.) (1987). *Children's literature in the reading program*. Newark, DE: International Reading Association.

Erickson, L.G. (1990). How improvement teams facilitate schoolwide reading reform. *Journal of Reading, 33*, 580-585.

Fullan, M. (1985). Change processes and strategies at the local level. *Elementary School Journal, 85*(3), 391-421.

Goodman, K. (1986). *What's whole in whole language?* Portsmouth, NH: Heinemann.

Havelock, R.G. (1973). *The change agents' guide to innovation in education*. Englewood Cliffs, NJ: Educational Technology.

Hord, S.M., & Goldstein, M.L. (1982). *What principals do to facilitate change: Their interventions*. Paper presented at the annual meeting of the American Educational Research Association, New York City, NY.

Macon, J., Bewell, D., & Vogt, M.E. (1989). *Responses to literature: K-8*. Newark, DE: International Reading Association.

Paulu, N. (1989). Principals and school improvement: Sixteen success stories. *NAASP Bulletin, 73*(517), 71-77.

Pearson, P.D. (1990, April). *Whole language: A coat of many colors (or should I say umbrella?)*. Keynote address presented at the 21st annual conference of the Massachusetts Reading Association, Sturbridge, MA.

Ridley, L. (1990). Enacting change in elementary school programs: Implementing a whole language perspective. *The Reading Teacher, 43*, 640-646.

Slavin, R.E. (1989). PET and the pendulum: Faddism in education and how to stop it. *Phi Delta Kappan 70*(10), 752-758.

Vanderpool, M. (1990). Innovations aren't for everyone. *Principal, 69*(4), 38-43.

Venezky, R., & Winfield, L. (1979). *Schools that succeed beyond expectations in teaching reading*. Newark, DE: University of Delaware.

Vogt, M.E. (1989). Toward literature-based reading instruction in California. *Reading Today, 6*(3), 19.

Vujea, C. (1990). Out of the basal and into literature to teach the basic skills. In N. Cecil (Ed.), *Literacy in the 90's: Reading in the language arts* (pp. 160-164). Dubuque, IA: Kendall/Hunt.

**Reprinted with permission of Mary Ellen Vogt and the International Reading Association.**

## Voices

Teachers are coming together. We're coming together across districts, across grade levels and disciplines, even within our own staffrooms, and we're coming together in the spirit of an old-fashioned barn raising. It's not a barn we're building but a better world for ourselves and our children.

*Lucy Calkins*
**Living Between the Lines**

Reprinted with permission from Lucy Calkins: Living Between the Lines (Heinemann Educational Books, Portsmouth, NH 1990).

Harold (Buzz) Bowers

# What Teachers Learn from "Kid Watching"

*Teacher-researchers in a Colorado district are expanding their understanding of teaching and learning by viewing their classrooms as "thoughtful communities," where they, too, are learners.*

RICHARD VANDEWEGHE

Recently I asked teachers participating in the Douglas County School District's Higher Literacy Project about their classroom-based research. One teacher talked excitedly about "an absolutely amazing event that happened just this morning." She then shared an anecdote about an at-risk 8th grader who wrote something longer than a sentence for the first time since September: a poem about his alienation from school. For this teacher-researcher, an unexpected event, like the poem suddenly and awkwardly composed by a marginally literate child, made her ask questions: Why did he do that now? What let loose in him? Has he learned to trust me? The class?

Another teacher looked down at his feet, hands in pockets, and admitted that his project is "taking turns I didn't expect" and that "the more I listen — really listen — to how these kids talk about their reading in the history textbook, the more I think I need to know about *reading*!" For him, realizing that he knows little about the problems kids have with reading history texts is seen as a professional opportunity rather than a shortcoming.

Another response came from a teacher who suddenly reached into her skirt pocket, pulled out a small notebook, flipped over pages of penciled notes, and read her observations of a class debate about a Hemingway short story. For her, getting some insight into the patterns of discourse in class debates is exciting.

These are typical responses of teacher-researchers who view their classrooms as places where they are the learners — learning from their students. As Mary W. Olson said recently, "These are confident teachers who research questions that intrigue and puzzle them, who seek answers and understanding about their students' learning and their own teaching, and who strive to be more knowledgeable in their responses to the teaching/ learning cycle" (1990, p. 13).

## Thoughtful Communities

Teacher research in Douglas County, Colorado, is sponsored by the district's Thoughtful Communities: The Douglas County Higher Literacy Project. Participants commit to

conducting two research projects in two years. They form "thoughtful communities" with other district teacher-researchers, who collaborate with and support one another in their research. At the same time, they seek to create thoughtful communities of learners in their classrooms: groups of students who collaborate with one another in constructing and refining their own knowledge. The second part of the program's title indicates its aim to promote and understand the nature of higher literacy, that complex of skills, attitudes, and abilities that mark the genuinely literate person of the 21st century (Brown 1988).

What makes this project distinctive is the individually designed programs of professional growth determined by the teacher-researchers themselves. To commit to doing research (in addition to all the other things that draw on their time and energy) constitutes a major investment in change. Then there is the large-scale district support for teachers-as-researchers: participating teachers receive release time for project research, university graduate credit, hourly pay for attending meetings, books to add to their professional libraries, and expenses paid for project-related professional conferences.

Project teachers meet regularly to discuss readings, issues and problems in higher literacy and classroom research; help one another (in writing workshops) to prepare project reports; and participate in institutes related to their professional development.

## The Research Projects

By observing their students at work, asking good questions about learning, and, as Glenda Bissex says, seeing "everything that happens in a classroom . . . as data to be understood rather than causes for blaming or

congratulating" (1986, p. 483), Thoughtful Communities teachers take on research projects that illuminate their understanding of teaching and learning, regardless of the projects' potential for success or failure. "We can learn from failures as well as successes, same as our kids," one teacher recently remarked. A sampling of their projects includes:

• investigation of ways to help students learn to write in visually articulate ways (using graphic, typographic, and spatial techniques);

• inquiry into the contradictions teachers face when they take time to promote higher literacy in their classrooms;

• development of a writing portfolio approach to outcomes-based assessment in social studies;

• exploration of the learning value of ambiguity and speculative thinking in language arts and social studies;

• development of classroom structures that address the needs of at-risk students.

The projects originate from a number of sources, and in each source

there exists some kind of tension. One source is *pedagogical experimentation,* where the tension is inherent in such speculation as "I wonder if this approach could work for me?" This was the case with one of our researchers, who came into the project intrigued by a teaching approach that encouraged active questions. He determined that he wanted to find out if, how, and why active questions contribute to higher literacy.

The second source of tension has to do with *self-reflection* and the corresponding doubt that gives rise to action. Like other reflective educators, project teachers engage in a "cycle of thought and action based on professional experience" (Wellington 1991, p. 4). For example, many teachers change completely their initial project area once they begin reading and talking with others about higher literacy. They say, in effect, "Why am I not promoting higher literacy in the way I teach?" The answers to that single question lead them to reflect on how they teach, how their kids learn, and how things could be.

Third, teachers *discover* projects through their research activities. They may tentatively commit to a project and in the course of reading about their topic, collecting classroom data, and reflecting on both, find their *real* project topic. They say, "Knowing *this* leads me to think in these ways now." This is what happened with a language arts teacher whose research topic began as an investigation of nonstandardized methods of assessing reading and writing. After seven months, her focus shifted to developing a learning environment in her classroom where assessment became integrated with, rather than separated from, her teaching.

Much professional growth occurs through trying to understand or resolve these tensions. Teachers discover that new techniques do or don't work for them — and because they are experimenting thoughtfully, they get insight into why or why not. That's much different from the teacher who tries and fails and never asks why. Similarly, teacher-researchers who doubt themselves or their approaches rely on their research to prove or disprove the legitimacy of their doubt. And those who think new thoughts reconceptualize their research because they know that doing so is a primary reason for such research to go on.

Classroom-research-as-professional-development becomes the impetus as well as the vehicle for change. I saw this idea brought out in one teacher's research report:

As an observer, I was able to examine "why" and "how" things happen as they do. For the first time ever I brought questions as well as answers to my classroom; questions that have helped me better evaluate not only my students but also myself. In a relatively short time I

**A wonderful sense of empowerment accrues to teachers who have a database for their teaching, who can say, "I know this works; let me show you these few hundred writing samples to illustrate what I mean."**

have made, and plan to continue making, significant changes in my classroom. My sense is that without a component of teacher-based research, change would be slow in coming (Groll 1990, p. 37).

## Teachers Reflect on Their Growth

The best indications of professional development in this project come from the teacher-researchers themselves, as they've contemplated their experiences in Thoughtful Communities. Here are just a few examples.

One teacher described how conducting classroom research altered the way she viewed herself:

I experienced many successes and frustrations along with some startling perceptions of myself as a teacher. . . . My successes include being a part of a happier, more exciting classroom experience with a minimum of "policewoman" responsibilities and the realization that it's okay not to be the ultimate expert in the eyes of my students.

Another teacher, whose project focused on the art of questioning, ended up with a rich and vastly expanded understanding of the heart of classroom inquiry:

Questions are not only a way of gaining knowledge — questions and knowledge fission to generate more questions and more knowledge. Questioning isn't a method or a technique; it has to be a habit — a lifestyle — if it is to lead students to higher levels of literacy.

Finally, a teacher whose research changed his view of school writing from "writing to present ideas" to "writing to learn" found that in addition to promoting a view of writing-as-a-way-of-learning, he needed to promote talking-as-a-way-of-learning:

I need to develop a skill in questioning that allows students to think. In the past, I usually orchestrated the discussion to get the answers I wanted to hear.

## Insight into Professional Development

What does teacher research of the kind described here teach us about professional development? First, *true* professional growth accompanies a skeptical stance toward oneself and toward one's classroom; it's a form of critical curiosity that many nonresearchers find hard to fathom.

Second, a collaborative network of teachers engaged in similar growth nourish and sustain one another in vital ways, especially during times of great challenge or doubt.

Third, collecting data — for example, observing and listening to kids, taking notes, reading learning logs and writing samples — forces teachers into the practice of monitoring learning in ways that demand reflection. That is, if things aren't going as one expects, one must ask why. Also, a wonderful sense of empowerment accrues to teachers who have a database for their teaching, who can say (with great

gusto), "I know this works; here, let me show you these few hundred writing samples to illustrate what I mean."

Finally, teacher-researchers challenge systems (curriculum, assessment, for example). But they do so from affective and cognitive knowledge based on firsthand observation, wide reading, and deep conviction.

Teacher-researchers constantly probe and question, listen and observe, notice and note — to them, professional development is driven by the vision, knowledge, and ambition generated by their research. They are, in Yetta Goodman's words, "kid watchers" (1989, p. 8), teachers who interact with students and who monitor class activities in order to understand more about teaching and learning, mostly learning. ☐

### References

Bissex, G. (1986). "On Becoming Teacher Experts: What's a Teacher-Researcher?" *Language Arts* 63, 5: 482-485.

Brown, R. (Spring 1988). "Schooling and Thoughtfulness." *Basic Education* 3, 3.

Goodman, Y. M. (1989). "Evaluation of Students." In *The Whole Language Evaluation Book,* edited by K. S. Goodman, Y. M. Goodman, and W. J. Hood. Portsmouth: Heinemann.

Groll, L. (1990). "Thoughtful Communities: A Reflection." In *Thoughtful Communities: Douglas County Higher Literacy Project.* Castle Rock, Colo.: Douglas County School District Reorganized 1.

Olson, M. (June/July 1990). "Teachers as Researchers." *Reading Today* 7, 6: 13.

Wellington, B. (1991). "The Promise of Reflective Practice." *Educational Leadership* 48, 6: 4-5.

**Richard VanDeWeghe** is English Department Chair, University of Colorado at Denver, Box 175, P.O. Box 173364, Denver, CO 80217-3364. He is also Director of the Higher Literacy Project, Douglas County Public School District.

## Voices

I f we know one thing from the last quarter-century of research and development, it is that literacy is a property of communities and that students are much more likely to go beyond decoding if they find themselves in the company of individuals who love to read and who turn naturally to writing as a means of working out their feelings, ideas and beliefs.

*Howard Gardner*
**Language Arts, March 1992**

**Reprinted with permission of the National Council of Teachers of English.**

**Van DeWeghe, Richard (1992). "What Teachers Learn From 'Kid Watching,'"** *Educational Leadership,* **49, 7:49-52.**
**Reprinted with permission of Richard VanDeWeghe and the Association for Supervision and Curriculum Development.**

# *Whole Language Professional Books*
## Bibliography
### Compiled by SDE Presenters
**If you would like help locating any of the books, contact Crystal Springs Books, 1-800-321-0401 or in N.H., (603) 924-9380.**

Allen, JoBeth, and Mason, Jana, eds. *Risk Makers, Risk Takers, Risk Breakers*. Portsmouth, NH: Heinemann, 1989.

Alvermann, Donna et al. *Using Discussion to Promote Reading Comprehension*. Newark, DE: International Reading Association, 1989.

Andrasick, Kathleen. *Opening Texts*. Portsmouth, NH: Heinemann, 1990.

Atwell, Nancie. *In the Middle*. Portsmouth, NH: Heinemann, 1987.

_____. *Coming to Know: Writing to Learn in the Middle Grades*. Portsmouth, NH: Heinemann, 1990.

_____. *Workshop 1: Writing and Literature*. Portsmouth, NH: Heinemann, 1989.

_____. *Workshop 2: Beyond the Basal*. Portsmouth, NH: Heinemann, 1990.

_____. *Workshop 3: The Politics of Process*. Portsmouth, NH: Heinemann, 1991.

_____. *Side by Side: Essays on Teaching to Learn*. Portsmouth, NH: Heinemann, 1991.

Baghban, Marcia. *Our Daughter Learns to Read and Write*. Newark, DE: International Reading Association, 1985.

Barrett, F.L. *A Teacher's Guide to Shared Reading*. Toronto, Ont.: Scholastic TAB, 1982.

Barron, Marlene. *I Learn to Read and Write the Way I Learn to Talk*. Katonah, NY: Richard C. Owen Publishers, 1990.

Barton, Bob. *Tell Me Another*. Portsmouth, NH: Heinemann, 1986.

Baskwill, Jane. *Connections — A Child's Natural Learning Tool*. Toronto, Ont.: Scholastic TAB, 1990.

Baskwill, Jane, and Whitman, Paulette. *Moving On: Whole Language Sourcebook for Grades 3 and 4*. Toronto, Ont.: Scholastic TAB, 1988.

_____. *Whole Language Sourcebook*. Toronto: Scholastic TAB, 1986.

_____. *A Guide to Classroom Publishing*. Toronto, Ont.: Scholastic TAB, 1988.

Bayer, Ann Shee. *Collaborative-Apprenticeship Learning*. Katonah, NY: Richard C. Owen Publishers, 1990.

Bean, Wendy, and Bouffler, Christine. *Spell by Writing*. Portsmouth, NH: Heinemann, 1988.

Bird, Lois Bridge. *Becoming a Whole Language School: The Fair Oaks Story*. Katonah, NY: Richard C. Owen Publishers, 1989.

Bissex, Glenda. *GNYS AT WRK*. Cambridge, MA: Harvard University Press, 1980.

Bissex, Glenda, and Bullock, Richard, eds. *Seeing for Ourselves*. Portsmouth, NH: Heinemann, 1987.

Bixby, Mary, and Pyle, Donelle et al. *Strategies That Make Sense! Invitations to Literacy for Secondary Students*. Katonah, NY: Richard C. Owen Publishers, 1987.

Blake, Robert, ed. *Whole Language — Explorations and Applications*. New York: New York State English Council, 1990.

Bosma, Bette. *Fairy Tales, Fables, Legends, and Myths*. New York: Teacher's College Press, 1987.

Britton, James, ed. *English Teaching: An International Exchange*. Portsmouth, NH: Heinemann, 1984.

Brown, Hazel, and Mathie, Vonne. *Inside Whole Language: A Classroom View*. Portsmouth, NH: Heinemann, 1991.

Buchanan, Ethel. *For the Love of Reading*. Winnipeg, Man.: The C.E.L. Group, 1980.

_____. *Spelling for Whole Language Classrooms*. Winnipeg, Man.: The C.E.L. Group, 1989.

Buncombe, Fran, and Peetoom, Adrian. *Literature-Based Learning: One School's Journey*. New York: Scholastic, 1988.

Buros, Jay. *Why Whole Language?* Rosemont, NJ: Programs for Education, 1991.

Butler, Andrea, and Turbill, Jan. *Towards a Reading-Writing Classroom*. Portsmouth, NH: Heinemann, 1984.

Butler, Dorothy. *Cushla and Her Books*. Boston: The Horn Book, 1980.

Calkins, Lucy McCormick. *Lessons from a Child: On the Teaching and Learning of Writing*. Portsmouth, NH: Heinemann, 1983.

_____. *The Art of Teaching Writing*. Portsmouth, NH: Heinemann, 1986.

_____. *Living Between the Lines*. Portsmouth, NH: Heinemann, 1991.

Cambourne, Brian. *The Whole Story*. New York: Scholastic, 1988.

Cambourne, Brian, and Turbill, Jan. *Coping with Chaos*. Portsmouth, NH: Heinemann, 1988.

Cambourne, Brian, and Brown, Hazel. *Read and Retell*. Portsmouth, NH: Heinemann, 1990.

Clay, Marie. *"Concepts about Print" Tests*. Portsmouth, NH: Heinemann, 1980.

_____. *Observing Young Readers*. Portsmouth, NH: Heinemann, 1982.

_____. *Reading: The Patterning of Complex Behaviour*. Portsmouth, NH: Heinemann, 1980.

_____. *What Did I Write?*. Portsmouth, NH: Heinemann, 1975.

_____. *Becoming Literate*. Portsmouth, NH: Heinemann, 1991.

Clifford, John. *The Experience of Reading — Louise Rosenblatt and Reader-Response Theory*. Portsmouth, NH: Heinemann, 1991.

Collis, Mark, and Dalton, Joan. *Becoming Responsible Learners*. Portsmouth, NH: Heinemann, 1991.

Cochrane, Orin et al. *Reading, Writing, and Caring*. Katonah, NY: Richard C. Owen Publishers, 1985.

Cullinan, Bernice. *Children's Literature in the Reading Program*. Newark, DE: International Reading Association, 1987.

Cutting, Brian. *Talk Your Way to Reading*. Auckland, New Zealand: Shortland Publications, 1985.

_____. *Getting Started in Whole Language*. Auckland, New Zealand: Applecross, 1989.

Dakos, Kalli. *What's There to Write About?* New York: Scholastic, 1989.

Davidson, Merrilyn et al. *Moving on with Big Books.* Auckland, New Zealand: Ashton Scholastic, 1989.

DeFord, Diane et al. *Bridges to Literacy.* Portsmouth, NH: Heinemann, 1991.

Department of Education, Wellington, New Zealand. *Reading in Junior Classes.* New York: Richard C. Owen Publishers,1985.

Department of Education, Victoria. *Beginning Reading.* Victoria: Department of Education, 1984.

Dewey, John. *The Child and the Curriculum and the School and Society.* Chicago: Phoenix Books, combined edition, 1956.

Edelsky, Carole; Altwerger, Bess; and Flores, Barbara. *Whole Language: What's the Difference?* Portsmouth, NH: Heinemann, 1990.

Eisele, Beverly. *Managing the Whole Language Classroom.* Cypress, CA: Creative Teaching Press, 1991.

Ferreiro, Emilia, and Teberosky, Ana. *Literacy Before Schooling.* Portsmouth, NH: Heinemann, 1979.

Fisher, Bobbi. *Joyful Learning: A Whole Language Kindergarten.* Portsmouth, NH: Heinemann, 1991.

Frank, Marjorie. *If You're Trying to Teach Kids How to Write, You Gotta Have This Book!.* Nashville, TN: Incentive Publications, 1979.

Froese, Victor, ed. *Whole Language: Theory and Practice.* Scarborough, Ont.: Prentice-Hall, 1990.

Fulwiler, Toby, ed. *The Journal Book.* Portsmouth, NH: Heinemann, 1987.

_____. *Programs That Work: Models and Methods for Writing Across the Curriculum.* Portsmouth, NH: Heinemann, 1990.

Gamberg, Ruth et al. *Learning and Loving It — Theme Studies in the Classroom.* Portsmouth, NH: Heinemann, 1988.

Garvey, Catherine. *Children's Talk.* Boston: Harvard Press, 1984. (Part of The Developing Child series).

Geller, Linda Gibson. *Word Play and Language Learning for Children.* Urbana, IL: National Council of Teachers of English, 1985.

Glover, Mary, and Sheppard, Linda. *Not on Your Own — The Power of Learning Together.* New York: Scholastic, 1990.

Gollasch, Fredrick, ed. *Language and Literacy — The Selected Writings of Kenneth S. Goodman, Vol. 1.* Boston: Routledge & Kegan Paul, 1982.

_____. *Language and Literacy — The Selected Writings of Kenneth S. Goodman, Vol. 2.* Boston: Routledge & Kegan Paul, 1985.

Goodman, Kenneth et al. *Language and Thinking in School: A Whole-Language Curriculum.* Katonah, NY: Richard C. Owen Publishers, 1987.

_____. *Report Card on Basals.* New York: Richard C. Owen Publishers, 1988.

Goodman, Yetta. *How Children Construct Literacy.* Newark, DE: International Reading Association, 1990.

Graves, Donald. *A Researcher Learns to Write.* Portsmouth, NH: Heinemann, 1984.

_____. *Discover Your Own Literacy.* Portsmouth, NH: Heinemann, 1990.

_____. *Experiment with Fiction*. Portsmouth, NH: Heinemann, 1989.

_____. *Investigate Nonfiction*. Portsmouth, NH: Heinemann, 1989.

_____. *Writing: Teachers and Children at Work*. Portsmouth, NH: Heinemann, 1983.

_____. *Build a Literate Classroom*. Portsmouth, NH: Heinemann, 1991.

Graves, Donald, and Stuart, Virginia. *Write from the Start*. New York: New American Library, 1985.

Greenwood, Barbara. *The Other Side of the Story*. Toronto, Ont.: Scholastic Tab, 1990.

Gunderson, Lee. *A Whole Language Primer*. New York: Scholastic, 1989.

Hall, Nigel, and Robertson, Anne. *"Some Day You Will No All About Me: Young Children's Explorations in the World of Letters."* Portsmouth, NH: Heinemann, 1991.

Hancock, Joelie, and Hill, Susan, eds. *Literature-Based Reading Programs at Work*. Portsmouth, NH: Heinemann, 1988.

Hansen, Jane. *When Writers Read*. Portsmouth, NH: Heinemann, 1987.

Hansen, Jane; Newkirk, Thomas; and Graves, Donald, eds. *Breaking Ground: Teachers Relate Reading and Writing in the Elementary School*. Portsmouth, NH: Heinemann, 1985.

Harste, Jerome, and Short, Kathy. *Creating Classrooms for Authors:The Reading-Writing Connection*. Portsmouth, NH: Heinemann, 1988.

Harste, Jerome; Woodward, Virginia; and Burke, Carolyn. *Language Stories and Literacy Lessons*. Portsmouth, NH: Heinemann, 1984.

Hayes, Martha. *Building on Books*. Bridgeport, CT: First Teacher Press, 1987.

Heald-Taylor, Gail. *Administrator's Guide to Whole Language*. Katonah, NY: Richard C. Owen Publishers, 1989.

Heard, Georgia. *For the Good of the Earth and Sun: Teaching Poetry*. Portsmouth, NH: Heinemann, 1989.

Holdaway, Don. *Independence in Reading*. New York: Scholastic, 1980.

_____. *The Foundations of Literacy*. New York: Scholastic, 1979.

_____. *Stability and Change in Literacy Learning*. Portsmouth, NH: Heinemann, 1984.

Holly, Mary Louise. *Writing to Grow: Keeping a Personal-Professional Journal*. Portsmouth, NH: Heinemann, 1989.

Hornsby, D. et al. *Read On: A Conference Approach to Reading*. Portsmouth, NH: Heinemann, 1986.

Hubbard, Ruth. *Authors of Pictures, Draughtsmen of Words*. Portsmouth, NH: Heinemann, 1989.

ILEA/Centre for Language in Primary Education. *The Primary Language Record: Handbook for Teachers*. Portsmouth, NH: Heinemann, 1989.

Infant Education Committee. *Beginning Reading*. Victoria: Education Department, 1984.

Jagger, Angela, and Smith-Burke, eds. *Observing the Language Learner*. Newark, DE: International Reading Association, 1985.

Jewell, Margaret, and Zintz, Miles. *Learning to Read Naturally*. Dubuque, IA: Kendall-Hunt, 1986.

Johnson, Terry, and Louis, Daphne. *Literacy through Literature*. Portsmouth, NH: Heinemann, 1987.

_____. *Bringing It All Together*. Portsmouth, NH: Heinemann, 1990.

Kitagawa, Mary, and Kitagawa, Chisato. *Making Connections with Writing*. Portsmouth, NH: Heinemann, 1987.

Kobrin, Beverly. *Eyeopeners! How to Choose and Use Children's Books about Real People, Places and Things*. New York: Penguin, 1988.

Lamme, Linda. *Highlights for Children, Growing up Reading*. Reston, VA: Acropolis Books, 1985.

_____. *Growing Up Writing*. Reston, VA: Acropolis Books, 1984.

Landsberg, Michele. *Michele Landsberg's Guide to Children's Books*. New York: Penguin, 1988.

Lloyd, Pamela. *How Writers Write*. Portsmouth, NH: Heinemann, 1987.

Lynch, Priscilla. *Using Big Books and Predictable Books*. New York: Scholastic, 1987.

McClure, Amy; Harrison, Peggy; and Reed, Sheryl. *Sunrises and Songs*. Portsmouth, NH: Heinemann, 1990.

McConaghy, June. *Children's Learning Through Literature*. Portsmouth, NH: Heinemann, 1990.

McCracken, Robert and Marlene. *Stories, Songs and Poetry to Teach Reading and Writing*. Chicago: American Library Association, 1986.

_____. *Reading, Writing and Language: A Practical Guide for Primary Teachers*. Winnipeg, Man.: Peguis, 1979.

McKenzie, Moira. *Journeys into Literacy*. Huddersfield: Schofield & Sims, 1986.

McVitty, Walter. *Word Magic — Poetry as a Shared Adventure*. PETA (Heinemann), 1985.

_____. *Children and Learning*. PETA (Heinemann), 1984.

_____. *Getting It Together: Organizing the Reading-Writing Classroom*. Portsmouth, NH: Heinemann,1986.

Meek, Margaret. *The Cool Web*. New York: Atheneum, 1978.

_____, ed. *Opening Moves*. London: University of London Institute of Education, 1983.

Miller, Joan. *Sharing Ideas: An Oral Language Programme*. Melbourne: Nelson Publishing Co., 1988.

Mills, Heidi, and Clyde, Jean Anne. *Portraits of Whole Language Classrooms*. Portsmouth, NH: Heinemann, 1990.

Mooney, Margaret. *Developing Life-Long Readers*. Katonah, NY: Richard C. Owen Publishers, 1988.

Morris, A. *Learning to Learn from Text*. Reading, MA: Addison-Wesley, 1984.

Murray, Donald. *Learning by Teaching*. Portsmouth, NH: Boynton-Cook, 1982.

Myers, Miles. *The Teacher-Researcher: How to Study Writing in the Classroom*. Urbana, IL: National Council of Teachers of English, 1985.

NCTE & IRA. *Cases in Literacy*. International Reading Association and National Council of Teachers of English, 1989.

Newman, Judith, ed. *Whole Language: Theory in Use*. Portsmouth, NH: Heinemann, 1985.

_____. *The Craft of Children's Writing*. Portsmouth, NH: Heinemann, 1985.

_____, ed. *Finding Our Own Way*. Portsmouth, NH: Heinemann, 1990.

Newkirk, Thomas. *More Than Stories*. Portsmouth, NH: Heinemann, 1989.

Nova Scotia Department of Education. *Language Arts in the Elementary School*. Curriculum Development Guide No. 86, 1986.

Paley, Vivian. *Molly Is Three*. Chicago: University of Chicago, 1986.

_____. *Wally's Stories*. Boston: Harvard Educational Press, 1981.

Parker, Robert P., and Davis, Francis, eds. *Developing Literacy: Young Children's Use of Language*. Newark, DE: International Reading Association, 1983.

Parry, Jo-Ann, and Hornsby, David. *Write On: A Conference Approach to Writing*. Portsmouth, NH: Heinemann, 1988.

Parsons, Les. *Writing in the Real Classroom*. Portsmouth, NH: Heinemann, 1991.

Peetboom, Adrian. *Shared Reading: Safe Risks with Whole Books*. Toronto, Ont.: Scholastic TAB, 1986.

Perl, Sondra. *Through Teachers' Eyes*. Portsmouth, NH: Heinemann, 1986.

Peterson, Ralph. *Grand Conversations*. New York: Scholastic, 1990.

Pinnell, Gay Su. *Teachers and Research — Language Learning in the Classroom*. Newark, DE: International Reading Association, 1989.

Raines, Shirley C., and Candy, Robert J. *The Whole Language Kindergarten*. New York: Teachers College Press, 1990

Raphael, Ray. *The Teacher's Voice: A Sense of Who We Are*. Portsmouth, NH: Heinemann, 1985.

Rief, Linda. *Seeking Diversity: Language Arts with Adolescents*. Portsmouth, NH: Heinemann, 1992.

Romano, Tom. *Clearing the Way*. Portsmouth, NH: Heinemann, 1987.

Routman, Regie. *Transitions: From Literature to Literacy*. Portsmouth, NH: Heinemann, 1988.

_____. *Invitations: Changing as Teachers and Learners, K-12*. Portsmouth, NH: Heinemann, 1991.

Roy, Susan, ed. *Young Imagination*. New South Wales: Primary English Teaching Association, 1988.

Sampson, Michael. *Literacy and Language Instruction*. Lexington, MA: Ginn Press, 1987.

_____. *The Pursuit of Literacy*. Dubuque, IA: Kendall-Hunt, 1986.

_____. *Pathways to Literacy*. New York: Holt, Rinehart & Winston, 1991.

Schickedanz, Judith. *Adam's Righting Revolutions*. Portsmouth, NH: Heinemann, 1990.

Shafer, Robert E., and Staab, Claire. *Language Functions and School Success*. New York: Scott Foresman, 1983.

Shannon, Patrick. *The Struggle to Continue*. Portsmouth, NH: Heinemann, 1990.

_____. *Broken Promises*. Portsmouth, NH: Heinemann, 1989.

Shedlock, Marie. *The Art of the Storyteller*. New York: Dover Press, 1951.

Silko, Leslie Marmon. *Storyteller*. New York: Seaver Books, 1981.

Sloan, Peter and Ross Latham. *Teaching Reading Is...* Melbourne: Nelson, 1981.

Smith, Frank. *Essays into Literacy*. Portsmouth, NH: Heinemann, 1983.

_____. *Insult to Intelligence.* Portsmouth, NH: Heinemann, 1986.

_____. *Joining the Literacy Club.* Portsmouth, NH: Heinemann, 1988.

_____. *Psycholinguistics and Reading.* New York: Holt, Rinehart & Winston, 1978.

_____. *Reading Without Nonsense.* New York: Teachers College Press, 1978.

_____. *Understanding Reading.* Hillsdale, NJ: Lawrence Erlbaum Publishers, 1986.

_____. *Writing and the Writer.* New York: Holt, Rinehart & Winston, 1982.

Somerfield, Muriel. *A Framework for Reading.* Portsmouth, NH: Heinemann, 1985.

Stephens, Diane. *What Matters? A Primer for Teaching Reading.* Portsmouth, NH: Heinemann, 1990.

Strickland, Dorothy. *Emerging Literacy: Young Children Learn to Read and Write.* Newark, DE: International Reading Association, 1989.

Taylor, Denny. *Family Literacy.* Portsmouth, NH: Heinemann, 1983.

_____. *Learning Denied.* Portsmouth, NH: Heinemann, 1990.

Taylor, Denny, and Dorsey-Gaines, Catherine. *Growing Up Literate.* Portsmouth, NH: Heinemann, 1988.

Temple, Charles et al. *The Beginnings of Writing.* Boston: Allyn & Bacon, 1988.

Tough, Joan. *Talk for Teaching and Learning.* Portsmouth, NH: Heinemann, 1981.

Tovey, Duane, and Kerber, James, ed. *Roles in Literacy Learning.* Newark, DE: International Reading Association, 1986.

Turbill, Jan, ed. *No Better Way to Teach Writing!* Portsmouth, NH: Heinemann, 1982.

_____. *Now, We Want to Write.* Portsmouth, NH: Heinemann, 1983.

Vail, Priscilla. *Common Ground: Whole Language and Phonics Working Together.* Rosemont, NJ: Programs for Education, 1991.

Van Manen, Max. *The Tone of Teaching.* Portsmouth, NH: Heinemann, 1986.

Vygotsy, Lev. *Mind in Society.* Cambridge, MA: Harvard University Press, 1978.

_____. *Thought and Language.* Cambridge, MA: MIT Press, 1986.

Ward, Geoff. *I've Got a Project.* Australia: PETA, 1988. (Distributed in the United States by Heinemann, Portsmouth, NH.)

Watson, Dorothy. *Whole Language: Inquiring Voices.* New York: Scholastic, 1989.

Weaver, Constance. *Reading Process and Practice.* Portsmouth, NH: Heinemann, 1988.

_____. *Understanding Whole Language.* Portsmouth, NH: Heinemann, 1990.

Wells, Gordon. *The Meaning Makers.* Portsmouth, NH: Heinemann, 1986.

Wittels, Harriet, and Greisman, Joan. *How to Spell It.* New York: Putnam, 1982.

# Assessment

Anthony, Robert. *Evaluating Literacy.* Portsmouth, NH: Heinemann, 1991.

*Resources*                                                                                                    *Resources*

Barrs, Myra et al. *The Primary Language Record: Handbook for Teachers*. Portsmouth, NH: Heinemann, 1989.

Baskwill, Jane, and Whitman, Paulette. *Evaluation: Whole Language, Whole Child*. Toronto, Ont.: Scholastic, 1988.

Belanoff, Pat, and Dickson, Marcia, eds. *Portfolios: Process and Product*, Portsmouth, NH: Heinemann, 1991.

Clay, Marie. *The Early Detection of Reading Difficulty*. Portsmouth, NH: Heinemann, 1985.

Cochrane, Orin, and Cochrane, Donna. *Whole Language Evaluation for Classrooms*. Bothell, WA: The Wright Group, 1992.

Eggleton, Jill. *Whole Language Evaluation*. Hong Kong: Applecross LTD, 1990.

Goodman, Kenneth, ed. *The Whole Language Evaluation Book*. Portsmouth, NH: Heinemann,1988.

Goodman, Yetta et al. *Reading Miscues Inventory: Alternative Procedures*. New York: Richard C. Owen Publishers, 1987.

Harp, Bill, ed. *Assessment and Evaluation in Whole Language Programs*. Norwood, MA: Christopher Gordon, 1991.

Parsons, Les. *Response Journals*. Portsmouth, NH: Heinemann, 1990.

Tierney, Robert J.; Carter, Mark A.; and Desai, Laura E. *Portfolio Assessment in the Reading-Writing Classroom*. Norwood, MA: Christopher Gordon, 1991.

# Parent Involvement

Baskwill, Jane. *Parents and Teachers — Partners in Learning*. Toronto, Ont.: Scholastic, 1990.

Butler, Dorothy, and Clay, Marie. *Reading Begins at Home*. Portsmouth, NH: Heinemann, 1982.

Clay, Marie. *Writing Begins at Home*. Portsmouth, NH: Heinemann, 1988.

Doake, David. *Reading Begins at Birth*. Toronto, Ont.: Scholastic, 1988.

Gentry, J. Richard. *Spel...Is a Four-Letter Word*. Portsmouth, NH: Heinemann, 1987.

Goodman, Kenneth. *What's Whole in Whole Language?* Portsmouth, NH: Heinemann, 1986.

Hill, Mary. *Home: Where Reading and Writing Begin*. Portsmouth, NH: Heinemann, 1989.

Lipson, Eden. *Parent's Guide to the Best Books for Children*. New York: Times Books, 1988.

Mooney, Margaret. *Reading to, with, and by Children*. Katonah, NY: Richard C. Owen Publishers, 1990.

Northeastern Local School District. *Every Child is a Promise: Early Childhood At-Home Learning Activities*. Springfield, OH, 1986.

_____. *Every Child is a Promise: Positive Parenting*. Springfield, Oh, 1986.

Rich, Dorothy. *Mega Skills*. Boston: Houghton Mifflin, 1988.

Taylor, Denny, and Strickland, Dorothy. *Family Storybook Reading*. Portsmouth, NH, 1986.

Trelease, Jim. *The New Read-Aloud Handbook*. New York: Penguin Books, 1989.

Wlodkowski, Raymond, and Jaynes, Judith H. *Eager to Learn*. San Francisco: Jossey-Bass, 1990.

**303**

# Great Idea Books

Cloonan, Kathryn. *Sing Me a Story, Read Me a Song, Book I.* Beverly Hills, FL: Rhythm & Reading Resources, 1991.

_____. *Sing Me A Story, Read Me a Song, Book II.* Beverly Hills, FL: Rhythm & Reading Resources, 1991.

Cochrane, Orin, ed. *Reading Experiences in Science.* Winnipeg, Man.: Peguis, 1985.

Drutman, Ava Deutsch, and Huston, Diane L. *150 Surefire Ways to Keep Them Reading All Year.* New York: Scholastic, 1992.

Gilbert, Labritta. *Do Touch: Instant, Easy Hands-on Learning Experiences for Young Children.* Mt. Ranier, MD: Gryphon House, 1989.

Haack, Pam, and Merrilees, Cynthia. *Write on Target.* Peterborough, NH: The Society for Developmental Education, 1991.

_____. *Ten Ways to Become a Better Reader.* Cleveland, OH: Modern Curriculum Press, 1991.

Hall, Mary. *Daily Writing Activities.* Frank Schaffer.

Hopkins, Lee. *Pass the Poetry Please.* New York: Harper & Row, 1987.

Huck, Charlotte and Hickman, Janet, eds. *The Best of the Web.* Columbus, OH: Ohio State University, 1982.

Irvine, Joan. How to Make Pop-ups. New York: Beech Tree Books, 1987.

Kovacs, Deborah, and Preller, James. *Meet the Authors and Illustrators: 60 Creators of Favorite Children's Books Talk about Their Work.* New York: Scholastic, 1991.

McCracken, Marlene and Robert. *Themes.* Winnipeg, Man.: Peguis, 1984-87.

Raines, Shirley C., and Canady, Robert J. *Story Stretchers.* Mt. Ranier, MD: Gryphon House, 1989

_____. *More Story Stretchers.* Mt. Ranier, MD: Gryphon House, 1991

_____. *Story Stretchers for the Primary Grades.* Mt. Ranier, MD: Gryphon House, 1992.

Ritter, Darlene. *Literature-Based Art Activities.* Cypress, CA: Creative Teaching Press, 1991.

Stangl, Jean. *Is Your Storytale Dragging?* Carthage, IL: Fearon Teaching Aids, 1989.

Spann, Mary Beth. *Literature-Based Seasonal and Holiday Activities.* New York; Scholastic, 1987.

Suid, Murray. *Writing Hangups.* Monday Morning Books.

# *Poetry In Motion*

## Bibliography
### Compiled by Bob Johnson and John Poeton

**If you would like help locating any of these books, contact Crystal Springs Books 1-800-321-0401 or in N.H., (603) 924-9380.**

Adoff, Arnold. *Chocolate Dreams.* New York: Lothrop, 1989.

_____. *Greens.* New York: Lothrop, 1988.

Bagert, Brod. *If Only I Could Fly.* Baton Rouge, LA: Juliahouse, 1984.

Behn, Harry. *The Little Hill.* New York: Harcourt Brace Jovanovich, 1949.

Baskwill, Jane. *Pass the Poems, Please.* Wildfire, 1989.

Blake, Quentin. *All Join In.* Boston: Little, Brown, & Co., 1990.

Booth, David. *'Till All the Stars Have Fallen.* New York: Viking, 1989.

Ciardi, John. *Doodle Soup.* Boston: Houghton Mifflin, 1985.

_____. *Fast and Slow.* Boston: Houghton Mifflin, 1975.

_____. *You Read to Me, I'll Read to You.* New York: Harper & Row, 1987.

_____. *The Monster Den or Look What Happened at My House—and to It.* Honesdale, PA: Boyds Mills Press, 1991.

Cole, William. *Poem Stew.* New York: Harper & Row, 1983.

Dakos, Kalli. *If You're Not Here Please Raise Your Hand.* New York: Four Winds, 1990.

Fleischman, Paul. *Joyful Noise.* New York: Harper & Row, 1988.

_____. *I Am Phoenix.* New York: Harper & Row, 1985.

Frost, Robert. *You Come Too.* New York: Holt, Rinehart & Winston, 1959.

Gander, Father. *Nursery Rhymes.* Santa Barbara, CA: Advocacy Press, 1985.

Giovanni, Nikki. *Spin a Soft Black Song.* New York: Farrar, Straus & Giroux, 1987.

Greenfield, Eloise. *Honey, I Love.* New York: Harper & Row, 1978.

_____. *Nathaniel Talking.* New York: Writers & Readers Publishing, 1989.

Hadjusiewicz, Babs. *Poetry Works.* Cleveland, OH: Modern Curriculum Press, 1990.

Halloran, Phyllis. *I'd Like to Hear a Flower Grow.* Oregon Ciry, OR: Reading, 1989.

Hopkins, Lee Bennett. *Creatures.* San Diego, CA: Harcourt Brace Jovanovich, 1986.

_____. *Dinosaurs*. San Diego, CA: Harcourt Brace Jovanovich, 1990.

_____. *The Sea Is Calling Me*. San Diego, CA: Harcourt Brace Jovanovich, 1986.

_____. *The Sky Is Full of Song*. New York: Harper & Row, 1987.

Hughes, Shirley. *Out and About*. New York: Lothrop, 1988.

Janeczko, Paul. *The Place My Words Are looking For*. New York: Bradbury, 1990.

Jeffers, Susan. *Robert Frost, Stopping by Woods on a Snowy Evening*.

Kennedy, X. J. *Ghastlies, Goops and Pincushions*. New York: McElderry, 1989.

_____. *Fresh Brats*. New York: McElderry, 1990.

Koch, Kenneth. *Talking to the Sun*. New York: Henry Holt, 1985.

Koeppen, Peter. *A Swinger of Birches, Poems of Robert Frost for Young People*.

Larrick, Nancy. *Cats Are Cats*. New York: Philomel, 1988.

_____. *When the Dark Comes Dancing*. New York: Philomel, 1983.

_____. *Mice are Nice*. New York: Philomel, 1990.

Lee, Dennis. *Alligator Pie*. New York: Macmillan, 1974.

_____. *Jelly Belly*. New York: Macmillan, 1983.

_____. *Garbage Delight*. New York: Macmillan.

Livingston, Myra Cohn. *Worlds I Know*. New York: Atheneum, 1986.

_____. *Celebrations*. New York: Holiday House, 1985.

_____. *There Was a Place and Other Poems*. New York: McElderry, 1990.

Lobel, Arnold. *The Random House Book of Mother Goose*. New York: Random House, 1986.

_____. *Whiskers and Rhymes*. New York: Greenwillow, 1985.

_____. *The Book of Pigericks*. New York: Harper & Row, 1988.

McNaughton, Colin. *There's an Awful Lot of Weirdos in Our Neighborhood*. New York: Walker & Co., 1987.

Merriam, Eve. *A Poem for a Pickle*. New York: Morrow, 1989.

_____. *A Sky Full of Poems*. New York: Dell, 1964.

_____. *You Be Good and I'll Be Night*. New York: Morrow, 1988.

Milne, A.A. *Now We Are Six*. New York: Dutton, 1988.

_____. *When We Were Very Young*. New York: Dutton, 1988.

Moss, Jeff. *The Butterfly Jar*. New York: Random House, 1989.

O'Neill, Mary. *Hailstones and Halibut Bones*. New York: Doubleday, 1990.

Prelutsky, Jack. *The New Kid on the Block*. New York: Greenwillow, 1984.

_____. *The Baby Uggs Are Hatching*. New York: Greenwillow, 1982.

_____. *My Parents Think I'm Sleeping*. New York: Greenwillow, 1985.

_____. *Nightmares*. New York: Greenwillow, 1976.

_____. *Poems of a Nonny Mouse*. New York: Greenwillow, 1989.

_____. *The Random House Book of Poetry for Children*. New York: Random House, 1983.

_____. *Rolling Harvey Down the Hill*. New York: Greenwillow, 1980.

_____. *Ride a Purple Pelican*. New York: Greenwillow, 1986.

_____. *The Sheriff of Rottenshot*. New York: Greenwillow, 1982.

_____. *Tyrannosaurus Was a Beast*. New York: Greenwillow, 1989.

_____. *What I Did Last Summer*. New York: Greenwillow, 1984.

_____. *Circus*. New York: Greenwillow, 1989.

_____. *Underneath a Blue Umbrella*. New York: Greenwillow, 1990.

_____. *For Laughing Out Loud*. New York: Greenwillow, 1991.

Ryder Joanne. *Inside Turtle's Shell*. New York: Macmillan, 1985.

Silverstein, Shel. *A Light in the Attic*. New York: Harper & Row, 1981.

_____. *Where the Sidewalk Ends*. New York: Harper & Row, 1974.

Singer, Marlyn. *Turtle in July*. New York: Macmillan, 1989.

Sneve, Virginia. *Dancing Teepees*. New York: Holiday, 1989.

Stopple, Libby. *A Box of Peppermints*. Austin, TX: American Universal Artforms, 1975.

Viorst, Judith. *If I Were in Charge of the World*. New York: Atheneum, 1983.

Voake, Charlotte, ill. *Over the Moon — A Book of Nursery Rhymes*. New York: C.N. Potter Books, 1985.

Wood, Nancy. *Many Winters*. New York: Doubleday, 1974.

Worth, Valerie. *All the Small Poems*. New York: Farrar, Straus & Giroux, 1987.

Yolen, Jane. *Dinosaur Dances*. New York: Putnam, 1990.

Zolotow, Charlotte. *Some Things Go Together*. New York: Harper & Row, 1987.

# More Than Books

## Expanding Children's Horizons Through Magazines

| Publication Subscription Address | Interest Area/Age Group | Publication Subscription Address | Interest Area/Age Group |
|---|---|---|---|
| *Boys' Life*<br>Boy Scouts of America<br>P.O. Box 152079<br>1325 Walnut Hill Lane<br>Irving, TX 75015-2079 | General Interest<br>7-17 | *Dolphin Log*<br>The Cousteau Society<br>870 Greenbrier Circle, Suite 402<br>Chesapeake, VA 23320 | Science/Ecology<br>7-15 |
| * *Chickadee*<br>Box 304, 255,Great Arrow Ave<br>Buffalo, NY 14207-3024 | Science/ Nature<br>4-9 | *Faces*<br>30 Grove St.<br>Peterborough, NH 03458 | World Cultures<br>8-14 |
| * *Child Life*<br>P.O. Box 7133<br>Red Oak, IA 51591-0133<br><br>Submissions:<br>P.O.Box 567<br>1100 Waterway Blvd.<br>Indianapolis, IN 46206 | Health/General Interest<br>9-11 | * *Highlights for Children*<br>2300 West Fifth Ave.<br>P.O. Box 269<br>Columbus, OH 43272<br><br>Submissions:<br>803 Church St.<br>Honesdale, PA 18431 | General Interest<br>2-12 |
| * *Children's Album*<br>P.O. Box 6086<br>Concord, CA 94524 | Writing/Crafts<br>8-14 | * *Humpty Dumpty's Magazine*<br>P.O. Box 7133<br>Red Oak, IA 51591-0133<br><br>Submissions: (*see Child Life*) | Health/General Interest<br>4-6 |
| * *Children's Digest*<br>P.O. Box 7133<br>Red Oak, IA 51591-0133<br><br>Submissions: (*see  Child Life*) | Health/General Interest<br>8-10 | *Images of Excellence*<br>Images of Excellence<br>   Foundation<br>P.O. Box 1131<br>Boiling Springs, NC 28017 | Social Studies<br>10-13 |
| * *Children's Playmate*<br>P.O. Box 7133<br>Red Oak, IA 51591-0133<br><br>Submissions: (*see  Child Life*) | Health/General Interest<br>6-8 | * *Jack and Jill*<br>P.O. Box 7133<br>Red Oak, IA 51591-0133<br><br>Submissions: (*see  Child Life*) | General Interest<br>6-8 |
| *Classical Calliope*<br>30 Grove St.<br>Peterborough, NH 03458 | World History<br>9-16 | * *Kid City*<br>P.O. Box 51277<br>Boulder, CO 80321-1277 | General Interest<br>6-9 |
| *Cobblestone*<br>30 Grove St.<br>Peterborough, NH 03458 | American History<br>8-14 | * *Kids Life and Times*<br>Kids Life<br>P.O. Box D<br>Bellport, NY 11713<br><br>Submissions:<br>Children's Television Workshop<br>One Lincoln Plaza<br>New York, NY 10023 | Entertainment/Education<br>6-12 |
| * *Creative Kids*<br>P.O. Box 637<br>Holmes, PA 19043<br><br>Submissions:<br>P.O. Box 6448<br>Mobile, AL 36660 | Student Art/Writing<br>8-14 | | |
| * *Cricket*<br>Box 51144<br>Boulder, CO 80321-1144<br><br>Submissions:<br>Open Court Publishing<br>P.O. Box 300<br>Peru, IL 61354 | Literature/Art<br>6-12 | *Koala Club News*<br>San Diego Zoo Membership<br>   Dept.<br>P.O. Box 271<br>San Diego, CA 92112 | Animals<br>3-15 |
| | | *Ladybug*<br>Cricket Country Lane<br>Box 50284<br>Boulder, CO 80321-0284 | Literature<br>2-7 |

| Publication Subscription Address | Interest Area/Age Group | Publication Subscription Address | Interest Area/Age Group |
|---|---|---|---|
| * The McGuffey Writer<br>400 A McGuffey Hall<br>Miami University<br>Oxford, OH 45056 | Student Writing<br>5-18 | Scienceland<br>501 Fifth Ave.<br>Suite 2108<br>New York, NY 10017-6165 | Science<br>5-11 |
| * Merlyn's Pen<br>The National Magazine of<br>Student Writing<br>P.O. Box 1058<br>East Greenwich, RI 02818 | Student Writing<br>12-16 | Seedling Short Story<br>International<br>P.O. Box 405<br>Great Neck, NY 11022 | Short Stories<br>9-12 |
| National Geographic World<br>P.O. Box 2330<br>Washington, DC 20077-9955 | Science/General Interest<br>8-14 | Sesame Street Magazine<br>P.O. Box 52000<br>Boulder, CO 80321-2000 | General Interest<br>2-6 |
| * Odyssey<br>30 Grove St.<br>Peterborough NH 03458 | Space Exploration/<br>Astronomy<br>8-14 | * Skipping Stones: A Multi-<br>Cultural Children's Forum<br>P.O. Box 3939<br>Eugene, OR 97403-0939 | Culture/Environment<br>All ages |
| Owl<br>Box 304<br>255 Great Ave.<br>Buffalo, NY 14207-3024 | Science/Nature<br>8-13 | Sports Illustrated for Kids<br>P.O. Box 830607<br>Birmingham, AL 35283-0607 | Sports<br>8-13 |
| Penny Power<br>Consumers Union<br>256 Washington St.<br>Mt. Vernon, NY 10553 | Consumer Education<br>8-14 | *Stone Soup<br>The Magazine by Children<br>P.O. Box 83<br>Santa Cruz, CA 95063 | Student Writing/Art<br>6-13 |
| Plays<br>120 Boylston St.<br>Boston, MA 02116-4615 | Drama<br>6-18 | 3-2-1 Contact<br>P.O. Box 51177<br>Boulder, CO 80321-1177 | Science<br>8-14 |
| * Prism<br>2455 E. Sunrise Blvd.<br>Ft. Lauderdale, FL 33304 | Student Writing<br>11-18 | Turtle<br>P.O. Box 7133<br>Red Oak, IA 51591-0133 | Health/General Interest<br>2-5 |
| Ranger Rick<br>National Wildlife Federation<br>8925 Leesburg Pike<br>Vienna, VA 22180-0001 | Science<br>6-12 | U.S. Kids<br>P.O. Box 50351<br>Boulder, CO 80321-0351 | Health/General Interest<br>5-10 |
| * Read Magazine<br>Field Publications<br>4343 Equrty Dr.<br>P.O. Box 16630<br>Columbus, OH 43216<br><br>Submissions:<br>245 Long Hill Rd.<br>Middletown, CT 06457 | Student Writing<br>12-15 | Your Big Backyard<br>National Wildlife Federation<br>8925 Leesburg Pike<br>Vienna, VA 22180 | Animals/Conservation<br>3-5 |
| * Reflections<br>P.O. Box 368<br>Duncan Falls, OH 43734 | Poetry<br>4-18 | Zoo Books<br>National Wildlife Federation<br>8925 Leesburg Pike<br>Vienna, VA 22180 | Wildlife<br>5-14 |
| School Mates<br>186 Route 9W<br>New Windsor, NY 12550 | Chess<br>7 and up | | |

**\*encourages children's submissions**

# VIDEOS

*Big Books: Practical Strategies.* (Available from Scholastic, Inc.)

Butler, Andrea. *Language, Learning and Literacy.*

_____. *Whole Language — A Framework for Thinking.*

_____. *The Elements of a Whole Language Classroom.*

_____. *Shared Book Experience.* (All four available from Rigby Education)

Calkins, Lucy McCormick. *The Writing Workshop: A World of Difference.* (Heinemann)

Hansen, Jane, and Graves, Donald. *The Writing and Reading Process: A Closer Look.*

_____. *The Writing and Reading Process: A New Approach to Literacy.* (Both available from Heinemann)

Harste, Jerome. *The Authoring Cycle: Read Better, Write Better, Reason Better.* (Heinemann)

*Learning Through Literature, Grade K-3.*

*Learning Through Literature, Grade 4-6.* (Both available from Scholastic, Inc.)

Martin, Bill. In-service and classroom videos. (DLM Teaching Resources)

*Natural Language Learning.* (Scholastic, Inc.)

# BIG BOOK PUBLISHERS

Holt Impressions
Modern Curriculum Press
Richard C. Owen Publishers, Inc.

Rigby Education
Scholastic, Inc.
Whole Language Consultants
The Wright Group

## *Addresses of Video and Big Book Order Departments:*

Crystal Springs Books
Northgate, Route 202
P.O. Box 577
Peterborough, NH 03458
1-800-321-0401

Curriculum Associates, Inc.
5 Espuire Rd.
N. Billerica, MA 01862-2589
1-800-225-0248

DLM Teaching Resources
P.O. Box 4000
One DLM Park
Allen, TX 75002

Heinemann
361 Hanover St.
Portsmouth, NH
1-800-541-2086

Holt Impressions
6277 Sea Harbor Dr.
Orlando, FL 32887
1-800-782-4479

Modern Curriculum Press
13900 Prospect Rd.
Cleveland, OH 44136
1-800-321-3106

Richard C. Owen Publishers, Inc.
P.O. Box 585
Katonah, NY 01536
1-800-336-5588

Rigby Education
P.O. Box 797
Crystal Lake, IL 60014
1-800-822-8661

Scholastic, Inc.
P.O. Box 7502
Jefferson City, MO 65102
1-800-325-6149

Whole Language
Consultants
#6-846 Marion St.
Winnipeg, Manitoba
Canada R2J OK4
1-204-235-1644

The Wright Group
19201 12th Ave. NE
Bothell, WA 98011-9512
1-800-523-2371

# PUBLICATIONS/SPECIAL INTEREST GROUPS

**Children's Literature**

*The Alan Review*
NCTE Assembly on Literature for Adolescents
111 Kenyon Rd.
Urbana, IL 61801

*The Bulletin*
Council on Interracial Books for Children
1841 Broadway
New York, NY 10023

*The Bulletin* of the Center for Children's Books
University of Illinois Press
54 E. Gregory Dr.
Champaign, Il 61820

*Chapters*
Hodge-Podge Books
272 Lark St.
Albany, NY 12210

*Children's Literature in Education*
Human Sciences Press, Inc.
233 Spring St.
New York, NY 10013-1578

*The CLA Bulletin*
Journal of the Children's Literature Assembly, NCTE
Membership:  Marjorie R. Hancock
                      2037 Plymouth Rd.
                      Manhattan, KS 66502

*The Five Owls*
2004 Sheridan Ave. S.
Minneapolis, MN 55408

*The Hornbook Magazine*
14 Beacon St.
Boston, MA 02105

*The Kobrin Letter* (reviews nonfiction books)
732 Greer Rd.
Palo Alto, CA 94303

*Literacy Matters*
Instructional Materials Laboratory
CETE/Ohio State University
1900 Kemy Rd.
Columbus, OH 43210

*The New Advocate*
Christopher Gordon Publishers, Inc.
480 Washington St.
Norwood, MA 02062

*Perspectives*
College of Education and Allied Professions
The University of Toledo
Toledo, OH 43606

SIGNAL (Special Interest Group Network on
        Adolescent Literature)
Martha Hartung, Chair
1194 A Kamahele St.
Kailua, HI 96734

*Telltales*
P.O. Box 614
Bath, ME 04530

*The WEB* (Wonderfully Exciting Books)
The Ohio State University
Room 200 Ramseyer Hall
29 West Woodruff
Columbus, OH 43210

**Early Childhood (See Developmental Education Resources)**

**General Education — Classroom Focus**

*Creative Classroom*
Children's Television Workshop
One Lincoln Plaza
New York, NY 10023

*Instructor Magazine*
Scholastic, Inc.
730 Broadway
New York, NY 10003

*Learning 91*
1111 Bethlehem Pike
Springhouse, PA 19477

*Teaching Pre-K-8*
40 Richards Ave.
Norwalk, CT 06854

**General Education — Issues/Research Focus**

*The American School Board Journal / Executive
  Educator*
National School Boards Association
1680 Duke St.
Alexandria, VA 22314

*Democracy and Education*
The Institute for Democracy and Education
College of Education
199 McCracken Hall
Ohio University
Athens, OH 45701-2979

*Education Week*
4301 Connecticut Ave. NW #250
Washington, DC 20008

*Educational Leadership*
Journal of the Association for Supervision and
  Curriculum Development (ASCD)
1250 N. Pitt St.
Alexandria, VA 22314-1403

*The Elementary School Journal*
University of Chicago Press
P.O. Box 37005
Chicago, IL 60637

*The Learning Disability Network*
25 Accord Park Dr.
Rockland, MD 02370

*Phi Delta Kappan*
Eighth and Union
P.O. Box 789
Bloomington, IN 47402

*Principal*
National Association of Elementary School
  Principals (NAESP)
1615 Duke St.
Alexandria, VA 22314-3483

*The School Administrator*
American Association of School Administrators
1801 North Moore St.
Arlington, VA 22209

*Teacher Magazine*
Subscription Services
P.O. Box 2091
Marion, OH 43305-2091

*TIP (Theory into Practice)*
Subscription Dept.
174 Arps Hall
1945 N. High St.
Columbus, OH 43210

### Language (See also Whole Language, this section)
*Language Arts*
National Council of Teachers of English
1111 Kenyon Rd.
Urbana, IL 61801

*Literacy*
The Journal of the International Institute

of Literacy Learning
Box 1414
Commerce, TX 75428

*The Reading Teacher*
International Reading Association
P.O. Box 8139
Newark, DE 19714-8139

(IRA also publishes *Journal of Reading, Reading Today,
  Reading Research Quarterly; lectura y
  yida* — a Spanish language journal.)

### Math and Science
*Arithmetic Teacher*
National Council of Teachers of Mathematics
1906 Association Dr.
Reston, VA 22091

*NatureScope*
National Wildlife Federation
1412 16th St.
Washington, DC 20036

*Science and Children*
National Science Teachers Association
1742 Connecticut Ave. NW
Washington, DC 20009-1171

### Whole Language
*Spotlight on Whole Language*
A Newsletter of the ASCD Whole Language Network
Hofstra University
Hempstead, NY 11550-9813

*Teachers Networking*
*The Whole Language Newsletter*
Richard C. Owen Publishers
135 Katonah Ave.
Katonah, NY 10536

*Whole Language Assembly of NCTE*
Paul Crowley
614 B Dufranedue
Sebastopal, CA 95472

*The Whole Idea*
*The Wright Group*
*19201 120th Ave. NE*
*Bothell, WA 98011-9512*

*Whole Language Network*
*Teaching K-8*
40 Richards Ave.
Norwalk, CT 06854

*The Whole Language Teachers Association*
　*Newsletter*
P.O. Box 216
Southboro, MA  01772

*WLSIG Newsletter*
*Whole Language Special Interest Group of the IRA*
Membership: Grace Vento Zogby
　　　　　　　125 Proctor Blvd.
　　　　　　　Utica, NY  13501

*Whole Language Umbrella*
President:　　Orin Cochrane
　　　　　　　#6-846 Marion St.
　　　　　　　Winnipeg, Manitoba
　　　　　　　Canada R2J OK4
Membership: Box 2029
　　　　　　　Bloomington, IN 47402-2029
Newsletter:　Debra Goodman, Chair
　　　　　　　P.O. Box 721236
　　　　　　　Berkley, MI  48072

## Whole Language Hotline

In the fall of 1991, the Center for the Expansion of Language and Thinking (CELT) began sponsoring a crisis hotline to support teachers and administrators who come under attack for their child-centered practices. For further information, contact:

The Center for Establishing Dialogue (CED)
325 E. Southern Ave.
Suite 14
Tempe, AZ  85282 • 1-602-929-0929

## Paperback Book Clubs (Compiled by Pam Haack and Cindy Merrilees)

Scholastic, Inc.
P.O. Box 7502
Jefferson City, MO  65102

Troll Book Club
2 Lethbridge Plaza
Mahwah, NJ  07430

The Trumpet Club
P.O. Box 604
Holmes, PA  19043

Weekly Reader Paperback Club
P.O. Box 16628
Columbus, OH  43216

## Authors' Addresses (Compiled by Sandy Cook)

Jerry Pallota
P.O. Box 760
Needham, MA  02192

Russell Hoban
c/o Harper & Row
Harper Junior Books
10 East 53rd St.
New York, NY  10022

Nonny Horgrogian
c/o Macmillan Pub. Co.
Children's Book Dept.
866 Third Ave.
New York, NY  10022

Mercer Mayer
E.P. Dutton
c/o Children's Marketing
2 Park Ave.
New York, NY  10016

Judith Viorst
c/o Atheneum
115 Fifth Ave.
New York, NY  10003

Thomas P. Lewis
c/o Harper & Row
Harper Junior Books
10 East 53rd St.
New York, NY  10022

Harry Allard
Houghton Mifflin Co.
215 Park Ave. South
New York, NY  10003

Verna Aaedema
E.P. Dutton
c/o Children's Marketing
2 Park Ave.
New York, NY  10016

Dr. Margaret Musgrave
Community College of Baltimore
　English Dept.
2901 Liberty Heights Ave.
Baltimore, MD  21215

Bernard Waber
Houghton Mifflin Co.
215 Park Ave. South
New York, NY 10003

Tomie dePaola
Box 444 RFD #1
New London, NH  03257

# MATERIALS
## Compiled by Kathryn Cloonan and Jay Buros

**Big Book Materials**
Sticky pockets, colored cotton balls — Demco Library Supplies and Equipment, 1-800-356-1200

Velour paper — Dick Blick Art Supply, 1-800-345-3042

Grommets — Hardware stores

Alphabet stickers — Childcraft, 1-800-631-6100

"Scribbles" Glitter Glue — Arts and crafts stores or Duncan Hobby, 1-209-291-2515

**Binding Machines and Spiral Binding**
Quill Discount Office Supply
100 S. Schelter Rd.
P.O. Box 4700
Lincolnshire, IL 60197-4700
(312) 634-4800

General Binding Corporation
One GBC Plaza
Northbrook, IL 60062
(708) 272-3700

Scholastic, Inc.
1-800-325-6149

**Book Racks/Easels**
Fixturecraft Corp.
443 East Westfield Ave.
P.O. Box 292
Roselle Park, NJ 07204-0292
1-800-275-1145

**Chart Paper/Sentence Strips**
New England Supply
P.O. Box 158
Springfield, MA 01101

J.L.Hammett Company
P.O. Box 9057
Braintree, MA 02184-9057
1-800-333-4600

**Computer Programs**
Magic Slate
Sunburst Communications
101 Castle St.
Pleasantville, NJ 10570-3493
1-800-628-8897

Letters, Labels, Lists
MECC
6160 Summit Dr. N.
Minneapolis, MN 55430-4003
1-800-685-MECC

Print Shop
Broderbund
17 Paul Dr.
San Rafael, CA 94903-2101
1-800-521-6263

SuperPrint
Scholastic
P.O. Box 7502
Jefferson City, MO 65102
1-800-325-6149

**Metal Shower Curtain Rings**
Department Stores

**Plastic Rings/Bird Bands**
Farm Feed Stores

**Plastic Slide Mounts**
"Lott 100" — photo stores or
Arel Inc., St. Louis, MO 63110

**Ribbons and Awards**
Hodges Badge Company, Inc. — 1-800-556-2440

**Stencil Machines**
Ellison Educational
P.O. Box 8209
Newport Beach, CA 92658-8209
1-714-724-0555

**Tutorettes**
Audiotronics — 1-800-821-6104
Language Masters — 1-800-771-4466

# GREAT SONGS AND WHERE TO GET THEM!
## Compiled by John and Janet Poeton

**Peter & Mary Alice Amidon**
6 Willow St.
Brattleboro, VT 05301
802-257-1006

*Things Are Going My Way & Traditional Songs
   for Children*
*All I Really Need*
*The Pretty Planet—Songs for the Earth*
*This Longest Night—Songs of Christmas,
   Chanukah, and the Winter Solstice*

**Bev Bos**
Turn the Page Press
203 Baldwin Ave.
Roseville, CA 95678

*Thumbprints*          *Handed Down*
*Thumbprints Too*      *Come on Over*
*Hand in Hand*         *I'll Tell you a Story* (Storytelling)

**Nancy & John Cassidy**
Klutz Press
Palo Alto, CA 94306

*Kids' Songs (book and tape)*

**Rick Charette**
Crystal Springs Books        Pine Point Records
Northgate, Route 202         P.O. Box 901
P.O. Box 577                 N. Windham, ME 04062
Peterborough, NH 03458       207-892-7175
1-800-462-1478

*Alligator in the Elevator*
*Where Do My Sneakers Go at Night?*
*Bubble Gum*
*I've Got Super Power*
*Chickens on Vacation*
*An Evening with Rick Charette* (video)

**Jon Gailmor**
Green Linnet Records
43 Beaver Brook Rd.
Danbury, CT 06810-6210

*Generations*
*Gonna Die with a Smile If It Kills Me*
*Dirt*
*Passing Through*

**Bill Harley**
Round River Records
301 Jacob St.
Seekonk, MA 02771 508-336-9703
*50 Ways to Fool Your Mother*
*Monsters in the Bathroom*
*Dinosaurs Never Say Please* (stories)
*You're in Trouble*
*Coyote* (stories)
*Cool in School* (stories)
*Come on Out and Play*
*Grownups are Strange* (stories)
*I'm Gonna Let It Shine*
*Who Made This Mess?* (video)

**Raffi**
Troubadour Records

Lots of titles — available at most bookstores

**Rosenshontz**
Lightyear Entertainment
350 Fifth Ave., Suite 5101
New York, NY 10118
1-800-229-STORY

*Family Vacation*        *It's the Truth*
*Share It*               *Tickles You*
*Rock 'n Roll Teddy Bear*  *Uh -Oh*

**Sharon, Lois & Bram**
Elephant Records         Silol/Alcazar, Inc.
P.O. Box 101 Station 2   P.O. Box 429, Main St.
Toronto, Ontario         Waterbury, VT 05676
Canada M5N 2Z3           1-800-342-0295

Many records and tapes — available in most bookstores

**Townshend School**
Townshend School
Townshend, VT 05353

*Townshend School Sings — 1986*
*Townshend Schools Sings — 1987*

**Wee Sing**
Price Stern Sloan, Inc.

Good variety of songs — comes with books too!

**Will Wright & Jim Reiman**
*Childhood's Greatest Hits*

Please add more and let us know about them.

# GREAT STORIES AND WHERE TO GET THEM!
## Compiled by John and Janet Poeton

**Marcia Lane**          Tales on the Wind
                         Stories and Songs for Children
                         Box 3103
                         Albany, NY  12203

**Joe Hayes**            Coyote and Native American Folk Tales
                         Silo/Alcazar, Inc.
                         P.O. Box 429 Main Street
                         Waterbury, VT 05676
                         1-800-342-0295

**Red Grammar**          Teaching Peace
                         Smilin' Atcha Music
                         81B Sugarloaf Mountain Rd.
                         Chester, NY 10918
                         914-469-9450

**Jay O'Callahan**       Vineyard Video Productions      **Titles:**
                         Elias Lane                      A Master Class in Storytelling
                         West Tisbury, MA  02575         Orange Cheeks
                         508-693-3584                    Six Stories About Little Heroes
                                                         Herman & Marguerite

**Laura Simms**          Laura Simms Tells Stories Just Right for Kids
                         Kids Records
                         Box 670 Station A
                         Toronto, Ontario
                         Canada M5W 1G2

**Odds Bodkin**          Wisdom Tree Records             **Titles:**
                         P.O. Box 410                    The Earthstone: A Musical Adventure Story
                         Bradford, NH  03221             The Teacup Fairy: Very Old Tales for Very Young Children
                                                         Giant's Cauldron: Viking Myths of Adventure
                                                         With a Twinkle in Your Eye: Funny Folk Tales
                                                             from Everywhere
                                                         The Wise Little Girl: Tales of the Feminine
                                                         Dark Tales of the Supernatural

---

**Voices**

*W*riters must have the experience of being readers. They cannot call up a felt sense of a reader unless they themselves have experienced what it means to be lost in a piece or to be excited about it. When writers do not have such experiences, it is easy for them to accept that readers merely require correctness.

*Sondra Perl, "Understanding Composing,"*
**College Composition and Communications,** *Dec. 1980.*

---

# INDEX

Assessment
strategies and tools, 259-284

Attention deficit disorder, 37-41

Benjamin, Susan
assessment, 259
thematic teaching, 164-168

Bibliography
anti-hurrying, 28
assessment, 302-303
developmental education, 25-28
differently abled, 67-68
grade replacement, 29
great idea books, 304
multiage, 83
parent involvement, 303
poetry, 305-307
whole language, 296-302

Buros, Jay
assessment, 260
goals, 177-178
schedule, 170
thematic teaching, 173
whole language, 171-172
writing, 174

Carpenter, Linda
multiage, 89-90
poetry, 186
reading, 184-185
thematic teaching, 179-182

Cloonan, Kathryn
assessment, 271
music, 195-197
parent involvement, 189-191
reading, 189, 194
schedule, 187
whole language, 188
writing, 190-193

Cook, Sandy
assessment, 265-266
goals, 198
reading, 184, 199
schedule, 198

Goodman, Gretchen
accommodations checklist, 66
differently abled, 57-63
inclusive education checklist, 64-65

Grant, Jim
developmental components, 22
notes, 23-24
self-esteem/discipline, 17-21

Haack, Pam
poetry, 220
reading, 218
schedule, 217
task sheet, 219

Johnson, Bob
whole language bill of rights, 91

Lessard, Ann
assessment, 261-264, 267-269
reading, 184, 199-202
spelling, 268
writing, 203

Lolli, Elizabeth
assessment, 272-275
multiage, 84-86
parent involvement, 87-89
schedule, 86

Magazines
children's, 308-309
professional, 29, 311-313

Mann, Jean
assessment, 276-280
reading, 204-213
writing, 214-216

Merrilees, Cynthia
assessment, 270
discipline, 223
math, 224-225
music, 223
schedule, 221
spelling, 226-227
task sheet, 219
writing, 222

Music
resources, 195, 223, 315

Parent involvement, 12-13, 87-88, 99-100, 119-124, 189-191, 203, 253-254, 255-258

Poeton, John
assessment, 281-284
music, 315
reading, 232-236
teachers, 228
whole language, 229-231
writing, 237

Reading
logs/journals/records, 179, 200-202, 234, 276-277
skills
readiness/pre-first, 259-260
first, 261-262, 264, 266
second, 267-268
strategies, 233
upper grades, 194

Resources
developmental education, 29-30
differently abled, 68
whole language, 310-316

Spelling
lists, 226-227, 268

Whole Language,
components, 231
definition, 230
principles, 230
schedules, 86, 170, 187, 198, 217, 221
thematic teaching, 164-168, 173, 179-182

Writing
authors' tea, 192,203
conferencing techniques, 216
editing, 269
invented spelling, 191
materials, 215
process, 192
publishing, 174, 193
records, 277-280
schedule,222
skills
readiness/pre-first, 259-260
first grade, 263-264, 266, 269
second grade, 267, 269
survey, 237

# Get 10 Issues of
## The Professional Journal for Education

◆

# PHI DELTA KAPPAN
## Now Only $35

Let the KAPPAN be your window to the wider world of education — from federal education policy to the latest in education research; from the most recent school restructuring plans to the hottest ideas in reading instruction, preschool education, and site-based management. The KAPPAN takes on controversial issues and presents all sides of the debate. From 1915 through today, the KAPPAN has pursued its editorial mission to:

- Inform readers about the most current issues and trends in education;
- Provide a balanced picture of policy matters in education;
- Present an amalgam of theoretical and practical thinking about the field of education;
- Provide a forum for debate on controversial subjects;
- Advocate research-based school reform.

Give your career a boost — subscribe today for only $35 a year. You'll receive:

- Ten issues, September through June, footnoted and with an annual index in June;
- Articles written by nationally known policy makers and researchers and by the most effective practitioners;
- Award-winning illustrations; great cartoons.

Here's what one reader says about the KAPPAN:

*"I find the KAPPAN stimulating and throught-provoking. I come away from reading it with a renewed sense of professionalism. It provides the philosophical/theoretical background for our work. It should be required reading."*

- - - - - - - - - - - - - - - - - - - - - - - - - - - - - - - - - - - - - - - -

☐ YES! Enter my KAPPAN subscription today.
☐ Please bill me $35 for a one-year subscription (10 issues).
☐ Payment enclosed.

_____
Name

_____

_____
Address

_____
City/State/Zip            KSDE

**Mail with payment to:**
**Phi Delta Kappa, Inc.**
**Eighth and Union**
**P.O. Box 789**
**Bloomington, IN 47402-0789**

Non-U.S. subscription rate is: 1 year $38.50 U.S. funds. Indiana residents please add 5% sales tax. This ad, or a photocopy, must accompany your order. Rates subject to change without further notice. Allow four to six weeks for delivery of first issue.

**Not A Race**

# The Society For Developmental Education . . .

The **SDE** seed began growing in the early 1970s when Jim Grant, the teaching principal of an elementary school in southwestern New Hampshire, began waging a personal campaign to promote developmentally appropriate education and to prevent school failure.

Jim's solo act, orchestrated from his dining room table, blossomed into Jim Grant Associates in 1986. With his wife Lillian, he co-founded The Society For Developmental Education in 1989. **SDE** branched out and broadened its scope to include whole language and process teaching. Now more than 35 SDE presenters are offering over 350 conferences a year to tens of thousands of elementary educators across the country.

Through the organization's astonishing growth and change, its main objective has remained the same — to support educators in creating child-centered classrooms where ALL children can learn, ALL children can succeed.

*Photo by Deborah Sumner*

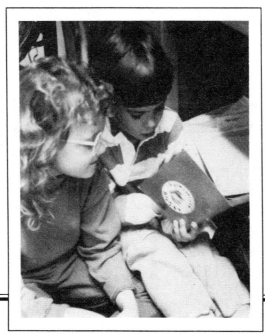

## Our services are designed for:
- Pre-K through Sixth Grade Teachers
- Chapter I Teachers/Directors
- Special Education Teachers/Directors
- Reading Specialists
- Speech and Language Teachers
- Curriculum Coordinators
- Administrators
- Librarians
- Staff Development Coordinators
- Guidance Counselors
- Primary Specialists
- Multi-age Primary Teachers

## Inservice • Speaker Service • Parent Involvement

Individual programs can be developed to fit the needs of specific schools or districts. We offer assistance with:

- Inservice Workshops/Presentations
- Conference Keynotes
  - Release Day Workshops
  - Education Retreats
  - School Openings
  - Make and Take Workshops
  - Program Follow-ups
  - Evening Parent Presentations

# helping to return childhood to our children.

## S eminars and Conferences— For School Success

**SDE** is the nation's primary provider of whole language and developmental education conferences and seminars.

One-day seminars during the school year and multi-day summer sessions offer information, inspiration and practical guidance to educators of all levels of experience who are striving to implement developmentally appropriate programs and practices.

**SDE**'s annual Whole Language and Developmental Education Conference in Nashua, N.H., attracts more than a thousand educators from across the country.

### Whole Language presentations include:
- Beginning Whole Language
- Writing Process
- Making the Transition from Basals to Literature-Based Reading
- Integrating Curriculum through Themes
- Authentic Assessment
- Songs,Chants and Rhymes to Enhance Literacy Learning
- Managing the Whole Language Classroom

### Developmental education presentations include:
- Clearing up Misconceptions about Developmental Education
- Creating Developmentally Appropriate Programs
- Parent Involvement
- The Self-Esteem/Discipline Connection
- Multi-age, Continuous Progress Programs
- School Readiness
- Differently-abled children

### Credit Options:
Each **SDE** seminar participant receives a certificate of attendance indicating the total hours of seminar or conference participation.

**SDE** is an approved provider of teacher recertification credit in many states. Continuing Education Units are available to all program participants from the American Council on Education Washington, DC.

Graduate college credit and/or professional growth credit will be available in most locations beginning in the spring of 1993.

For more information on SDE, our presenters, services or conference schedules, call us toll-free: 1-800-462-1478, Mon - Fri., 9 a.m. to 9 p.m. EST.

**321**

1993 CATALOG

TO ORDER CALL 1-800-421-30

Zaner-B

INTEGRATED LANGUAGE ARTS

DECISION MAKIN

SPELLING

# Zaner-Bloser
## Educational Publishers:
### *Brings Learning to Life*

Zaner-Bloser offers the following quality materials for students:

*Breakthroughs: Strategies for Thinking* — Grades 1-8, teaches critical thinking and science.

*Literacy Plus* — Grades K-8, applies critical thinking to literacy and the language arts with a whole language approach to reading, writing, vocabulary and reasoning.

*Spelling Connections: Words into Language* — Grades 1-8, introduces a network of the most successful spelling strategies developed through extensive research and the experience of classroom teachers.

*Zaner-Bloser Handwriting: A Way to Self-Expression* — Grades K-8, offers students opportunities for self-expression, meaningful practice, and building self-esteem.

*Feelings Like Yours* — Grades K-6, helps students develop self-esteem, make responsible decisions, and prevent substance abuse.

The employees at Zaner-Bloser believe their mission is to make a significant contribution to the education of children in pre-kindergarten through eighth grade by publishing materials of the highest quality. Their commitment is reflected in the company's motto: Zaner-Bloser brings learning to life.

*For more information about Zaner-Bloser materials, write 2200 West Fifth Ave., P.O. Box 16764, Columbus, OH 43216-6764 or call 1-800-421-3018.*

# Modern Curriculum Press

## When professional educators need new choices.

Creating learning environments that stir the imagination, inspire discovery, and empower children to expand their own knowledge is what professional teachers like you do every day.

Providing professional educators with new choices for creating these learning environments is what we at Modern Curriculum Press do for you. For over 35 years we have created the kinds of materials that have reflected your choices and we are still doing that today.

Come take a look at our new choices! We're sure they can help you create the best learning environments for your students.

# Choices for Today's Educator

**Multicultural Celebrations**
Discover the common bond that different cultures share when they celebrate in America.

**Poetry Works! and
Poetry Works! The Second Stanza**
Thematically grouped poetry posters designed to develop language skills and an appreciation for poetry in primary and intermediate students.

**MCP Phonics**
The trusted classic for 35 years has been revised and updated for the '90s.

**Young Explorers**
18 predictable stories that use rhyme, rhythm and repetition to integrate science, math and social studies with language development.

**Literature Links To Social Studies**
Discover fresh ideas for integrating literature with your social studies curriculum.

**Literary Life Lines**
Build an understanding for the process of writing with insights into the lives and times of well-known authors.

**Concept Science / Concept Health**
Big books that introduce primary students to science concepts, health and safety through clear, easy-to-read expository text.

**Bilingual and ESL**
New programs covering science, health, poetry, language development and self-esteem.

- - - - - - - - - - - - - - - - - - - - - - - - - - - - - -

**MODERN CURRICULUM PRESS**
13900 Prospect Rd. Cleveland, Ohio 44136

**1-800-321-3106**

Mail in this coupon or call us today for more information on these programs.
**Please check only one box.**

❏ Multicultural Celebrations
❏ Poetry Works! Poetry Works! The Second Stanza
❏ Discovery Phonics

❏ MCP Phonics
❏ Young Explorers
❏ Literary Links to Social Studies
❏ Literary Lifelines

❏ Concept Science/ Concept Health
❏ Bilingual and ESL
❏ I would like to have a representative contact me.

Name_____

Position_____Grade Level_____

School_____

Address_____

City_____State_____Zip_____

Phone No._____

Best time to call_____

America's Leader in Whole Language

19201 120th Ave. NE • Bothell WA 98011-9512

# THE SUNSHINE™ SERIES

## Light the window to a child's world with SUNSHINE's complete Whole Language reading program

From the start, the SUNSHINE series immerses children in stories they can understand, written in language *they* can read. Special story features—including rhyme, rhythm, predictable sentence patterns, and illustrations that match the text—support every reader, while the natural language text allows children to make use of their own already-developed sense of oral language.

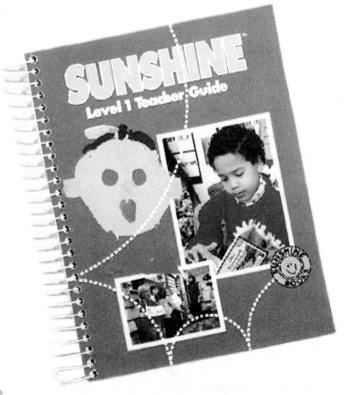

## SUNSHINE Emergent Level
## (Grades K–1; ages 5–6)

SUNSHINE's emergent level provides the strong support that is critical to the success of beginning readers. The stories increase gradually in difficulty, providing children with a gentle, natural progression to early fluency. Many favorite Level 1 titles are also available as Big Books, which are crucial to the success of Shared Reading.

## SUNSHINE Early Fluency Level
## (Grades 1–2; ages 6–7)

While books at this level are more complex and varied, they continue to provide the needed support structures and to build on vocabulary already introduced. SUNSHINE's early fluency level offers fun-filled stories, informative Fact and Fantasy titles, Big Rhyme Books, and more.

## SUNSHINE Fluency Level
## (Grades 2–3; ages 7–8)

Children at the fluency level need books that spark their imaginations and broaden their perspectives. They are also ready to enjoy such literary elements as plot, character development, figurative language, and theme. SUNSHINE answers these needs with rich, well-written literature of many genres.

## SUNSHINE Teacher Guides

Comprehensive teacher guides are available for each level of SUNSHINE. Each provides a helpful introduction to the Whole Language approach, plus ideas and activities for each title to help you make the most of SUNSHINE in your classroom.

FOR MORE INFORMATION CALL TOLL-FREE
## 1-800-523-2371

America's Leader in Whole Language

19201 120th Ave. NE • Bothell WA 98011-9512

# SUNSHINE™ SCIENCE

## Investigate our world with SUNSHINE Science!

Engage children in the exciting *real world* of science, using books that spark their natural curiosity about why things are the way they are. The 24 titles in SUNSHINE Science explore such topics as spiders, seeds, machines, and outer space to draw students into the life, earth, and physical sciences. Special language-based activity and observation pages (in the Duplicate Masters Book) will involve children in ways that no basal program ever could—and are excellent for use in student evaluation.

SUNSHINE Science has been carefully developed to correspond to the early, middle, and upper ranges of the emergent level of reading. All of the reading cues that SUNSHINE is known for—repetitive structures, meaningful text, illustrations keyed to the text, and more—can be found in these books. Your students will look forward to learning science with this fun and fascinating Whole Language approach.

◀ *Early Emergent*
*Students get a "first look" at each topic and at the idea of the theme. Concepts are kept very simple. Photos / illustrations match text.*

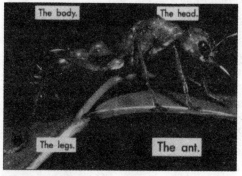

◀ *Middle Emergent*
*The text is now slightly more difficult, but photos and illustrations continue to support the text. Subjects are studied in more detail.*

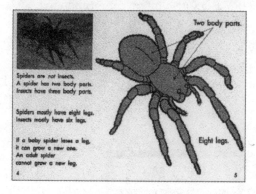

◀ *Upper Emergent*
*Here, texts focus on specific topics, and ideas grow slightly more complex.*

## SUNSHINE Science Teacher Guide

Science is not just a collection of facts to be memorized! Engage children in the exciting, hands-on aspects of scientific exploration at the emergent level. With this guide, you'll explore science with your students as fellow investigators, offering them suggestions and possibilities so that they can explore and appreciate the world they live in.

### FOR MORE INFORMATION CALL TOLL-FREE
# 1-800-523-2371

# THE STORY BOX®

## An integrated language arts collection that encourages instant success and lifelong learning

THE STORY BOX has been the leader in Whole Language programs for years. This imaginative series has all the essential elements that support new readers: rhyme, rhythm, repetition, illustrations that match the text, and stories that are relevant and appealing to children. THE STORY BOX makes learning to read a natural and pleasurable experience.

THE STORY BOX contains 111 storybooks graded into seven levels, including both pupil-size books and Big Books. Level 1 books (emergent) allow children to experience success in their first efforts at reading: pictures correlate directly to text; repetitive, rhythmic language and fun rhymes aid in prediction; and story lines are predictable but never boring. Levels 2–7 (early fluency) also feature these elements, but language, punctuation, and plot become more sophis–ticated, gradually guiding students toward fluency. THE STORY BOX also offers comprehensive teacher guides for Level 1 and for Levels 2–7.

### THE STORY BOX Emergent Level (Level 1: grades K–1; ages 5–6)

These emergent level stories are written in a child's own natural language, making the stories irresistible to young readers. The simple, clear language and the fun, colorful illustrations will encourage your students as they discover the enchantment of reading.

### THE STORY BOX Early Fluency Level (Levels 2–7: grades 1–2; ages 6–7)

As children become more comfortable with their reading ability, they are ready to appreciate such literary elements as character development, plot, dialogue, and figurative language. THE STORY BOX early fluency books bring an early appreciation of both traditional and contemporary literature into children's lives.

FOR MORE INFORMATION CALL TOLL-FREE
**1-800-523-2371**

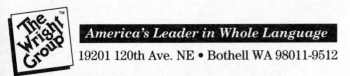
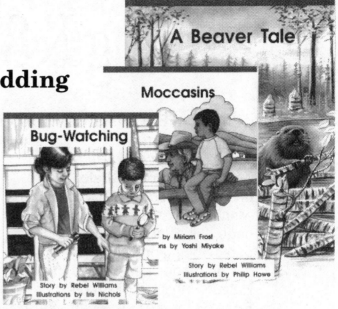

329

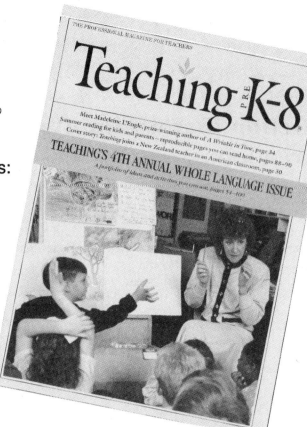

# Crystal Springs Books

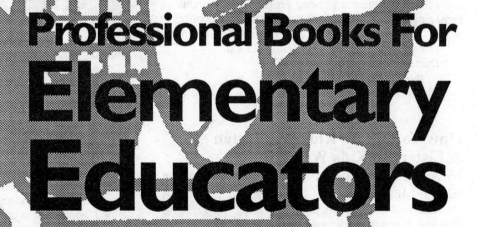

## Professional Books For
## Elementary
## Educators

**Behavior/Development** ♦ **Page 332**
**Spelling** ♦ **Page 336**
**Assessment** ♦ **Page 337**
**Extension Activities** ♦ **Page 339**
**Whole Language** ♦ **Page 341**
**Order form** ♦ **Page 347**

♦**1992-93**

## To Order Call Toll Free 1-800-321-0401

   **Purchase orders and personal checks accepted.**

## Discipline Without Shouting or Spanking: Practical Solutions to the Most Common Preschool Behavior Problems
by Jerry Wyckoff, Ph.D. and Barbara Unell

*Discipline Without Shouting or Spanking* offers effective, practical, nonviolent options for correcting the most common behavior problems of preschoolers. This book shows how to deal with temper tantrums, whining, negativity, sibling rivalry, possessiveness, aggressive behavior, resisting bedtime, playing with food, and many more problems—without shouting or spanking.

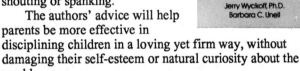

The authors' advice will help parents be more effective in disciplining children in a loving yet firm way, without damaging their self-esteem or natural curiosity about the world.

"Helps you keep your cool with your kid."
Diane Crowley, *Chicago Sun-Times*
> *paper, 141 pp. 1984*
> *order no. 3048E* ........................................... *$5.95*

## How To Talk So Kids Will Listen & Listen So Kids Will Talk
by Adele Faber and Elaine Mazlish

This best-selling book offers practical, innovative methods for solving common parent/child communication problems.

Adele Faber and Elaine Mazlish have won nationwide praise from parents and professional educators. They offer skills based on the work of the late child psychologist Dr. Haim Ginott, new

psychological insights, their own experience as parents, and what they have learned from parents throughout the country.

Using their supportive, friendly and effective methods, learn how to: • listen to—and understand your child's concerns; • have cooperation without nagging; • find alternatives to punishment; • help your child attain a positive self-image.
> *paper, 253 pp. 1980*
> *order no. 2020E* ........................................... *$9.00*

## How to Give a Child a Great Self-Image: Proven Techniques to Build Confidence from Infancy to Adolescence
by Dr. Debora Phillips with Fred Bernstein

Give your child the most valuable asset of all— a great self-image. This book by a distinguished behavioral therapist provides a program to help your child grow up feeling esteemed, confident, productive, and worthy of love. Based on techniques that Dr. Debora Phillips has used with hundreds of parents and children, these easy-to-do strategies describe the ways in which you can build a strong foundation of self-esteem in your child. Includes: • the power of positive reinforcement; • helping your child focus on his or her strengths; • the art of accepting a compliment; • rejection without pain (almost); • the importance of being imperfect.
> *paper, 271 pp. 1989*
> *order no. 1159E* ........................................... *$8.95*

## Self-Esteem: A Classroom Affair, Vol. 1 and 2
by Michele and Craig Borba

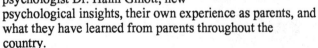

In *Self-Esteem: A Classroom Affair*, Michele and Craig Borba share activities and ideas that have helped them create a positive, self-enhancing atmosphere for children.

Each of the 101 activities is complete in itself but also adapts to use with most academic subjects. The activities are designed to help children gain confidence in their ability to communicate both verbally and in written form.

These field-tested ideas will be useful for classroom and special education teachers, early childhood personnel, resource specialists, program developers, and parents.
*vol. 1,*
> *paper, 143 pp. 1978*
> *order no. 3042E* ........................................... *$10.95*
*vol. 2,*
> *paper, 138 pp. 1982*
> *order no. 3043E* ........................................... *$10.95*

To Order Call Toll Free 1-800-321-0401

   **Purchase orders and personal checks accepted.**

## A Parent's Guide to Attention Deficit Disorders

by Lisa J. Bain

Is your child frequently inattentive, restless, easily distracted, moody, or impulsive? Does he or she have difficulty playing quietly or concentrating in school? These symptoms may indicate Attention Deficit Disorders (ADD).

*A Parent's Guide to Attention Deficit Disorders* helps parents understand their child with ADD and find the appropriate treatment and support.

The book includes information on the causes of ADD, diagnosis, treatment, therapy, and support groups and organizations that specialize in ADD.

*paper, 221 pp. 1991*
*order no. 3061E ........................................ $10.00*

## Why Johnny Can't Concentrate: Coping with Attention Deficit Problems

by Robert A. Moss, M.D, with Helen Huff Dunlap

From his extensive experience evaluating and treating hundreds of children with attention deficit disorders (ADD), Dr. Robert A. Moss provides not only a comprehensive treatment plan, but the support and knowledge a parent or teacher needs to help a child with ADD reach his or her full potential and promise.

*Why Johnny Can't Concentrate* supplies information on identifying and evaluating ADD in both children and adults; finding a knowledgeable, caring team of professionals who can provide safe, effective therapy; treating ADD at home with behavior-modification techniques; and devising an educational therapy for ADD children.

*paper, 233 pp. 1990*
*order no. 1209E ........................................ $9.95*

## Smart Kids With School Problems: Things to Know & Ways to Help

by Priscilla Vail

They are known as "conundrum kids": the math whiz who can't read, the wonderfully coordinated athlete with the undecipherable handwriting. They are a puzzle—smart kids who do poorly in school.

Learning specialist, diagnostician, teacher, and parent, Priscilla Vail has created a much-needed, authoritative

guide to spot conundrum kids, evaluate their problems, and use the right strategies for dealing with them in school and at home. She provides specific remedial programs and techniques for taking standardized tests so that they work *for* conundrum kids instead of against them. This book shows how to break the cycle of anger, fear, pressure, self-doubt, and frustration and make it possible to turn school failure into school success.

*paper, 265 pp. 1987*
*order no. P016E ........................................ $8.95*

## Gifted, Precocious, or Just Plain Smart: A Story for Puzzled Parents

by Priscilla L. Vail

The story of Evan — Everything is the "inside story" of what it feels like to be a gifted child. The 7-year-old knows only the frustrations of being gifted until his needs are recognized and school problems eliminated.

Priscilla Vail shares her insights as a teacher and a parent in the hopes she may help caregivers better understand the needs of gifted children and support them as they grow into whole adults.

*paper, 37 pp. 1987*
*order no. P039E ........................................ $5.95*

## Ages and Stages: Developmental Descriptions & Activities Birth Through Eight Years

by Karen Miller

*Ages and Stages* focuses on how developmental stages and behaviors show up in group child care situations. Author Karen Miller describes young children at each stage, including their emotional, social, physical, intellectual, and language development, and provides a wealth of suitable activities for children at each developmental stage.

But, she advises readers to remember that growth is a continuum. "A child doesn't suddenly stop being 'two' and start being 'three' on her third birthday."

*paper, 167 pp. 1985*
*order no. 2095E ........................................ $10.95*

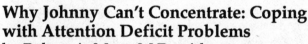
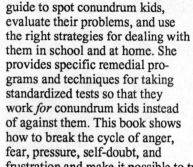
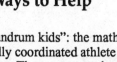

## I Hate School: Some Commonsense Answers for Parents Who Wonder Why
### by Jim Grant

*I Hate School* has helped thousands of teachers and parents become ardent supporters of developmental placement.

The book focuses on the dilemma of children placed in the wrong grade. It includes signs and signals that identify the overplaced child in kindergarten through sixth grade, in junior and senior high school, and in college.

In the final section of his book, Jim Grant answers questions parents ask most often about school readiness.

> *paper, 124 pp. 1986*
> *order no. P007E ......................................... $9.95*

## Every Parent's Owner's Manuals
### by Jim Grant and Margot Azen

*Owner's Manuals* is a series of concise, humorous booklets (written as take-off's on car manuals) that outlines predictable developmental behaviors of three, four, five, six, and seven-year-old models at home and in school.

Each manual presents information about the particular model's parts, language control panel, and operation and maintenance for home and school use.

> *paper, 16 pp. (each manual) 1987, 1988*
> *order no. P011E (specify model year) ........ $.75*

## Jim Grant's Book of Parent Pages

Jim Grant developed these helpful handouts so that teachers could communicate more easily with parents. Important messages about children and school are presented in an inviting format—an 8" x 11 ½" page that folds into an attractively illustrated note for individualized addressing. *Jim Grant's Book of Parent Pages* includes 16 photocopiable masters that can be used year after year.

Topics include: childhood stress checklist, school and divorce, accepting the readiness idea, love and limits, and seven secrets to school success.

> *paper, 16 photocopiable masters 1988*
> *order no. P012E ................................... $24.95*

## Worth Repeating: Giving Children a Second Chance at School Success
### by Jim Grant

*Worth Repeating* squarely confronts the controversial topic of grade retention for young students. Jim Grant addresses important considerations that are often overlooked or misstated. He examines this critical issue without jargon and challenges those academic voices that study the statistics and forget the child. Giving children the best chance at school success is the responsibility of both educators and parents; this book has that focus clearly in mind.

"...If its advice is followed, it could rescue thousands of children from academic failure. I endorse it whole heartedly."

Louise Bates-Ames, Author and Co-founder of the Gesell Institute.

> *paper, 205 pp. 1989*
> *order no. P024E ......................................... $9.95*

## Developmental Education in the 1990's
### by Jim Grant

Working with thousands of educators across the country, Jim Grant understands the kinds of questions educators will be facing in the coming decade. In *Developmental Education in the 1990's*, he helps clarify developmental issues by answering 93 of the questions most frequently asked by teachers and parents. The book focuses attention on the condition of children who are entering the education system in this decade and the need for teachers to clarify their goals and become more active participants in the reform efforts.

In his clear, no nonsense style, Grant addresses questions about extra-year programs, developmentally appropriate practices, whole language, multiage classrooms, assessment, political implications of developmental education issues, and the president's national reform proposals.

> *paper, 144 pp. 1991*
> *order no. P015E ..................................... $10.95*

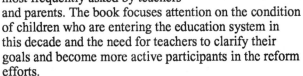

## Positively Kindergarten: A Classroom-proven, Theme-based, Developmental Guide for the Kindergarten Teacher
by Beth Lamb, Ph.D. and
Phyllis Logsdon, Ph.D.

Based on the authors' and other teachers' years of experience in developmental classrooms, this comprehensive guide provides vital information, advice, and an extensive resource section full of learning games, activities, finger plays, crafts, songs, poems, and unit themes. You will be able to create many of the projects without having to purchase expensive, pre-packaged materials.

*Positively Kindergarten* offers information for understanding the developmental philosophy and stages of children; organizing the classroom and the school day; planning and using theme units; and working with peers, parents, and administrators.

*paper, 146 pp. 1991*
*order no. P038E* ........................................ *$14.95*

## Childhood Should Be A Journey . . . Not A Race: The Readiness Guidelist Series, Kindergarten Through Third Grade
By Jim Grant and Bob Johnson

"School readiness" is not only important for children beginning school, but continues to be a relevant concept as they progress through the grades. This four-book series provides parents and teachers with a checklist of developmental benchmarks as well as suggestions and alternatives to help ease the transition between grades. The series is designed to help improve communication and strengthen the parent-teacher partnership.

*Kindergarten Readiness* .................. available fall 1992
*order no. 3072E* ..............................$16.95
*First Grade Readiness* .................... available fall 1992
*order no. 3073E* ..............................$16.95
*Second Grade Readiness* ........... available spring 1993
*order no. 3074E* ..............................$16.95
*Third Grade Readiness* .............. available spring 1993
*order no. 3075E* ..............................$16.95

## Real Facts From Real Schools
by James K. Uphoff, Ed.D.

In *Real Facts From Real Schools*, James Uphoff, recognized as one of seven experts on school readiness by the National Education Association, provides a historical perspective on the development of readiness and transition programs, presents an in-depth look at the major issues raised by recent attacks on such programs, and summarizes more than three dozen research studies.

Uphoff hopes that "this book will help the entire educational community move beyond the divisive, counter-productive debate about readiness and transition, so that we can all work together on the constructive changes in curriculum needed by young children."

*paper, 113 pp. 1990*
*order no. P037E* ......................................... *$6.95*

## Childhood Should Be A ~~Pressure~~ Precious Time:
Anthology of Poems
compiled by Jim Grant

*Childhood Should Be A Precious Time* is a charming collection of poems, with illustrations, centering around the theme of not hurrying children. Poems are from many sources: children who have been replaced, parents, grandparents, teachers, songwriters, and even ancient philosophers.

*paper, 36 pp. 1989*
*order no. P014E* ......................................... *$6.95*

### Other books on child development and behavior available through Crystal Springs Books:

| Order no. | Title | Author | Price |
|---|---|---|---|
| 1003E | All Grown Up | David Elkind | 9.95 |
| P002E | Child Behavior | Ilg/Ames/Baker | 8.95 |
| 2073E | The Difficult Child | Stanley Turecki | 9.95 |
| 1260E | First Grade Can Wait | Lorraine Aseltine | 11.95 |
| 1031E | First Grade Takes a Test | Miriam Cohen | 2.95 |
| 1073E | Miseducation | David Elkind | 8.95 |
| 1082E | Notebook for Teachers | Greenfield Ctr. School | 19.95 |
| P013E | Parents in a Pressure Cooker | Bluestein/Collins | 10.95 |
| 2030E | What's Best for Kids? | Anthony Coletta | 14.95 |
| 1151E | Your Child's Growing Mind | Jane Healy | 9.95 |

## Words I Use When I Write, Grades 1-2 *and* More Words I Use When I Write, Grades 3-4
by Alana Trisler and Patrice Howe Cardiel

Personal spelling guides that let students expand their vocabulary, practice their handwriting, and have their own dictionary of words important to them. Contains spelling for commonly used words such as colors, contractions, numbers, days, and months, etc.

*Words,*
 *paper, 64 pp. 1989*
 *order no. P023E ....... $2.50 (30 copies $52.50)*
*More Words,*
 *paper, 88 pp. 1990*
 *order no. P008E ....... $2.75 (30 copies $60.00)*

## Common Ground: Whole Language and Phonics Working Together
by Priscilla L. Vail

A guide for educators who want to provide students with the phonics instruction and skills they need within the context of a whole language learning approach. *Common Ground* provides an overview of appropriate reading and instructional methods for kindergarten through 4th grade.

"Replete with hands-on practicality, this book shows us how foolish we are to fragment the reading process."
Jane M. Healy, Ph.D, author of *Endangered Minds: Why Children Don't Think & What We Can Do About It*
 *paper, 86 pp. 1991*
 *order no. P040E ......................................... $8.95*

## Spelling for Whole Language Classrooms
by Ethel Buchanan

An experienced classroom teacher explains how increased spelling proficiency is a developmental process. Buchanan outlines the stages of spelling development and shows how to develop grade level expectations, evaluate spelling growth, and create a spelling environment.

The content is really a whole language spelling curriculum presented within the framework of a theory of spelling development.
 *paper, 156 pp. 1989*
 *order no. 3039E ....................................... $18.95*

## Spel...Is a Four-Letter Word
by J. Richard Gentry

Often spelling is taught in a way offensive to children. This creates a set of false dichotomies that prejudice children against spelling. This practical book demonstrates how children can learn to speak. *Spel...Is a Four-Letter Word* is devoted to helping teachers and parents to teach spelling as part of the reading-writing process.
 *paper, 56 pp. 1987, Heinemann*
 *order no. 1113E ......................................... $7.95*

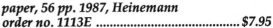

## How to Spell It: A Handbook of Commonly Misspelled Words
by Harriet Wittels and Joan Greisman

*How to Spell It: A Handbook of Commonly Misspelled Words* is an easy-to-use and complete reference book for spelling. Look up the word as you think it should be spelled and you'll either find you're right or find the correct spelling listed beside your guess. This book contains thousands of words that frequently confuse people.

Usefull too peeple of all agez!
 *paper, 333 pp. 1973*
 *order no. 1044E ....................................... $10.95*

# Assessment

## Assessment and Evaluation in Whole Language Programs
### Edited by Bill Harp

*Assessment and Evaluation in Whole Language Programs* examines the basic principles of whole language, past assessment and evaluation practices, and offers guiding principles for future practice. The book includes strategies for assessment in the primary, intermediate, special education, bilingual, and multicultural settings.

"...attempts to answer many of the critical questions being asked about the role of whole language in our schools. In pulling this volume together we called on some of the most talented educators working in the whole language area, and gave them a challenge. We asked them to create a scholarly, yet practical work that not only examines the growing research base that supports whole language, but offers realistic suggestions for tackling the many thorny issues involved in the assessment and evaluation of students."

> *hardbound, 266 pp. 1991*
> *order no. 2075E* .......................................... *$29.95*

## The Early Detection of Reading Difficulties, Third Edition
### by Marie M. Clay

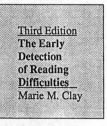

Part One of the third edition of *The Early Detection of Reading Difficulties* provides for the systematic observation of young children's responses to classroom reading instruction. Part Two contains a set of Reading Recovery procedures for use in an early intervention program with young children having difficulty with beginning reading.

Teachers working successfully with an earlier edition of this book and another by Dr. Clay asked that a set of procedures be developed to help them re-teach young children identified as having difficulty.

> *paper, 144 pp. 1985, Heinemann*
> *order no. 1025E* .......................................... *$17.95*

## Sand *and* Stones — "Concepts About Print" Tests
### by Marie Clay

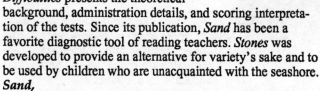

The "*Concepts About Print*" tests can be used with the new entrant or non-reader because the child is asked to help the examiner by pointing to certain features as the examiner reads the book. *The Early Detection of Reading Difficulties* presents the theoretical background, administration details, and scoring interpretation of the tests. Since its publication, *Sand* has been a favorite diagnostic tool of reading teachers. *Stones* was developed to provide an alternative for variety's sake and to be used by children who are unacquainted with the seashore.

*Sand,*
> *paper, 20 pp. 1972, Heinemann*
> *order no. 1107E* .......................................... *$3.50*

*Stones,*
> *paper, 20 pp. 1979, Heinemann*
> *order no. 1117E* .......................................... *$3.50*

## The Primary Language Record: Handbook for Teachers
### by Myra Barrs, Sue Ellis, Hilary Tester, and Anne Thomas

*The Primary Language Record* is a tool for teachers who want to keep meticulous records of their students' progress in achieving literacy. The three main purposes of record keeping outlined in this book are: to inform and guide other teachers who do not yet know the child; to inform the administrators of a child's work: and to provide parents with information and assessment of the child's progress. It presumes involvement of parents in their children's education.

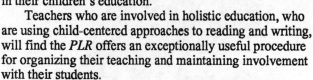

Teachers who are involved in holistic education, who are using child-centered approaches to reading and writing, will find the *PLR* offers an exceptionally useful procedure for organizing their teaching and maintaining involvement with their students.

*The PLR includes the handbook and eight photocopiable record keeping forms.*
> *paper, 64 pp. plus 8 masters, 1989, Heinemann*
> *order no. 1095E* .......................................... *$21.95*

## The Whole Language Evaluation Book

Edited by Kenneth S. Goodman,
Yetta M. Goodman, and Wendy J. Hood

• How do whole language teachers evaluate their students?

• How can evaluation fit the principles and requirements of whole language?
• How can evaluation help whole language teachers learn more about their students?
• How can evaluation be made an integral part of the whole language program?

The authors of this book— classroom teachers from all over North America representing kindergarten through adult education — attempt to answer such questions with ideas that are grounded in proven, working methods of evaluation. Through descriptions of their classrooms and vignettes of their students, they demonstrate how they have created environments that facilitate whole language evaluation. They discuss strategies they use in assessing students' growth across many curricular areas, including reading, writing, and second language growth, and suggest alternatives to standardized tests in mainstream, resource, and special education programs.

*paper, 296 pp. 1988, Heinemann*
*order no. 1147E* ......................................... *$18.50*

## Portfolio Assessment in the Reading-Writing Classroom

by Robert J. Tierney,
Mark A. Carter, and
Laura E. Desai

*Portfolio Assessment in the Reading-Writing Classroom* grew out of a three-year collaborative research study with teachers in the authors' attempts to find a sensible and workable alternative to standardized testing.

The book's stated purpose is to give teachers ideas about how they can implement portfolios in their classrooms. It contains reproductions of actual teacher materials, examples of student portfolios across subjects and grades, and research-based information to help teachers explain portfolio concepts to parents, the community, administrators, and other interested parties.

The authors repeatedly warn that there is no "right" way to implement portfolios, that each classroom reflects a unique approach to authentic assessment. They suggest that, "If we approach portfolios with a research and development orientation, we simply ask ourselves to identify possible goals for portfolios and consider possible procedures and ways we can keep tabs on what is happening. Thus we are open to revamping our processes, reexamining possibilities, and exploring promising avenues."

*paper, 215 pp. 1991*
*order no. 2079E* ......................................... *$19.95*

## Portfolios: Process and Product

Edited by Pat Belanoff and
Marcia Dickson

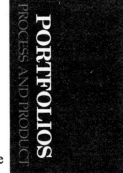

This book, the first to focus exclusively on portfolio assessment, is both practical and theoretical, broad in scope, offering places to start rather than claiming to be definitive. The articles, all by teachers with considerable experience in using portfolio grading, are free of jargon, making sound composition and assessment theory available to every reader regardless of what level of writing is taught. Because the book covers the most recent developments readers can expect a thorough introduction to portfolio practice and many suggestions for implementing a portfolio program. The diversity of the projects described will allow readers to compose systems ideally suited to their own situations.

*paper, 315 pp. 1991, Heinemann*
*order no. 3072E* ......................................... *$20.00*

# Extension Activities

## Is Your Storytale Dragging?
by Jean Stangl

Introduce children to the art of storytelling with 26 original stories written by Jean Stangl. These charming stories, imaginative props, and innovative presentation techniques will captivate and delight your young listeners.

Use string boards, flip charts, edible props, and fold-and-cut paper illustrations to help children discover art, science and movement concepts.

Each story provides easy-to-follow directions, reproducible patterns, and creative suggestions for related activities. Now you can become a master storyteller and inspire your listeners to create stories of their own.

> *paper, 79 pp. 1988*
> *order no. 2062E ........................................... $8.95*

## Sing Me A Story, Read Me A Song, Book I, II *and* Cassette

by Kathryn L. Cloonan

The *Sing Me A Story, Read Me A Song* cassette is a collection of traditional songs that can be made into big books, mini books, and classbooks. Ideas and easy-to-make patterns for making books that go along with the songs are available in the two companion books.

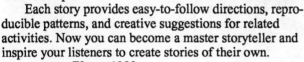
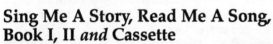
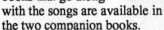

This collection of favorite children's songs makes integrating music into the whole language classroom fun and gives children reading successes they can sing about.

The books include ideas and related activities to accompany 16 songs such as Wheels on the Bus, Five Green Frogs, We Have a Friend, Baa Baa Black Sheep, Tiny Tim, Ten in the Bed — and more.

*Book I,*
> *paper, 66 pp. 1991*
> *order no. 1012E ........................................... $9.95*

*Book II,*
> *paper, 66 pp. 1991*
> *order no. 1242E ........................................... $9.95*

*Cassette,*
> *order no. 1166E ........................................... $11.95*

## Story Stretchers, More Story Stretchers, *and* Story Stretchers for the Primary Grades

by Shirley C. Raines and Robert J. Canady

*Story Stretchers, More Story Stretchers* and *Story Stretchers for the Primary Grades* each offer 450 ways to expand the impact and interest of 90 popular children's picture books. The activities are arranged in chapters with suggestions for integrating them into childhood curriculum units, including friends, feelings, science and nature, and the four seasons.

Shirley Raines and Robert Canady offer a wealth of ideas for extending the book experiences through math, art, circle time, science, creative dramatics, snack time, music and movement activities — and more.

All three books are a wonderful resource for teachers, parents, and children's librarians.

*Story Stretchers,*
> *paper, 250 pp. 1989*
> *order no. 1119E ........................................ $14.95*

*More Story Stretchers,*
> *paper, 254 pp. 1991*
> *order no. 1245E ........................................ $14.95*

*Story Stretchers for the Primary Grades,*
> *paper, 254 pp. 1992*
> *order no. 3078E ........................................ $14.95*

## Do Touch: Instant, Easy Hands-on Learning Experiences for Young Children
by Labritta Gilbert

Touching and doing stimulate learning. Children want to explore. They are curious. They need to touch, to find out, and to know. We need to surround them with things to explore, wonder about, do and discover.

The activities developed for 2½ through 7-year-olds in *Do Touch* use simple materials and can be prepared easily. Chapters include sticks, sponges, stickers, cups, pockets, gadgets, transparencies, and rings. Simple, yes. Intriguing, yes. Boring, never!

> *paper, 225 pp. 1989*
> *order no. 3049E ........................................ $14.95*

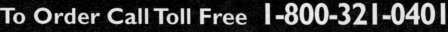

To Order Call Toll Free **1-800-321-0401**

**339**

   **Purchase orders and personal checks accepted.**

## How to Make Pop-ups
### by Joan Irvine

Anyone can make pop-ups. Find a piece of paper, a pair of scissors, some crayons, and a little glue. In minutes make greeting cards that talk, rockets that fly, or a zoo full of animals.

*How to Make Pop-ups* features:
• easy to follow directions; • step-by-step instructions; • illustrations for each pop-up creation; • projects for all levels and abilities; • ideas for birthday cards, invitations, holiday decorations, gifts — and more.

*paper, 93 pp. 1987*
*order no. 1043E* .......................................... *$6.95*

## Meet The Authors And Illustrators: 60 Creators of Favorite Children's Books Talk About Their Work
### by Deborah Kovacs and James Preller

Anno, Eric Carle, E.B. White, Chris Van Allsburg, Bruce Degen and dozens of other favorite children's authors and illustrators provide easy-to-read profiles, with bibliographies, extension activities, index of authors and illustrators by birthdate. Appropriate for grades K-6.

*paper, 144 pp. 1991*
*order no. 3074E* .......................................... *$19.95*

## 150 Surefire Ways to Keep Them Reading All Year
### by Ava Deutsch Drutman and Diane L. Huston

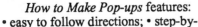

Celebrate reading with this collection of book-related activities, including games, awards, contests, book display and storage ideas, unique parties, author birthday calendars and projects, bibliographies, and more. Build reading excitement through reading-related holidays, celebrations of book formats, buddy reading projects with classmates and family members, read-alouds by the principal, the custodian and mystery guests. Through fun and motivation, these surefire activities will give a boost to lifelong reading. For grades K-6.

*paper, 112 pp, 1992*
*order no. 3076E* .......................................... *$12.95*

## Literature-Based Art Activities
### by Darlene Ritter

Fun to make art projects inspired by 45 favorite children's books. Common classroom art materials are used to create these original projects. What a way to build a life-long love of literature! Includes a list of related literature titles and integrated learning activities for each project. For Grades K-3.

*paper, pp. 1991*
*order no. 3079E* .......................................... *$9.95*

## Literature-Based Seasonal and Holiday Activities
### by Mary Beth Spann

Dozens of games, arts and crafts projects, writing ideas, recipes, and other activities based on 28 seasonal and holiday-related children's books, including *Angelina's Christmas, Arthur's Valentine, Ira Says Goodbye, The Legend of the Indian Paintbrush, Pet Show, Sarah Morton's Day.* Includes reproducible game boards, patterns, and step-by-step instructions.

*paper, 112 pp. 1992*
*order no. 3075E* .......................................... *$12.95*

### Other Extension Activity Books Available through Crystal Springs Books:

| Order no. | Title | Author | Price |
|---|---|---|---|
| 3065E | Good Earth Art: Environmental Art for Kids | MaryAnn F. Kohl | 16.95 |
| 3064E | Mudworks: Creative Clay, Dough, and Modeling Experiences | MaryAnn F. Kohl | 14.95 |
| 3066E | Scribble Cookies — And Other Independent Art Experiences | MaryAnn F. Kohl | 12.95 |
| 3004E | Steven Kellogg Connection | Will C. Howell | 9.95 |
| 3022E | Robert McCloskey Connection | Will C. Howell | 9.95 |
| 3019E | Bill Martin Connection | Will C. Howell | 9.95 |
| 1220E | Make & Take Games | Liz & Dick Wilmes | 12.95 |

## Literacy through Literature
by Terry D. Johnson and Daphne R. Louis

With *Literacy through Literature*, all teachers interested in learning, literacy, and children will be better able to implement a literature-based language program. This book provides a feast of original ideas on offering literature in the classroom as part of a whole language/literacy program for children ages five to fifteen.

*paper, 160 pp. 1987, Heinemann order no. 1068E ............... $17.95*

## Bringing It All Together: A Program for Literacy
by Terry D. Johnson and Daphne R. Louis

In their follow-up to *Literacy through Literature*, the authors provide a more thorough and coordinated program for using literature in any K-8 classroom. They offer practical, class-tested methods for integrating children's literature in the class. They also offer advice on assessment, parental involvement, and the development of a genuine whole language curriculum.

*paper, 258 pp. 1990, Heinemann order no. 1008E ......................... $17.50*

## Ten Ways to Become a Better Reader
by Cindy Merrilees and Pamela Haack

*Ten Ways to Become a Better Reader* is especially valuable for parents and teachers who are searching for classroom-proven, practical advice on making the transition from traditional reading groups to whole-group reading.

Although the title says there are 10 ways to become a better reader, there is really only one — read! This book includes ideas and activities that encouraged Merrilees and Haack's students to do just that.

*paper, 48 pp. 1991 order no. 1221E ......................... $7.95*

*Ten Ways . . . Poster, color, 21"x 34" order no. 3093E ......................... $3.95*

## The Foundations of Literacy
by Don Holdaway

Written with remarkable clarity by the founding father of New Zealand's Shared Book Experience, this is an important book for anyone who wishes to understand the "great debate" about literacy.

The practical aspects of the study, presented with lively clarity and humor, provide a valuable resource to help children towards joyful competence in reading and writing.

*paper, 232 pp. 1979 order no. 1032E $14.95*

## Independence in Reading
by Don Holdaway

In this third edition of a highly practical guide to reading instruction, Don Holdaway writes with freshness, enthusiasm, and simplicity about a complex area of learning. The emphasis he places on using a wide range of children's books in making literacy more relevant and fulfilling for children is always welcome, and his championing of children's need to be independent in learning at all stages of development characterizes the book. He argues his case strongly from a sound body of research and practice.

*paper, 219 pp. 1991, Heinemann order no. 1052E ......................... $15.50*

## Write On Target
by Cindy Merrilees and Pamela Haack

*Write On Target* offers a wealth of easily-implemented ideas to help generate student interest in writing and meet the needs of a wide range of learners.

Experienced classroom teachers, Cindy Merrilees and Pamela Haack give suggestions for writing individual student books, whole-group big books, journals, and creative writing booklets. They also explain how they solved the most frequently encountered problems of students writing every day.

*paper, 61 pp. 1990 order no. 1120E ......................... $8.95*

## The Craft of Children's Writing
by Judith Newman

Looking at children's writing can provide guidelines to understanding how a child develops as she or he begins the two-way process of communicating with the world. In this book for teachers and parents, Judith Newman explains not only how children learn to write, but shows how writing reveals a child's growing awareness of and use of language in every context.

> *paper, 72 pp. 1985, Heinemann*
> *order no. 1016E ........ $7.95*

## What's Whole in Whole Language?
by Kenneth S. Goodman

This book's major purpose is to describe the essence of the whole language movement — its basis, its features, and its future. More specifically it:
• presents a whole language perspective on literacy; development, both reading and writing; • provides criteria that parents and teachers can use in helping children to develop literacy; • mentions examples of whole language programs that are already at work; • suggests directions for building whole language programs and transforming existing programs into whole language programs.

> *paper, 80 pp. 1986, Heinemann*
> *order no. 1140E ......................... $8.95*

## Transitions: From Literature to Literacy
by Regie Routman

In *Transitions*, Regie Routman attempts to provide support, encouragement, and ideas to teachers who are looking for alternatives to a reading program emphasizing skill-oriented basal texts and worksheets.

Drawing from her own experience, she describes an existing literature-based whole language program that has worked well for students and teachers and offers suggestions of how any elementary classroom can benefit from the transition from standardized texts to literature. She presents material designed to demonstrate the alternatives available, to stimulate thinking, and to give teachers, parents, and administrators the knowledge and procedures that are necessary to make a change.

> *paper, 352 pp. 1988, Heinemann*
> *order no. 1132E ......................... $17.00*

## Invitations: Changing as Teachers and Learners, K-12
by Regie Routman

*Invitations* is an invaluable, practical, easy-to-read text that has been written to support and encourage K-12 educators as they translate whole language theory into practice. This remarkably complete and well-organized resource provides specific strategies for the daily management and educational issues teachers think about and struggle with in their efforts to make teaching more relevant for their students and themselves.

In a candid, personal, and reassuring voice, Regie Routman invites all teachers to reflect upon their teaching and learning, and in so doing, she ensures that the book will help to make whole language teaching and learning possible for everyone.

> *paper, 672 pp. 1991, Heinemann*
> *order no. 3023E ......................................... $25.00*

## Joyful Learning: A Whole Language Kindergarten
by Bobbi Fisher

A valuable resource for curriculum planners and administrators, *Joyful Learning* is written primarily to assist kindergarten and other pre-primary teachers in developing whole language programs to match their own teaching styles and school cultures, to meet the needs of their student and parent populations, and to satisfy the curriculum goals of their school systems.

Bobbi Fisher discusses whole language theory and offers practical, applicable advice on such topics as shared reading, the reading and writing process, math manipulatives, dramatic play, assessment, and communication with parents.

> *paper, 243 pp. 1991, Heinemann*
> *order no. 3025E ......................................... $17.50*

## Learning and Loving It: Theme Studies in the Classroom
by Ruth Gamberg, Winniefred Kwak, Meredith Hutchings, and Judy Altheim with Gail Edwards

*Learning and Loving It* explains what a theme studies approach to education means and illustrates how it works with real case studies — descriptions of theme studies that were conducted at an award-winning elementary school in Nova Scotia.

The authors explain that theme studies is a productive, child-centered approach to teaching that can be used in any classroom and that is successful with all children. While helping children develop thinking and problem-solving skills, it promotes responsibility, confidence, and self-discipline through a learning process that children can actually enjoy.

> *paper, 256 pp. 1988, Heinemann*
> *order no. 1062E .......................................... $18.95*

## Living Between the Lines
by Lucy McCormick Calkins, with Shelley Harwayne

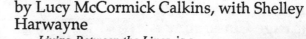

*Living Between the Lines* is a heartening invitation to bring new life into reading-writing workshops. Lucy Calkins has woven insights, practical suggestions, references, and anecdotes into this inspirational story of a community of educators who have pushed back the frontiers of what we know about teaching writing and reading.

This book includes: • the story of how writers' notebooks and a new attention to rehearsal have led to important revisions in many writing workshops; • establishing courses of study in which children read and write memoir, nonfiction, and picture books; • an invitation to pioneer new ideas about workshop conferring, record keeping, mini-lessons, and organizational structures.

> *paper, 336 pp. 1990, Heinemann*
> *order no. 2064E .......................................... $19.50*

## Lessons from a Child
by Lucy McCormick Calkins

A story of one child's growth in writing, *Lessons from a Child* follows Susie from her introduction to the writing process through her early efforts at revision and at writing for real audiences to her becoming a committed writer. The story of Susie is part of a larger drama encompassing 150 children, their teachers, and classrooms.

Lucy Calkins explains how teachers can work with children, helping them to teach themselves and each other. Matters of classroom management, methods for helping children to use the peer conference, ways mini-lessons can extend children's understanding of good writing, and the sequences of writing development and growth are all covered here.

> *paper, 192 pp. 1983, Heinemann*
> *order no. 1066E .......................................... $14.00*

## Literature-Based Reading Programs at Work
edited by Joelie Hancock and Susan Hill

This is a book about change, specifically about teachers, administrators, specialists, and parents making the change from a basal-based reading program to a literature-based reading program. It is a book about beliefs, about teachers' questions and answers, and about problems and solutions.

The articles offer detailed explanations of how educators made the change and include: • step-by-step suggestions for initiating a literature-based reading program; • recommendations for selecting and obtaining materials; • alternatives for the physical arrangement of classrooms; • ways of enlisting the aid of school resource people and parents in the transition; • explanations of *why* the transition should be made.

> *paper, 128 pp. 1988, Heinemann*
> *order no. 1069E .......................................... $14.50*

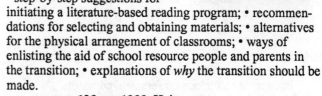

## Managing the Whole Language Classroom: A Complete Teaching Resource Guide for K-6 Teachers
by Beverly Eisele

*Managing the Whole Language Classroom* has been designed to meet the needs of teachers who are just beginning to read about and understand the benefits of the whole language philosophy as well as those who are already experiencing the excitement it creates. The book is filled with meaningful activities, strategies, checklists, and resources to help you manage your classroom.

Beverly Eisele offers practical, classroom-proven advice on: •setting up a child-centered classroom environment; • planning effective activities using the four language arts components; • using themes to integrate the curriculum; • scheduling; • organizing; • communicating with peers, parents, and administrators; • assessing student progress.

> *paper, 136 pp. 1991*
> *order no. 3001E ........................................ $15.00*

## Into Teachers' Hands, 5th ed. *and* A Child's Window to the World, 4th ed.

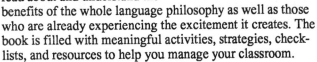

The SDE Sourcebooks contain up-to-date information, articles, reports, presenter handouts, and resources on developmental education, whole language, literature-based reading, helping ALL children succeed, and more.

The Sourcebooks offer practical, classroom-proven ideas for implementing whole language and the writing process; building self-esteem through a positive discipline approach; integrating the curriculum through themes; using poetry, songs, and chants to enhance literacy learning; and understanding and using authentic assessment in your classroom.

Both editions include professional educators' bibliographies. The 5th edition contains sections on multiage and the "differently abled."

*Child's Window,*
> *paper, 336 pp. 1991*
> *order no. 1259E ........................................ $24.95*

*Into Teachers' Hands,*
> *paper, 352 pp. 1992*
> *order no. 3101E .................... $24.95*

## Towards a Reading-Writing Classroom
by Andrea Butler and Jan Turbill

This thoroughly practical book discusses ways in which the process approach that revolutionized teaching writing may be applied effectively to the teaching of reading. The integration of reading and writing instruction has been proved to be a valuable instructional approach, and this book not only outlines the basic research on this method, but offers sensible applications for the classroom teacher.

> *paper, 96 pp. 1984, Heinemann*
> *order no. 1131E ........................................ $12.50*

## Understanding Whole Language: From Principles to Practice
by Constance Weaver, with Diane Stephens and Janet Vance

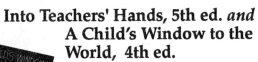

As the term "whole language" becomes more widely used, whole language educators are concerned that this philosophy is in danger of being increasingly misunderstood and misapplied. There is concern that this reform movement will be curtailed because practices that are contrary to a holistic philosophy are being promoted in the name of whole language. The aim of this book is to demonstrate that whole language is good education that can help to develop literate citizens and lifelong learners.

*Understanding Whole Language* is directed toward teachers, teacher educators, and administrators. It includes sections on research in literacy development, implementing whole language, and assessment.

> *paper, 336 pp. 1990, Heinemann*
> *order no. 3058E ........................................ $18.50*

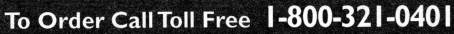

## To Order Call Toll Free 1-800-321-0401

   **Purchase orders and personal checks accepted.**

## Whole Language: What's the Difference?
by Carole Edelsky, Bess Altwerger, and Barbara Flores

Just what is whole language? Does the term have a core meaning? As teachers, researchers, and teacher educators, the authors of this book maintain that it does and, having worked expensively with the concept of whole language, they recognize the need to clarify that meaning.

Readers who want to increase their understanding of this trend in American education will learn that whole language is much more than a label; it is a perspective, a theory-in-practice, a powerful alternative with a history.

*paper, 120 pp. 1990, Heinemann*
*order no. 2063E .......................... $10.95*

## Why Whole Language
by Jay Buros

Based on Jay Buros' extensive experience as a teacher and consultant, this book explains the whole language approach through a detailed examination of classroom techniques. *Why Whole Language* provides information to help you set up a whole language classroom, find appropriate materials, integrate the curriculum through themes, and develop parental support.

Buros emphasizes that whole language teaching is a growing, reflecting process. "You have to do what you believe," she writes, "and finding out what that is is part of the process."

*paper, 123 pp. 1991*
*order no. P022E .......................... $8.95*

## Writing: Teachers & Children at Work
by Donald H. Graves

This book has become the basic text in the movement that established writing as a central part of literacy education and gave impetus to the whole language approach in classrooms.

*Writing: Teachers & Children at Work* was written to help both experienced and inexperienced teachers with children's writing. It presents no lists of what teachers ought to do. Rather it shows real teachers in the midst of helping children learn to express themselves — conferring with children, keeping records, talking to parents, and organizing their classrooms.

Features of children's development in spelling, handwriting, use of concepts, revision, use of the page, and process are charted through descriptions of their behaviors in writing and the classroom.

*paper, 336 pp. 1983, Heinemann*
*order no. 1153E .......................... $16.95*

## The New Read-Aloud Handbook
by Jim Trelease

In this new edition of his classic book, Jim Trelease shows you how to raise a reader and bring your family closer at the same time. He explains: • how to begin reading aloud — and which books to choose; • how reading aloud awakens children's imaginations, improves their language skills, and opens new worlds of enjoyment; • how to coax children away from the television; • how time shared reading together is valuable to parents and children; • how individuals across America have raised reading scores and united communities.

This new edition offers a chance for you — whether you're a parent, teacher, grandparent, sibling, or librarian —to discover the joys and rewards of reading aloud.

*paper, 316 pp. 1989*
*order no. 1097E .......................... $10.95*

## The Whole Language Kindergarten
by Shirley C. Raines and Robert J. Candy

The authors demonstrate that by involving children in the world of play, cultural awareness and creative expression fuse with "emerging literacy."

This practical volume includes an abundance of whole language activities within the classical content areas of reading, writing, science, art, music, and mathematics. It offers clear suggestions on how to interest children in books and print; how to structure groupwork to emphasize whole language philosophy; and how parents can reevaluate their roles to better understand and effect classroom change. In addition, each chapter contains examples of kindergartens where programs have been implemented and describes how the changes were organized, as well as how the children reacted.

*paper, 272 pp. 1990*
*order no. 3095E .......................... $24.95*

## Coming to Know: Writing to Learn in the Intermediate Grades
### edited by Nancie Atwell

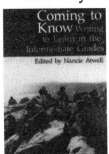

*Coming to Know* is for teachers who are ready to put writing to work across the curriculum. It is written by teachers of grades 3 through 6 who, dissatisfied with encyclopedia-based approaches to content area writing, asked their students to write as scientists, historians, mathematicians, and literary critics do — to use the process of writing to discover meaning.

One of the subjects of this book is report writing and ways to help children produce content area writing that is as personal and meaningful as their own stories. In addition, the book explores uses of academic journals, or learning logs.

*paper, 248 pp. 1989, Heinemann*
*order no. 1212E ........................................ $17.50*

## Other books on whole language and literacy available through Crystal Springs Books:

| Order no. | Title | Author | Price |
|---|---|---|---|
| 1211E | Art of Teaching Writing* | Lucy Calkins | 19.50 |
| 2065E | Build a Literate Classroom* | Donald Graves | 12.50 |
| 1023E | Discover Your Own Literacy* | Donald Graves | 10.95 |
| 1027E | Experiment With Fiction* | Donald Graves | 8.95 |
| 1035E | Getting it Together* | Walter McVitty, ed. | 13.95 |
| 1040E | Home: Where Reading and Writing Begin* | | |
| | | Mary W. Hill | 9.95 |
| 1045E | How Writers Write* | Pamela Lloyd | 12.50 |
| 1055E | Investigate Nonfiction* | Donald Graves | 8.95 |
| 1210E | Portraits of a WL Classroom* | Mills/Clyde | 18.95 |
| 1096E | Read & Retell* | Brown/Cambourne | 12.95 |
| 1098E | Read On* | Hornsby/Sukarna/Parry | 16.95 |
| 1099E | Readers & Writers with a Difference* | | |
| | | Rhodes/Dudley-Marling | 19.95 |
| 1100E | Reading Process and Practice* | C. Weaver | 29.95 |
| 1101E | Reading with the Troubled Reader* | M. Phinney | 14.50 |
| 1102E | Reading, Writing & Caring | Cochrane et al. | 15.95 |
| 1118E | Stories in the Classroom* | Barton/Booth | 15.95 |
| 1138E | What Did I Write?* | Marie Clay | 11.95 |
| 1141E | When Will I Read?* | Miriam Cohen | 2.95 |
| 1142E | When Writers Read* | Jane Hansen | 17.95 |
| 1148E | Whole Language Theory in Use* | J. Newman | 16.95 |
| 1150E | Workshop 1-By & For Teachers* | N. Atwell | 11.50 |
| 1152E | Write On* | Parry/Hornsby | 13.95 |
| 2090E | Writing Road to Reading* | R. Spaulding | 17.95 |

*Heinemann*

## In the Middle: Writing, Reading, and Learning with Adolescents
### by Nancie Atwell

The author, an eighth-grade English teacher when she wrote the book, provides a convincing model of what classroom research can accomplish. *In the Middle* is a story about her and her students, about what she and they learned together as collaborating writers and readers, and about what went on in one eighth-grade classroom where writing and reading instruction was transformed by a teacher who was concerned enough to question her beliefs about teaching.

This book is also about adolescents themselves — how they learn, what they believe, and what we can learn from and about them.

*paper, 320 pp. 1987, Heinemann*
*order no. 1051E ........................................ $19.00*

## Seeking Diversity: Language Arts with Adolescents
### by Linda Rief

Seeking Diversity is organized chronologically, following Linda and her students from September through June. Teachers will find especially helpful:

• Organization techniques— materials, the room, and expectations
• Ways of using life experiences and literature to immerse the students in meaningful writing and reading
• Evaluation beliefs and techniques that focus on process as well as product, and on self-evaluation over outside assessment
• Portfolios from a range of students – what's in them, who chooses, and what they show us
• A new look at art as an integral part of students, literacy
• An appendix filled with handouts for both students and parents
• Numerous lists of best-liked books for individualized reading, reading aloud, and reading together

*paper, 336 pp, 1992, Heinemann*
*order no. 3096E ........................................ $19.50*

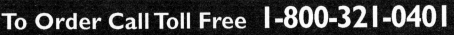

# Crystal Springs Books    ORDER FORM

Northgate • PO Box 577 • Peterborough, NH 03458
You may charge credit card orders by phone on our toll-free number 1-800-321-0401 or by FAX 603-924-6688

SB 93

SHIP TO:   Name _____   Grade/Title _____

Mailing Address (street address) _____

City _____   State _____   Zip _____

Telephone (    ) _____

**PAYMENT BY:**    ☐ Check Enclosed

☐ MasterCard (16 digits)    ☐ Visa (13 or 16 digits)    ☐ Discover (16 digits)

☐☐☐☐☐☐☐☐☐☐☐☐☐☐☐☐

Card Number

☐☐ — ☐☐   _____

Expiration Date     Cardholder Signature

Purchase Order # _____

School Name _____

Billing Address _____

City _____ State ____ Zip _____

Billing Office Phone (    ) _____

| Item No. | Description | Qty. | Price | Amount |
|---|---|---|---|---|
| 3098E | Whole Language Lesson Plan Book (see back cover) | | 6.95 | |
| 3100E | School Readiness Library (see back cover) | | 35.80 | |
| | | | | |
| | | | | |
| | | | | |
| | | | | |
| | | | | |
| | | | | |
| | | | | |
| | | | | |
| | | | | |
| | | | | |
| | | | | |
| | | | | |
| | | | | |
| | | | | |

**Shipping, Handling, and Insurance:**
Up to $24.99 ................................. $3.00
$25.00 to $49.99 ......................... $5.00
$50.00 to $79.99 ......................... $8.00
Over $80.00 .............. add 10% of order
**FREE shipping and handling for orders over $500.**

Prices Subject to Change

Subtotal _____
Shipping & Handling _____
**TOTAL** _____

Photocopy this form as needed.

*Thank you for your order!*

*fold along this line*

- - - - - - - - - - - - - - - - - - - - - - - - - - - - - - - - - - - - - - - - - - -

_____
_____
_____

## Crystal Springs Books

Route 202 Northgate • PO Box 577
Peterborough, NH 03458

**SB93**

- - - - - - - - - - - - - - - - - - - - - - - - - - - - - - - - - - - - - - - - - - -

*fold along this line*

# Program Notes

# Program Notes

# Program Notes

# Program Notes